Sixth Form College

KT-523-135

This book belongs to ...

| Name | Year | Cond. |
|---|---|---|
| Summer Cool | 17 | N |
| Ellie Chissell | 18 | |
| Emily Spence | 19 | |
| | | |
| | | |
| | | |
| | | |
| | | |
| | | |
| | | |
| | | |

**Sixth Form Studies**

Bournemouth & Poole College
The Lansdowne
Bournemouth
Dorset BH1 3JJ
Tel: 01202 205811 Fax: 01202 205739

Condition

N = New, G = Good, A = Acceptable, P = Poor

### Approval message from AQA

This textbook has been approved by AQA for use with our qualification. This means that we have checked that it broadly covers the specification and we are satisfied with the overall quality. Full details of our approval process can be found on our website.

We approve textbooks because we know how important it is for teachers and students to have the right resources to support their teaching and learning. However, the publisher is ultimately responsible for the editorial control and quality of this book.

Please note that when teaching the **AQA A–level Law** course, you must refer to AQA's specification as your definitive source of information. While this book has been written to match the specification, it cannot provide complete coverage of every aspect of the course.

A wide range of other useful resources can be found on the relevant subject pages of our website: www.aqa.org.uk.

The Publishers would like to thank the following for permission to reproduce copyright material.

**Photo credits**

**p.6** © Lordprice Collection/Alamy Stock Photo; **p.13** © dade72 – Shutterstock; **p.31** © Richard Sowersby/REX/Shutterstock; **p.73** © REUTERS/Alamy Stock Photo; **p.81** © Anibal Trejo – Fotolia; **p.96** © Photofusion Picture Library/Alamy Stock Photo; **p.102** © Dan Atkin/Alamy Stock Photo; **p.111** © Ian Dagnall/Alamy Stock Photo; **p.130** © Peter Dazeley/Getty Images; **p.131** © Stockbyte/Getty Images; **p.138** © REUTERS/Alamy Stock Photo; **p.139** © Gareth Fuller/PA Wire/Press Association Images; **p.220** © kavalenkau – Shutterstock; **p.232** © Mr Z – Shutterstock; **p.242** © schankz – Shutterstock.

**Acknowledgements**

**p.5** Rip-off plumber danced jig of joy in OAP's garden after overcharging her £6,000. Used by permission of Express Newspapers.; **p.31** © Croydon UK; **pp.39–40** Cheeseman v Director of Public Prosecutions (1990) The Times, 2 November 1990. © The Times. Used with permission.; **p.99** 'Man admits murder in first UK double jeopardy case' © Daily Mail. Used with permission.; **p.101** © Crown copyright 2011.

Every effort has been made to trace all copyright holders, but if any have been inadvertently overlooked, the Publishers will be pleased to make the necessary arrangements at the first opportunity.

Although every effort has been made to ensure that website addresses are correct at time of going to press, Hodder Education cannot be held responsible for the content of any website mentioned in this book. It is sometimes possible to find a relocated web page by typing in the address of the home page for a website in the URL window of your browser.

Hachette UK's policy is to use papers that are natural, renewable and recyclable products and made from wood grown in sustainable forests. The logging and manufacturing processes are expected to conform to the environmental regulations of the country of origin.

Orders: please contact Bookpoint Ltd, 130 Milton Park, Abingdon, Oxon OX14 4SE. Telephone: +44 (0)1235 827720. Fax: +44 (0)1235 400454. Email: education@bookpoint.co.uk. Lines are open from 9 a.m. to 5 p.m., Monday to Saturday, with a 24-hour message answering service. You can also order through our website: www.hoddereducation.co.uk

ISBN: 978 1 5104 0164 8

© Jacqueline Martin, Nicholas Price 2017

First published in 2017 by

Hodder Education,
An Hachette UK Company
Carmelite House
50 Victoria Embankment
London EC4Y 0DZ

www.hoddereducation.co.uk

Impression number    10 9 8 7 6 5 4 3 2 1

Year    2021 2020 2019 2018 2017

Cover photo © UK Stock Images Ltd / Alamy Stock Photo

Illustrations by Aptara Inc., Peter Lubach and Ian Foulis

Typeset in Caecilia LT Std/ 45 Light, 9.5/13.5 pts. by Aptara Inc.

Printed in Italy

A catalogue record for this title is available from the British Library.

# Contents

# Criminal law

## Tort

# Preface

This book and the follow on Book 2 are written for the AQA Specification for A-level Law. All the topics for AS Law for the English legal system, criminal law and the law of tort are included in this book. The order of topics follows that of AQA's AS specification. There is also a chart setting out the coverage and where to find the related material in this book.

As well as the factual material on the topics, evaluation is included for all areas where it is required by AQA's specification.

The text is broken up into manageable 'bites' and throughout the text we have used features which have proved popular in previous texts for A and AS level Law. These include key facts charts, case charts, highlighting cases and diagrams.

Activities for students are also included. These are based on a variety of material such as newspaper and internet articles, research material and cases. There are also application tasks for students to practice applying the law to given scenarios.

The law is as we believe it to be on 1 March 2017.

Jacqueline Martin

Nick Price

# Tables of Legislation

## Acts

## Statutory Instruments

## EU Directives

## Treaties

# Table of Cases

# Introduction

This book has been written and designed for the new AQA Law specifications introduced for first teaching in September 2017.

**AQA A-level Law for Year 1/AS** covers the content required for year 1 and AQA AS Law for first examination in 2017. To view the full specifications, and examples of assessment material for AQA AS or AQA A-level Law, please visit AQA's website: www.aqa.org.uk.

## How to use this book

Each chapter has a range of features that have been designed to present the course content in a clear and accessible way, to give you confidence and to support you in your revision.

### Learning objectives

Each chapter starts with a list of what is to be studied and how these relate to the specification.

### Key terms

Key terms, in bold in the text, are defined.

## Key fact tables

Key fact tables provide a summary of key facts.

## Tables of key cases

Tables of key cases include a description of a case and a comment on the point of law it illustrates.

### Tips

These are suggestions to help clarify what you should aim to learn.

### Case studies

Relevant examples of cases to illustrate points of law.

### Extension tasks

These include challenging questions and activities to help advance your understanding.

### Look online

These weblinks will help you with further research and reading on the internet.

## In the news

Real events relating to specific areas of law are covered.

### Summary

These boxes contain summaries of what you have learned in each section.

### Activities

Activities appear throughout the book and have been designed to help you apply your knowledge and develop your understanding of various topics.

### Practice questions

These are questions to help you get used to the type of questions you may encounter.

Text highlighted with a pale tint is A-level only content.

# Book coverage of specification content

| AS content | A-level content | Covered in |
|---|---|---|
| **3.1 THE NATURE OF LAW AND THE ENGLISH LEGAL SYSTEM** | | |
| **Nature of law** | **Nature of law** | |
| Distinction between rules and principles | Distinction between rules and principles | Book 1, Chapter 1.1, 1.2 |
| Difference between criminal and civil law | Difference between criminal and civil law | Book 1, Chapter 1.3 |
| Sources of law | Sources of law | Book 1, Chapter 1.4 |
| **The rule of law** | **The rule of law** | |
| Doctrine of the rule of law | Doctrine of the rule of law | Book 1, Chapter 2.1 |
| Law making | Law making | Book 1, Chapter 2.3 |
| The legal system | The legal system | Book 1, Chapter 2.4 |
| Substantive law | Substantive law | Book 1, Chapter 2.5 |
| **Law making: parliamentary law making** | **Law making: parliamentary law making** | |
| Parliamentary law making | Parliamentary law making | Book 1, Chapter 3.1 |
| Green and White Papers | Green and White Papers | Book 1, Chapter 3.2 |
| The formal legislative process | The formal legislative process | Book 1, Chapter 3.3 |
| The influences on parliament | The influences on parliament | Book 1, Chapter 3.4 |
| The doctrine of parliamentary supremacy and limitations on it | The doctrine of parliamentary supremacy and limitations on it | Book 1, Chapter 3.5 |
| The advantages and disadvantages of influences on parliamentary law making | The advantages and disadvantages of influences on parliamentary law making | Book 1, Chapter 3.4 |
| **Law making: delegated legislation** | **Law making: delegated legislation** | |
| Types of delegated legislation: orders in council, statutory instruments, by-laws | Types of delegated legislation: orders in council, statutory instruments, by-laws | Book 1, Chapter 4.1 |
| Parliamentary and judicial controls on delegated legislation | Parliamentary and judicial controls on delegated legislation | Book 1, Chapter 4.2 |
| The reasons for the use of delegated legislation | The reasons for the use of delegated legislation | Book 1, Chapter 4.3 |
| The advantages and disadvantages of delegated legislation | The advantages and disadvantages of delegated legislation | Book 1, Chapter 4.4 |
| **Law making: statutory interpretation** | **Law making: statutory interpretation** | |
| The rules of statutory interpretation: literal, golden and mischief rules; the purposive approach | The rules of statutory interpretation: literal, golden and mischief rules; the purposive approach | Book 1, Chapter 5.1, 5.2, 5.3 |
| Internal (intrinsic) and external (extrinsic) aids | Internal (intrinsic) and external (extrinsic) aids | Book 1, Chapter 5.4 |
| The impact of European Union law and of the Human Rights Act 1998 on statutory interpretation | The impact of European Union law and of the Human Rights Act 1998 on statutory interpretation | Book 1, Chapter 5.5 and 5.6 |

| AS content | A-level content | Covered in |
|---|---|---|
| **Nature of law** | **Nature of law** | |
| The advantages and disadvantages of the different approaches to statutory interpretation | The advantages and disadvantages of the different approaches to statutory interpretation | Book 1, Chapter 5.7 |
| **Law making: judicial precedent** | **Law making: judicial precedent** | |
| The doctrine of judicial precedent | The doctrine of judicial precedent | Book 1, Chapter 6.1 |
| The hierarchy of the courts including the Supreme Court | The hierarchy of the courts including the Supreme Court | Book 1, Chapter 6.2, 6.3, 6.4 |
| *Stare decisis*, *ratio decidendi* and *obiter dicta*; law reporting in outline and the reasons for it | *Stare decisis*, *ratio decidendi* and *obiter dicta*; law reporting in outline and the reasons for it | Book 1, Chapter 6.5 |
| The operation of judicial precedent: following, overruling and distinguishing | The operation of judicial precedent: following, overruling and distinguishing | Book 1, Chapter 6.6 |
| The advantages and disadvantages of the doctrine of judicial precedent and the operation of precedent | The advantages and disadvantages of the doctrine of judicial precedent and the operation of precedent | Book 1, Chapter 6.8 |
| **Law making: law reform** | **Law making: law reform** | |
| The work of the Law Commission: reform, codification, consolidation and repeal | The work of the Law Commission: reform, codification, consolidation and repeal | Book 1, Chapter 7.1 |
| The advantages and disadvantages of reform through the Law Commission | The advantages and disadvantages of reform through the Law Commission | Book 1, Chapter 7.2 |
| **Law making: the European Union** | **Law making: the European Union** | |
| The institutions of the European Union: the Council, the Commission, the Parliament and the Court of Justice of the European Union and their functions | The institutions of the European Union: the Council, the Commission, the Parliament and the Court of Justice of the European Union and their functions | Book 1, Chapter 8.2, 8.3 |
| The different sources of European Union law: treaties, regulations and directives | The different sources of European Union law: treaties, regulations and directives | Book 1, Chapter 8.4 |
| The impact of European Union law on the law of England and Wales | The impact of European Union law on the law of England and Wales | Book 1, Chapter 8.5 |
| **The legal system: the civil courts and other forms of dispute resolution** | **The legal system: the civil courts and other forms of dispute resolution** | |
| Basic understanding of civil courts | Basic understanding of civil courts | Book 1, Chapter 9.2 |
| The track system | The track system | Book 1, Chapter 9.4 |
| The appeal system | The appeal system | Book 1, Chapter 9.6 |
| **Other forms of dispute resolution** | **Other forms of dispute resolution** | |
| The tribunal structure and the role of tribunals | The tribunal structure and the role of tribunals | Book 1, Chapter 10.1 |
| The roles of mediation and negotiation | The roles of mediation and negotiation | Book 1, Chapter 10.2 |

| AS content<br><br>Nature of law | A-level content<br><br>Nature of law | Covered in |
|---|---|---|
| **The criminal courts and lay people** | **The criminal courts and lay people** | |
| The classification of offences | The classification of offences | Book 1, Chapter 11.1 |
| The appeal system | The appeal system | Book 1, Chapter 11.3, 11.5 |
| Criminal court powers | Criminal court powers | Book 1, Chapter 12.2 |
| Sentencing of adult offenders | Sentencing of adult offenders | Book 1, Chapter 12.3 |
| The role and powers of magistrates in criminal courts | The role and powers of magistrates in criminal courts | Book 1, Chapter 13 |
| The role of juries in criminal courts | The role of juries in criminal courts | Book 1, Chapter 14.4 |
| The advantages and disadvantages of using juries in criminal courts | The advantages and disadvantages of using juries in criminal courts | Book 1, Chapter 14.5 and 14.6 |
| **The legal system: legal personnel** | **The legal system: legal personnel** | |
| Basic understanding of the different roles of barristers, solicitors and legal executives | Basic understanding of the different roles of barristers, solicitors and legal executives | Book 1, Chapter 15.1–15.6 |
| Basic understanding of the regulation of legal personnel | Basic understanding of the regulation of legal personnel | Book 1, Chapter 15.7 |
| The judiciary: types of judge | The judiciary: types of judge | Book 1, Chapter 16.2 |
| The role of judges in civil and criminal courts | The role of judges in civil and criminal courts | Book 1, Chapter 16.4 |
| The independence of the judiciary: security of tenure, immunity from suit, independence from the executive | The independence of the judiciary: security of tenure, immunity from suit, independence from the executive | Book 1, Chapter 16.5 |
| Reason for and advantages of judicial independence and the methods by which it is achieved | Reason for and advantages of judicial independence and the methods by which it is achieved | Book 1, Chapter 16.6, 16.7 |
| **The legal system: access to justice and funding** | **The legal system: access to justice and funding** | |
| Basic understanding of alternative sources of legal advice: help lines, Citizens Advice Bureau (CAB), law centres and trade unions | Basic understanding of alternative sources of legal advice: help lines, Citizens Advice Bureau (CAB), law centres and trade unions | Book 1, Chapter 17.2 |
| Private funding: own resources, insurance and conditional fee agreements | Private funding: own resources, insurance and conditional fee agreements | Book 1, Chapter 17.3 |
| Basic understanding of public funding: criminal and civil state funding | Basic understanding of public funding: criminal and civil state funding | Book 1, Chapter 17.4, 17.5 |
| **3.2 CRIMINAL LAW** | | |
| **The rules of criminal law** | **The rules of criminal law** | |
| Rules and principles concerning general elements of criminal liability and liability for non-fatal offences against the person | Rules and principles concerning general elements of criminal liability and liability for non-fatal offences against the person | Book 1, Chapter 18 |

| AS content<br>Nature of law | A-level content<br>Nature of law | Covered in |
|---|---|---|
| **General elements of liability** | **General elements of liability** | |
| Actus reus: | Actus reus: | |
| conduct; acts and omissions and state of affairs | conduct; acts and omissions and state of affairs | Book 1, Chapter 19.1.1, 19.2, 19.1.3 |
| voluntariness and involuntariness | voluntariness and involuntariness | Book 1, Chapter 19.1.4, 19.1.5 |
| causation | causation | Book 1, Chapter 19.3 |
| consequences | consequences | Book 1, Chapter 19.1.2, 19.3 |
| Additional fault elements: | Additional fault elements: | |
| mens rea; intention and subjective recklessness | mens rea; intention and subjective recklessness | Book 1, Chapter 20.1, 20.2, 20.3 |
| negligence | negligence | Book 1, Chapter 20.4 |
| transferred malice | transferred malice | Book 1, Chapter 20.5 |
| No fault: strict liability | No fault: strict liability | Book 1, Chapter 21 |
| Coincidence of actus reus and mens rea | Coincidence of actus reus and mens rea | Book 1, Chapter 20.6 |
| **Non-fatal offences against the person** | **Non-fatal offences against the person** | |
| Common assault:<br>assault<br>battery | Common assault:<br>assault<br>battery | Book 1, Chapter 22.1 |
| Offences Against the Person Act 1861:<br>s 47 assault/battery occasioning actual bodily harm | Offences Against the Person Act 1861:<br>s 47 assault/battery occasioning actual bodily harm | Book 1, Chapter 22.2 |
| S 20 unlawful and malicious wounding or inflicting grievous bodily harm | S 20 unlawful and malicious wounding or inflicting grievous bodily harm | Book 1, Chapter 22.3 |
| S 18 unlawful and malicious wounding or causing grievous bodily harm with intent to cause grievous bodily harm | S 18 unlawful and malicious wounding or causing grievous bodily harm with intent to cause grievous bodily harm | Book 1, Chapter 22.4 |
| **3.3 TORT** | | |
| **The rules of tort law** | **The rules of tort law** | |
| Rules and principles concerning liability and fault in actions | Rules and principles concerning liability and fault in actions | Book 1, Chapter 23.1 |
| Rules and principles of liability in negligence and occupiers' liability | Rules and principles of liability in negligence and occupiers' liability | Book 1, Chapter 23.2 |
| | Rules and principles of liability in nuisance and vicarious liability | Book 1, Chapter 23.1.4 |
| Associated remedies | Associated remedies | Book 1, Chapter 23.3 |
| | Associated defences | Book 1, Chapter 23.1.5 |

| AS content<br><br>Nature of law | A-level content<br><br>Nature of law | Covered in |
|---|---|---|
| **Liability in negligence for physical injury to people and damage to property** | **Liability in negligence for physical injury to people and damage to property** | |
| Duty of care: the 'neighbour' principle; the Caparo three-part test | Duty of care: the 'neighbour' principle; the Caparo three-part test | Book 1, Chapter 24.1 |
| Breach of duty: the objective standard of care | Breach of duty: the objective standard of care | Book 1, Chapter 24.2 |
| Damage: factual causation and legal causation (remoteness of damage) | Damage: factual causation and legal causation (remoteness of damage) | Book 1, Chapter 24.3 |
| | **Defences** | |
| | Contributory negligence | Book 1, Chapter 24.5.1 |
| | Consent (*volenti non fit injuria*) | Book 1, Chapter 24.5.2 |
| **Occupiers' liability** | **Occupiers' liability** | |
| Liability in respect of visitors (Occupiers' Liability Act 1957) | Liability in respect of visitors (Occupiers' Liability Act 1957) | Book 1, Chapter 25.2 |
| | Defences and remedies | Book 1, Chapter 25.2.5, 25.2.6 |
| Liability in respect of trespassers (Occupiers' Liability Act 1984) | Liability in respect of trespassers (Occupiers' Liability Act 1984) | Book 1, Chapter 25.3 |
| | Defences and remedies | Book 1, Chapter 25.3.3, 25.3.4 |
| **Remedy of compensatory damages** | **Remedies** | |
| Basic understanding of compensatory damages for physical injury to people and damage to property | Basic understanding of compensatory damages for physical injury to people, damage to property and economic loss | Book 1, Chapter 26.1 |
| Basic understanding of the principle of mitigation of loss | Basic understanding of the principle of mitigation of loss | Book 1, Chapter 26.2 |
| | Injunctions | Book 1, Chapter 26.4 |

# The nature of law and the English legal system

# 1 The nature of law

After reading this chapter you should be able to:
- Understand the distinction between legal rules and other rules or norms of behaviour
- Understand the differences between criminal and civil law
- Have a basic understanding of the sources of law

## 1.1 The character of a rule

In all societies there are rules for keeping order. These rules often develop from the 'norms of behaviour': that is, from the behaviour that the particular society has, over a long period of time, accepted as the 'correct' or 'normal' behaviour. Many of these norms of behaviour will be rules about morality.

Rules exist in many contexts. The term 'rule' has been defined by academics Twining and Miers as 'a general norm, mandating or guiding conduct'. In other words, a rule is something that determines the way in which we behave. This can be either because we submit ourselves to it voluntarily, as would be the case with moral rules, or because it is enforceable in some way, as would be the case with the law.

As well as legal rules and moral rules there are other types of rules which operate in specific contexts. A classic example of this is the rules that operate in sport. These rules started to define the sport, and have evolved over time to ensure fair play. In some instances a rule may have developed for the protection of the players. These rules will also be enforced through a set of sanctions.

For example, in football, a breach of the rules may mean that a free kick is given to the other side, or a player may be sent off, or in serious cases or repeated breaches of rules a player may even be banned from playing for a certain number of games.

Rules that come about through custom or practice will involve the disapproval of the community rather than any legal sanction if such a rule is broken. Also the individual may become conditioned to accept the rules and so such rules are enforced by a feeling of self-guilt. Some such rules may 'harden into rights' and can be so widely accepted that they become the law. The early common law of England and Wales developed out of customs that were commonly accepted.

Rules are generally obeyed for one of three reasons:
1. because they carry with them a sense of moral obligation
2. because the rule is reasonable and relevant
3. because a penalty may be imposed if the rule is broken.

## 1.2 Legal rules

Law has been described as a formal mechanism of social control. It is a set of rules imposed and enforced by the state. There is a system of courts which apply and enforce the law.

Legal rules are enforced through the courts. In criminal law there are penalties for breaking the law. The most severe penalty is imprisonment for life. In civil law the courts can order the party who has broken the rules to compensate the innocent party or the courts can make some other order trying to put right the wrong that was done.

Figure 1.1 Differences between norms of behaviour and law

| Norms of behaviour | Law |
| --- | --- |
| Develop over time | Can change instantly |
| Ought to be obeyed | Must be obeyed |
| Are enforced by disapproval of the community | Are enforced by the courts |
| Are voluntary and apply only to those who accept them | Are obligatory and apply to everyone |

## 1.3 Criminal and civil law

In the English legal system criminal and civil law are quite separate. The purpose of the law is different and the cases are dealt with in different courts.

### 1.3.1 Criminal law

Criminal law sets out the types of behaviour which are forbidden at risk of punishment. A person who commits a crime is said to have offended against the state, and so the state has the right to prosecute them. This is so even though there is often an individual victim of a crime as well. For example, if a defendant commits the crime of burglary by breaking into a house and stealing, the state prosecutes the defendant for that burglary, although it is also possible for the victim to bring a private prosecution if the state does not take proceedings. This very rarely happens in cases where the victim is an individual. However, some private organisations do bring cases against offenders. An example is the RSPCA which will often prosecute in cases of cruelty to animals.

The criminal courts have the right to punish those who break the criminal law. So, at the end of the case where the defendant is found guilty, that defendant will be sentenced. The courts have a wide range of sentences that they can use. These include sending the defendant to prison, making an order that the defendant do a certain number of hours of unpaid work, fining the defendant or disqualifying the defendant from driving for a certain period of time.

Any individual victim of the crime will not necessarily be given any compensation though, where possible, the courts will order the offender to pay the victim compensation, as well as passing a sentence on him.

## 1.3.2 Civil law

Civil law is about private disputes between individuals and/or businesses. There are several different types of civil law. Some important ones are:

- law of tort
- contract law
- human rights
- family law
- employment law
- company law.

If you are doing AQA AS Law you will study topics from the law of tort. These are covered in Chapters 23 to 26 of this book. If you are doing AQA A-level Law you will study both law of tort and either the law of contract or human rights. The further areas of law of tort and the areas of contract law or human rights that you need are covered in Book 2.

In order to give you a basic understanding of the areas covered by tort, contract and human rights some examples of each are given in the following sections.

### Law of tort

Consider the following situations:

a   A child passenger in a car is injured in a collision (the tort of negligence).

b   A family complains that their health is being affected by the noise and dust from a factory which has just been built near their house (the tort of nuisance).

c   A woman is injured by faulty machinery at work (the tort of negligence, but may also involve occupiers' liability and/or employer's duty under health and safety regulations).

d   A man complains that a newspaper has written an untrue article about him, which has affected his reputation (the tort of defamation).

All these cases come under the law of tort. A tort occurs where the civil law holds that, even though there is no contract between them, one person owes a legal responsibility of some kind to another person, and there has been a breach of that responsibility. If there is a breach of this responsibility, then the person affected can make a claim under the law of tort. If successful the court can award damages – that is a sum of money to compensate the person.

Where there is a situation which is continuing (such as in (b) above), it is also possible for the court to award an injunction. This is an order to the defendant to do or to stop doing something.

There are many different types of tort, and the above examples demonstrate only some of them. Many cases arise from road traffic crashes, since drivers owe a duty of care to anyone who might be injured by their negligent driving.

### Law of contract

Look at the following situations:

a   A family complains that their package holiday did not match what was promised by the tour operator and that they were put into a lower-grade hotel than the one they had paid for.

b   A woman has bought a new car and discovers the engine is faulty.

c   A man who bought a new car on hire purchase has failed to pay the instalments due to the hire-purchase company.

All these situations come under the law of contract. There are, of course, many other situations in which contracts can be involved. A contract is where the parties have made an agreement and each side has put something into the agreement. In (a) the tour operator provided the holiday and the family paid for that holiday. In (b) a garage had sold the car to the woman and she had paid for it. In (c) the hire-purchase company had provided the money for the man to have the car, while the man promised to pay back that money in instalments to the company.

If one party to the contract has not kept their side of the bargain, then the other party can bring a claim against them.

## Human rights

Consider the following situations:

a   A man is arrested and held in a police station for longer than the law allows.

b   At the trial of a woman in the Crown Court, one of the jurors is a police officer. This officer knows (and has worked with) one of the police who gives important evidence in the case.

c   The eight-year-old child of a well-known author is photographed by a journalist as he goes to school. The journalist does not have permission to take the child's photo. The photo is then published in a newspaper.

All these situations involve breaches of human rights. In (a) there is a breach of Article 5 of the European Convention on Human Rights – the right to liberty. In (b) there is a breach of Article 6(1) of the Convention – the right to a fair trial. In (c) there is a breach of Article 8 of the Convention – the right to respect for private life. These rights will be upheld in the English courts. There is also a right to take the case to the European Court of Human Rights.

Compensation can be awarded where there is a breach of human rights. It is also possible for other remedies to be given, such as an injunction to prevent the future publication of photographs.

## 1.3.3 Differences between criminal and civil law

There are many differences between civil cases and criminal cases. It is important to understand fully the distinctions between civil and criminal cases.

### Purpose of the law

Criminal law is aimed at trying to maintain law and order. So, when a person is found guilty of an offence, that offender will be punished. There is also the aim of trying to protect society and this is the justification for sending offenders to prison.

Civil law upholds the rights of individuals and the courts can order compensation in an effort at putting the parties back to the position they would have been in if there had not been any breach of the civil law.

### Person starting the case

Criminal cases are taken on behalf of the state, and so there is a Crown Prosecution Service responsible for conducting most cases. However, there are other State agencies which may prosecute certain types of offence, for example the Environment Agency which prosecutes pollution cases.

In civil cases, the person starting the case is the individual or business which has suffered as a result of the breach of civil law.

The person starting the case is given a different name in criminal and civil cases. In criminal cases they are referred to as the **prosecutor**, while in civil cases they are called the **claimant**.

> ### Key terms
>
> **Prosecutor** – the legal term for the person or organisation bringing a criminal charge against a defendant.
>
> **Claimant** – the legal term for a person or organisation starting a civil claim in the courts.

### Courts

Criminal cases will be tried in either the Magistrates' Courts or the Crown Court. The Magistrates' Courts deal with less serious offences and the case is tried by a panel of lay magistrates or by a single legally qualified District Judge. Serious offences are tried in the Crown Court. The case is tried by a judge sitting with a jury. The judge decides points of law and the jury decide the verdict of 'guilty' or 'not guilty'.

The cases take place in different courts. In general, civil cases are heard in the High Court or the County Court. The High Court deals with more serious cases while the County Court deals with cases of lower value.

In both the High Court and the County Court a judge will try the case. It is very rare to have a case tried by a jury in a civil matter.

### Standard of proof

Criminal cases must be proved 'beyond reasonable doubt'. This is a very high standard of proof, and is necessary since a conviction could result in the defendant serving a long prison sentence.

Civil cases have to be proved 'on the balance of probabilities'. This is a much lower standard of proof, where the judge decides who is most likely to be right. This difference in the standard of proof means that it is possible for a defendant who has been acquitted in a criminal case to be found liable in a civil case based on the same facts.

This can happen in driving cases where a driver may be found not guilty of dangerous driving but can still be liable in the law of tort for damage or injury caused by negligent driving.

## Outcome of case

A defendant in a criminal case is found 'guilty' or 'not guilty'. Another way of stating this in criminal cases is to say that the defendant is 'convicted' or 'acquitted'. A defendant in a civil case is found 'liable' or 'not liable'.

At the end of a criminal case a defendant found guilty of an offence may be punished. The courts have various penalties available depending on the seriousness of the offence. A defendant may be sent to prison, given a community order, fined or (for driving cases) disqualified from driving.

At the end of a civil case, anyone found liable will be ordered to put right the matter as far as possible. This is usually done by an award of money in compensation, known as damages, though the court can make other orders such as an injunction to prevent similar actions in the future or an order for specific performance (where the defendant who broke a contract is ordered to complete that contract).

**Figure 1.2** Key facts table on differences between criminal and civil cases

|  | Criminal cases | Civil cases |
| --- | --- | --- |
| **Purpose of the law** | To maintain law and order: to protect society | To uphold the rights of individuals |
| **Person starting the case** | Usually the state through the Crown Prosecution Service | The individual whose rights have been affected |
| **Legal name for that person** | Prosecutor | Claimant |
| **Courts hearing cases** | Magistrates' Court Crown Court | County Court High Court |
| **Standard of proof** | Beyond reasonable doubt | The balance of probabilities |
| **Person/s making the decision** | Magistrates in Magistrates' Court A judge and jury in Crown Court | Judge Very rarely a jury |
| **Decision** | Guilty (convicted) or not guilty (acquitted) | Liable or not liable |
| **Powers of the court** | Prison, community order, fine, driving ban | Usually an award of damages (compensation); also possible – injunction, specific performance of a contract |

## Activity

Read the newspaper article below and say whether it is a criminal or a civil case. What specific points or words in the article led to your decision?

### Rip-off plumber danced jig of joy in OAP's garden after overcharging her £6,000

A rogue plumber was spotted dancing a jig outside a frail pensioner's house after he conned her out of nearly £8,000, a court heard.

Tradesman Russell Lane, 38, made no attempt to hide his joy after shamelessly ripping off Patricia Binks, 72, who had called for help after suffering a blocked drain.

But yesterday he was counting the cost of his dishonesty after the company he worked for was fined £15,000 in fines and costs.

Lane was also found guilty of fraud and is due to be sentenced in March. Bournemouth Crown Court heard Mrs Binks contacted Plumbers 24/7 Ltd after finding the number in *Yellow Pages*.

Lane, who was with a second unnamed man, produced paperwork he ordered Mrs Binks to sign. It had no prices on and the men told her that if she didn't sign they wouldn't be able to carry out the work.

The men worked on the drains for five hours – then handed Mrs Binks a bill for £7,800. They produced a card machine and ordered her to pay the full amount immediately.

Officials called in an expert to examine the work who found Lane overcharged Mrs Binks by £6,000.

The jury agreed the price charged by Lane was so significantly above a reasonable charge that the demand to pay that amount could only have been made dishonestly.

*Source: Adapted from an article by David Pilditch, in the Daily Express online, 21 January 2016*

## 1.4 Sources of law

There are several sources of law: custom, common law, statute law.

### 1.4.1 Custom

A custom is a rule of behaviour which develops in a community without being deliberately invented. Historically these are believed to have been very important in that they were, effectively, the basis of our common law (see below). It is thought that following the Norman Conquest, judges appointed by the king travelled around the land making decisions in the king's name. The judges based at least some of their decisions on the common customs. This idea caused Lord Justice Coke in the seventeenth century to describe these customs as being 'one of the main triangles of the laws of England'. Custom is an historical source and is unlikely to create new law today.

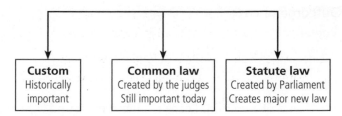

```
Custom              Common law              Statute law
Historically        Created by the judges   Created by Parliament
important           Still important today   Creates major new law
```

**Figure 1.3** Sources of law

### 1.4.3 Statute law

An Act of Parliament is law that has been passed by both Houses of Parliament and received Royal Assent. Law can be changed by an Act of Parliament or new law can be created. This is useful for new situations or inventions such as computer technology. Parliament has created new offences involving computer hacking. It has also created new rules in respect of 'designer babies' and what is allowed (the laws surrounding choices which can be made when creating a baby through in-vitro fertilisation).

Statute law can bring together all the existing law in one area in a single Act of Parliament. This was done in the Consumer Rights Act 2015.

Statute law can create, change or revoke any law. It is useful for make wide-sweeping changes to the law.

> The process for enacting a new Act of Parliament is explained in Chapter 3.

However, statutes often recognise the common law and create laws which rely on the common law. For example, the criminal offences of assault and battery are common law offences but s 39 of the Criminal Justice Act 1988 sets out the maximum penalty for these offences.

> In addition the judges still play an important role as they may have to interpret the meaning of words in a statute if they are not clear. This problem of statutory interpretation is dealt with in Chapter 5.

The Court of the King's Bench, 1805

### 1.4.2 Common law

Common law is the basis of our law today: it is unwritten law that developed from customs and judicial decisions. The phrase 'common law' is still used to distinguish laws that have been developed by judicial decisions from laws that have been created by statute or other legislation. For example, murder is a common law crime while theft is a statutory crime. This means that murder has never been defined in any Act of Parliament, but theft is defined by the Theft Act 1968. Involuntary manslaughter is also a common law offence.

In tort law most of the law on negligence has been developed by the judges. Also in the law regarding formation of a contract many of the rules on offer and acceptance come from decisions by the judges in the nineteenth century. The judges can still create new law today. However, they can only do this when a relevant case comes before them. And then they can only rule on the point in that case. This then becomes the law for future cases. Judges cannot make wide-ranging changes to the law. This can only be done by statute law.

## Check your understanding

1  In which court would a defendant, who has committed minor criminal offence, be dealt with?

   A  Crown Court

   B  High Court

   C  Magistrates' Court

   D  County Court

2  Which one of the following statements accurately defines the standard of proof required in a civil case?

   A  It must be proved beyond reasonable doubt

   B  It must be proved on the balance of probabilities

   C  There must be sufficient evidence

   D  There is a low standard of proof

3  Using an example from both civil and criminal law to illustrate your answer, explain two differences in the way civil and criminal cases are dealt with in court.

## Summary

- A rule is something that determines the way in which we behave.
- Rules often develop from the 'norms of behaviour'.
- Norms of behaviour are enforced by the attitudes of the community and by self-guilt.
- Law is a formal mechanism of social control and legal rules are enforced by the state.
- Criminal law sets out the types of behaviour which are forbidden at risk of punishment.
- Civil law governs private disputes between individuals and/or businesses.
- Criminal cases are heard in the Magistrates' Court and the Crown Court.
- Civil cases are heard in the County Court and the High Court.
- The standard of proof for criminal cases is 'beyond reasonable doubt': the standard of proof for civil cases is the 'balance of probabilities'.
- The earliest source of law was custom.
- The common law was developed from custom and the decisions of the judges.
- Today most law is made by Acts of Parliament.
- Judges still have a role in the interpretation of statutes.

# 2 The rule of law

After reading this chapter you should be able to:
- Have a basic understanding of the constitutional doctrine of the rule of law
- Explain the principles upon which the rule of law is based
- Understand the application of the rule of law to law making, the legal system and substantive law

## 2.1 Concept of the rule of law

The 'rule of law' is a symbolic idea. It is difficult to give a precise meaning to the concept and academic writers have defined it in different ways. However, the main principle is that all people are subject to and accountable to law that is fairly applied and enforced. Also the process by which the laws of the country are enacted, administered and enforced must be fair.

The rule of law is a safeguard against dictatorship. It supports democracy. This is because the government and its officials are accountable under the law. Also authority is distributed in a manner that ensures that no single organ of government can exercise power in an unchecked way.

Tony Honoré, an academic lawyer, points out that the rule of law exists when a government's powers are limited by law and citizens have a core of rights that the government are bound to uphold.

These principles mean that:
- no person shall be sanctioned except in accordance with the law: this is in both civil and criminal cases
- there is equality before the law: there must be no discrimination on any grounds
- there must be fairness and clarity of the law.

## 2.2 Academic views

Many academics have written about the rule of law. The best-known explanation of the 'rule of law' was given by Professor A.V. Dicey in the nineteenth century, but there have been other writers with different views on the topic.

### 2.2.1 Dicey

Dicey thought that the rule of law was an important feature that distinguished English law from law in other countries in Europe. He held that there were three elements that created the rule of law.

These were:
- an absence of arbitrary power on the part of the state
- equality before the law
- supremacy of ordinary law.

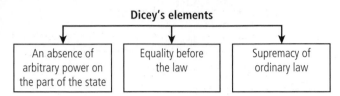

**Figure 2.1** Dicey's elements in the rule of law

### An absence of arbitrary power of the state

The state's power must be controlled by the law. The law must set limits on what the state can or cannot do. In our legal system actions of, and decisions by, government ministers can be challenged by judicial review. One of the main aims of the rule of law is to avoid the state having wide discretionary powers. Dicey recognised that discretion can be exercised in an arbitrary way and this should be avoided to comply with the rule of law.

### Everyone must be equal before the law

No person must be above the law. It does not matter how rich or powerful a person is, the law must deal with them in the same way as it would anyone else. Another side of this part of the rule of law is that those who carry out functions of state must be accountable under the law for their actions.

### The law must be supreme

This is particularly true in the law of England and Wales in the time of Dicey, as many of the main developments up to that time were through judicial decisions rather than being created by Parliament. Today most laws are through legislation, that is Acts of Parliament and delegated legislation, though judicial decisions do still create law.

### 2.2.2 Problems with Dicey's views

A major problem with Dicey's view of the rule of law is that it conflicts with another fundamental principle, that of parliamentary supremacy. This concept holds that an Act of Parliament can overrule any other law. The concept also holds that no other body has the right to override or set aside an Act of Parliament.

See section 3.5 for fuller details of the concept of parliamentary supremacy.

So under the rule of law there should be no arbitrary power on the part of the state, yet under parliamentary supremacy Parliament has the right to make any law it wishes and these can include granting arbitrary powers to the state.

Also, laws passed by Parliament cannot be challenged through judicial review. This is different from some other countries where the legislative body is subject to the rule of law, so that laws passed by them can be challenged in the courts.

Another problem is that equality before the law in Dicey's theory refers to formal equality. It disregards the differences between people in terms of wealth, power and connections. Real equality can only be achieved if there are mechanisms in place to address these differences. For example, the cost of taking legal cases to court is very high. In order to allow the poorest in society to be able to enforce their rights and so be equal under the law, it is necessary to have some form of state help in financing their case.

Dicey's view of the rule of law is based on abstract ideas. This makes it difficult to apply in real-life situations.

## 2.2.3 Other views

F.A. von Hayek, a twentieth-century academic economist, agreed with Dicey that the key component of the rule of law is the absence of any arbitrary power on the part of the state. However, von Hayek thought that the rule of law had become weaker. His reason for this was that, provided actions of the state were authorised by legislation, any act in accordance with this legislation was lawful. He also pointed out that the modern state is directly involved in regulating economic activity and this is in conflict with the rule of law.

Another academic, Joseph Raz (1939– ), recognised that the rule of law was a way of controlling discretion rather than preventing it completely. He saw the rule of law as of negative value, acting to minimise the danger of the use of discretionary power in an arbitrary way. He thought that the key point which emerged from the rule of law was that the law must be capable of guiding the individual's behaviour.

He set out a number of principles which come from this wider idea. Some of these are:

- There should be clear rules and procedures for making laws.
- The independence of the judiciary must be guaranteed.
- The principles of natural justice should be observed; these require an open and fair hearing with all parties being given the opportunity to put their case.
- The courts should have the power to review the way in which the other principles are implemented to ensure that they are being operated as demanded by the rule of law.

Within our legal system there have been changes in the twenty-first century which support these principles. A major example is the Constitutional Reform Act 2005 which recognised the rule of law and the importance of the independence of the judiciary. Section 1 of that Act states:

**This Act does not adversely affect**

a    the existing constitutional principle of the rule of law; or

b    the Lord Chancellor's existing constitutional role in relation to that principle

## While s 3(1) states:

> The Lord Chancellor, other Ministers of the Crown and all with responsibility for matters relating to the judiciary or otherwise to the administration of justice must uphold the continued independence of the judiciary.

For more on the independence of the judiciary see Chapter 21.

These safeguards in the Constitutional Reform Act 2005 show the importance that is attached to the rule of law.

### Look online

Look up the Constitutional Reform Act 2005 on www. legislation.gov.uk. What other changes were introduced by the Act?

**Figure 2.2** Comparing views of the rule of law

| Dicey | von Hayek | Raz |
|---|---|---|
| Absence of arbitrary power on the part of the state | Absence of arbitrary power on the part of the state | Clear rules and procedures for making laws |
| Equality before the law | Rule of law weakened by an increasingly interventionist state | Judicial independence must be guaranteed |
| Supremacy of ordinary law | Modern state is directly involved in regulating economic activity in conflict with the rule of law | Principles of natural justice should be observed |
| | | Courts should have the power to review the way in which the other principles are implemented |

## 2.3 The rule of law and law making

The rule of law is very important when it comes to law making. The process by which laws are made must be open and fair.

In our legislative system, Acts of Parliament have to be passed by both Houses of Parliament. In practice the government of the day usually has a majority in the House of Commons. So most proposed new laws will be passed by the House of Commons, although there will be debate on all contentious issues which can lead to changes being made.

The House of Lords exercises a check on the law-making process as all new laws have also to be passed by them. One area where the House of Lords has consistently voted against change in the law has been in relation to allowing trials in the Crown Court without a jury.

The government can also make regulations through statutory instruments (delegated legislation). As these regulations do not always have to be considered by Parliament as a whole, there are several checks on this method of law making. First, Parliament must pass an Act granting power to make regulations. Then Parliament also has various powers to scrutinise and check the regulations. Finally, the regulations can be challenged in the courts through the process of judicial review to make sure that they have not gone beyond the powers granted by Parliament.

See Chapter 4 at section 4.2 for more information on control of delegated legislation.

## 2.4 The rule of law and the legal system

The way in which the legal system works is also covered by the rule of law. One of the most important points is that every defendant in criminal cases must have a fair trial. Trial by jury is seen as an important factor in maintaining fairness and protecting citizens' rights.

Another very important point is that no person can be imprisoned without a trial. In countries where the rule of law is disregarded, people are likely to be detained without a trial, particularly if they are opponents of the government.

The rule of law is also important in the civil justice system. Ordinary people need to be able to resolve their disputes effectively through the civil justice system. This means that the system should be free from discrimination. It must also be free from corruption and not improperly influenced by public officials. Our system is trusted and recognised for being impartial.

The civil justice system should be accessible and affordable. This point is open to debate as there have been major cuts to public funding of cases in the past 20 or so years. At the same time the costs of taking civil cases to court has increased. People of modest means are unlikely to be able to afford to take a case to court. However, there has been an increase in alternative ways of resolving civil disputes which are much cheaper to use.

See Chapter 10 for details on alternative dispute resolution.

## 2.5 The rule of law and substantive law

Substantive means the law in the different areas of law. There is the substantive law of criminal law which sets out the definitions of the various criminal offences. There is the substantive law of tort which sets out what rights and responsibilities people owe to each other in everyday life. The substantive law of contract lays down the rules on such issues as when a contract is formed, what events may make that contract void or voidable and what will breach a contract. The substantive law of human rights sets out the various rights that individuals are entitled to expect.

Whatever the area of substantive law it is important that the rules recognise that people have key rights and that the laws are not oppressive.

Many criminal laws are aimed at protecting people, such as murder, manslaughter and non-fatal offences against the person. Other offences are aimed at protecting property, such as theft, burglary or criminal damage. Other offences can be aimed at preventing disruptive behaviour and protecting public order. There are also regulatory offences aimed at such issues as preventing pollution, ensuring that food sold in shops is fit for human consumption and a wide range of driving offences aimed at safety on the roads.

For all offences the law has to be clear and the prosecution have to prove that the defendant has committed the offence. All offences also have a stated maximum penalty and the courts cannot impose a higher penalty. In fact in nearly all cases the penalty imposed will be much lower than the maximum allowed.

Many torts are aimed at protecting people and their property and give the right to claim compensation for damage caused by breaches of the law. Unlike criminal law, where the prosecution is nearly always brought by the state, it is the person affected by the tort who claims. For example, if one person drives negligently and knocks down a pedestrian, that pedestrian has the right to claim compensation for his injuries.

One of the problems, as mentioned in section 2.4, is that public funding for making claims in tort through the courts is no longer available. This means that although everyone has the right to claim, so there appears to be equality before the law, in fact financial problems can make it difficult for many people to claim. Conditional fee agreements can be used to fund such cases, but there are still problems.

Contract law recognises that, in most cases, people should be free to make what agreements they wish. However, it does recognise that consumers may have very little choice when making contracts with businesses and that there is not really equality between the parties. In order to bring about greater equality, contract law provides some rights for consumers.

An example is the Consumer Protection Act 1987 which gives consumers much wider rights where they are injured or their property is damaged by faulty goods. The Act allows any consumer to claim, not just the buyer of the goods. So where an item is bought as a present for another person, that person can claim if there is a fault in the goods which causes him injury. Another example is the Consumer Rights Act 2015 which applies to contracts between a trader and a consumer to supply goods, digital content or services. The Act sets out statutory rights of the consumer. These include that the goods must be of satisfactory quality and fit for purpose.

Human rights law supports the rule of law in many ways. For example, all rights must be applied without discrimination. The European Convention on Human Rights sets out the right to liberty. This right should only be taken away where it is in accordance with the law, such as imprisoning someone who has been found guilty of murder. The Convention also states that there is a right to a fair trial.

So the rule of law is central to any legal claim.

**Tip**

When discussing the rule of law use examples from the different areas of law.

## Check your understanding

1  Which one of the following Acts of Parliament provides that it does not adversely affect previously existing constitutional principle of the rule of law?

    A  Legal Services Act 2007

    B  Law Commissions Act 1965

    C  Constitutional Reform Act 2005

    D  Parliament Act 1949

2  Explain Professor Dicey's three elements of the rule of law.

## Summary

- The rule of law is important in a democratic country.
- All people are subject to and accountable to law that is fairly applied and enforced.
- There is equality before the law.
- Dicey held that there were three elements that created the rule of law:
    - an absence of arbitrary power on the part of the state
    - equality before the law
    - supremacy of ordinary law.
- F.A. von Hayek stated: 'Stripped of all technicalities the Rule of Law means that the government in all its actions is bound by rules fixed and announced in advance.'

- Joseph Raz recognised that the rule of law was a way of controlling discretion rather than preventing it completely.
- The process by which laws are made must be open and fair:
    - Acts of Parliament have to be passed by both Houses of Parliament
    - delegated legislation is subject to controls.
- Both criminal and civil justice systems must be fair.
- The rule of law is an important element in all areas of substantive law.

# 3 Law making: parliamentary law making

After reading this chapter you should be able to:
- Understand the way law is made by Parliament
- Understand the influences on parliamentary law making
- Discuss the advantages and disadvantages of influences on parliamentary law making
- Understand the doctrine of parliamentary supremacy
- Comment on the limitations on parliamentary supremacy

## 3.1 Parliament

A key principle in a democracy is that laws should be made by the elected representatives of society. In the United Kingdom this means that major laws are made by Parliament. Parliament consists of the House of Commons, the House of Lords and the Crown.

### 3.1.1 House of Commons

The members of the House of Commons are elected by the electorate. The country is divided into constituencies and each of these votes for one Member of Parliament (MP).

There must be a general election every five years. In addition, there may be individual by-elections in constituencies where the MP has died or retired during the current session of Parliament.

The government of the day is formed by the political party which has a majority in the House of Commons, and it is the government which has the main say in formulating new Acts of Parliament.

### 3.1.2 House of Lords

The House of Lords is a non-elected body. Before 1999, there were over 1,100 members of the House of Lords of whom 750 were hereditary peers. The rest consisted of life peers (people who have been given a title for their service to the country), judges and bishops.

In 1999 the Labour Government reviewed membership of the House of Lords and decided that it should consist of some nominated members (like the life peers) and some elected members. In particular they decided that an inherited title should not automatically allow that person to take part in the law-making process. Temporary changes were made to the membership of the House of Lords so that it consisted of:

- 92 hereditary peers
- about 700 life peers
- the 26 most senior bishops in the Church of England.

This was meant to be a temporary solution while the government consulted on the final make-up of the House of Lords. However, there has not yet been agreement on how many of the House of Lords should be elected and how many should be nominated (and by whom).

Note that the 12 most senior judges used to sit in the House of Lords, but they no longer do so. They are now separate from Parliament and sit as the Supreme Court. See Chapter 16 for more information.

## 3.2 Green and White Papers

Each government minister has a department of civil servants and advisers. The particular ministry which is responsible for the area in which a change in the law is being considered will draft ideas for change.

On major matters a **Green Paper** may be issued by the Minister with responsibility for that matter. A Green Paper is a consultative document on a topic in which the government's view is put forward with proposals for law reform. Interested parties are then invited to send comments to the relevant government department, so that a full consideration of all sides can be made and necessary changes made to the government's proposals. Following this the

The Palace of Westminster, London

government may publish a **White Paper** with its firm proposals for new law.

An unusual example was seen following the decision by the Supreme Court in January 2017 that Parliament had to be consulted on leaving the European Union (Brexit). The Government issued a White Paper before a Bill was put before Parliament. The White Paper set out twelve principles including 'taking control of our own laws'.

Consultation before any new law is framed is valuable as it allows time for mature consideration. Governments have been criticised for sometimes responding in a 'knee-jerk' fashion to incidents and, as a result, rushing law through that has subsequently proved to be unworkable.

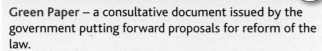

> ### Key terms
>
> **Green Paper** – a consultative document issued by the government putting forward proposals for reform of the law.
>
> **White Paper** – a document issued by the government stating their decisions as to how they are going to reform the law.

## 3.3 The formal legislative process

Major legislation is usually made through Acts of Parliament. Acts of Parliament are also known as statutes. There is a very long and formal process which has to be followed before an Act of Parliament becomes law.

### 3.3.1 Introducing an Act of Parliament

The great majority of Acts of Parliament are introduced by the government and these are initially drafted by lawyers in the Civil Service who are known as parliamentary counsel to the Treasury. The government department which is responsible for the new law gives instructions as to what is to be included and the intended effect of the proposed law.

### Bills

When the proposed Act has been drafted it is published, and at this stage it is called a **Bill**. It will only become an Act of Parliament if it successfully completes all the necessary stages in Parliament and receives the Royal Assent. Where it is a Bill put forward by the government it will be introduced into Parliament by a government minister. For example,

the Minister of Justice (or a junior minister in that department) will introduce any Bills about the justice system, while the Minister for the Department for the Environment, Food and Rural Affairs (or an MP in that department) will introduce any Bills on issues about the environment.

Even at this early stage there are difficulties, as the draftsmen face problems in trying to frame the Bill. It has to be drawn up so that it represents the government's wishes, while at the same time using correct legal wording so that there will not be any difficulties in the courts applying it. It must be unambiguous, precise and comprehensive. Achieving all this is not easy, and there may be unforeseen problems from the language used, as discussed in Chapter 5.

In addition, there is usually a pressure on time, as the government will have a timetable of when they wish to introduce the draft Bill into Parliament.

> ### Key term
>
> **Bill** – the name for a draft law going through Parliament before it passes all the parliamentary stages to become an Act of Parliament.

### Private members' Bills

As well as Bills being introduced into Parliament by the government, it is possible for individual (private) Members of Parliament to introduce a Bill. These MPs are those who are not government ministers. They can be from any political party. They are also known as 'backbenchers' because they do not sit in the front row in the actual House of Commons. (The government ministers sit in the front row.)

Relatively few private members' Bills became law, but there have been some important laws passed as the result of such Bills. A major example was the Abortion Act 1967 which legalised abortion in this country. Others include the Marriage Act 1994 which allows people to marry in any registered place, not only in Register Offices or religious buildings, and the Household Waste Recycling Act 2003 which places local authorities under a duty to recycle waste.

There are two ways a private MP can introduce a Bill. These are:

- by ballot
- through the 'ten-minute' rule.

### Ballot

The parliamentary process allows for a ballot each parliamentary session in which 20 private members are selected who can then take their turn in presenting a Bill to Parliament. The time for debate of private members' Bills is limited, usually only being debated on Fridays, so that only the first six or seven members in the ballot have a realistic chance of introducing a Bill on their chosen topic.

### Ten-minute rule

Backbenchers can also try to introduce a Bill through the 'ten-minute' rule, under which any MP can make a speech of up to ten minutes supporting the introduction of new legislation. This method is rarely successful unless there is no opposition to the Bill, but some Acts of Parliament have been introduced in this way, for example the Bail (Amendment) Act 1993 which gave the prosecution the right to appeal against the granting of bail to a defendant. Members of the House of Lords can also introduce private members' Bills.

## Public Bills

Most Bills introduced into Parliament involve matters of public policy which will affect either the whole country or a large section of it. These Bills are known as Public Bills. Most government Bills are in this category. For example the Legal Services Act 2007, the Legal Aid, Sentencing and Punishment of Offenders Act 2012 and the Criminal Justice and Courts Act 2015 all started as Public Bills.

## Private Bills

A small number of Bills are designed to pass a law which will affect only individual people or corporations. These do not affect the whole community. They are known as Private Bills. A recent example of such a Bill was the Faversham Oyster Fisheries Bill 2016. This Bill changes the way the company is run.

**Look online**

This Bill should have been passed by the time you read this textbook. Search for it as an Act on www.legislation.gov.uk.

## Hybrid Bills

These are a cross between Public Bills and Private Bills. They are introduced by the government, but if they become law they will affect a particular person, organisation or place. Recent examples are the various Crossrail Bills. These Bills allow for the construction of underground rail links in London which affect people in the area. The Bills give power to acquire land, grant planning permission and authorise the necessary work. Individuals directly and specially affected by the construction of the route have been able to petition about it, so their views could be considered before the various Acts have been passed.

## 3.3.2 Role of the House of Commons

As the members of the House of Commons are democratically elected, most Bills are introduced into the House of Commons first. If the House of Commons votes against a Bill, then that is the end of the Bill.

During the course of a Bill through the House of Commons, there will be debates on issues of the policy behind the law as well as on the specific details of the Bill.

**Figure 3.1** Types of bill

| Type of Bill | Explanation | Example of statute |
|---|---|---|
| **Government Bill** | Introduced by the government | Criminal Justice and Courts Act 2015 |
| **Private members' Bill** | Introduced by a private MP | Household Waste Recycling Act 2003 |
| **Public Bill** | Involves matters of public policy and affects the general public | Legal Aid, Sentencing and Punishment Act 2012 |
| **Private Bill** | Affects a particular organisation, person or place | Faversham Oyster Fishery Company Bill 2016 |
| **Hybrid Bill** | Introduced by the government but affects an organisation, person or place | Crossrail Acts |

The government will have a majority in the House of Commons, so that it is likely that policies supported by the government will become law.

### 3.3.3 Role of the House of Lords

The House of Lords acts as a check on the House of Commons. All Bills go through the House of Lords and they can vote against proposed changes to the law. In some cases this may alert the House of Commons to a problem with the proposal and it will be dropped or amended.

However, the power of the House of Lords is limited by the Parliament Acts 1911 and 1949. These allow a Bill to become law even if the House of Lords rejects it, provided that the Bill is reintroduced into the House of Commons in the next session of Parliament and passes all the stages again there. So the House of Lords can only delay a law by up to one year.

The principle behind the Parliament Acts is that the House of Lords is not an elected body. Its function is to refine and add to the law rather than oppose the will of the democratically elected House of Commons. In fact there have only been four occasions when this procedure has been used to by-pass the House of Lords after they had voted against a Bill. These were for the:

■ War Crimes Act 1991
■ European Parliamentary Elections Act 1999
■ Sexual Offences (Amendment) Act 2000
■ Hunting Act 2004.

Following the passing of the Hunting Act 2004 under the use of the Parliament Acts, there was a challenge as to whether the Act was constitutionally valid. This was in R (Jackson and others) v Attorney General (2005). The challenge was on the basis that the Parliament Act 1949 could not be used as it had increased the House of Commons' power without the agreement of the House of Lords. It was held that the Parliament Act 1949 merely placed limits on the power of the unelected House of Lords. It did not increase the power of the House of Commons. Therefore the Hunting Act 2004 had been validly enacted and was law.

### 3.3.4 The parliamentary process

In order to become an Act of Parliament, the Bill will usually have to be passed by both Houses of Parliament, and in each House there is a long and complex process. A Bill may start in either the House of Commons or the House of Lords, with the exception of Finance Bills which must start in the House of Commons. All Bills must go through the following stages.

### First reading

This is a formal procedure where the name of the Bill is read out. No discussion or vote takes place.

### Second reading

This is the main debate on the whole Bill in which MPs debate the principles behind the Bill. The debate usually focuses on the main principles rather than the smaller details. Those MPs who wish to speak in the debate must catch the Speaker's eye, since the Speaker controls all debates and no one may speak without being called on by the Speaker. At the end of this a vote is taken. The vote may be verbal, that is the Speaker of the House asks the members as a whole how they vote and the members shout out 'Aye' or 'No'. If it is clear that nearly all members are in agreement, either for or against, there is no need for a more formal vote.

If it is not possible to judge whether more people are shouting 'Aye' or 'No', there will be a formal vote in which the members of the House vote by leaving the Chamber and then walking back in through one of two special doors on one side or the other of the Chamber. There will be two 'tellers' positioned at each of these two voting doors to make a list of the members voting on each side. These tellers count up the number of MPs who voted for and against and declare these numbers to the Speaker in front of the members of the House.

Obviously there must be a majority in favour for the Bill to progress any further.

### Committee stage

At this stage a detailed examination of each clause of the Bill is undertaken by a committee of between 16 and 50 MPs. This is usually done by what is called a Standing Committee, which, contrary to its name, is a committee chosen specifically for that Bill. In such a committee the government will have a majority and the opposition and minority parties are represented proportionately to the number of seats they have in the House of Commons.

The Members of Parliament nominated for each Standing Committee will usually be those with a special interest in or knowledge of the subject of the Bill which is being considered. For Finance Bills the whole House will sit in committee.

### Report stage

At the Committee stage amendments to various clauses in the Bill may have been voted on and passed, so this Report stage is where the committee report back to the House on those amendments. (If there were no amendments at the Committee stage, there will not be a Report stage – instead the Bill will go straight on to the Third reading.) The amendments will be debated in the House and accepted or rejected. Further amendments may also be added. The Report stage has been described as 'a useful safeguard against a small Committee amending a Bill against the wishes of the House, and a necessary opportunity for second thoughts'.

## Third reading

This is the final vote on the Bill. It is almost a formality since a Bill that has passed through all the stages above is unlikely to fail at this late stage. In fact in the House of Commons there will only be an actual further debate on the Bill as a whole if at least six MPs request it.

> **Tip**
>
> The process in the House of Commons is similar to that in the House of Lords but there are some important differences. It is important to be able to describe the process at each stage and in each House.

## The House of Lords

If the Bill started life in the House of Commons it is now passed to the House of Lords where it goes through the same five stages outlined above. If the House of Lords makes amendments to the Bill, then it will go back to the House of Commons for them to consider those amendments. If the Commons do not accept the Lords' amendments, they then send those amendments back to the Lords. This sending to and fro can go on for some time and is referred to as 'ping-pong'.

## Royal Assent

The final stage is where the monarch formally gives approval to the Bill and it then becomes an Act of Parliament. This is now a formality and, under the Royal Assent Act 1967, the monarch will not even have the text of the Bill to which she is assenting; she will only have the short title. The last time that a monarch refused assent was in 1707, when Queen Anne refused to assent to the Scottish Militia Bill.

These stages in the parliamentary procedure are shown in a flow chart in Figure 3.2.

> **Tip**
>
> The parliamentary process is relatively easy, but it is important to know it well.

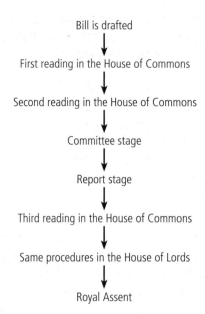

**Figure 3.2** Flow chart of the passing of an Act of Parliament starting in the House of Commons

## 3.3.5 Commencement of an Act of Parliament

Following the Royal Assent the Act of Parliament will come into force on midnight of that day, unless another date has been set. However, very few Acts are implemented immediately. Instead the Act itself states the date when it will commence or passes responsibility on to the appropriate minister to fix the commencement date. In the latter case the minister will bring the Act into force by issuing a commencement order.

This can cause problems as it can be necessary to keep checking which sections have been brought into force. It may be that some sections or even a whole Act will never become law. An example of this is the Easter Act 1928, which was intended to fix the date of Easter Day. Although this Act passed all the necessary parliamentary stages, and was given the Royal Assent, it has never come into force.

## 3.3.6 Example of an Act of Parliament

Figure 3.3 shows a reproduction of an Act of Parliament – the Lords Spiritual (Women) Act 2015. This shows what an Act of Parliament looks like. The name of the Act is given immediately under the Royal coat of arms. Underneath the name, '2015 CHAPTER 18' means that it was the eighteenth Act to be passed in 2015.

Next follows a short statement or preamble about the purpose of the Act. Then there is a formal statement starting 'BE IT ENACTED' showing that the Act has been passed by both Houses of Parliament and received the Royal Assent. This is included in all Acts. After this comes the body of the Act, which is set out in sections. This is a very short Act with only two sections.

Section 1 has five subsections. The effect is to allow for women bishops to become members of the House of Lords when there is a vacancy. Remember that the 26 most senior bishops in the Church of England are entitled to sit in the House of Lords.

Section 2 has three subsections. These give the commencement (that is when the Act will come into force), the area of the country that it applies to – here it is England and Wales, Scotland and Northern Ireland. The final subsection states the name by which the Act is to be known.

**ELIZABETH II**                                                **c. 18**

# Lords Spiritual (Women) Act 2015

## 2015 CHAPTER 18

An Act to make time-limited provision for vacancies among the Lords Spiritual to be filled by bishops who are women.          [26th March 2015]

B E IT ENACTED by the Queen's most Excellent Majesty, by and with the advice and consent of the Lords Spiritual and Temporal, and Commons, in this present Parliament assembled, and by the authority of the same, as follows:—

**1      Vacancies among the Lords Spiritual**

(1)    This section applies where—
   (a)   a vacancy arises among the Lords Spiritual in the House of Lords in the 10 years beginning with the day on which this Act comes into force,
   (b)   at the time the vacancy arises there is at least one eligible bishop who is a woman, and
   (c)   the person who would otherwise be entitled to fill the vacancy under section 5 of the Bishoprics Act 1878 is a man.

(2)    If at the time the vacancy arises there is only one eligible bishop who is a woman, the vacancy is to be filled by the issue of writs of summons to her.

(3)    If at the time the vacancy arises there are two or more eligible bishops who are women, the vacancy is to be filled by the issue of writs of summons to the one whose election as a bishop of a diocese in England was confirmed first.

**Figure 3.3a** The Lords Spiritual (Women) Act 2015

(4)    In this section "eligible bishop" means a bishop of a diocese in England who is not yet entitled in that capacity to the issue of writs of summons.

(5)    The reference in subsection (1) to a vacancy does not include a vacancy arising by the avoidance of the see of Canterbury, York, London, Durham or Winchester.

**2        Commencement, extent and short title**

(1)    This Act comes into force on the day Parliament first meets following the first parliamentary general election after this Act is passed.

(2)    This Act extends to England and Wales, Scotland and Northern Ireland.

(3)    This Act may be cited as the Lords Spiritual (Women) Act 2015.

**Figure 3.3b** The Lords Spiritual (Women) Act 2015 (continued)

**Look online**

1.  Look up a recent Act of Parliament on the internet. You can find Acts on www.legislation.gov.uk. Try to find the commencement section.

2.  Look up any Bill that is currently going through Parliament. These can be seen on www.parliament. uk. What stage in the parliamentary process has the Bill you have chosen reached?

## 3.3.7 Advantages of law making in Parliament

The main advantage of parliamentary-made law is that it is made by our elected representatives. This means it is democratic. Also, as there has to be a general election at least once every five years, the public can vote out any government if it has not performed as the public expected.

Another advantage is that Acts of Parliament can reform whole areas of law in the one Act. An example is in the criminal law with the Fraud Act 2006, which abolished all the old offences of deception and fraud and created a newer and, hopefully, simpler structure of offences. Judges can only change the law on very

small areas of law as they can only rule on the point of law in the case they are deciding.

Acts of Parliament can also set broad policies and give the power to others to make detailed regulations. This is known as delegated legislation (see Chapter 4). This is an advantage because the general structure is laid down by Parliament but it allows greater detail in the law than if it was just contained in an Act of Parliament.

Also before a Bill is presented to Parliament there will have been consultation on the proposed changes to the law. This allows the government to take into consideration objections to the proposals. Also, as all Bills have to go through the lengthy process in both Houses of Parliament, the new law will be thoroughly discussed in Parliament.

Law made by Parliament is also certain as it cannot be challenged under the doctrine of parliamentary supremacy (see section 3.5).

## 3.3.8 Disadvantages of law making in Parliament

Although there are major advantages to having law made in Parliament, there are also some disadvantages. One is that Parliament does not always have time to deal with all the reforms that are proposed. This is particularly true of reform of 'lawyers' law' such as criminal law or the law of contract.

An example of law that is still awaiting reform is the law on assaults and other offences against the person. The Law Commission proposed changes to the law on offences against the person in 1993. Reform was needed because the old law dated back to an Act of 1861 which was very difficult to understand. In 1997 the government accepted that there was a need for reform and published a draft Bill in 1998. However, this was not put before Parliament and the law has not yet been reformed.

Even where the government introduces a Bill into Parliament the process of becoming an Act with all the different reading, committee and report stages can take several months.

The government is in control of the parliamentary timetable and allows very little time for private members' Bills. Even when a private member does manage to introduce a Bill, it can be easily voted out by the government as they have the majority in the House of Commons. The result is that very few private members' Bills become law.

Another disadvantage is that Acts of Parliament are often very long and complex. This can make them difficult to understand. In fact many of the cases that go to the Supreme Court on appeals are about what the words in an Act of Parliament mean.

The law can become even more complicated where one Act amends another so that it is necessary to consult two or more Acts to find out exactly what the law is.

## 3.4 The influences on Parliament

There are several influences that lead to Parliament deciding what new law to bring in or what law needs to be changed.

### 3.4.1 Political influence

When there is a general election all the political parties publish a list of the reforms they would carry out if they were elected as the next government. This is called the party's manifesto, and it is one of the ways in which the party tries to persuade people to vote for them.

The party that has the most members of Parliament after a general election becomes the government. This party then has the whole life of the Parliament

(this can be up to five years) to bring in the reforms they promised in their manifesto. Most of the reforms will gradually be put before Parliament to pass as an Act of Parliament.

Throughout any session of Parliament, the government has the major say on what new laws will be put before the House of Commons and the House of Lords for debate.

At the opening of each session of Parliament (usually about once a year) the government announces its plans for new laws in that session. This is done in the Queen's speech. This speech is written for the Queen by the Prime Minister and other senior ministers. This is shown in the speech as the Queen will usually use the words 'my government will …'.

### Advantages

Each political party has its proposals for reform ready so that if they are elected as the government they know what they wish to do. Also the fact that the government has a majority in the House of Commons means that virtually every law it proposes will be passed. This makes the law-making process efficient.

### Disadvantages

If a different party is elected at the next general election, they may decide to repeal or alter some of the laws that the previous government passed. This is because their policies are likely to be quite different from those of the previous government. Changes in the law in this way can be costly and open to criticism.

Where the government has a very small majority it may restrict what laws they can get passed in Parliament. In particular, when there is a coalition government (that is where two parties have to combine in order to have the majority of MPs in the House of Commons) then they will have to compromise on what policies are followed. This happened in the Coalition Government of 2010–15 where the Conservative and Liberal Democrat parties joined together to form the government.

### 3.4.2 Public opinion/media

Where there is strong public opinion about a change to the law, the government may bow to such opinion. This is more likely towards the end of a term of government when there will be a general election soon and the government wants to remain popular with the majority of people.

The term 'media' means the ways in which information is supplied to the public. It includes television and radio, newspapers and magazines. The media play a large role in bringing public opinion to the government's attention. Where an issue is given a high profile on television and in the newspapers, then this also brings it to the attention of other members of the public and may add to the weight of public opinion.

## Advantages

Sometimes public opinion will be affected by specific events and these may also play a role in formulating the law. A particularly tragic example was the massacre in 1996 of 16 young children and their teacher in Dunblane by a lone gunman with a legally owned gun. An enquiry into the ownership of guns was set up and a pressure group organised a petition asking for guns to be banned. Eventually Parliament banned private ownership of most handguns.
This has helped prevent many further such tragic incidents. In America, where private ownership of guns is allowed, there are frequent examples of mass shootings each year.

We have a free press. This is an advantage as they are able to criticise government policy or bring any other issue to the attention of the government. An example of the media highlighting bad practice was seen in 2009 over Members of Parliaments' expenses claims. Expenses claims made by various MPs were detailed in a national newspaper. Some of the claims were for quite large amounts of money and some were even for items which the MP had not paid for. This caused a public outrage at the system of MPs' expenses. Parliament then had to reform the whole system.

## Disadvantages

The government may respond too quickly to high-profile incidents (a 'knee-jerk reaction'). This can lead to law being created too quickly and not thought through, so that the law is poorly drafted. This was seen with the Dangerous Dogs Act 1991 where the wording in the Act has led to many disputed cases in the courts. The Act has also failed to protect people from dangerous dogs as thousands of people need hospital treatment each year after being attacked by dogs. Also each year there are incidents in which people, especially children, die as a result of being attacked by a dog.

There is also the disadvantage that, in some cases, it can be argued that the media manipulate the news and create public opinion.

## 3.4.3 Pressure groups

These are groups which have a particular interest. They try to bring matters they are interested in to the attention of the general public and the government. There are two types of pressure group: sectional and cause.

**Sectional pressure groups** exist to represent the interests of a particular group of people. They often represent work groups or professions. Examples include the Law Society which represents solicitors' interests, the British Medical Association which represents doctors and trade unions which represent workers in different types of jobs.

**Cause pressure groups** exist to promote a particular cause. There are many different types of 'cause' pressure group. Examples include environmental groups such as Greenpeace, animal welfare groups, human rights groups, such as Amnesty and ASH, the anti-smoking group.

Pressure groups may make the government reconsider the law on certain areas. This was seen in 2000 when the government finally agreed to reduce the age of consent for homosexual acts in private to 16. Another example of the government bowing to public opinion and the efforts of the pressure group the League against Cruel Sports was the passing of the Hunting Act 2004, which banned hunting foxes with dogs. In 2007 strict laws against smoking in public places were introduced because of public opinion and medical opinion.

Sometimes pressure groups will campaign against a proposed change to the law. This was seen when the government tried to restrict the right to trial by jury. Pressure groups such as Justice and Liberty campaigned against this as they thought the changes infringed human rights.

### Key terms

**Sectional pressure group** – a pressure group that represents the interests of a particular group of people.

**Cause pressure group** – a pressure group that exists to promote a particular cause.

## Lobbying

Some pressure groups try to persuade individual Members of Parliament to support their cause. This is called lobbying (because members of the public can meet MPs in the lobbies (small hallways) through which MPs go to get to the House of Commons). If a pressure group is successful, it may persuade an MP to ask questions in Parliament about a particular problem. It is also possible that a backbench MP may use the private members' Bill session (see section 3.3.1) to introduce a Bill trying to reform the law in the way that the pressure group wants. However, it is very unlikely that such a Bill will be passed by Parliament unless there is widespread support for it.

## Advantages

A wide range of issues is drawn to the attention of the government as there are so many pressure groups with different aims and issues.

Pressure groups often raise important issues. Environmental groups have made the government much more aware of the damage being done to our environment by greenhouse gases and other pollutants.

## Disadvantages

It can be argued that pressure groups are seeking to impose their ideas, even where the majority of the public do not support their views.

There are also occasions when two pressure groups have conflicting interests and want opposing things.

This was seen when the ban against fox hunting was considered. The League against Cruel Sports wanted it banned, but the Countryside Alliance wanted it to be allowed to continue.

## 3.4.4 Law reform bodies

There are some official law reform bodies which consider what reforms of the law are needed and report on these. The most important of these is the Law Commission.

The Law Commission is a permanent panel of legal experts who research areas of law and recommend which laws need to be reformed. They usually look at whole areas and make comprehensive proposals for reform. Before setting out their final proposals for reform they issue a consultation paper so that they can get the views of interested parties. In most cases their final report includes a draft Bill setting out the exact way they think the law should be reformed. These reports go to Parliament and most of the recommendations are eventually made law.

See Chapter 7 for fuller details on the work of the Law Commission.

**Figure 3.4** Influences on parliamentary law making

| Influence | Explanation | Advantages | Disadvantages |
|---|---|---|---|
| **Political** | Each political party has its own policies and drafts a manifesto before a general election<br><br>When elected as the government, these will be a major influence on the laws they introduce into Parliament | Each political party has its proposals ready if it is elected<br><br>A government majority means that most of the laws it introduces will be passed | New governments may repeal or alter laws made by previous governments |
| **Public opinion/Media** | Strong public opinion can lead to a change in the law<br><br>The media play an important role in highlighting issues of social concern | Brings the attention of the government to areas of law that need reforming | Responding too quickly to high-profile incidents may lead to poorly drafted law<br><br>Media manipulating the news and creating public opinion |
| **Pressure groups** | Groups that have a particular interest and bring issues to the attention of the general public and the government | Raise important issues<br><br>Wide range of issues is drawn to the attention of Parliament | Trying to impose their will on the majority<br><br>Pressure groups may have conflicting interests |
| **Law Commission** | An independent body to review the law and propose reform | Law is researched by legal experts<br><br>Consults before finalising proposals<br><br>Whole areas of law are considered | Parliament does not implement all proposals |

## Advantages

The main advantages of having the Law Commission issue reports on areas of law are:

- areas of law are researched by legal experts
- the Law Commission consults before finalising its proposals
- whole areas of law can be considered, not just isolated issues
- enacting the law on an area in one Act (such as the Fraud Act 2006) makes the law easier to find and understand.

## Disadvantages

The government does not always implement the reforms it suggests. This is partly because of lack of parliamentary time for pure law reform. Parliamentary time has to be given to major issues such as finance and taxation, foreign affairs, health and education. The reform of substantive areas of law is not a priority.

### Look online

Look up websites of pressure groups such as Liberty (www.liberty-human-rights.org.uk), Justice (www.justice.org.uk) or Greenpeace (www.greenpeace.org.uk). (These are only suggestions. You can find many other websites by searching.)

Choose one pressure group and write a brief summary of any changes in the law it is suggesting or any success in changing the law that it has had.

# 3.5 The doctrine of parliamentary supremacy

## 3.5.1 Definition of parliamentary supremacy

The most widely recognised definition of parliamentary supremacy was given by Dicey in the nineteenth century. He made three main points:

1. Parliament can legislate on any subject-matter.
2. No Parliament can be bound by any previous Parliament, nor can a Parliament pass any Act that will bind a later Parliament.
3. No other body has the right to override or set aside an Act of Parliament.

Parliamentary supremacy is also referred to as the sovereignty of Parliament.

## Legislating on any subject-matter

There are no limits on what Parliament can make laws about. It can make any law it wants. For example, in the past Parliament changed the rule on who should succeed to the throne. This was in 1700 when Parliament passed the Act of Settlement which stated that the children of King James II (who were the direct line of the monarchy) could not succeed to the throne. Also in modern times the rule that the eldest son had the right to be the next monarch even though he may have had elder sisters has been changed. This was done by the Succession to the Crown Act 2013.

Parliament can also change its own powers. It did this with the Parliament Acts 1911 and 1949 which placed limits on the right of the House of Lords to block a Bill by voting against it (see section 3.3.3).

## Cannot bind successor

Each new Parliament should be free to make or change what laws they wish. They cannot be bound by a law made by a previous Parliament. They can repeal any previous Act of Parliament.

There are, however, some laws that become such an important part of the British constitution that they cannot realistically be repealed. For example, the Act of Settlement in 1700 changed the line of succession to the throne. It affected who was entitled to become king or queen. Realistically, after 300 years, this cannot now be repealed.

Another example where it would be impractical to repeal the law is the Statute of Westminster 1931. Before 1931 the United Kingdom had the right to make law for Dominion countries (now Commonwealth countries). Section 4 of the Statute of Westminster stated that no future United Kingdom statute should extend to law in those countries unless the countries requested and consented to the legislation. These countries included Australia, Canada and New Zealand.

Technically, the Statute of Westminster 1931 could be repealed and the UK could pass a law extending to one or more of these countries, but obviously none of those countries would accept such a law. So, it is impracticable to repeal the Statute of Westminster.

There are other modern limitations which have been self-imposed by Parliament. These are dealt with in section 3.5.2 below.

## Cannot be overruled by others

This rule is kept to even where the Act of Parliament may have been made because of incorrect information. This was shown by *British Railways Board v Pickin* (1974).

### British Railways Board v Pickin (1974)

A private Act of Parliament, the British Railways Act 1968, was enacted by Parliament. Pickin challenged the Act on the basis that the British Railways Board had fraudulently concealed certain matters from Parliament. This alleged fraud had led to Parliament passing the Act which had the effect of depriving Pickin of his land or proprietary rights. The action was struck out because no court is entitled to go behind an Act once it has been passed. A challenge cannot be made to an Act of Parliament even if there was fraud.

A more modern example is shown by the case taken in the courts over the UK leaving the European Union. The government (the executive) announced that it would trigger Article 50 of the Treaty on European Union to leave the EU in 2017.

The right to do this was challenged in the case of *R (on the application of Miller and another) v The Secretary of State for Exiting the European Union* (2016) where the Supreme Court held that leaving the EU would effectively overrule the European Communities Act 1972. As an Act of Parliament was involved, Parliament had to pass another Act to give authority to start the prosess of leaving.

## 3.5.2 Limitations on parliamentary supremacy

There are now some limitations on Parliament's supremacy but all these limits have been self-imposed by previous Parliaments. The main limitations are through:

■ the effect of the Human Rights Act 1998
■ devolution
■ EU membership.

### Effect of the Human Rights Act 1998

This states that all Acts of Parliament have to be compatible with the European Convention on Human Rights. It is possible to challenge an Act on the ground that it does not comply with the Convention. Under s 4 of the Human Rights Act, the courts have the power to declare an Act incompatible with the Convention.

This happened in *H v Mental Health Review Tribunal* (2001). When a patient was making an application to

be released, the Mental Health Act 1983 placed the burden of proof on the patient to show that he should be released. Human rights meant that it should be up to the state to justify the continuing detention of such a patient. The court made a declaration that the law was not compatible with human rights. Following this declaration of incompatibility, the government changed the law.

However, a declaration of incompatibility does not mean that the government has to change the law. Also, if Parliament wishes it can pass a new Act which contravenes the European Convention on Human Rights.

### Devolution

The Scotland Act 1998 and the Wales Act 1998 have devolved (handed down) certain powers to the Scottish Parliament and to the Welsh Parliament. As a result they can make laws on some matters for their own countries without having to get Parliament's approval. This means that Parliament's supremacy has been lost in these areas.

It is theoretically possible that a future Parliament could repeal the Scotland Act 1998 and the Wales Act 1998, but it seems unlikely as such a move would be very unpopular and would lose support for any political party which proposed it.

### EU membership

In 1973 Britain became a member of the European Union. In 2016 the British people voted in a referendum to leave the European Union and the arrangements to leave were being made while this book was being published.

While Britain is a member of the EU, there are limitations on parliamentary supremacy. EU law takes priority over British law. This was shown by the Merchant Shipping Act 1998 which set down rules for who could own or manage fishing boats registered in Britain. This Act was meant to protect British fishing stocks and the industry in this country. The Act stated that 75 per cent of directors and shareholders had to be British. The Court of Justice of the European Union ruled that this was contrary to EU law and the Merchant Shipping Act could not be enforced so far as EU citizens were concerned.

**Figure 3.5** Parliament and Acts of Parliament

| Pre-legislative procedure | Green Papers<br>White Papers<br>Consultation |
|---|---|
| Parliamentary procedure | First reading<br>Second reading<br>Committee stage<br>Report stage<br>Third reading<br>Same procedure in the other House<br>Royal Assent |
| Advantages and disadvantages | **Advantages**<br>Democratic<br>Allows full reform of law<br>Consultation before Bill is presented to Parliament<br>Discussion in both Houses during legislative process<br>**Disadvantages**<br>Long process<br>Limited parliamentary time may prevent some laws from being reformed<br>Acts can be long and complex<br>Wording of an Act may be difficult to understand and lead to court case on interpretation of meaning |
| Influences | Political policies<br>Public opinion/media<br>Pressure groups<br>Law Commission |
| Parliamentary supremacy | Can legislate on any subject-matter<br>Cannot bind successor<br>Cannot be overruled by others |
| Limitations on parliamentary supremacy | Where impractical to repeal a law<br>Human rights<br>Devolution<br>While a member of the EU – EU law |

## Check your understanding

1 Which one of the following is the correct term for a draft Act of Parliament?

   A Green Paper

   B White Paper

   C Bill

   D Report

2 Explain two limitations on parliamentary supremacy.

3 Explain any one influence on Parliamentary law making and discuss its importance to that process.

## Summary

- Acts of Parliament are laws made by both Houses of Parliament and given Royal Assent.
- There is usually pre-legislative consultation and Green and White Papers will set out the government's proposals for changing the law.
- Bills can be put before Parliament by the government or by individual MPs.
- There are several formal stages in Parliament in both Houses before a Bill can become an Act. These are: First reading, Second reading, Committee stage, Report stage, Third reading and Royal Assent.
- Parliament may be influenced in its law making by political policies, public opinion/media, pressure groups and law reform bodies, especially the Law Commission.
- Parliamentary supremacy means that:
  - Parliament can make law on any subject- matter
  - no Parliament can bind its successors
  - no other body has the right to override or set aside an Act of Parliament.
- The Human Rights Act 1998, devolution and EU Membership have placed some limitations on parliamentary supremacy.

# 4 Law making: delegated legislation

After reading this chapter you should be able to:
- Understand and explain the different types of delegated legislation
- Understand and explain parliamentary and judicial controls on delegated legislation
- Explain the reasons for the use of delegated legislation
- Discuss the advantages and disadvantages of delegated legislation

## Key term

**Delegated legislation** – law made by some person or body other than Parliament, but with the authority of Parliament.

Parliament's authority to make delegated legislation is usually laid down in a 'parent' Act of Parliament known as an enabling Act. The enabling Act creates the framework of the law and then delegates power to others to make more detailed law in the area.

## 4.1 Types of delegated legislation

There are three different types of **delegated legislation**:
- Orders in Council
- statutory instruments
- by-laws.

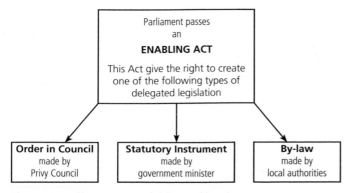

**Figure 4.1** Different types of delegated legislation

Figure 4.1 shows these in diagram form.

### 4.1.1 Orders in Council

The Queen and the Privy Council have the authority to make Orders in Council. The Privy Council is made up of the Prime Minister and other leading members of the government. So this type of delegated legislation effectively allows the government to make laws without going through Parliament.

Orders in Council can be made on a wide range of matters, especially:

- transferring responsibility between government departments, e.g. when the Ministry of Justice was created, the powers of the previous Department of Constitutional Affairs and some of the powers of the Home Office were transferred to what was then a new ministry
- bringing Acts (or parts of Acts) of Parliament into force
- as a member of the European Union, giving legal effect to European Directives.

In addition, the Privy Council has power to make law in emergency situations under the Civil Contingencies Act 2004. This power will usually only be exercised in times of emergency when Parliament is not sitting.

Orders in Council can also be used to make other types of law. For example, in 2003 an Order in Council was used to alter the Misuse of Drugs Act 1971 so as to make cannabis a class C drug. Five years later, the government decided that it had been a mistake to downgrade cannabis and another Order in Council was issued changing cannabis back to a class B drug (see Figure 4.2).

There must be an enabling Act allowing the Privy Council to make Orders in Council on the particular topic. For the change of category of cannabis, the enabling Act was the Misuse of Drugs Act 1971.

Another enabling Act giving power to make Orders in Council is the Constitutional Reform Act 2005. This allows the Privy Council to alter the number of judges in the Supreme Court.

## Look online

Look up recent Orders in Council on the Privy Council website at https://privycouncil.independent.gov.uk/. On the Home page, click on Privy Council, then click on Privy Council Meetings. There will be a list of years, choose a year and you should now see a series of dates on which meetings took place. Click on some of these dates to find Orders in Council made by the Privy Council. When you find some look to see which enabling Acts have allowed recent orders to be made. The Enabling Act is usually given on the left-hand side of the list of orders.

## 2008 No. 3130

# DANGEROUS DRUGS

### The Misuse of Drugs Act 1971 (Amendment) Order 2008

| | |
|---|---|
| *Made* | *10th December 2008* |
| *Coming into force* | *26th January 2009* |

At the Court at Buckingham Palace, the 10th day of December 2008

Present,

The Queen's Most Excellent Majesty in Council

In accordance with section 2(5) of the Misuse of Drugs Act 1971 a draft of this Order has been laid before Parliament after consultation with the Advisory Council on the Misuse of Drugs and approved by a resolution of each House of Parliament.

Accordingly, Her Majesty, in exercise of the powers conferred upon Her by sections 2(2) and 2(4) of that Act, is pleased, by and with the advice of Her Privy Council, to order as follows:

**Citation, commencement and revocation**

1.—(1) This Order may be cited as the Misuse of Drugs Act 1971 (Amendment) Order 2008 and shall come into force on 26th January 2009.

(2) The Misuse of Drugs Act 1971 (Modification) (No. 2) Order 2003 is revoked.

**Amendments to the Misuse of Drugs Act 1971**

2.—(1) Schedule 2 to the Misuse of Drugs Act 1971 (which specifies the drugs which are subject to control under that Act) is amended as follows.

(2) In Part 2 (Class B drugs)—

(a) in paragraph 1(a), after "Amphetamine" insert—

"Cannabinol

Cannabinol derivatives

Cannabis and cannabis resin";

(b) after paragraph 2 insert—

"**2A**. Any ester or ether of cannabinol or of a cannabinol derivative."; and

(c) in paragraph 3, for "or 2" substitute ", 2 or 2A".

(3) In Part 3 (Class C drugs) the following words are repealed —

(a) in paragraph 1(a), "Cannabinol", "Cannabinol derivatives" and "Cannabis and cannabis resin"; and

(b) in paragraph 1(d), "or of cannabinol or a cannabinol derivative".

*Judith Simpson*
Clerk of the Privy Council

**Figure 4.2** Example of an Order in Council

## 4.1.2 Statutory instruments

> ### Key term
>
> Statutory instruments – rules and regulations made by government ministers.

Ministers and government departments are given authority to make regulations for areas under their particular responsibility. There are about 15 departments in the government. Each one deals with a different area of policy and can make rules and regulations in respect of matters it deals with. So the Minister for Work and Pensions will be able to make regulations on work-related matters, such as health and safety at work, while the Minister for Transport will be able to deal with necessary road traffic regulations.

**Statutory instruments** can be very short, covering one point such as making the annual change to the minimum wage. However, other statutory instruments may be very long with detailed regulations which were too complex to include in an Act of Parliament.

Examples of statutory instruments which include a lot of detail are:

- Building Regulations 2010 – these have ten parts and six schedules. They have been amended a number of times by further regulations. They were made under the European Union Act 1972 and the Building Act 1984.
- Police codes of practice in relation to such powers as stop and search, arrest and detention. These are made by the Minister for Justice under powers in the Police and Criminal Evidence Act 1984 and are updated from time to time.

Statutory instruments are an important way of making law, as over 3,000 are made each year.

## 4.1.3 By-laws

These can be made by local authorities to cover matters within their own area, for example a county council can pass laws affecting the whole county while a district or town council can only make by-laws for its district or town. Many local by-laws will involve traffic control, such as parking restrictions. Other by-laws may be for such matters as banning drinking in public places or banning people from riding cycles in local parks.

By-laws can also be made by public corporations and certain companies for matters within their jurisdiction, which involve the public. This means that bodies such as the British Airports Authority and the railways can enforce rules about public behaviour on their premises.

**Figure 4.3** Different types of delegated legislation with examples

| Types of delegated legislation | Made by | Examples |
|---|---|---|
| **Orders in Council** | Made by Queen and Privy Council | The Misuse of Drugs Act 1971 (Amendment) Order 2008 |
| **Statutory instruments** | Made by government ministers | Codes of Practice under PACE |
| **By-laws** | Made by local authorities or public corporations | Local parking regulations |

## Activity

Look at the following two sources and answer the questions below.

**Source A**

## 2016 No. 719

## PENSIONS

## The Employers' Duties (Implementation) (Amendment) Regulations 2016

|  |  |
|---|---|
| *Made* - - - - | *7th July 2016* |
| *Laid before Parliament* | *11th July 2016* |
| *Coming into force* - - | *1st October 2016* |

The Secretary of State makes the following Regulations in exercise of the powers conferred by sections 29(2) and (4) and 30(8) of the Pensions Act 2008(**a**):

**Citation and commencement**

**1.** These Regulations may be cited as the Employers' Duties (Implementation) (Amendment) Regulations 2016 and come into force on 1st October 2016.

**Amendment of the Employers' Duties (Implementation) Regulations 2010**

**2.**—(1) The Employers' Duties (Implementation) Regulations 2010(**b**) are amended as follows.

(2) In regulation 5 (transitional periods for money purchase and personal pension schemes)—

   (a)  in paragraph (a) (prescription of first transitional period)—

      (i)  omit "is five years and three months"; and

      (ii)  after the words in parentheses, add ", ends on, but includes, 5th April 2018".

   (b)  in paragraph (b) (prescription of second transitional period), for the words following the comma, substitute "beginning with 6th April 2018 and ending on, but including, 5th April 2019".

(3) In regulation 6 (transitional periods for defined benefits and hybrid schemes)—

   (a)  omit "is five years and three months"; and

   (b)  after the words "comes into force", add ", ends on, but includes, 30th September 2017".

*Altmann*
Minister of State,
Department for Work and Pensions

7th July 2016

---

(**a**)  2008 c. 30. Section 99 defines "prescribed" and "regulations".
(**b**)  S.I. 2010/4. Regulations 5 and 6 were amended by S.I. 2012/1813.

**Source B**

**Drinking ban zones**

The Safer Croydon Partnership has implemented four drinking ban zones in four areas.

How do they work?

The correct term for a drinking ban zone is a Designated Public Place Order. These were introduced as part of the Criminal Justice and Police Act 2001. Prior to

implementing a drinking ban zone, consultation must take place with the police and local residents, businesses and all of the licensed premises within the proposed area. Within the designated area, alcohol consumption is restricted in any open space, other than licensed premises.

It is important to note that this is a discretionary power, so where alcohol is being consumed without causing a problem (e.g. a family picnic in the park) the police would be unlikely to take action.

What happens to people who don't comply?

People are required to hand over alcohol in their possession when requested to do so by a police officer. The police officer will generally dispose of the alcohol by pouring it away. Failure to surrender alcohol on request may result in an arrest.

*Source: Adapted from the Croydon Council website, August 2016*

**Questions**

1 What type of delegated legislation is Source A?
2 Which Act is the enabling Act which allowed this delegated legislation to be made?
3 Which government department was responsible for producing the regulations?
4 To which type of delegated legislation does Source B refer?
5 Who made the orders referred to in the source?
6 What effect do these orders have?

# 4.2 Control of delegated legislation

As delegated legislation in many instances is made by non-elected bodies and, since there are so many people with the power to make delegated legislation, it is important that there should be some control over delegated legislation. Control is exercised by Parliament and by the courts. In addition there may sometimes be a Public Enquiry before a law is passed on an especially sensitive matter, such as planning laws which may affect the environment.

## 4.2.1 Control by Parliament
### Checks on the enabling Act

Parliament has the initial control over what powers are delegated as the enabling Act sets out the limits within which any delegated legislation must be made. For example, the Act will state which government minister can make the regulations. It will also state the type of

laws to be made and whether they can be made for the whole country or only for certain places. The Act can also set out whether the government department must consult other people before making the regulations.

Parliament also retains control over the delegated legislation as it can repeal the powers in the enabling Act at any time. If it does this then the right to make regulations will cease.

There is also a Delegated Powers Scrutiny Committee in the House of Lords which considers whether the provisions of any Bills going through Parliament delegate legislative power inappropriately. It reports its findings to the House of Lords before the Committee stage of the Bill, but it has no power to amend Bills.

It is sensible that checks are made on what powers are proposed to be delegated. If the powers in the original enabling Act are appropriate, then the delegated legislation is more likely to be properly drawn up.

## Checks on the delegated legislation

There also need to be checks to make sure that powers are not being used wrongly. Parliament has the following ways of checking on the actual delegated legislation:

- affirmative resolution
- negative resolution
- questioning of government ministers
- Joint Select Committee on Statutory Instruments (Scrutiny Committee).

In addition there are special controls for any delegated legislation made under the Legislative and Regulatory Reform Act 2006 (see section 4.2.2).

### Affirmative resolutions

A small number of statutory instruments will be subject to an affirmative resolution. This means that the statutory instrument will not become law unless specifically approved by Parliament. The need for an affirmative resolution will be included in the enabling Act. For example, an affirmative resolution is required before new or revised police Codes of Practice under the Police and Criminal Evidence Act 1984 can come into force. One of the disadvantages of this procedure is that Parliament cannot amend the statutory instrument; it can only be approved, annulled or withdrawn.

### Negative resolutions

Most other statutory instruments will be subject to a negative resolution, which means that the relevant statutory instrument will be law unless rejected by Parliament within 40 days. The main problem with this procedure is that very few of the statutory instruments will be looked at. They are available for MPs to consider, but, as there are so many statutory instruments, it is likely that only a few will be looked at.

### Questioning of government ministers

Individual ministers may also be questioned by MPs in Parliament on the work of their departments, and this can include questions about proposed regulations.

### Scrutiny Committee

A more effective check is the Joint Select Committee on Statutory Instruments, usually called the Scrutiny Committee. This committee reviews all statutory instruments and, where necessary, will draw the attention of both Houses of Parliament to points that need further consideration. However, the review is a technical one and not based on policy. The main grounds for referring a statutory instrument back to the Houses of Parliament are that:

- it imposes a tax or charge – this is because only an elected body has such a right
- it appears to have retrospective effect which was not provided for by the enabling Act
- it appears to have gone beyond the powers given under the enabling legislation
- it makes some unusual or unexpected use of those powers
- it is unclear or defective in some way.

The Scrutiny Committee can only report back its findings; it has no power to alter any statutory instrument.

The two main problems are, first, that the review is only a technical one limited to the points set out above. Second, even if the Committee discovers a breach of one of these points, the Committee cannot alter the regulations or stop them from becoming law. The Committee can only draw the attention of Parliament to the matter.

## 4.2.2 The Legislative and Regulatory Reform Act 2006

This Act sets procedure for the making of statutory instruments which are aimed at repealing an existing law in order to remove a 'burden'. For the purpose of the Act 'burden' means any of the following:

a a financial cost
b an administrative inconvenience
c an obstacle to efficiency, productivity or profitability or
d a sanction, criminal or otherwise, which affects the carrying on of any lawful activity.

Any minister making a statutory instrument under the powers of this Act must consult various people and organisations. These include:

- organisations which are representative of interests substantially affected by the proposals
- the Welsh Parliament in relation to matters upon which the Assembly exercises functions
- the Law Commission where appropriate.

Orders made under this power of this Act must be laid before Parliament. There are three possible procedures:

1 **Negative resolution procedure** – where the minister recommends that this procedure should be used, it will be used unless within 30 days one of the Houses of Parliament objects to this. If the negative resolution procedure is adopted, the delegated legislation will not become law until it has been laid before Parliament for 40 days.

2 **Affirmative resolution procedure** – this requires both Houses of Parliament to approve the order; even though the minister has recommended this procedure Parliament can still require the super-affirmative resolution procedure to be used.

3 **Super-affirmative resolution procedure** – under this the minister must have regard to:
   – any representations
   – any resolution of either House of Parliament
   – any recommendations by a committee of either House of Parliament who are asked to report on the draft order.

This super-affirmative resolution procedure gives Parliament more control over delegated legislation made under the Legislative and Regulatory Reform Act 2006. It is important that this is the position as the Act gives ministers very wide powers to amend Acts of Parliament.

## 4.2.3 Control by the courts

Delegated legislation can be challenged in the courts on the ground that it is **ultra vires**.

### Key term

Ultra vires – it goes beyond the powers that Parliament granted in the enabling Act. Where any delegated legislation is ultra vires, then it is not valid law.

The validity of delegated legislation may be challenged through the judicial review procedure, or it may arise in a civil claim between two parties. Any delegated legislation which is ruled to be ultra vires is void and not effective. This was illustrated by *R v Home Secretary, ex parte Fire Brigades Union* (1995) where changes made by the Home Secretary to the Criminal Injuries Compensation Scheme were held to have gone beyond the power given to him in the Criminal Justice Act 1988.

The courts will presume that unless an enabling act expressly allows it, there is no power to do any of the following:

- make unreasonable regulations – in *Strickland v Hayes Borough Council* (1896) a by-law prohibiting the singing or reciting of any obscene song or ballad and the use of obscene language generally, was held to be unreasonable and so ultra vires, because it was too widely drawn in that it covered acts done in private as well as those in public
- levy taxes
- allow sub-delegation.

It is also possible for the courts to hold that delegated legislation is ultra vires because the correct procedure has not been followed. Two examples of this are the *Aylesbury Mushroom case* (1972) and *R v Secretary of State for Education and Employment, ex parte National Union of Teachers* (2000).

### Aylesbury Mushroom case (1972)

The Minister of Labour had to consult 'any organisation … appearing to him to be representative of substantial numbers of employers engaging in the activity concerned'. His failure to consult the Mushroom Growers' Association, which represented about 85 per cent of all mushroom growers, meant that his order establishing a training board was invalid as against mushroom growers. However, it was valid in relation to others affected by the order, such as farmers, as the Minister had consulted with the National Farmers Union.

### R v Secretary of State for Education and Employment, ex parte National Union of Teachers (2000)

A High Court Judge ruled that a statutory instrument setting conditions for appraisal and access to higher rates of pay for teachers was beyond the powers given under the Education Act 1996. In addition, the procedure used was unfair as only four days had been allowed for consultation.

While the UK remains a member of the European Union, statutory instruments can also be declared void if they conflict with European Union legislation.

Figure 4.4 Advantages and disadvantages of controls over delegated legislation

|  | Advantages | Disadvantages |
|---|---|---|
| **CONTROL BY PARLIAMENT** | | |
| **Enabling Act** | Parliament sets limits<br>Parliament can amend or repeal Act | The powers in the Act may be very wide |
| **Delegated Powers Scrutiny Committee** | Looks at proposed powers before they are enacted<br>Should ensure that only appropriate powers are given | Can only report – cannot amend Bill |
| **Affirmative resolution** | Means Parliament must agree with the regulations | Time consuming – cannot be used for all SIs |
| **Negative resolution** | Gives MPs the opportunity to check SIs before they come into force | Unlikely that many SIs will be looked at under this procedure |
| **Scrutiny Committee** | Ensures:<br>■ do not impose taxes or<br>■ go beyond the powers<br>■ are not retrospective<br>■ do not make unusual or unexpected use of powers<br>■ are not unclear or defective | Only a technical check – cannot check substance of the SI<br>Committee can only report to Parliament – it cannot make changes |
| **CONTROL BY THE COURTS** | | |
| **Judicial review**<br>**Doctrine of ultra vires** | Anyone affected by the delegated legislation can ask for a judicial review<br>Court can declare delegated legislation void | It is expensive to take court proceedings<br>Can normally only do this if the correct procedure has not been followed OR if the delegated legislation goes beyond the power given by the enabling Act |

# 4.3 The reasons for the use of delegated legislation

## 4.3.1 Need for detailed law

In our modern society there are a large number of rules and regulations. These are needed to make society work more safely and efficiently. Parliament does not have the time to deal with all the detail needed. Using delegated legislation means that Parliament has control, through the use of enabling Acts, of what regulations are passed. At the same time use of delegated legislation means that other bodies do the rest of the work.

## 4.3.2 Need for expert knowledge

Many regulations need expert knowledge of the subject-matter in order to draw up the most effective laws. It is impossible for Parliament to have all the knowledge needed to draw up laws for such things as controlling the use of technology, ensuring environmental safety, dealing with a vast array of different industrial problems or operating complex taxation schemes.

It is thought that it is better for Parliament to debate the main principles thoroughly, but leave the detail to be filled in by those who have expert knowledge of it.

## 4.3.3 Need for local knowledge

For local by-laws, the local councils know their own areas and can decide which areas need drinking bans or what local parking regulations there should be. It would be impossible for Parliament to deal with all the local requirements for every city, town and village in the country.

### 4.3.4 Need for consultation

Consultation is particularly important for rules on technical matters, where it is necessary to make sure that the regulations are technically accurate and workable. By creating law through delegated legislation ministers can have the benefit of consultation before having regulations drawn up.

Also some enabling Acts giving the power to make delegated legislation set out that there must be consultation before the regulations are created. An example is that before any new or revised police Code of Practice under the Police and Criminal Evidence Act 1984 is issued, there must be consultation with a wide range of people including:

- persons representing the interests of police authorities
- the General Council of the Bar
- the Law Society.

## 4.4 Advantages and disadvantages of delegated legislation

### 4.4.1 Advantages

#### Saves parliamentary time

Parliament does not have time to consider and debate every small detail of complex regulations. Making such regulations through delegated legislation saves parliamentary time.

#### Access to technical expertise

Modern society has become very complicated and technical, so that it is impossible that members of parliament can have all the knowledge needed to draw up laws on complex areas. By using delegated legislation, the necessary experts can be consulted.

#### Allows consultation

Ministers can have the benefit of further consultation before regulations are drawn up. Consultation is particularly important for rules on technical matters, where it is necessary to make sure that the regulations are technically workable.

#### Allows quick law making

As already seen, the process of passing an Act of Parliament can take a considerable time and in an emergency Parliament may not be able to pass law quickly enough. Orders in Council, especially, can be made very quickly.

#### Easy to amend

Delegated legislation can be amended or revoked easily when necessary so that the law can be kept up to date. This is useful where monetary limits have to change each year as, for example, the minimum wage or the limits for legal aid. Ministers can also respond to new or unforeseen situations by amending regulations made through a statutory instrument. This is another reason why use of delegated legislation is sometimes preferred to an Act of Parliament.

### 4.4.2 Disadvantages

#### Undemocratic

The main criticism is that delegated legislation takes law making away from the democratically elected House of Commons and allows non-elected people to make law. This is acceptable provided there is sufficient control, but, as already seen, Parliament's control is fairly limited. This criticism cannot be made of by-laws made by local authorities since these are elected bodies and accountable to the local citizens.

#### Sub-delegation

Another problem is that of sub-delegation, which means that the law making authority is handed down another level. This causes comments that much of our law is made by civil servants and merely 'rubber stamped' by the minister of that department.

#### Large volume and lack of publicity

The large volume of delegated legislation also gives rise to criticism, since it makes it difficult to discover what the present law is. This problem is aggravated by a lack of publicity, as much delegated legislation is made in private, in contrast to the public debates of Parliament.

#### Difficult wording

Finally, delegated legislation shares with Acts of Parliament the same problem of obscure wording that can lead to difficulty in understanding the law. Complex regulations may be difficult to understand. This difficulty of how to understand or interpret the law is dealt with in the next chapter.

**Figure 4.5** Delegated legislation

| | Facts |
|---|---|
| **Types of delegated legislation** | ■ Orders in Council<br>■ Statutory instruments<br>■ By-laws |
| **Reason for delegated legislation** | Need for:<br>■ detailed law<br>■ expert knowledge<br>■ local knowledge<br>■ consultation |
| **Advantages of delegated legislation** | ■ saves parliamentary time<br>■ allows use of expert or local knowledge<br>■ allows consultation<br>■ quick to make<br>■ easy to amend |
| **Disadvantages of delegated legislation** | ■ undemocratic<br>■ risk of sub-delegation<br>■ large volume and lack of publicity<br>■ complex wording |

## Check your understanding

1  Which one statement most accurately describes a statutory instrument?

   A  It is a law made by Parliament

   B  It is a law made by a local council

   C  It is a law made by a government minister within a department

   D  It is a law made by a private organisation such as a railway or bus company.

2  A local council intends to introduce a law banning dogs from walking on beaches in its area in the summer months. From the following list, choose the best form of legislation for the council to use:

   A  Statutory instrument

   B  Order in Council

   C  By-law

   D  Act of Parliament.

3  Detailed rules on health and safety are needed for using a new form of technology. Suggest why delegated legislation would be the most suitable form for the new rules.

## Tip

It is important to read the questions carefully and do what is asked. For example if the question states 'describe any two types', make sure that you do describe two types.

## Summary

- There are three types of delegated legislation:
  - Orders in Council made by the Privy Council
  - statutory instruments made by government ministers and departments
  - by-laws made by local councils or other bodies such as the railways.
- Parliament controls delegated legislation by:
  - the enabling Act setting limits on the powers
  - Delegated Powers Scrutiny Committee
  - affirmative or negative resolutions
  - questioning of ministers
  - Joint Select Committee on statutory instruments
  - super-affirmative resolutions.

- The courts control delegated legislation through the judicial review process where:
  - it is beyond the powers
  - it is unreasonable
  - it does not go through the correct procedure and consultation.
- Delegated legislation is needed because of the detail needed, the consultation required, and for expert or local knowledge.
- The advantages of delegated legislation are: saving parliamentary time, use of expert or local knowledge, use of consultation, relatively quick to make and easy to amend.
- The disadvantages of delegated legislation are: undemocratic, sub-delegation, large volume, lack of publicity and can be difficult to interpret.

# 5 Law making: statutory interpretation

After reading this chapter you should be able to:
- Understand why it may be necessary for judges to interpret the law
- Understand the 'three rules' of interpretation and the differences between them
- Understand the purposive approach
- Understand the use of internal and external aids to interpretation
- Understand the impact of European Union law on interpretation
- Understand the impact of the Human Rights Act 1998 on interpretation
- Discuss and evaluate the advantages and disadvantages of the different approaches to interpretation

## 5.1 The need for statutory interpretation

As seen in Chapter 3, many Acts of Parliament are passed by Parliament each year. The meaning of the law in these statutes should be clear and explicit but this is not always achieved. In order to help with the understanding of a statute Parliament sometimes includes sections defining certain words used in that statute. Such sections are called interpretation sections. In the Theft Act 1968, for example, the definition of theft is given in s 1, and then ss 2–6 define the key words in that definition. To help the judges with general words Parliament has also passed the Interpretation Act 1978 which makes it clear that, unless the contrary appears, he includes she, and singular includes plural.

Despite the aids mentioned above, many cases come before the courts because there is a dispute over the meaning of an Act of Parliament. In such cases the court's task is to decide the exact meaning of a particular word or phrase. There are many reasons why meaning may be unclear:

- A broad term
  There may be words designed to cover several possibilities; this can lead to problems as to how wide this should go. In the Dangerous Dogs Act 1991 there is a phrase 'any dog of the type known as the pit bull terrier'. This seems a simple phrase but has led to problems. What is meant by type? Does it mean the same as 'breed'? In *Brock v DPP* (1993) this was the key point in dispute and the Queen's Bench Divisional Court decided that 'type' had a wider meaning than 'breed'. It could cover dogs which were not pedigree pit bull terriers, but had a substantial number of the characteristics of such a dog.
- Ambiguity
  This is where a word has two or more meanings; it may not be clear which meaning should be used.
- A drafting error
  The Parliamentary Counsel who drafted the original Bill may have made an error which has not been noticed by Parliament; this is particularly likely to occur where the Bill is amended several times while going through Parliament. Also where several old Acts have been brought together in one Act, there may be differences in the wording of sections, which causes confusion. This is seen in ss 18 and 20 of the Offences against the Person Act. Section 18 uses the word 'cause' while s 20 uses the word 'inflict'. Both sections are concerned with assaults where there has been grievous bodily harm. The use of different words has caused problems of interpretation in the courts. Finally in *R v Burstow* (1997) the House of Lords stated that although the words did not have exactly the same meaning, it 'would be absurd to differentiate between ss 18 and 20'. See section 22.3.3.
- New developments
  New technology may mean that an old Act of Parliament does not apparently cover present day situations. This is seen in the case of *Royal College of Nursing v DHSS* (1981) where medical science and methods had changed since the passing of the Abortion Act in 1967. This case is discussed more fully at section 5.2.3.
- Changes in the use of language
  The meaning of words can change over the years. This was one of the problems in the case of *Cheeseman v DPP* (1990). The Times law report of this case is set out later in this section as an Activity.

# 5.2 The three rules

In English law the judges have not been able to agree on which approach should be used, but instead, over the years they have developed three different rules of (or approaches to) interpretation. These are:

- the literal rule
- the golden rule
- the mischief rule.

These rules take different approaches to interpretation and some judges prefer to use one rule, while other judges prefer another rule. This means that the interpretation of a statute may differ according to which judge is hearing the case. However, once an interpretation has been laid down, it may then form a precedent for future cases under the normal rules of judicial precedent. Since the three rules can result in very different decisions, it is important to understand them.

## 5.2.1 The literal rule

Under the literal rule, courts will give words their plain, ordinary or literal meaning, even if the result is not very sensible. This idea was expressed by Lord Esher in *R v Judge of the City of London Court* (1892) when he said:

> If the words of an act are clear then you must follow them even though they lead to a manifest absurdity. The court has nothing to do with the question whether the legislature has committed an absurdity.

The rule developed in the early nineteenth century and was the main rule used for the first part of the twentieth century. It is still used as the starting point for interpreting any legislation.

## Key term

**Literal rule** – a rule of statutory interpretation that gives the words their plain ordinary or dictionary meaning.

### Cases using the literal rule

The rule was used in *Whiteley v Chappell* (1868).

### *Whiteley v Chappell* (1868)

In this case the defendant was charged under a section which made it an offence to impersonate 'any person entitled to vote'. The defendant had pretended to be a person whose name was on the voters' list, but who had died. The court held that the defendant was not guilty since a dead person is not, in the literal meaning of the words, 'entitled to vote'.

Using the literal rule in *Whiteley v Chappell* made the law absurd.

The rule can also lead to what are considered harsh decisions. This occurred in *London & North Eastern Railway Co. v Berriman* (1946)

### *London & North Eastern Railway Co. v Berriman* (1946)

A railway worker was killed while doing maintenance work, oiling points along a railway line. His widow tried to claim compensation because there had not been a look-out man provided by the railway company in accordance with a regulation under the Fatal Accidents Act which stated that a look-out should be provided for men working on or near the railway line 'for the purposes of relaying or repairing' it. The court took the words 'relaying' and 'repairing' in their literal meaning and said that oiling points was maintaining the line and not relaying or repairing so that Mrs Berriman's claim failed.

## Activity

Read the following law report and answer the questions below.

### Lurking policeman not 'passengers'

*Cheeseman v Director of Public Prosecutions* (1990)

Police officers who witnessed a man masturbating in a public lavatory were not 'passengers' within the meaning of section 28 of the Town Police Clauses Act 1847 when they had been stationed in the lavatory following complaints.

The Queen's Bench Divisional Court so held in allowing an appeal by way of case stated by Ashley Frederick Cheeseman against his conviction of an offence of wilfully and indecently exposing his person in a street to the annoyance of passengers.

Section 81 of the Public Health Acts Amendment Act 1907 extended the meaning of the word 'street' in section 28 to include, inter alia, any place of public resort under the control of the local authority.

LORD JUSTICE BINGHAM, concurring with Mr Justice Waterhouse, said that The Oxford English Dictionary showed that in 1847 when the Act was passed 'passenger' had a meaning, now unusual except in the expression 'foot-passenger' of 'a passer by or through; a traveller (usually on foot); a wayfarer'.

Before the meaning of 'street' was enlarged in 1907 that dictionary definition of passenger was not hard to apply: it clearly covered anyone using the street for ordinary purposes of passage or travel.

The dictionary definition could not be so aptly applied to a place of public resort such as a public lavatory, but on a commonsense reading when applied in context 'passenger' had to mean anyone resorting in the ordinary way to a place for one of the purposes for which people would normally resort to it.

If that was the correct approach, the two police officers were not 'passengers'. They were stationed in the public lavatory in order to apprehend persons committing acts which had given rise to earlier complaints. They were not resorting to that place of public resort in the ordinary way but for a special purpose and thus were not passengers.

Source: *The Times*, 2 November 1990

**Questions**

1 In this case the meaning of the word 'street' was important. Why did the court decide the word 'street' in the Act included a public lavatory?

2 The meaning of the word 'passenger' was also important. How did the court discover what this word meant in 1847?

3 The court decided that 'passenger' meant 'a passer by or through; a traveller (usually on foot); a wayfarer'. Why did that definition not apply to the police officers who arrested the defendant?

4 The defendant was found not guilty because of the way the court interpreted 'passenger'. Do you think this was a correct decision or not? Give reasons for your answer.

## 5.2.2 The golden rule

This rule is a modification of the literal rule. The **golden rule** starts by looking at the literal meaning but the court is then allowed to avoid an interpretation which would lead to an absurd result. There are two views on how far the golden rule should be used. The first is very narrow and is shown by Lord Reid's comments in *Jones v DPP* (1962) when he said:

> ❝ It is a cardinal principle applicable to all kinds of statutes that you may not for any reason attach to a statutory provision a meaning which the words of that provision cannot reasonably bear. If they are capable of more than one meaning, then you can choose between those meanings, but beyond this you cannot go. ❞

So under the narrow application of the golden rule the court may only choose between the possible meanings of a word or phrase. If there is only one meaning then that must be taken.

The second and wider application of the golden rule is where the words have only one clear meaning, but that meaning would lead to a repugnant situation. This is a situation in which the court feels that using the clear meaning would produce a result which should not be allowed. In such a case the court will use the golden rule to modify the words of the statute in order to avoid this problem.

### Key term

Golden rule – a rule of statutory interpretation. It is a modification of the literal rule and avoids an interpretation that is absurd.

### Cases using the golden rule

The narrow view of the golden rule can be seen in practice in *Adler v George* (1964).

### Adler v George (1964)

The Official Secrets Act 1920 made it an offence to obstruct Her Majesty's Forces 'in the vicinity' of a prohibited place. The defendants had obstructed HM Forces actually in the prohibited place. They argued they were not guilty as the literal wording of the Act did not apply to anyone in the prohibited place. It only applied to those 'in the vicinity', i.e. outside but close to it. The Divisional Court found the defendants guilty as it would be absurd if those causing an obstruction outside the prohibited place were guilty, but anyone inside was not. The words should be read as being 'in or in the vicinity of' the prohibited place.

A very clear example of the use of the wider application of the golden rule was the case of *Re Sigsworth* (1935).

### Re Sigsworth (1935)

In this case the son had murdered his mother. The mother had not made a will, so normally her estate would have been inherited by her next of kin according to the rules set out in the Administration of Justice Act 1925. This meant that the murderer son would have inherited as her 'issue'.

There was no ambiguity in the words of the Act, but the court was not prepared to let a murderer benefit from his crime, so it was held that the literal rule should not apply. The golden rule would be used to prevent the repugnant situation of the son inheriting.

Although the meaning was clear, the court was effectively writing into the Act that the 'issue' would not be entitled to inherit where he had killed the person he would be inheriting from.

## 5.2.3 The mischief rule

This rule gives a judge more discretion than the other two rules. The definition of the **mischief rule** comes from *Heydon's case* (1584), where it was said that there were four points the court should consider. These, in the original language of that old case, were:

1 'What was the common law before the making of the Act?'
2 'What was the mischief and defect for which the common law did not provide?'
3 'What was the remedy the Parliament hath resolved and appointed to cure the disease of the commonwealth?'
4 'The true reason of the remedy. Then the office of all the judges is always to make such construction as shall suppress the mischief and advance the remedy.'

So, under this rule, the court should look to see what the law was before the Act was passed in order to discover what gap or 'mischief' the Act was intended to cover. The court should then interpret the Act in such a way that the gap is covered. This is clearly a quite different approach to the literal rule.

### Key term

**Mischief rule** – a rule of statutory interpretation that looks back to the gap in the previous law and interprets the Act so as to cover the gap.

### Cases using the mischief rule

The mischief rule was used in *Smith v Hughes* (1960) to interpret s 1(1) of the Street Offences Act 1959 which said 'it shall be an offence for a common prostitute to loiter or solicit in a street or public place for the purpose of prostitution'.

### *Smith v Hughes* (1960)

The court considered appeals against the conviction under this section of six different women. In each case the women had not been 'in a street'. One had been on a balcony and the others had been at the windows of ground floor rooms, with the window either half open or closed. In each case the women were attracting the attention of men by calling to them or tapping on the window, but they argued that they were not guilty under this section since they were not literally 'in a street or public place'. The court decided that they were guilty, with Lord Parker saying:

> For my part I approach the matter by considering what is the mischief aimed at by this Act. Everybody knows that this was an Act to clean up the streets, to enable people to walk along the streets without being molested or solicited by common prostitutes. Viewed in this way it can matter little whether the prostitute is soliciting while in the street or is standing in the doorway or on a balcony, or at a window, or whether the window is shut or open or half open.

A similar point to *Smith v Hughes* arose in *Eastbourne Borough Council v Stirling* (2000).

### *Eastbourne Borough Council v Stirling* (2000)

A taxi driver was charged with 'plying for hire in any street' without a licence to do so. His vehicle was parked on a taxi rank on the station forecourt, not on a street.

He was found guilty as, although the taxi was on private land, he was likely to get customers from the street. The court referred to *Smith v Hughes* and said that it was the same point.

Another case in which the House of Lords used the mischief rule was the *Royal College of Nursing v DHSS* (1981).

### Royal College of Nursing v DHSS (1981)

In this case the wording of the Abortion Act 1967, which provided that a pregnancy should be 'terminated by a registered medical practitioner', was in issue.

When the Act was passed in 1967 the procedure to carry out an abortion was such that only a doctor (a registered medical practitioner) could do it. From 1972 onwards improvements in medical technique meant that the normal method of terminating a pregnancy was to induce premature labour with drugs. The first part of the procedure was carried out by a doctor, but the second part was performed by nurses without a doctor present. The court had to decide if this procedure was lawful under the Abortion Act. The case went to the House of Lords where the majority (three) of the judges held that it was lawful, while the other two said that it was not lawful.

The three judges in the majority based their decision on the mischief rule. They pointed out that the mischief Parliament was trying to remedy was the unsatisfactory state of the law before 1967 and the number of illegal abortions which put the lives of women at risk. They also said that the policy of the Act was to broaden the grounds for abortion and ensure that they were carried out with proper skill in hospital.

However, this was a majority decision and the other two judges took the literal view. They said that the words of the Act were clear and that terminations could only be carried out by a registered medical practitioner. They said that the other judges were not interpreting the Act but 'redrafting it with a vengeance'.

It is clear that the three rules (literal, golden and mischief) can lead to different decisions on the meanings of words and phrases. See below for an activity based on a real case in which the different rules could result in different decisions.

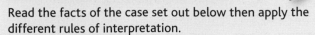

### Activity

Read the facts of the case set out below then apply the different rules of interpretation.

CASE: *Fisher v Bell* [1960] 1 QB 394

The Restriction of Offensive Weapons Act 1959, s 1(1):

> Any person who manufactures, sells or hires or offers for sale or hire or lends or gives to any other person – (a) any knife which has a blade which opens automatically by hand pressure applied to a button, spring or other device in or attached to the handle of the knife, sometimes known as a 'flick knife' ... shall be guilty of an offence.

FACTS: The defendant was a shopkeeper, who had displayed a flick knife marked with a price in his shop window; he had not actually sold any. He was charged under s 1(1) and the court had to decide whether he was guilty of offering the knife for sale. There is a technical legal meaning of 'offers for sale', under which putting an article in a shop window is not an offer to sell (students of contract law will learn this rule).

Consider the phrase 'offers for sale' and explain how you think the case would have been decided using:

a the literal rule

b the golden rule

c the mischief rule.

Note: the court's decision on the case is given on page 47.

Note: the court's decision on the case is given on page 47.

**Figure 5.1** The three 'rules' of statutory interpretation

| Literal rule | Golden rule | Mischief rule |
| --- | --- | --- |
| Words given their plain ordinary dictionary meaning | Can choose best interpretation of ambiguous words OR avoid an absurd or repugnant result | Looks at the gap on the law prior to the Act and interprets words to 'suppress the mischief' |
| **Cases** | **Cases** | **Cases** |
| *Whiteley v Chappell* | *Adler v George* | *Smith v Hughes* |
| Not guilty of impersonating someone entitled to vote because a dead person was not entitled to vote | The words 'in the vicinity' held to include being in the place | Prostitutes calling from doorways, windows or balconies were 'in a street or public place' |
| *LNER v Berriman* | *Re Sigsworth* | *Royal College of Nursing v DHSS* |
| Not literally 'relaying or repairing' track so widow could not get compensation | A son who murdered his mother could not inherit her estate as it would be repugnant | Even though the second part of an abortion procedure was not carried out by a doctor, the procedure was lawful as it prevent the mischief of illegal abortions |

# 5.3 The purposive approach

This goes beyond the mischief rule in that the court is not just looking to see what the gap was in the old law. The judges are deciding what they believe Parliament meant to achieve.

## Key term

Purposive approach – an approach to statutory interpretation in which the courts look to see what is the purpose of the law.

## Cases using the purposive approach

The purposive approach was used in *R v Registrar-General, ex parte Smith* (1990).

### R v Registrar-General, ex parte Smith (1990)

The court had to consider s 51 of the Adoption Act 1976 which stated:

> (1) Subject to subsections (4) and (6), the Registrar-General shall on an application made in the prescribed manner by an adopted person a record of whose birth is kept by the Registrar-General and who has attained the age of 18 years supply to that person ... such information as is necessary to enable that person to obtain a certified copy of the record of his birth.

Subsection 4 said that before supplying that information the Registrar-General had to inform the applicant about counselling services available. Subsection 6 stated that if the adoption was before 1975 the Registrar-General could not give the information unless the applicant had attended an interview with a counsellor.

An application was made by Charles Smith for information to enable him to obtain his birth certificate. Mr Smith had made his application in the correct manner and was prepared to see a counsellor. On a literal view of the Act the Registrar-General had to supply him with the information, since the Act uses the phrase 'shall ... supply'.

The problem was that Mr Smith had been convicted of two murders and was detained in Broadmoor as he suffered from recurring bouts of psychotic illness. A psychiatrist thought that it was possible he might be hostile towards his natural mother.

This posed a difficulty for the court: should they apply the clear meaning of the words in this situation? The judges in the Court of Appeal decided that the case called for the purposive approach. They said that, despite the plain language of the Act, Parliament could not have intended to promote serious crime. So, in view of the risk to the applicant's natural mother if he discovered her identity, they ruled that the Registrar-General did not have to supply any information.

Another case in which the purposive approach was used was *R (on the application of Quintavalle) v Human Fertilisation and Embryology Authority* (2003).

### R (on the application of Quintavalle) v Human Fertilisation and Embryology Authority (2003)

The House of Lords had to decide whether organisms created by cell nuclear replacement (CNR) came within the definition of 'embryo' in the Human Fertilisation and Embryology Act 1990. Section 1(1)(a) of this Act states that 'embryo means a live human embryo where fertilisation is complete'.

When the Act was passed in 1990 there was only one way of creating an embryo outside the human body. This was by taking an egg from a woman and sperm from a man and fertilising the egg with the sperm. The fertilised egg could then be placed in a woman's uterus and, if it established itself, she would be pregnant. This is the normal method of helping those unable to conceive naturally to have children.

However, by 2003 another method of producing an embryo had become possible. This was through cell nuclear replacement (CNR). Fertilisation is not used in CNR. Instead, the nucleus from one cell of an unfertilised egg is removed. It is then replaced with the nucleus from an adult cell and, if the cell now divides, it is possible to produce an embryo. This technique is known as cloning.

Using the purposive approach, the House of Lords decided that embryos produced through CNR were covered by the 1990 Act. In his judgment in the case Lord Bingham said:

> [T]he court's task, within permissible bounds of interpretation is to give effect to Parliament's purpose ... Parliament could not have intended to distinguish between embryos produced by, or without, fertilisation since it was unaware of the latter possibility.

## 5.3.1 Literal approach versus purposive approach

The case of *Cheeseman* in the activity in section 5.2.1 illustrates several of the problems of statutory interpretation. It is an example of the courts taking the words literally.

However, it can be argued that the defendant was 'wilfully and indecently exposing his person in a street' and that he was caught doing that. Is it important whether the police officers were 'passengers'? After all they were there because of

**Figure 5.2** Comparing the literal approach and the purposive approach

| Literal approach | Purposive approach |
|---|---|
| Words taken in their ordinary grammatical meaning | Looks for the purpose of Parliament and interprets the law to ensure that purpose |
| **Case: *LNER v Berriman*** <br> Not 'relaying or repairing' track, but was oiling points (maintenance) <br> Literal approach – held maintenance was not within the literal meaning of the words 'relaying or repairing' <br> Could not claim compensation | **Case: *R (Quintavelle) v Sec of State for Health*** <br> Act stated embryo meant 'a live human embryo where fertilisation is complete' <br> Embryos were created by cell nuclear replacement, so there was no fertilisation <br> Purposive approach – Parliament could not have intended to distinguish between embryos, so the Act applied |
| **Advantages of literal approach** <br> ■ leaves law making to Parliament <br> ■ makes law more certain | **Advantages of purposive approach** <br> ■ leads to justice in individual cases <br> ■ broad approach covering more situations <br> ■ allows for new technology |
| **Disadvantages of literal approach** <br> ■ assumes that every Act is perfectly crafted <br> ■ words have more than one meaning <br> ■ can lead to absurd results <br> ■ can lead to unjust decisions | **Disadvantages of purposive approach** <br> ■ leads to judicial law making <br> ■ can make law uncertain <br> ■ difficult to discover the intention of Parliament |

previous complaints about this type of behaviour and presumably the defendant thought they were ordinary members of the public.

Some people would argue that the whole purpose of the act was to prevent this type of behaviour; this is the purposive approach to statutory interpretation. Instead of looking at the precise meaning of each word a broader approach is taken.

This conflict between the literal approach and the purposive approach is one of the major issues in statutory interpretation. Should judges examine each word and take the words literally or should it be accepted that an Act of Parliament cannot cover every situation and that meanings of words cannot always be exact?

In European law the purposive approach is taken. This is important since as European laws are issued in several languages, it would be difficult, if not impossible, to take the meanings of words literally. It is not always possible to have an exact translation from one language to another.

## 5.4 Internal and external aids

There are some aids to help the judges with interpretation. These can be either internal (intrinsic) aids or external (extrinsic) aids.

### 5.4.1 Internal (intrinsic) aids

These are matters within the statute itself that may help to make its meaning clearer. The court can consider the long title, the short title and the preamble, if any. Older statutes usually have a preamble which sets out Parliament's purpose in enacting that statute. Modern statutes either do not have a preamble or contain a very brief one, for example the Theft Act 1968 states that it is an Act to modernise the law of theft. The long title may also explain briefly Parliament's intentions.

Some Acts will have an interpretation section in them. For example, s 4(1) of the Theft Act 1968 states that 'property' includes 'money and all other property real or personal, including things in action and other intangible property'. See Chapter 5 of Book 2.

The other useful internal aids are any headings before a group of sections, and any schedules attached to the Act. There are often also marginal notes explaining different sections but these are not generally regarded as giving Parliament's intention as they will have been inserted after the parliamentary debates and are only helpful comments put in by the printer.

It is also possible to look at other sections in the Act as these may help. An example of this is shown by the case of *Harrow LBC v Shah and Shah* (1999).

### *Harrow LBC v Shah and Shah* (1999)

The defendants were charged under s 13(1)(c) of the National Lottery Act 1993. This subsection does not include any words indicating either that *mens rea* (intention) is required or not, nor does it contain any provision for a defence of 'due diligence'. However, another subsection, s 13(1)(a), clearly allows a defence of 'due diligence'. The inclusion of a 'due diligence' defence in subsection (1)(a) of s 13 but not in the section under which the defendants were charged, was an important point in the Divisional Court coming to the decision that s 13(1)(c) was an offence of strict liability.

## 5.4.2 External (extrinsic) aids

These are matters which are outside the Act and it has always been accepted that some external sources can help explain the meaning of an Act. These undisputed sources are:

- previous Acts of Parliament on the same topic
- the historical setting
- earlier case law
- dictionaries of the time.

Where a dictionary is used, it must be a dictionary published at the time when the Act was passed. This is because the meanings of words change over time. A dictionary of 1847 was used in the case of *Cheeseman v DPP* because the Act in question was passed in 1847. See section 5.2.1 for the case of *Cheeseman v DPP*.

As far as other external aids are concerned attitudes have changed. Originally the courts had very strict rules that other extrinsic aids should not be considered. However, for the following three aids the courts' attitude has changed. These three main external aids are:

- Hansard – that is the official report of what was said in Parliament when the Act was debated
- reports of law reform bodies such as the Law Commission which led to the passing of the Act
- international conventions, regulations or directives which have been implemented by English legislation.

### The use of Hansard

Until 1992 there was a firm rule that the courts could not look at what was said in the debates in Parliament. Some years earlier Lord Denning had tried to attack this ban on Hansard in *Davis v Johnson* (1979), which involved the interpretation of the Domestic Violence and Matrimonial Proceedings Act 1976. He admitted that he had indeed read Hansard before making his decision saying:

> Some may say ... that judges should not pay any attention to what is said in Parliament. They should grope about in the dark for the meaning of an Act without switching on the light. I do not accede to this view.

The House of Lords disapproved of this and Lord Scarman explained their reasons by saying:

> Such material is an unreliable guide to the meaning of what is enacted. It promotes confusion, not clarity. The cut and thrust of debate and the pressures of executive responsibility ... are not always conducive to a clear and unbiased explanation of the meaning of statutory language.

However, in *Pepper v Hart* (1993) the House of Lords relaxed the rule and accepted that Hansard could be used in a limited way. This case was unusual in that seven judges heard the appeal, rather than the normal panel of five. Those seven judges included the Lord Chancellor, who was the only judge to disagree with the use of Hansard. The majority ruled that Hansard could be consulted. Lord Browne-Wilkinson said in his judgment that:

> the exclusionary rule should be relaxed so as to permit reference to parliamentary materials where: (a) legislation is ambiguous or obscure, or leads to an absurdity; (b) the material relied on consists of one or more statements by a minister or other promoter of the Bill together if necessary with such other parliamentary material as is necessary to understand such statements and their effect; (c) the statements relied on are clear. Further than this I would not at present go.

So Hansard may be considered but only where the words of the Act are ambiguous or obscure or lead to an absurdity. Even then Hansard should only be used if there was a clear statement by the minister introducing the legislation, which would resolve the ambiguity or absurdity. The Lord Chancellor opposed the use of Hansard on practical grounds, pointing out the time and cost it would take to research Hansard in every case.

The only time that a wider use of Hansard is permitted is where the court is considering an Act that introduced an international convention or European Directive into English law. This was pointed out by the Queen's Bench Divisional Court in *Three Rivers District Council and others v Bank of England (No. 2) (1996)*. In such a situation it is important to interpret the statute purposively and consistently with any European materials and the court can look at ministerial statements, even if the statute does not appear to be ambiguous or obscure.

Since 1992, Hansard has been referred to in a number of cases. The Lord Chancellor's predictions on cost have been confirmed by some solicitors, with one estimating that it had added 25 per cent to the bill. On other occasions it is clear that Hansard has not been helpful or that the court would have reached the same conclusion in any event.

### Law reform reports

As with Hansard, the courts used to hold that reports by law reform agencies such as the Law Reform Agency should not be considered by the courts. However this rule was relaxed in the *Black-Clawson case* in 1975, when it was accepted that such a report should be looked at to discover the mischief or gap in the law which the legislation based on the report was designed to deal with.

> See Chapter 7 for detail on the Law Commission.

With increased use of the purposive approach, the courts have become much more prepared to look at Law Commission reports. In the Law Commission's report for 2014–15 it was pointed out that the Law Commission's work had been cited in 404 cases in the United Kingdom and in three cases in other common law jurisdictions such as Canada.

So today Law Commission reports are an important external aid to statutory interpretation.

## 5.5 The effect of EU law

The purposive approach is the one preferred by most European countries when interpreting their own legislation. It is also the approach which has been adopted by the European Court of Justice in interpreting European law.

From the time when the United Kingdom became a member of the European Union in 1973 the influence of the European preference for the purposive approach has affected the English courts in two ways. First, they have had to accept that for law which has been passed as a result of having to conform to a European law, the purposive approach is the correct one to use. Second, the fact that judges have had to use the purposive approach for European law for over 40 years has made them more accustomed to it and, therefore, more likely to apply it to English law.

Even though it is likely that the UK is leaving the EU, judges are likely to continue to use the purposive approach.

### 5.5.1 Interpreting EU Law

Where the law to be interpreted is based on European law, the English courts have had to interpret it in the light of the wording and purpose of the European law. This is because the Treaty of Rome, which set out the duties of European member states, stated that all member states were required to 'take all appropriate measures ... to ensure fulfilment of the obligations'.

The European Court of Justice in the *Marleasing case* (1992) ruled that this included interpreting national law in the light and the aim of the European law.

If the UK leaves the EU this will no longer apply.

## 5.6 The effect of the Human Rights Act 1998

Section 3 of the Human Rights Act says that, so far as it is possible to do so, legislation must be read and given effect in a way which is compatible with the rights in the European Convention on Human Rights. This applies to any case where one of the rights is concerned, but it does not apply where there is no involvement of human rights.

An example of the effect of the Human Rights Act on interpretation is *Mendoza v Ghaidan* (2002) which involved interpretation of the Rent Act 1977.

## Mendoza v Ghaidan (2002)

The Rent Act applied where a person who had the tenancy of a property died. It allowed unmarried partners to succeed to the tenancy as it stated that 'a person who was living with the original tenant as his or her wife or husband shall be treated as the spouse of the original tenant'.

The question was whether same sex partners had the right to take over the tenancy. A House of Lords' decision, made before the Human Rights Act came into effect, had ruled that same sex partners did not have the right under the Rent Act to take over the tenancy.

The Court of Appeal held that the Rent Act had to be interpreted to conform to the European Convention on Human Rights which forbids discrimination on the ground of gender. In order to make the Act compatible with human rights, the Court of Appeal read the words 'living with the original tenant as his or her wife or husband' to mean 'as if they were his or her wife or husband'. This allowed same sex partners to have the same rights as unmarried opposite sex couples.

The Court of Appeal pointed out the importance of conforming to the Convention rights when they said:

> " In order to remedy this breach of the Convention the court must, if it can, read the Schedule so that its provisions are rendered compatible with the Convention rights of the survivors of same-sex partnerships. "

In 2004 the House of Lords confirmed the Court of Appeal's decision in this case.

## Fisher v Bell

The court used the literal rule in coming to the decision in this case. They pointed out that there is a legal meaning of the words 'offer for sale' in contract law. This meaning does not include where goods are displayed in shop a window. In contract law this is only an 'invitation to treat' (this is explained in Book 2).

So, under the literal rule, the shop keeper was not guilty of offering the knives for sale.

**Figure 5.3** Statutory interpretation

|  | Brief definition | Case example |
|---|---|---|
| **Literal approach** | Words given plain, ordinary meaning | *London & North Eastern Railway Co. v Berriman* |
| **Purposive approach** | Looking at the reasons why the law was passed and interpreting it accordingly | *Royal College of Nursing v DHSS* |
| **Internal aids** | Within the Act | *Harrow LBC v Shah and Shah* |
| **External aids** | Outside the Act – includes: <br>■ Hansard <br>■ Law Commission reports <br>■ dictionaries | *Pepper v Hart* <br><br>*Black-Clawson case* <br><br>*Cheeseman v DPP* |
| **Impact of EU law** | EU law uses the purposive approach <br>■ interpreting national law in the light and the aim of the European law <br>■ has made our judges more ready to use the purposive approach | *Marleasing case* |
| **Impact of the Human Rights Act 1998** | Legislation must be read and given effect in a way which is compatible with the rights in the European Convention on Human Rights | *Mendoza v Ghaidan* |

# 5.7 Advantages and disadvantages of the different approaches to statutory interpretation

## 5.7.1 The literal rule

### Advantages

The main advantage of the literal rule is that the rule follows the words that Parliament has used. Parliament is our law-making body and it is right that judges should apply the law exactly as it is written. Using the literal rule to interpret Acts of Parliament prevents unelected judges from making law.

Another advantage is that using the literal rule should make the law more certain, as the law will be interpreted exactly as it is written. This makes it easier for people to know what the law is and how judges will apply it.

### Disadvantages

There are also serious disadvantages to the rule. The literal rule assumes every Act will be perfectly drafted. In fact it is not always possible to word an Act so that it covers every situation Parliament meant it to. This was seen in the case of *Whiteley v Chappell* (1868) where the defendant was not guilty of voting under another person's name.

Another problem is that words may have more than one meaning, so that the Act is unclear. Often in dictionaries words are defined with several different meanings. At section 5.1 we have already seen that there was difficulty in interpreting the word 'type' in the Dangerous Dogs Act 1991.

Following the words exactly can lead to unfair or unjust decisions. This was seen in *London & North Eastern Railway Co. v Berriman* (1946) where a workman's widow was unable to claim compensation when he was killed while maintaining the track. Her claim failed because literally he was not 'relaying or repairing' it.

With decisions such as *Whiteley v Chappell* and the *Berriman case*, it is not surprising that Professor Michael Zander has denounced the literal rule as being mechanical and divorced from the realities of the use of language.

## 5.7.2 The golden rule

### Advantages

The golden rule respects the exact words of Parliament except in limited situations. Its main advantage is that where there is a problem with using the literal rule, it provides an 'escape route'.

Another important advantage is that it allows the judge to choose the most sensible meaning where there is more than one meaning to the words in the Act. It can also provide sensible decisions in cases where the literal rule would lead to a repugnant situation. It would clearly have been unjust to allow the son in *Re Sigsworth* to benefit from his crime.

Effectively it avoids the worst problems of the literal rule.

### Disadvantages

The main disadvantage is that it is very limited in its use. It is only used on rare occasions. Another problem is that it is not always possible to predict when courts will use the golden rule. Michael Zander has described it as a 'feeble parachute'. In other words, it is an escape route but it cannot do very much.

## 5.7.3 The mischief rule

### Advantages

The main advantage is that the mischief rule promotes the purpose of the law as it allows judges to look back at the gap in the law which the Act was designed to cover. The emphasis is on making sure that the gap in the law is filled.

Another advantage is that this approach is more likely to produce a 'just' result. It also means that judges try to interpret the law in the way that Parliament meant it to work. The Law Commission prefers the mischief rule and, as long ago as 1969, recommended that it should be the only rule used in statutory interpretation.

### Disadvantages

The main disadvantage is that there is the risk of judicial law making. Judges are trying to fill the gaps in the law with their own views on how the law should remedy the gap. The case of *Royal College of Nursing v DHSS* (see section 5.2.3) shows that judges do not always agree on the use of the mischief rule.

Use of the mischief rule may lead to uncertainty in the law. It is impossible to know when judges will use the rule and also what result it might lead to. This makes it difficult for lawyers to advise clients on the law.

The mischief rule is not as wide as the purposive approach as it is limited to looking back at the gap in the old law. It cannot be used for a more general consideration of the purpose of the law.

## 5.7.4 The purposive approach

### Advantages

The main advantage of the purposive approach is that it leads to justice in individual cases. It is a broad approach which allows the law to cover more situations than applying words literally.

The purposive approach is particularly useful where there is new technology which was unknown when the law was enacted. This is demonstrated by *R (Quintavalle) v Secretary of State*, the embryo case explained in section 5.3. If the literal rule/approach had been used in that case, it would have been necessary for Parliament to make a new law to deal with the situation.

It also gives judges more discretion than using the literal meanings of words. This allows judges to avoid the literal meaning where it would create an absurd situation. If the purposive approach had been

used in *Whiteley v Chappell* (see section 5.2.1) then it is probable that the judges would have decided that Parliament's intention was to prevent people voting in another person's name and found the defendant guilty.

### Disadvantages

The main disadvantage of the purposive approach is that it may mean the judges refuse to follow the clear words of Parliament. How do the judges know what Parliament's intentions were? Opponents of the purposive approach say that it is impossible to discover Parliament's intentions; only the words of the statute can show what Parliament wanted. So using the purposive approach allows unelected judges to 'make' law as they are deciding what they think the law should be rather than using the words that Parliament enacted.

Another problem with the purposive approach is that it is difficult to discover the intention of Parliament. There are reports of debates in Parliament in Hansard (see section 5.4.2), but these give every detail of debates including those MPs who did not agree with the law that was under discussion. The final version of what Parliament agreed is the actual words used in the Act.

It also leads to uncertainty in the law. It is impossible to know when judges will use this approach or what result it might lead to. This makes it difficult for lawyers to advise clients on the law.

**Figure 5.4** Advantages and disadvantages of the rules and approaches of statutory interpretation

| Literal rule | Golden rule | Mischief rule | Purposive approach |
|---|---|---|---|
| **Advantages**<br>■ follows wording of Parliament<br>■ prevents unelected judge making law<br>■ makes the law more certain<br>■ easier to predict how the judges will interpret the law | **Advantages**<br>■ respects the words of Parliament<br>■ allows the judge to choose the most sensible meaning<br>■ avoids the worst problems of the literal rule | **Advantages**<br>■ promotes the purpose of the law<br>■ fills in the gap in the law<br>■ produces a 'just' result | **Advantages**<br>■ leads to justice in individual cases<br>■ allows for new developments in technology<br>■ avoids absurd decisions |
| **Disadvantages**<br>■ not all Acts are perfectly drafted<br>■ words have more than one meaning<br>■ can lead to unfair or unjust decisions | **Disadvantages**<br>■ can only be used in limited situations<br>■ not possible to predict when the courts will use it<br>■ it is a 'feeble parachute' (Zander) | **Disadvantages**<br>■ risk of judicial law making<br>■ not as wide as the purposive approach<br>■ limited to looking back at the old law<br>■ can make the law uncertain | **Disadvantages**<br>■ difficult to find Parliament's intention<br>■ allows judges to make law<br>■ leads to uncertainty in the law |

## Check your understanding

1 Which one statement most accurately describes the literal rule of statutory interpretation?

   A It gives words their ordinary grammatical meaning

   B It allows judges to look at Hansard

   C It avoids results that are repugnant or absurd

   D The judges look for the intention of Parliament

2 Which one statement most accurately describes the effect of the decision in Pepper v Hart?

   A Judges can look for the gap in the law that the Act was meant to fill

   B It allows judges to look at Hansard

   C It allows judges to look at the dictionary meaning of a word

   D It avoids results that are repugnant or absurd

3 A judge hearing a case has to decide the meaning of some words in a relevant Act of Parliament.

   Using illustrations in support, suggest why might be more advantageous for the judge to use the purposive approach as opposed to the literal rule.

## Summary

- Interpretation is needed because of such problems as:
  - failure of legislation to cover a specific point
  - a broad term
  - ambiguity
  - drafting errors
  - new technological developments.
- The original three rules of statutory interpretation are:
  - the literal rule – the plain ordinary grammatical meaning
  - the golden rule – allows modification of words where the literal rule would lead to absurdity, repugnance or inconsistency
  - the mischief rule – considers the 'mischief' or gap in the old law and interprets the Act in such a way that the gap is covered.

- The purposive approach is more modern and looks for the intention of Parliament.
- Internal aids are those in the Act and include:
  - the short title and preamble
  - interpretation sections
  - headings
  - schedules.
- External aids to interpretation include:
  - previous Acts of Parliament
  - the historical setting
  - earlier case law
  - dictionaries
  - Hansard
  - Law Commission reports
  - international conventions.
- There are advantages and disadvantages to all the rules and approaches of statutory interpretation.

# 6 Law making: judicial precedent

After reading this chapter you should be able to:

- Understand what is meant by the doctrine of precedent
- Understand the hierarchy of the courts and its importance in judicial precedent
- Understand the meaning of *stare decisis*, *ratio decidendi* and *obiter dicta*
- Have an outline knowledge of law reporting and understand the reasons for it
- Explain the operation of judicial precedent
- Explain and evaluate the advantages and disadvantages of the doctrine of judicial precedent

## 6.1 The doctrine of precedent

Judicial precedent refers to the source of law where past decisions of the judges create law for future judges to follow. This source of law is also known as case law. It is a major source of law, both historically and today.

The **doctrine of precedent** is based on the Latin maxim *stare decisis et non quieta movere*, usually shortened to *stare decisis*. This means stand by what has been decided and do not unsettle the established. So precedent is 'standing by' or following decisions in previous cases.

### Key term

Doctrine of precedent – following the decisions of previous cases, especially of higher courts.

So, where the point of law in the previous case and the present case is the same, the court hearing the present case should follow the decision in the previous case. This concept of treating similar cases in the same way promotes the idea of fairness and provides certainty in the law.

Law in the English legal system developed from custom and the decisions of judges in cases. This system of law is known as common law. Judicial precedent is very important in common law legal systems. In the English legal system, the doctrine of precedent means that courts must follow decisions of the courts above. Also appeal courts will usually follow their own previous decisions.

In countries that operate a civil legal system, previous cases are used as a guide but they do not have to be followed.

### Example

In our legal system, once there has been a decision on a point of law, that decision immediately becomes a precedent for later cases. This is illustrated by *Automatic Telephone and Electric Co. Ltd v Registrar of Restrictive Trading Agreements* (1965).

The Court of Appeal had made a decision in *Schweppes Ltd Registrar of Restrictive Trading Agreements* (1965) on discovery of documents. One judge (Willmer LJ) disagreed with the other two. Later on the same day, the same point of law arose in *Automatic Telephone and Electric Co. Ltd v Registrar of Restrictive Trading Agreements*. This case was heard by the same three judges. This time the judges did not disagree. Willmer LJ pointed out:

> ❝ I am now bound by the decision of the majority in the previous case. In these circumstances, I have no alternative but to concur in saying that the appeal in the present case should be allowed. ❞

The decision in the *Schweppes case* had become a precedent that had to be followed in the next case.

### 6.1.1 Original precedent

If the point of law in a case has never been decided before, then whatever the judge decides will form a new precedent for future cases to follow. It is an **original precedent**. As there are no past cases for the judge to base his decision on he is likely to look at cases which are the closest in principle and he may decide to use similar rules. This way of arriving at a judgment is called reasoning by analogy.

### Key term

Original precedent – a decision on a point of law that has never been decided before.

### 6.1.2 Binding precedent

This is a precedent from an earlier case which must be followed even if the judge in the later case does not agree with the legal principle. A **binding precedent** is only created when the facts of the second case are sufficiently similar to the original case and the decision was made by a court which is senior to (or in some cases the same level as) the court hearing the later case.

Binding precedent – a decision in an earlier case which must be followed in later cases.

## 6.1.3 Persuasive precedent

This is a precedent that is not binding on the court but the judge may consider it and decide that it is a correct principle so he is persuaded that he should follow it. **Persuasive precedent** comes from a number of sources as explained below.

**Key term**

Persuasive precedent – a decision which does not have to be followed by later cases, but which a judge may decide to follow.

### Courts lower in the hierarchy

An example can be seen in R v R (1991) where the House of Lords agreed with and followed the same reasoning as the Court of Appeal in deciding that a man could be guilty of raping his wife.

### Decisions of the Judicial Committee of the Privy Council

This court is not part of the court hierarchy in England and Wales and so its decisions are not binding. However, as many of its judges are also members of the Supreme Court (formerly the House of Lords), the judgments of the Privy Council are treated with respect and may often be followed. An example of this can be seen in the law on remoteness of damage in the law of tort and the decision made by the Privy Council in the case of *The Wagon Mound (No. 1)* (1961).

> Full details of this case are given at section 24.3.2.

More recently, in *A-G for Jersey v Holley* (2005) the Privy Council ruled that in the defence of provocation a defendant is to be judged by the standard of a person having ordinary powers of self-control. This was contrary to an earlier judgment by the House of Lords. In cases in 2005 and 2006 the Court of Appeal followed the Privy Council decision rather than the decision of the House of Lords.

### Statements made *obiter dicta*

*Obiter dicta* means statements made in a judgment that were not part of the point of law in deciding

the case. This is clearly seen in the law on duress as a defence to a criminal charge. The House of Lords in *R v Howe* (1987) ruled that duress could not be a defence to a charge of murder. In the judgment the Lords also commented, as an *obiter dicta* statement, that duress would not be available as a defence to someone charged with attempted murder. When, later, in *R v Gotts* (1992) a defendant charged with attempted murder tried to argue that he could use the defence of duress, the *obiter* statement from *Howe* was followed as persuasive precedent by the Court of Appeal.

### A dissenting judgment

When a case has been decided by a majority of judges, for example 2:1 in the Court of Appeal, the judge who disagreed will have explained his reasons. This is a **dissenting judgment**. If that case goes on appeal to the Supreme Court, or if there is a later case on the same point which goes to the Supreme Court, it is possible that the Supreme Court may prefer the dissenting judgment and decide the case in the same way. The dissenting judgment has persuaded them to follow it.

Dissenting judgment – a judgment given by a judge who disagrees with the reasoning of the majority of judges in the case.

## Decisions of courts in other countries

This is especially so where the other country uses the same ideas of common law as in our system. This applies to Commonwealth countries such as Canada, Australia and New Zealand.

# 6.2 The hierarchy of the courts

In England and Wales our courts operate a very rigid doctrine of judicial precedent which has the effect that:

- every court is bound to follow any decision made by a court above it in the hierarchy and
- in general, appellate courts are bound by their own past decisions.

There are two exceptions where lower courts in our legal system are not bound to follow decisions by the English appellate courts. These are:

1 where there is a decision of the Court of Justice of the European Union when the English courts have to follow that decision (this will remain the situation until the UK leaves the European Union).

2 in cases involving human rights – for these the Human Rights Act 1998 requires courts to take into account judgments, decisions and opinions of the European Court of Human Rights.

So the hierarchy of the courts is the next important point to get clear. Which courts come where in the hierarchy? Figure 6.1 shows this in the form of a cascade model and Figure 6.2 gives each court and its position in respect of the other courts. The position of each court is considered in this section. Extra detail on the use of precedent in the Supreme Court (formerly the House of Lords) and Court of Appeal is given in sections 6.3 and 6.4.

## 6.2.1 Appellate courts

Appellate courts are those that hear appeals. In our legal system these are:

- Supreme Court
- Court of Appeal
- Divisional Courts.

### Supreme Court

The most senior national court is the Supreme Court and its decisions bind all other courts in the English legal system. It replaced the House of Lords in 2009. Decisions by the House of Lords also bind all lower courts in the English legal system. The Supreme Court is not bound by its own past decisions, nor by decisions of the House of Lords, although it generally will follow them. This point is discussed in detail at section 6.3.

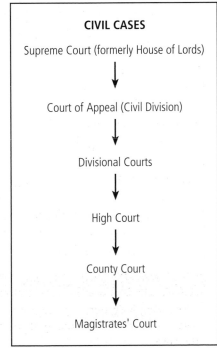

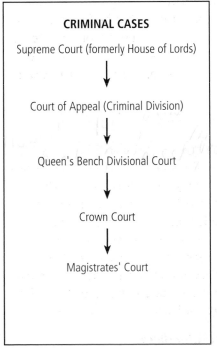

**Figure 6.1** Cascade model of judicial precedent operating in the hierarchy of the courts

## Court of Appeal

At the next level down in the hierarchy is the Court of Appeal; this has two divisions, Civil and Criminal. Both divisions of the Court of Appeal are bound to follow decisions of the Supreme Court. In addition they must usually follow past decisions of their own, although there are some limited exceptions to this rule. The Court of Appeal (Criminal Division) is more flexible where the point involves the liberty of the subject. The position of the two divisions is discussed in detail in section 6.4.

## Divisional Courts

The three Divisional Courts (Queen's Bench, Chancery and Family) are bound by decisions of the Supreme Court and the Court of Appeal. In addition the Divisional Courts are bound by their own past decisions. However, they operate similar exceptions to those operated by the Court of Appeal (see section 6.4.2).

# 6.2.2 Courts of first instance

The term 'courts of first instance' refers to any court where the original trial of a case is held. The appellate courts considered in the previous section do not hear any original trials. They only deal with appeals from decisions of other courts. Quite often an appeal will be about a point of law. This allows the appellate courts to decide the law. This is why appellate courts are much more important than courts of first instance when it comes to creating precedent.

## High Court

This is bound by decisions of all the courts above and in turn it binds the lower courts. High Court Judges do not have to follow each others' decisions but will usually do so. In *Colchester Estates (Cardiff) v Carlton Industries plc* (1984) it was held that where there were two earlier decisions which conflicted, then, provided the first decision had been fully considered in the later case, that later decision should be followed.

## Inferior courts

These are the Crown Court, the County Court and the Magistrates' Court. They are bound to follow decisions by all higher courts and it is unlikely that a decision by an inferior court can create precedent. The one exception is that a ruling on a point of law by a judge in the Crown Court technically creates precedent for the Magistrates' Court. However, since such rulings are rarely recorded in the law reports, this is of little practical effect.

# 6.2.3 The Court of Justice of the European Union

From 1973, and until the UK leaves the European Union, the highest court affecting our legal system is the Court of Justice of the European Union. Points of EU law can be referred to it by courts in England and Wales. The Court of Justice of the European Union only decides the point of law; the case then comes back to the court in this country to apply that law to the case.

Points of EU law decisions made by the Court of Justice of the European Union are binding on all courts in England and Wales. It does not affect other areas of law.

An important feature of the Court of Justice of the European Union is that it is prepared to overrule its own past decisions if it feels it is necessary. This flexible approach to past precedents is seen in other legal systems in Europe, and it is a contrast to the more rigid approach of our national courts.

**Figure 6.2** The courts and precedent

| Court | Courts bound by it | Courts it must follow |
|---|---|---|
| **Supreme Court** | All other courts in the English legal system | European Court |
| **Court of Appeal** | Itself (with some exceptions) Divisional Courts All other lower courts | European Court Supreme Court |
| **Divisional Courts** | Itself (with some exceptions) High Court All other lower courts | European Court Supreme Court Court of Appeal |
| **High Court** | County Court Magistrates' Court | European Court Supreme Court Court of Appeal Divisional Courts |
| **Crown Court** | Possibly Magistrates' Court | All higher courts |
| **County Court** | Possibly Magistrates' Court | All higher courts |

County Court and Magistrates' Court do not create precedent and are bound by all higher courts.

# 6.3 The Supreme Court (formerly the House of Lords)

The main debate about the former House of Lords and precedent was the extent to which it should follow its own past decisions and the ideas on this changed over the years.

Originally the view was that the House of Lords had the right to overrule past decisions, but gradually during the nineteenth century this more flexible approach disappeared. By the end of that century, in *London Street Tramways v London County Council (1898)*, the House of Lords held that certainty in the law was more important than the possibility of individual hardship being caused through having to follow a past decision.

So, from 1898 to 1966 the House of Lords regarded itself as being completely bound by its own past decisions unless the decision had been made *per incuriam*, that is 'in error'. However, this idea of error referred only to situations where a decision had been made without considering the effect of a relevant statute.

This was not felt to be satisfactory. The law could not change to meet changing social conditions and opinions, nor could any possible 'wrong' decisions be changed by the courts. If there was an unsatisfactory decision by the House of Lords, then the only way it could be changed was by Parliament passing a new Act of Parliament.

This happened in the law on intention as an element of a criminal offence. The House of Lords in *DPP v Smith (1961)* had ruled that an accused could be guilty of murder if a reasonable person would have foreseen that death or very serious injury might result from the accused's actions. This decision was criticised as it meant that the defendant could be guilty even if he had not intended to cause death or serious injury, nor even realised that his actions might have that effect. Eventually Parliament changed the law by passing the Criminal Justice Act 1967.

## 6.3.1 The Practice Statement

It was realised that the House of Lords should have more flexibility, so in 1966 the Lord Chancellor issued a Practice Statement announcing a change to the rule in *London Street Tramways v London County Council*. The Practice Statement said:

> Their Lordships regard the use of precedent as an indispensable foundation upon which to decide what is the law and its application to individual cases. It provides at least some degree of certainty upon which individuals can rely in the conduct of their affairs, as well as a basis for orderly development of legal rules.

> Their Lordships nevertheless recognise that the rigid adherence to precedent may lead to injustice in a particular case and also unduly restrict the proper development of the law. They, therefore, propose to modify their present practice and while treating former decisions of this House as normally binding, to depart from a previous decision when it appears right to do so.

> In this connection they will bear in mind the danger of disturbing retrospectively the basis on which contracts, settlement of property and fiscal arrangements have been entered into and also the especial need for certainty as to the criminal law.

> This announcement is not intended to affect the use of precedent elsewhere than in this House.

## Activity

Read the following passage which comes from an extra explanatory note given to the press when the Practice Statement was issued and answer the questions below.

> The statement is one of great importance, although it should not be supposed that there will frequently be cases in which the House thinks it right not to follow their own precedent. An example of a case in which the House might think it right to depart from a precedent is where they consider that the earlier decision was influenced by the existence of conditions which no longer prevail, and that in modern conditions the law ought to be different.

> One consequence of this change is of major importance. The relaxation of the rule of judicial precedent will enable the House of

Lords to pay greater attention to judicial decisions reached in the superior courts of the Commonwealth, where they differ from earlier decisions of the House of Lords. That could be of great help in the development of our own law. The superior courts of many other countries are not rigidly bound by their own decisions and the change in the practice of the House of Lords will bring us more into line with them. **"**

### Questions

1 Why was the Practice Statement of great importance?

2 Did the note suggest that the Practice Statement was likely to be used often?

3 Do you agree that 'in modern conditions' (see the passage above) the law ought to be different from earlier law decided when social or other conditions in this country were different? Give reasons and examples to support your answer.

4 Why should the House of Lords (now the Supreme Court) want to consider decisions from Commonwealth countries? What authority do such decisions have in the English legal system?

## 6.3.2 Use of the Practice Statement

From 1966, this Practice Statement allowed the House of Lords to change the law if they believed that an earlier case was wrongly decided. They had the flexibility to refuse to follow an earlier case when 'it appears right to do so'. This phrase is, of course, very vague and gave little guidance as to when the House of Lords might overrule a previous decision. In fact the House of Lords was reluctant to use this power, especially in the first few years after 1966. The first case in which the Practice Statement was used was *Conway v Rimmer* (1968), but this only involved a technical point on discovery of documents.

The first major use did not occur until 1972 in *Herrington v British Railways Board* (1972), which involved the law on the duty of care owed to a child trespasser. The earlier case of *Addie v Dumbreck* (1929) had decided that an occupier of land would only owe a duty of care for injuries to a child trespasser if those injuries had been caused deliberately or recklessly. In *Herrington* the Lords held that social and physical conditions had changed since 1929, and the law should also change.

There was still great reluctance in the House of Lords to use the Practice Statement, as can be seen by the case of *Jones v Secretary of State for Social*

*Services* (1972). This case involved the interpretation of the National Insurance (Industrial Injuries) Act 1946 and four out of the seven judges hearing the case regarded the earlier decision in *Re Dowling* (1967) as being wrong. Despite this the Lords refused to overrule that earlier case, preferring to keep to the idea that certainty was the most important feature of precedent. The same attitude was shown in *Knuller (Publishing, Printing and Promotions) Ltd v DPP* (1973) when Lord Reid said:

**"** Our change of practice in no longer regarding previous decisions of this House as absolutely binding does not mean that whenever we think a previous precedent was wrong we should reverse it. In the general interest of certainty in the law we must be sure that there is some very good reason before we so act. **"**

From the mid-1970s onwards the House of Lords showed a little more willingness to make use of the Practice Statement. For example in *Miliangos v George Frank (Textiles) Ltd* (1976) the House of Lords used the Practice Statement to overrule a previous judgment that damages could only be awarded in sterling. Another major case was *Pepper v Hart* (1993) where the previous ban on the use of Hansard in statutory interpretation was overruled.

## 6.3.3 The Practice Statement in criminal law

The Practice Statement stressed that criminal law needs to be certain, so it was not surprising that the House of Lords did not rush to overrule any judgments in criminal cases. The first use in a criminal case was in *R v Shivpuri* (1986) which overruled the decision in *Anderton v Ryan* (1985) on attempts to do the impossible. The interesting point was that the decision in *Anderton* had been made less than a year before, but it had been severely criticised by academic lawyers. In *Shivpuri* Lord Bridge said:

**"** I am undeterred by the consideration that the decision in *Anderton v Ryan* was so recent. The Practice Statement is an effective abandonment of our pretention to infallibility. If a serious error embodied in a decision of this House has distorted the law, the sooner it is corrected the better. **"**

In other words, the House of Lords recognised that they might sometimes make errors and the most important thing then was to put the law right. Where the Practice Statement is used to overrule a previous decision, that past case is then effectively ignored. The law is now that set out in the new case.

A major case on the use of the Practice Statement by the House of Lords in criminal law is *R v G* (2003).

> Full details of this case are given at section 20.3.2.

The House of Lords overruled their previous decision in the case of *Metropolitan Police Commissioner v Caldwell* (1982) on the law of criminal damage.

In *Caldwell* the House of Lords had ruled that recklessness included the situation where the defendant had not realised the risk of his action causing damage, but an ordinary careful adult would have realised there was a risk. In *R v G* it was held that this was the wrong test to use. The Law Lords overruled *Caldwell* and held that a defendant is only reckless if he realised there is risk and goes ahead and takes that risk.

## 6.3.4 The Supreme Court

When the Supreme Court replaced the House of Lords in 2009, the Constitutional Reform Act 2005 transferred the House of Lords' powers to the Supreme Court. It was initially not sure if this included the Practice Direction.

In *Austin v London Borough of Southwark* (2010), which was about tenancy law, the Supreme Court confirmed that the power to use the Practice Statement had been transferred to them. However, they did not use it in *Austin* to depart from an earlier decision as they took the view that certainty in tenancy law was important.

They quoted from the judgment in *Knuller (Publishing, Printing and Promotions) Ltd v DPP* (1973) where it was said that 'In the general interest of certainty in the law we must be sure that there is some very good reason [to depart from the previous law]'. (See section 6.3.2 for fuller quotation from *Knuller*.)

In 2016 the Supreme Court used the Practice Statement to overrule two previous decisions of the House of Lords in cases on regarding what date damages should be calculated in the law of tort.

**Figure 6.3** The operation of judicial precedent in the House of Lords and Supreme Court

| Case year | Case name | Outcome |
| --- | --- | --- |
| 1898 | *London Street Tramways v London County Council* | House of Lords decide they are bound by their own previous decisions |
| 1966 | Practice Statement | House of Lords will depart from their own previous decisions when 'it is right to do so' |
| 1968 | *Conway v Rimmer* | First use of Practice Statement<br>Only involves technical law on discovery of documents |
| 1972 | *Herrington v British Railways Board* | First major use of Practice Statement on the duty of care owed to child trespassers |
| 1973 | *Knuller (Publishing, Printing and Promotions) Ltd v DPP* | Certainty in law was important and would not always use Practice Statement |
| 1986 | *R v Shivpuri* | First use of Practice Statement in a criminal case |
| 1993 | *Pepper v Hart* | Practice Statement used to allow courts to look at Hansard for the purpose of statutory interpretation |
| 2003 | *R v G and R* | Practice Statement used to overrule the decision in *Caldwell* on recklessness in criminal law |
| 2010 | *Austin v London Borough of Southwark* | Supreme Court states that the Practice Statement applies to it |

## 6.4 The Court of Appeal

As already stated there are two divisions of this court, the Civil Division and the Criminal Division, and the rules for precedent are not quite the same in these two divisions.

## 6.4.1 Decisions of courts above the Court of Appeal

Both divisions of the Court of Appeal are bound by decisions of the Court of Justice of the European Union and the House of Lords (now the Supreme Court). This is true even though there were attempts in the past, mainly by Lord Denning, to argue that the Court of Appeal should not be bound by the House of Lords. In *Broome v Cassell & Co. Ltd* (1971) Lord Denning refused to follow an earlier decision of the House of Lords in *Rookes v Barnard* (1964) on the circumstances in which exemplary damages could be awarded.

Again in the cases of *Schorsch Meier GmbH v Hennin* (1975) and *Miliangos v George Frank (Textiles) Ltd* (1976) the Court of Appeal under Lord Denning's leadership refused to follow a decision of the House of Lords in *Havana Railways* (1961) which said that damages could only be awarded in sterling (English money). Lord Denning's argument for refusing to follow the House of Lords' decision was that the economic climate of the world had changed, and sterling was no longer a stable currency; there were some situations in which justice could only be done by awarding damages in another currency. The case of *Schorsch Meier GmbH v Hennin* did not get appealed to the House of Lords, but *Miliangos v George Frank (Textiles) Ltd* did go on appeal to the Lords where it was pointed out that the Court of Appeal had no right to ignore or overrule decisions of the House of Lords. The more unusual feature of *Miliangos* was that the House of Lords then used the Practice Statement to overrule their own decision in *Havana Railways*.

## 6.4.2 The Court of Appeal and its own decisions

The first rule is that decisions by one division of the Court of Appeal will not bind the other division. However, within each division, decisions are normally binding, especially for the Civil Division. This rule comes from the case of *Young v Bristol Aeroplane Co. Ltd* (1944) and the only exceptions allowed by that case are:

- where there are conflicting decisions in past Court of Appeal cases, the court can choose which one it will follow and which it will reject;
- where there is a decision of the Supreme Court/ House of Lords which effectively overrules a Court of Appeal decision, the Court of Appeal must follow the decision of the Supreme Court/House of Lords;
- where the decision was made *per incuriam*, that is carelessly or by mistake because a relevant Act of Parliament or other regulation has not been considered by the court.

The rule in *Young's case* was confirmed in *Davis v Johnson* (1979). In this case the Court of Appeal refused to follow a decision made only days earlier regarding the interpretation of the Domestic Violence and Matrimonial Proceedings Act 1976. The case went to the House of Lords on appeal, where the Law Lords, despite agreeing with the actual interpretation of the law, ruled that the Court of Appeal had to follow its own previous decisions and said that they 'expressly, unequivocally and unanimously reaffirmed the rule in *Young v Bristol Aeroplane*'.

Since this case the Court of Appeal has not challenged the rule in *Young's case*, though it has made some use of the *per incuriam* exception allowed by that case. For example in *Williams v Fawcett* (1986) the Court refused to follow previous decisions because these had been based on a misunderstanding of the County Court rules dealing with procedure for committing to prison those who break court undertakings.

In *Rickards v Rickards* (1989) Lord Donaldson said that it would only be in 'rare and exceptional cases' that the Court of Appeal would be justified in refusing to follow a previous decision. *Rickards v Rickards* was considered a 'rare and exceptional case' because the mistake was over the critical point of whether the court had the power to hear that particular type of case. Also it was very unlikely that the case would be appealed to the House of Lords.

**Figure 6.4** The Court of Appeal and the doctrine of precedent

| General rules | Comment |
| --- | --- |
| Bound by European Court of Justice | Since 1973 all courts in England and Wales are bound by the European Court of Justice |
| Bound by Supreme Court/House of Lords | This is because the House of Lords (now the Supreme Court) is above the Court of Appeal in the court hierarchy. Also necessary for certainty in the law. The Court of Appeal tried to challenge this rule in *Broome v Cassell* (1971) and also in *Miliangos* (1976). The House of Lords rejected this challenge. The Court of Appeal must follow decisions of the Supreme Court/House of Lords. |
| Bound by its own past decisions | Decided by the Court of Appeal in *Young's case* (1944), though there are minor exceptions (see below). In *Davis v Johnson* (1979) the Court of Appeal tried to challenge this rule but the House of Lords confirmed that the Court of Appeal had to follow its own previous decisions. |
| **Exceptions** | **Comment** |
| Exceptions in *Young's case* | The Court of Appeal need not follow its own previous decisions where:<br>■ there are conflicting past decisions<br>■ there is a House of Lords/Supreme Court decision which effectively overrules the Court of Appeal decision<br>■ the decision was made *per incuriam* (in error) |
| Limitation of *per incuriam* | Only used in 'rare and exceptional cases' |
| Special exception for the Criminal Division | If the law has been 'misapplied or misunderstood' (*R v Gould* (1968)) |

## Comment

The main argument in favour of the Court of Appeal being able to ignore House of Lords (now the Supreme Court) decisions is that very few cases reach the Supreme Court, so that if there is an error in the law it may take years before a suitable case is appealed all the way to the Supreme Court.

The cases of *Schorsch Meier* and *Miliangos* illustrate the potential for injustice if there is no appeal to the Supreme Court. What would have happened if the Court of Appeal in *Schorsch Meier* had decided that it had to follow the House of Lords' decision in *Havana Railways*? It is quite possible that the later case of *Miliangos* would not have even been appealed to the Court of Appeal. After all, why waste money on an appeal when there have been previous cases in both the Court of Appeal and the House of Lords ruling on that point of law. The law would have been regarded as fixed and it might never have been changed.

On the other hand, if the Court of Appeal could overrule the Supreme Court, the system of precedent would break down and the law would become uncertain. There would be two conflicting precedents for lower courts to choose from. This would make it difficult for the judge in the lower court. It would also make the law so uncertain that it would be difficult for lawyers to advise clients on the law. However, since the case of *Miliangos*, there has been no further challenge by the Court of Appeal to this basic idea in our system of judicial precedent that lower courts must follow decisions of courts above them in the hierarchy.

### Activity

Read the following comments by Lord Scarman in his judgment in *Tiverton Estates Ltd v Wearwell Ltd* (1975) and answer the questions below.

❝ The Court of Appeal occupies a central, but intermediate position in our legal system. To a large extent, the consistency and certainty of the law depend upon it … If, therefore, one division of the court should refuse to follow another because it believed the other's decision to be wrong, there would be a risk of confusion and doubt arising where there should be consistency and certainty. ❞

❝ The appropriate forum for the correction of the Court of Appeal's errors is the House of Lords, where the decision will at least have the merit of being final and binding, subject only to the House's power to review its own decisions. The House of Lords as the court of last resort needs this power of review; it does not follow that an intermediate court needs it. **"**

**Questions**

1 Why did Lord Scarman describe the Court of Appeal as occupying 'a central but intermediate position'?

2 Do you agree with his view that there would be a 'risk of confusion and doubt' if the Court of Appeal was not obliged to follow its own past decisions?

3 Describe the situations in which the Court of Appeal may refuse to follow its own past decisions.

4 Why did the House of Lords (and now the Supreme Court) need the power of review?

### 6.4.3 The Court of Appeal (Criminal Division)

The Criminal Division, as well as using the exceptions from *Young's case*, can also refuse to follow a past decision of its own if the law has been 'misapplied or misunderstood'. This extra exception arises because in criminal cases people's liberty is involved. This idea was recognised in *R v Taylor* (1950). The same point was made in *R v Gould* (1968).

Also in *R v Spencer* (1985) the judges said that there should not in general be any difference in the way that precedent was followed in the Criminal Division and in the Civil Division, 'save that we must remember that we may be dealing with the liberty of the subject and if a departure from authority is necessary in the interests of justice to an appellant, then this court should not shrink from so acting'.

**Tip**

The hierarchy of the courts and the rules on when the Supreme Court and the Court of Appeal follow their own previous precedents are complicated. It might be an idea to go over these sections again and make sure of the topic.

## 6.5 Judgments: *stare decisis, ratio decidendi, obiter dicta*

### 6.5.1 *Stare decisis*

The doctrine of precedent is based on the Latin maxim *stare decisis et non quieta movere*, usually shortened to *stare decisis*. This means stand by what has been decided and do not unsettle the established.

So precedent is 'standing by' or following decisions in previous cases.

This means that, where the point of law in the previous case and the present case is the same, the court hearing the present case should follow the decision in the previous case. This concept of treating similar cases in the same way promotes the idea of fairness and provides certainty in the law.

It is particularly important in the English legal system as our laws developed from custom and the decisions of judges in cases.

**Key term**

*Stare decisis* – this means 'stand by what has been decided and do not unsettle the established'. It is the foundation of judicial precedent.

Precedent can only operate if the legal reasons for past decisions are known, so at the end of a case there will be a judgment. This is a speech made by the judge (or judges) hearing the case giving the decision and explaining the reasons for the decision. In a judgment the judge usually gives a summary of the facts of the case, reviews the arguments put to him by the advocates in the case, and then explains the principles of law he is using to come to the decision.

### 6.5.2 *Ratio decidendi*

The principles which the judges use are the important part of the judgment and are known as the *ratio decidendi* which means the reason for deciding (and is pronounced ray-she-o dess-i-dend-i). This is what creates a precedent for judges to follow in future cases.

It is also worth realising that there can be more than one speech at the end of a case depending on the number of judges hearing the case. In courts of first instance there will be only one judge and therefore one judgment. However, in the Divisional Courts and the Court of Appeal cases are heard by at least two judges and usually three. In the Supreme Court, the panel of judges must consist of an uneven number, so it could be three, five, seven, nine or even eleven.

The fact that there are two or more judges does not mean that there will always be several judgments as it is quite common for one judge to give the judgment and the other judge/judges simply to say 'I agree'! However, in cases where there is a particularly important or complicated point of law, more than one judge may want to explain his legal reasoning on the point. This can cause problems in later cases as each judge may have had a different reason for his decision, so there will be more than one *ratio decidendi*.

---

### Key term

*Ratio decidendi* – the reason for the decision. This forms a precedent for future cases.

---

A major problem when looking at a past judgment is to divide the *ratio decidendi* from the *obiter dicta*. Older judgments are usually in a continuous form, without any headings specifying what is meant to be part of the *ratio* and what is not. This means that the person reading the judgment (especially a judge in a later case) will have to decide what the *ratio* is.

Sir Rupert Cross defined the *ratio decidendi* as 'any rule expressly or impliedly treated by the judge as a necessary step in reaching his conclusion'. Michael Zander says that it is 'a proposition of law which decides the case, in the light or in the context of the material facts.

It depends on the level of the court making the decision as to whether the *ratio* has to be followed by a later court (a binding precedent) or whether it merely has to be considered by that court.

As stated at the beginning of this section, the *ratio decidendi* is the part of the judgment that creates law for future cases to follow. So when looking at the substantive areas of law in this specification you will be considering the *ratio decidendi* in many cases.

For example, in the law of negligence in tort the tests for establishing a duty of care in 'new' situations of negligence are set out in the *ratio* of *Caparo v Dickman* (1990). See 24.1.

When considering whether there was a breach of duty of care in negligence cases, the rule that children are judged in the way that other children would have acted comes from the *ratio* in *Mullin v Richards* (1998). See 24.2.1. And the rule that if the claimant has a weakness or disability, the defendant should take extra precautions comes from the *ratio* in *Paris v Stepney* (1951). See 24.2.2.

In criminal law in offences against the person, the *ratio* in *R v Chan Fook* (1994) states that actual bodily harm includes psychiatric injury to the victim. See 22.2.1.

While for 'grievous bodily harm' the *ratio* in *DPP v Smith* (1961) is that this means really serious harm. See 22.3.2.

### 6.5.3 *Obiter dicta*

The *ratio decidendi* is the only part of a judgment that forms a precedent. The rest of the judgment is known as *obiter dicta* (other things said). *Obiter dicta* are not binding on other courts.

Sometimes a judge will speculate on what his decision would have been if the facts of the case had been different. This hypothetical situation is part of the *obiter dicta* and the legal reasoning put forward in it may be considered in future cases, although as with all *obiter* statements it is not binding precedent.

An example of *obiter dicta* which occurred in *R v Howe* (1987) in respect of the criminal defence of duress is given at section 6.1.3.

---

### Key term

*Obiter dicta* – this means 'other things said'. So it is all the rest of the judgment apart from the *ratio decidendi*. Judges in future cases do not have to follow it.

---

### 6.5.4 Law reporting

In order to follow past decisions there must be an accurate record of what those decisions were. Written reports have existed in England and Wales since the thirteenth century, but many of the early reports were very brief and, it is thought, not always accurate. The earliest reports from about 1275 to 1535 were called Year Books, and contained short reports of cases, usually written in French. From 1535 to 1865 cases were reported by individuals who made a business out of selling the reports to lawyers. The detail and accuracy of these reports varied enormously. However, some are still occasionally used today.

In 1865 the Incorporated Council of Law Reporting was set up. This was controlled by the courts. Reports became accurate, with the judgment usually noted down word for word. This accuracy of reports was one of the factors in the development of the strict doctrine of precedent. These reports still exist and are published according to the court that the case took place in. For example, case references abbreviated to Ch stand for Chancery and the case will have been decided in the Chancery Division; while QB stands for Queen's Bench Division.

There are also other well-established reports today, notably the All England Reports (abbreviated to All ER) and the Weekly Law Reports (WLR).

Today there are also law reports where the citations (the reference number for cases) show which court heard the case:

- UKSC – a Supreme Court case
- UKHL – a House of Lords case
- EWCA Civ – a case from the Court of Appeal (Civil Division)
- EWCA Crim – a case from the Court of Appeal (Criminal Division)
- EWHC – a case from the High Court.

### Internet reports

All High Court, Court of Appeal, Supreme Court (and House of Lords for 1996–2009) cases are now reported on the internet. Some websites give the full report free; others give summaries or an index of cases. There are also subscription sites which contain virtually all the cases. The main ones of these are LexisNexis and Westlaw.

### Activity

In the Table of Cases at the beginning of this book, look at the case citations and find:

1 a case decided in the House of Lords
2 a case reported in the All England Reports
3 a case decided in the Criminal Division of the Court of Appeal
4 a case reported in the Weekly Law Reports.

## 6.6 The operation of precedent

When a new case is being decided the judges can follow a past decision; appellate courts can also overrule past cases. In addition, it is possible to distinguish the present case from an earlier one and avoid having to follow it.

### 6.6.1 Following

Where there is a previous precedent and the judge in the present case decides that it is relevant, the judge should follow that decision. This means he applies the same principle of law to the case now before him.

If the decision is by a court above or on the same level as the present court (see the hierarchy of the courts in section 6.2) then the judge must normally follow the previous precedent.

### 6.6.2 Overruling

This is where a court in a later case states that the legal rule decided in an earlier case is wrong. Overruling may occur when a higher court overrules a decision made in an earlier case by a lower court, for example the Supreme Court overruling a decision of the Court of Appeal. It can also occur where the Court of Justice of the European Union overrules a past decision it has made; or when the Supreme Court uses the Practice Statement to overrule a past decision of its own.

### 6.6.3 Distinguishing

Distinguishing is a method which can be used by a judge to avoid following a past decision which he would otherwise have to follow. It means that the judge finds that the material facts of the case he is deciding are sufficiently different for him to draw a distinction between the present case and the previous precedent. He is not then bound by the previous case.

### Key term

Distinguishing – a method by which a judge avoids having to follow what would otherwise be a binding precedent.

Two cases demonstrating this process are *Balfour v Balfour* (1919) and *Merritt v Merritt* (1971).

### *Balfour v Balfour* (1919) and *Merritt v Merritt* (1971)

Both cases involved a wife making a claim against her husband for breach of contract. In *Balfour* it was decided that the claim could not succeed because there was no intention to create legal relations; there was merely a domestic arrangement between a husband and wife and so there was no legally binding contract. The second case was successful because the court held that the facts of the two cases were sufficiently different in that, although the parties were husband and wife, the agreement was made after they had separated. Furthermore the agreement was made in writing. This distinguished the case from *Balfour*; the agreement in *Merritt* was not just a domestic arrangement but meant as a legally enforceable contract.

**Figure 6.5** The basic concepts of judicial precedent

| Concept | Definition | Comment |
|---|---|---|
| *Stare decisis* | Stand by what has been decided | Follow the law decided in previous cases for certainty and fairness |
| *Ratio decidendi* | Reason for deciding | The part of the judgment which creates the law |
| *Obiter dicta* | Other things said | The other parts of the judgment – these do not create law |
| Binding precedent | A previous decision which has to be followed | Decisions of higher courts bind lower courts |
| Persuasive precedent | A previous decision which does not have to be followed | The court may be 'persuaded' that the same legal decision should be made |
| Original precedent | A decision in a case where there is no previous legal decision or law for the judge to use | This leads to judges 'making' law |
| Distinguishing | A method of avoiding a previous decision because facts in the present case are different | e.g. *Balfour v Balfour* not followed in *Merritt v Merritt* |
| Overruling | A decision which states that a legal rule in an earlier case is wrong | e.g. in *Pepper v Hart* the House of Lords overruled *Davis v Johnson* on the use of Hansard |

# 6.7 Precedent and Acts of Parliament

When a new Act of Parliament is passed which contains a provision which contradicts a previously decided case, that case decision will cease to have effect. The Act of Parliament is now the law on that point.

An example is when Parliament passed the Law Reform (Year and a Day Rule) Act in 1996. Up to then judicial decisions meant that a person could only be charged with murder or manslaughter if the victim died within a year and a day of receiving his injuries. The Act enacted that there was no time limit, and a person could be guilty even if the victim died several years later, so cases after 1996 follow the Act and not the previous judicial decisions.

However, where an act is unclear and needs to be interpreted by the courts then that decision on the interpretation of the words is a precedent for future cases. An example of this is seen in the Theft Act 1968. This Act defined theft as being where a person 'dishonestly appropriates property belonging to another with the intention of permanently depriving the other of it'. However, the Act did not define 'dishonestly' and it was defined in *R v Ghosh* (1992).

Another example is in the Offences against the Person Act 1861 with the offences under ss 18 and 20. Section 18 uses the wording 'cause any grievous bodily harm' but s 20 uses the wording 'inflict any grievous bodily harm'. There have been several cases on whether there is any difference in the meaning of 'cause and 'inflict'. These problems were finally settled when the House of Lords in *R v Burstow* (1997) stated that although the words did not have exactly the same meaning, it 'would be absurd to differentiate between ss 18 and 20'.

So, there is an important relationship between precedent and Acts of Parliament.

# 6.8 Advantages and disadvantages of precedent

As can be seen from the previous sections there are both advantages and disadvantages to the way in which judicial precedent operates in England and Wales. In fact it could be said that every advantage has a corresponding disadvantage.

## 6.8.1 Advantages

1 Certainty
   Because the courts follow past decisions people know what the law is and how it is likely to be applied in their case; it allows lawyers to advise clients on the likely outcome of cases; it also allows people to operate their businesses knowing

that financial and other arrangements they make are recognised by law. The House of Lords Practice Statement points out how important certainty is.

**2 Consistency and fairness in the law**

It is seen as just and fair that similar cases should be decided in a similar way, just as in any sport it is seen as fair that the rules of the game apply equally to each side. The law must be consistent if it is to be credible.

**3 Precision**

As the principles of law are set out in actual cases the law becomes very precise; it is well illustrated and gradually builds up through the different variations of facts in the cases that come before the courts.

**4 Flexibility**

There is room for the law to change as the Supreme Court can use the Practice Statement to overrule cases. The use of distinguishing also gives all courts some freedom to avoid decisions and develop the law.

**5 Time saving**

Precedent can be considered a useful time-saving device. Where a principle has been established, cases with similar facts are unlikely to go through the lengthy process of litigation.

## 6.8.2 Disadvantages

**1 Rigidity**

The fact that lower courts have to follow decisions of higher courts together with the fact that the Court of Appeal has to follow its own past decisions can make the law too inflexible so that bad decisions made in the past may be perpetuated. There is the added problem that so few cases go to the Supreme Court. Change in

the law will only take place if parties have the courage, the persistence and the money to appeal their case.

**2 Complexity**

Since there are nearly half a million reported cases it is not easy to find all the relevant case law even with computerised databases. Another problem is in the judgments themselves, which are often very long with no clear distinction between comments and the reasons for the decision. This makes it difficult in some cases to extract the *ratio decidendi*; indeed in *Central Asbestos Co. Ltd v Dodd* (1973) the judges in the Court of Appeal said they were unable to find the *ratio* in a decision of the House of Lords.

**3 Illogical distinctions**

The use of distinguishing to avoid past decisions can lead to 'hair-splitting' so that some areas of the law have become very complex. The differences between some cases may be very small and appear illogical.

**4 Slowness of growth**

Judges are well aware that some areas of the law are unclear or in need of reform; however they cannot make a decision unless there is a case before the courts to be decided. This is one of the criticisms of the need for the Court of Appeal to follow its own previous decisions, as only about 50 cases go to the Supreme Court each year. There may be a long wait for a suitable case to be appealed as far as the Supreme Court.

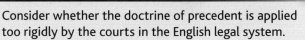

**Extension essay**

Consider whether the doctrine of precedent is applied too rigidly by the courts in the English legal system.

## Check your understanding

1   Which one statement most accurately describes the term *ratio decidendi*?

   A   A decision which forms a new precedent

   B   The reason for the decision in the judgment of a case

   C   A decision by a court which a lower court has to follow

   D   Other things said in a judgment

2   Which one statement most accurately describes the effect of the Practice Statement 1966?

   A   The Court of Appeal must follow a past decision of the Supreme Court

   B   The Supreme Court must follow its own past decisions

   C   The Supreme Court can depart from its own past decision when it is right to do so

   D   The Supreme Court must follow a past decision of the Court of Justice of the European Union when it is right to do so

3   Using an example from civil or criminal law, explain how judges can use distinguishing to avoid following a previous decision.

4   Using examples from civil and/or criminal law, explain how judges can avoid following a binding precedent and suggest why it may be advantageous for them to use this approach.

## Summary

- The doctrine of precedent is based on *stare decisis* (keep to the decision).

- Courts lower in the hierarchy must follow precedents set by higher courts.

- The Supreme Court is normally bound by its own previous decisions, but the Practice Statement allows the court to depart from a previous decision where it is right to do so.

- The Court of Appeal is bound by its own previous decisions: the only exceptions are those set out in *Young's case*.

- The Human Rights Act 1998 means that past decisions in breach of human rights should not be followed.

- *Ratio decidendi* is the reason for the decision and creates a precedent for future cases: the *ratio* is identified by judges in later cases.

- *Obiter dicta* is the rest of the judgment and does not create a binding precedent.

- Judges in later cases do not have to follow precedent if they can distinguish their case from the previous one.

- Courts higher in the hierarchy can overrule a previous precedent.

- The advantages of judicial precedent are: certainty, consistency and fairness, precision, flexibility and time saving.

- The disadvantages of judicial precedent are: rigidity, complexity, illogical distinctions and slowness of growth.

# 7 Law making: law reform

After reading this chapter you should be able to:
- Understand the work of the Law Commission
- Understand the need to reform, codify, consolidate or repeal areas of law
- Explain the advantages and disadvantages of reform through the Law Commission

## 7.1 The work of the Law Commission

The Law Commission was set up in 1965 by the Law Commissions Act 1965. It is a full-time body and consists of a Chairman who is a High Court Judge, and four other Law Commissioners who are all highly qualified lawyers. There are also support staff to assist with research.

The role of the Law Commission is set out in s 3 of the Law Commissions Act which states:

> It shall be the duty of each of the Commissions to take and keep under review all the law with which they are respectively concerned with a view to its systematic development and reform, including in particular the codification of such law, the elimination of anomalies, the repeal of obsolete and unnecessary enactments, the reduction of the number of separate enactments and generally the simplification and modernisation of the law. ""

This is a very wide-ranging brief as it covers 'keep under review all the law'. It also specifically states that the Law Commission is to be concerned with:
- 'systematic development and reform'
- codification
- repeal.

### 7.1.1 Reform

The Law Commission considers areas of law which are believed to be in need of reform. The actual topics may be referred to it by the Lord Chancellor on behalf

of the government, or the Law Commission may itself select areas in need of reform and seek governmental approval to draft a report on them. It concentrates on what is sometimes called 'lawyers' law' or 'pure law'. In other words it is concerned with substantive law, such as criminal law, contract law, law of tort, land law and family law.

The Law Commission works by researching the area of law that is thought to be in need of reform. It then publishes a consultation paper seeking views on possible reform. The consultation paper will describe the current law, set out the problems and look at options for reform (often including explanations of the law in other countries).

Following the response to the consultation paper, the Commission will then draw up positive proposals for reform. These will be presented in a report which will also set out the research that led to the conclusions. There will often be a draft Bill attached to the report with the intention that this is the exact way in which the new law should be formed. Such a draft Bill must, of course, go before Parliament and go through the necessary parliamentary stages if it is to become law.

See section 3.3.1 for more information on a Bill's journey through Parliament.

**Figure 7.1** The way the Law Commission works

### 7.1.2 Codification

**Codification** involves reviewing all the law on the particular topic and then creating a code to cover all aspects of the law on that topic. The code is likely to include existing law as well as creating new law where the previous law was unsatisfactory. In this way all the law is in one place and it makes the law simpler and easier to find. Codification was specifically referred to by s 3 of the Law Commissions Act 1965 as part of the Law Commission's role.

When the Law Commission was first formed in 1965 an ambitious programme of codification was announced, aimed at codifying family law, contract law, landlord and tenant laws and the law of evidence. However, the Law Commission has gradually abandoned these massive schemes of codification in favour of what might be termed the 'building-block' approach. Under this it has concentrated on codifying small sections of the law that can be added to later.

In particular, the Law Commission spent many years writing a draft criminal code which aimed to include the main general principles of criminal law. The draft Criminal Code was first published in 1985. However, the government has never implemented it. In 2008, the Law Commission stated that it would be concentrating on smaller areas of the code, as there was more chance that the government would be prepared to make such reforms of the law.

In its 2015–16 Annual Report the Law Commission pointed out that 'the pattern in future is likely to be codification rather than a simple consolidation'. However, this would only happen in areas where 'statute law is incoherent or confusing and where codification would bring genuine practical benefits'.

## 7.1.3 Consolidation

The aim of **consolidation** is to draw all the existing provisions together in one Act. It is different to codification as the law is not reviewed or changed. It is simply brought together in one Act. This is needed because in some areas of law there are a number of statutes, each of which sets out a small part of the total law. This is another way in which the law is being made more accessible.

Up to 2006 the Law Commission produced about five or six Consolidation Bills each year. By 2006 they were responsible for 220 consolidation Acts. From 2006 to 2016 only two were produced, the Charities Act 2011 and the Co-operative and Community Benefit Societies Act 2014.

In some areas the law that was consolidated has been fragmented by further Acts of Parliament! This happened with the law on sentencing. The law was consolidated in the Powers of Criminal Courts (Sentencing) Act 2000. However, within a few months the law was changed again by the Criminal Justice and Courts Services Act 2000, which renamed some of the community penalties and also created new powers of sentencing.

Then in 2003 the Criminal Justice Act 2003 changed much of the sentencing law again. Other reforms have since been put in place for young offenders and, in 2012, the Legal Aid, Sentencing and Punishment of Offenders Act made further changes in the law on sentencing. It is not surprising that it has now been suggested that there should be a new Consolidated Bill for sentencing.

In its 2015–16 Annual Report the Law Commission stated that work was currently being undertaken by their criminal law team on important but technical provisions dealing with transitional arrangements in sentencing. This work is intended to pave the way for a Consolidation Bill to introduce a new Sentencing Code.

## 7.1.4 Repeal

Another of the Law Commission's roles is to identify old Acts which are no longer used, so that Parliament can **repeal** these Acts. The Law Commission has been very successful in this. By 2015 there had been 19 Statute Law (Repeals) Acts. Over 3,000 out-of-date Acts of Parliament have been completely repealed. In addition, parts of thousands of other Acts have also been repealed.

The Statute Law (Repeals) Act 2013 repealed several Acts that were very old and now completely useless such as an Act of 1696 about the rebuilding of St Paul's Cathedral, London.

In 2015 the twentieth Statute Law (Repeals) Bill was published. This will result in the repeal of another 209 complete Acts and the removal of redundant provisions from 63 other Acts. Many of the Acts that will be repealed by this were passed during the 1940s to deal with the aftermath of the Second World War and are now completely redundant.

> ### Look online
>
> 1   Look at the Law Commission's website (www. lawcom.gov.uk) and make a list of three areas of law which the Law Commission is currently researching.
> 2   Look for a Statute Law (Repeals) Act on the website www.legislation.gov.uk and find three old Acts that have been repealed. What is the oldest Act that you can find?

## 7.1.5 Implementation of the Law Commission's proposals for reform

The Law Commission has produced over 300 reports proposing reform of the law in a wide variety of areas of law. However, in order to be effective, their proposals then have to be passed as law by Parliament.

In the first ten years of its existence the Law Commission had a high success rate with 85 per cent of its proposals being enacted by Parliament. During the next ten years, however, only 50 per cent of its suggested reforms became law. This lack of success was due to lack of parliamentary time, and an apparent disinterest by Parliament in technical law reform. The rate hit an all-time low in 1990 when not one of its reforms was enacted by Parliament.

Since then there has been an improvement and there have been three measures to ensure that more reforms are implemented. The three measures are:

1   the Law Commission Act 2009 amending the 1965 Act, and which places a requirement on the Lord Chancellor to report to Parliament annually on the government's progress in implementing reports
2   a Protocol agreed between the government and the Law Commission in March 2010. The Protocol sets out that the minister for the relevant department will provide an interim response as soon as possible (but not later than six months after publication of the report), and will give a final response as soon as possible but within a year of the report being published
3   a dedicated parliamentary procedure to implement Law Commission reports. regarded as 'uncontroversial'. This has operated since 2010 and six Acts have been passed through this procedure.

### Implementation rate

By March 2016 the Law Commission had published a total of 217 law reform reports. Of these 143 (66 per cent) had been implemented in whole or in part and another eight had been accepted in whole or in part and were awaiting implementation. A response from the government was still being waited for in respect of 19 reports. Of the rest, the government had rejected 31 reports.

### Examples of law implemented

Some important reforms have been passed in recent years. These include:

■ Land Registration Act 2002, which reformed and modernised the method of registering land. This is important as it affects everyone who buys and sells a house, flat or any other land or building
■ Corporate Manslaughter and Corporate Homicide Act 2007, which made corporations and organisations criminally liable for deaths caused by their working practices
■ Coroners and Justice Act 2009, which abolished the defence to murder of provocation and replaced it with the defence of loss of control
■ Criminal Justice and Courts Act 2015, which includes reform of **contempt of court** by jurors and the creation of new offences of juror misconduct in relation to using the internet
■ Consumer Rights Act 2015, which gives consumers the legal right to reject faulty goods and the right to a refund if they act within a reasonable time.

> ### Key term
>
>
> Contempt of court – disobeying a court's order: for example where a juror uses a mobile phone in the court room when he has been told that it is not allowed.

**Figure 7.2 The Law Commission**

| Set up | By the Law Commissions Act 1965 |
|---|---|
| Personnel | Chairman and four other Commissioners Support staff |
| Function | To keep the law under review with a view to its systematic development and reform, including codification and repeal |
| Recent reforms | Coroners and Justice Act 2009 abolishing defence of provocation<br><br>Criminal Justice and Courts Act 2015 creating offences of jury misconduct in using the internet<br><br>Consumer Rights Act 2015 giving consumers the legal right to reject faulty goods |
| Success rate | First 10 years 85%<br>Second 10 years 50%<br>Since improved<br>Overall (1965–2016) 66% of reform reports became law |

# 7.2 Advantages and disadvantages of reform through the Law Commission

The Law Commission has made a large contribution to law reform in England and Wales. Before it was set up in 1965 there was no full-time law reform body. There were only part-time committees that considered small areas of law.

## 7.2.1 Advantages

The main advantages of having the Law Commission issue reports on areas of law are:

- areas of law are researched by legal experts
- the Law Commission consults before finalising its proposals
- whole areas of law can be considered, not just small issues
- if Parliament enacts the reform of a whole area of law, then the law is in one Act, such as the Land Registration Act 2002 (see page 68) and it is easier to find and to understand
- reform can simplify and modernise the law.

## 7.2.2 Disadvantages

### Failure of Parliament to implement reforms

The main disadvantage is that the Law Commission has to wait for the government to bring in the reforms it proposes. The government is often slow to enact reforms and some Law Commission reports have not yet been made law.

Each year in its Annual Report, the Law Commission highlights the number of reports which are still awaiting implementation by Parliament.

A major area of criminal law that is still awaiting reform is non-fatal offences against the person. (This is an area of law you have to study for Unit 2 of both the AS and A-level.)

In 1993 the Law Commission issued a report, Offences Against the Person (Law Com No. 218) recommending reform to this area of law. Five years later, in 1998, the government issued a consultation paper which included a draft Bill on this area of law. However, the government did not proceed with the Bill and the reforms proposed by the Law Commission have never been made.

Another example of law where the proposals for reform have not been made is in the civil law of negligence. In 1998 the Commission issued a report, Liability for Psychiatric Illness (Law Com No. 249) suggesting changes to the law where a person suffers psychiatric illness because of another person's negligence. This reform to the law has not been made by the government.

These two examples show how slow Parliament can be over taking action on the Law Commission's proposals. Clearly the Law Commission can only be effective if the government and Parliament are prepared to find time to enact reforms.

### Lack of parliamentary time

There is a problem with the amount of time available in Parliament. A lot of time has to be given to financial matters such as the budget and taxation, health, education and foreign policy, especially at this time of our withdrawal from the European Union. So only a limited time is left for 'pure' law reform.

In fact, in the Lord Chancellor's report in 2012 on implementation, he stated that the Report on Participating in Crime (2007) (Law Com No. 305) and the Report on Conspiracy and Attempts (2009) (Law Com No. 318) were not priority areas and would not be implemented during the lifetime of the then current Parliament which lasted until early 2015. They have still not been implemented.

## Other disadvantages

The government may accept the Law Commission's recommendations in principle. However, when reforming the law, the government may not follow all the recommendations. In addition, as a Bill goes through Parliament, changes to the wording may be made so that the final law is very different to that proposed by the Law Commission. This can cause the law to be less satisfactory than the original proposals.

The government does not have to consult the Law Commission on changes to the law. This can mean that major changes are made without the benefit of the Law Commission's legal knowledge and extensive research.

## Check your understanding

1 Which one of the following is not part of the work of the Law Commission?

A Keeping the law under review

B Passing new laws

C Proposing consolidation of an existing area of law

D Researching the operation of current law

2 Suggest why the Law Commission plays an effective role in law reform.

3 Examine and discuss the difficulties involved in implementing reforms proposed by the Law Commission.

## Summary

- The Law Commission was set up by the Law Commission Act 1965. Its role is to keep all the law under review. This is done by:
  - researching existing law
  - consulting
  - drawing up proposals for reform.
- It can make proposals for:
  - reforming the law
  - codifying the law
  - consolidating the law
  - repealing out-of-date law.
- Its proposals are put before Parliament who decides whether or not to implement them.
- Parliament does not always implement the Law Commission's law reform reports but the rate of implementation is improving.

- Advantages of reform through the Law Commission are:
  - law is researched by legal experts
  - there is consultation before drawing up proposals
  - whole areas of law are considered
  - can bring the law on one topic together in one Act
  - simplifies and modernises the law.
- Disadvantages are:
  - the government is slow to implement the reforms
  - some reforms may never be implemented
  - the lack of parliamentary time to discuss the proposed reforms
  - Parliament may make changes to the proposed reforms without the benefit of legal expertise.

# 8 Law making: the European Union

After reading this chapter you should be able to:
- Understand the functions of the main institutions of the European Union
- Understand the different sources of European Union law
- Understand the impact of the law of England and Wales

## 8.1 Formation of the European Union

On 1 January 1973 the United Kingdom joined what was then the European Economic Community, and another source of law came into being: European Union law. Since then it has had increasing significance as a source of law. The European Economic Community was originally set up by Germany, France, Italy, Belgium, the Netherlands and Luxembourg in 1957 by the Treaty of Rome. The name 'European Union' was introduced by the Treaty of European Union in 1993. Denmark and Ireland joined at the same time as the United Kingdom. In the 1980s and 1990s Greece, Spain, Portugal, Austria, Finland and Sweden joined. Then on 1 May 2004 another ten countries joined the EU. These were Cyprus, Czech Republic, Estonia, Hungary, Latvia, Lithuania, Malta, Poland, Slovak Republic and Slovenia. Bulgaria and Romania joined on 1 January 2007 and Croatia joined in 2013. There are now 28 Member States (see Figure 8.1).

In 2016 Britain voted to leave the European Union.

## 8.2 The institutions of the European Union

In 2009 the Treaty of Lisbon restructured the European Union. There are now two treaties setting out its rules. These are:
- the Treaty of European Union (TEU)
- the Treaty of the Functioning of the European Union (TFEU).

The European Union has a vast and complex organisation with institutions established originally by the Treaty of Rome. The main institutions which exercise the functions of the Union are:
- the Council of the European Union
- the Commission
- the European Parliament
- the Court of Justice of the European Union.

### 8.2.1 The Council of the European Union

The government of each nation in the Union sends a representative to the Council. The Foreign Minister is usually a country's main representative, but a government is free to send any of its ministers to Council meetings. This means that usually the minister responsible for the topic under consideration will attend the meetings of the Council, so that the precise membership will vary with the subject being discussed. For example, the Minister for Agriculture will attend when the issue to be discussed involves agriculture. Usually, twice a year government heads meet in the European Council or 'Summit' to discuss broad matters of policy.

**Figure 8.1** The Member States of the European Union

| Date | Countries joining | Comment |
|---|---|---|
| 1957 | Belgium France Germany Italy Luxembourg The Netherlands | These are the founder members Treaty of Rome signed |
| 1973 | Denmark Ireland United Kingdom | UK passes the European Communities Act 1972 on joining |
| 1981 | Greece | |
| 1986 | Portugal Spain | |
| 1995 | Austria Finland Sweden | |
| 2004 | Cyprus, Czech Republic, Estonia, Hungary, Latvia, Lithuania, Malta, Poland, Slovak Republic and Slovenia | |
| 2007 | Bulgaria Romania | |
| 2013 | Croatia | |

The Member States take it in turns to provide the President of the Council, each for a six-month period. To assist with the day-to-day work of the Council there is a committee of permanent representatives.

The Council is the principal law making body of the Union. Voting in the Council is, in 80 per cent of decisions, by qualified majority which is reached if two conditions are met:

- 55 per cent of member states vote in favour – meaning 16 out of 28 member states, and
- the proposal is supported by member states representing at least 65 per cent of the total EU population.

This new procedure is also known as the 'double majority' rule.

## 8.2.2 The Commission

This consists of 28 Commissioners who are supposed to act independently of their national origin. Each Member State has one Commissioner.

The Commissioners are appointed for a five-year term and can only be removed during this term of office by a vote of censure by the European Parliament. Each Commissioner heads a department with special responsibility for one area of Union policy, such as economic affairs, agriculture or the environment.

The Commission as a whole has several functions as follows:

- It puts forward proposals for new laws to be adopted by the Parliament and the Council.
- It is the 'guardian' of the treaties and ensures that treaty provisions and other measures adopted by the Union are properly implemented. If a Member State has failed to implement Union law within its own country, or has infringed a Provision in some way, the Commission has a duty to intervene and, if necessary, refer the matter to the Court of Justice of the European Union. The Commission has performed this duty very effectively, and as a result there have been judgments given by the Court against Britain and other Member States.
- It is responsible for the administration of the Union and has executive powers to implement the Union's budget and supervise how the money is spent.

## 8.2.3 The European Parliament

The members of the European Parliament (MEPs) are directly elected by the electorate of the Member States in elections which take place once every

**Figure 8.2** Map showing countries of the European Union

five years. The number of MEPS from each country is determined by the size of the population of the country. There are 751 MEPs at the moment.

Within the Parliament the members do not operate in national groups, but form political groups with those of the same political allegiance. The Parliament meets on average about once a month for sessions that can last up to a week. It has standing committees which discuss proposals made by the Commission and then report to the full Parliament for debate. Decisions are made by the Parliament Council of Ministers.

The Parliament used to have only a consultative role, but it can now co-legislate on an equal footing with the Council in most areas. It can approve or reject a legislative proposal made by the Commission, or propose amendments to it. There are some areas, such as competition laws, where the Parliament cannot make law but only has the right to be consulted and put forward its opinion.

The Parliament also:

- decides on international agreements
- decides on whether to admit new member States
- reviews the Commission's work programme and asks it to propose legislation.

Members of the European Parliament in Strasbourg, France, 2016

# 8.3 The Court of Justice of the European Union

Its function is set out in Article 19 of the TEU. This states that the Court must 'ensure that in the interpretation and application of the Treaty the law is observed'. The Court sits in Luxembourg and has 28 judges, one from each Member State.

For a full court 11 judges will sit. The Court sits as a full court in the particular cases prescribed by the Statute of the Court (including proceedings to dismiss the European Ombudsman or a Member of the European Commission who has failed to fulfil his obligations) and where the Court considers that a case is of exceptional importance. For other cases the Court sits in chambers of five judges or three judges.

Judges are appointed under Article 253 TFEU from those who are eligible for appointment to the highest judicial posts in their own country or who are leading academic lawyers. Each judge is appointed for a term of six years, and can be reappointed for a further term of six years. The judges select one of themselves to be President of the Court.

The Court is assisted by 11 Advocates General who also hold office for six years. Each case is assigned to an Advocate General whose task under Article 253 is to research all the legal points involved and

**"** **to present publicly, with complete impartiality and independence, reasoned conclusions on cases submitted to the Court of Justice with a view to assisting the latter in the performance of its duties. "**

## 8.3.1 Key functions

The Court's task is to ensure that the law is applied uniformly in all Member States and it does this by performing two key functions.

The first is that it hears cases to decide whether Member States have failed to fulfil obligations under the Treaties. Such actions are usually initiated by the European Commission, although they can also be started by another Member State. An early example of such a case was *Re Tachographs: The Commission v United Kingdom* (1979) in which the court held that the United Kingdom had to implement a Council regulation on the use of mechanical recording equipment (tachographs) in road vehicles used for the carriage of goods (see section 8.3.2 for further information on the effect of regulations).

The second function is that it hears references from national courts for preliminary rulings on points of European law.

## 8.3.2 Preliminary rulings

This function is a very important one, since rulings made by the Court of Justice of the European Union are then binding on courts in all Member States. This ensures that the law is indeed uniform throughout the European Union.

### Article 267

A request for a preliminary ruling is made under Article 267 TFEU. This says that:
the Court of Justice shall have jurisdiction to give preliminary rulings concerning:

a  the interpretation of treaties;
b  the validity and interpretation of acts of the institutions of the Union;
c  the interpretation of the statutes of bodies established by an act of the Council, where those statutes so provide.

Article 267 goes on to state that where there is no appeal from the national court within the national system, then such a court must refer points of European law to the Court of Justice of the European Union. Other national courts are allowed to make an Article 267 reference, but as there is still an appeal available within their own system, such courts do not have to do so. They have discretion (i.e. they can choose whether or not to refer the case).

Applied to the court structure in England and Wales, this means that, while we remain a member of the European Union, the Supreme Court must refer questions of European law, since it is the highest appeal court in our system. However, the Court of Appeal does not have to refer questions. It has a choice: it may refer if it wishes or it may decide the case without any referral. The same is true of all the lower courts in the English court hierarchy.

However, even courts at the bottom of the hierarchy can refer questions of law under Article 267, if they feel that a preliminary ruling is necessary to enable a judgment to be given.

Whenever a reference is made, the Court of Justice of the European Union only makes a preliminary ruling on the point of law; it does not actually decide the case. The case then returns to the original court for it to apply the ruling to the facts in the case.

The first case to be referred to the Court of Justice of the European Union by an English court was *Van Duyn v Home Office* (1974).

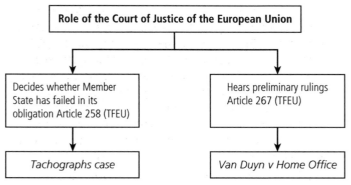

**Figure 8.3** Role of the Court of Justice of the European Union

### 8.3.3 The operation of the Court of Justice of the European Union

When compared with English courts there are several major differences in the way the Court of Justice of the European Union operates. First the emphasis is on presenting cases 'on paper'. Lawyers are required to present their arguments in a written form and there is far less reliance on oral presentation of a case. This requirement is, of course, partly because of the wide range of languages involved, though French is the traditional language of the Court. It also represents the traditional method of case presentation in other European countries. An interesting point to note is that the English system in some areas is now beginning to use this 'paper' submission.

A second major difference is the use of the Advocate General. This independent lawyer is not used in the English system. However in the Court of Justice of the European Union the Advocate General who was assigned to the case will present his findings on the law after the parties have made their submissions. The court, therefore, has the advantage of having all aspects of the law presented to them.

The deliberations of the judges are secret and where necessary the decision will be made by a majority vote. However, when the judgment is delivered, again in a written form, it is signed by all the judges who formed part of the panel, so that it is not known if any judges disagreed with the majority. This contrasts strongly with the English system, whereby a dissenting judge not only makes it known that he disagrees with the majority, but also usually delivers a judgment explaining his reasoning.

The other points to be noted are that the Court of Justice of the European Union is not bound by its own previous decisions and that it prefers the purposive approach to interpretation.

> See section 5.3 for an explanation of the purposive approach.

The court has wide rights to study extrinsic material when deciding the meaning of provisions and may study preparatory documents. The Court of Justice of the European Union is important, not only because its decisions are binding on English courts, but also because its attitude to interpretation is increasingly being followed by English courts. The Court of Justice of the European Union pointed this out in *von Colson v Land Nordrhein-Westfalen* (1984) when it said: 'national courts are required to interpret their national law in the light of the wording and the purpose of the directive.'

**Figure 8.4** The institutions of the European Union

| Council of Ministers | ■ Consists of ministers from each Member State<br>■ Responsible for broad policy decisions |
|---|---|
| Commission | ■ 28 Commissioners whose duty it is to act in the Union's interest<br>■ Proposes legislation<br>■ Tries to ensure that the Treaties are implemented in each Member State |
| European Parliament | ■ Members elected by citizens in each Member State<br>■ Can co-legislate on an equal footing with the Council in most areas |
| Court of Justice of the European Union | ■ One judge from each Member State<br>■ Decides whether Member States have failed in obligations<br>■ Rules on points of European law when cases are referred to it under Article 267 TFEU |

# 8.4 Sources of European Union law

There are primary and secondary sources of law. Primary sources are mainly the Treaties, the most important of which was originally the Treaty of Rome itself and now is the Treaty of the European Union. Secondary sources are legislation passed by the institutions of the Union under Article 288 TFEU. This secondary legislation is of three types: treaties, regulations and directives, all of which are considered below.

## 8.4.1 Treaties

While the UK is a member of the European Union any Treaties made by the Union are automatically part of our law. This is as a result of the European Communities Act 1972, s 2(1) which states that:

> **66** All such rights, powers, liabilities, obligations and restrictions from time to time created or arising by or under the Treaties and all such remedies and procedures from time to time provided for by or under the Treaties, as in accordance with the Treaties are without further enactment to be given legal effect or used in the United Kingdom, shall be recognised and available in law and be enforced, allowed and followed accordingly. **99**

This not only makes European Union law part of our law but also allows individuals to rely on it. In the case of *Van Duyn v Home Office* (1974) the Court of Justice of the European Union held that an individual was entitled to rely on Article 45 in the Treaty of Rome giving the right of freedom of movement. The Article had direct effect and conferred rights on individuals which could be enforced not only in the Court of Justice of the European Union, but also in national courts.

This means that while the UK is a member of the EU, citizens of the United Kingdom are entitled to rely on the rights in the Treaty of Rome and other treaties, even though those rights may not have been specifically enacted in English law. This is clearly illustrated by the case of *Macarthys Ltd v Smith* (1980).

### Macarthys Ltd v Smith (1980)

Wendy Smith's employers paid her less than her male predecessor for exactly the same job. As the two people were not employed at the same time by the employer there was no breach of English domestic law. However, Wendy Smith was able to claim that the company which employed her was in breach of Article 157 TFEU over equal pay for men and women and this claim was confirmed by the Court of Justice of the European Union.

UK courts can apply European Treaty law directly rather than wait for the Court of Justice of the European Union to make a ruling on the point. An example is *Diocese of Hallam Trustee v Connaughton* (1996).

### Diocese of Hallam Trustee v Connaughton (1996)

In this case the Employment Appeal Tribunal had to consider facts which had some similarity to the *Wendy Smith case*. Josephine Connaughton was employed as director of music by the Diocese of Hallam from 1990 to September 1994, at which time her salary was £11,138. When she left the position, the post was advertised at a salary of £13,434, but the successful applicant, a man, was actually appointed at a salary of £20,000. In other words, where in Wendy Smith's case she had discovered that her male predecessor was paid more than she was, in the *Connaughton case* it was the immediate successor who was receiving considerably higher pay.

The Employment Appeal Tribunal considered Article 157 TFEU and decided as a preliminary point that its provisions were wide enough to allow Miss Connaughton to make a claim, saying:

> **66** We are sufficiently satisfied as to the scope of Article 141 so as to decide this appeal without further reference to the Court of Justice of the European Union. **99**

## 8.4.2 Regulations

Under Article 288 TFEU the European Union has the power to issue **regulations** which are 'binding in every respect and directly applicable in each Member State'.

### Key term

**EU regulations** – laws issued by the EU which are binding on Member States and automatically apply in each member country.

Such regulations do not have to be adopted in any way by the individual states as Article 288 makes it clear that they automatically become law in each member country.

This 'direct applicability' point was tested in *Re Tachographs: Commission v United Kingdom* (1979).

### Re Tachographs: Commission v United Kingdom (1979)

A regulation requiring mechanical recording equipment to be installed in lorries was issued. The United Kingdom government of the day decided not to implement the regulation, but to leave it to lorry owners to decide whether or not to put in such equipment. When the matter was referred to the Court of Justice of the European Union it was held that Member States had no discretion in the case of regulations. The wording of Article 288 was explicit and meant that regulations were automatically law in all Member States.

This prevents states from picking and choosing which regulations they implement. As a result laws are uniform across all the Member States.

## 8.4.3 Directives

**Directives** are the main way in which harmonisation of laws within Member States is reached. There have been directives covering many topics including company laws, banking, insurance, health and safety of workers, equal rights, consumer law and social security.

### Key term

**EU directives** – these are issued by the EU and direct all Member States to bring in the same laws throughout all the countries.

As with regulations, it is Article 288 TFEU that gives the power to the Union to issue directives. There is, however, a difference from regulations in that Article 288 says such directives 'bind any Member State to which they are addressed as to the result to be achieved, while leaving to domestic agencies a competence as to form and means'.

This means that Member States will pass their own laws to bring directives into effect (or implement them) and such laws have to be brought in within a time limit set by the European Commission.

The usual method of implementing directives in the United Kingdom is by statutory instrument. An example is the Restriction of the Use of Certain Hazardous Substances in Electrical and Electronic Equipment Regulations 2012 which implemented EU Directive 2011/65/EU (Restriction of the Use of Certain Hazardous Substances in Electronic and Electrical Equipment).

Directives can, however, be implemented by other law-making methods such as Acts of Parliament. An example was the Consumer Protection Act 1987. A directive on liability for defective products was issued in July 1985. The directive had to be implemented by 30 July 1988. This was done in Britain by Parliament passing the Consumer Protection Act 1987, which came into force on 1 March 1988.

Directives can also be implemented by an order in Council made by the Privy Council.

### Direct effect

Where Member States have not implemented a directive within the time laid down, the Court of Justice of the European Union has developed the concept of 'direct effect'.

If the purpose of a directive is to grant rights to individuals and that directive is sufficiently clear, it may be directly enforceable by an individual against the Member State. This will be so even though that state has not implemented the directive, or has implemented it in a defective way. The important point is that an individual who is adversely affected by the failure to implement only has rights against the state. This is because of the concepts of vertical direct effect and horizontal direct effect (see Figure 8.5).

### Vertical direct effect

Vertical direct effect is where the individual can claim against the state even when a directive has not been implemented. This happened in *Marshall v Southampton and South West Hampshire Area Health Authority* (1986).

### Marshall v Southampton and South West Hampshire Area Health Authority (1986)

Miss Marshall was required to retire at the age of 62 when men doing the same work did not have to retire until age 65. Under the Sex Discrimination Act 1975 in English law this was not discriminatory. However, she was able to succeed in an action for unfair dismissal by relying on the Equal Treatment Directive 76/207. This directive had not been fully implemented in the United Kingdom but the Court of Justice of the European Union held that it was sufficiently clear and imposed obligations on the Member State. This ruling allowed Miss Marshall to succeed in her claim against her employers because her employers were 'an arm of the state', i.e. they were considered as being part of the state.

The Equal Treatment Directive had vertical effect allowing individuals to rely on it and take action against the state. This idea of vertical direct effect is shown in diagram form in Figure 8.5.

The concept of the state for these purposes is quite wide, as it was ruled by the Court of Justice of the European Union in *Foster v British Gas plc* (1990) that the state was:

> ❝ a body, whatever its legal form, which has been made responsible, pursuant to a measure adopted by the State, for providing a public service under the control of the State and has for that purpose special powers beyond those which result from the normal rules applicable in relations between individuals. ❞

In view of this wide definition the House of Lords decided that British Gas, which at the time was a nationalised industry, was part of the state, and *Foster* could rely on the Equal Treatment Directive.

The concept of vertical direct effect means that a Member State cannot take advantage of its own failure to comply with European law and implement a directive. Individuals can rely on the directive when bringing a claim against the state.

## Horizontal direct effect

Directives which have not been implemented do not, however, give an individual any rights against other people. So in *Duke v GEC Reliance Ltd* (1988), Mrs Duke was unable to rely on the Equal Treatment Directive as her employer was a private company. This illustrates that directives do not have horizontal direct effect and this was confirmed by an Italian case, *Paola Faccini Dori v Recreb Srl* (1995), in which the Italian government failed to implement Directive 85/447 in respect of consumer rights to cancel certain contracts. *Dori* could not rely on the directive in order to claim a right of cancellation against a private trader.

Clearly it is unfair that these conflicting doctrines of vertical and horizontal effect should give rights to individuals in some cases and not in others. The Court of Justice of the European Union has developed law under which it is possible to take an action to claim damages against the Member State that failed to implement the European directive. This was decided in *Francovich v Italian Republic* (1991).

### *Francovich v Italian Republic* (1991)

The Italian government failed to implement a directive aimed at protecting wages of employees whose employer became insolvent. The firm for which *Francovich* worked went into liquidation owing him wages which he was unable to get from the firm. So, he sued the state for his financial loss. The Court of Justice of the European Union held that he was entitled to compensation.

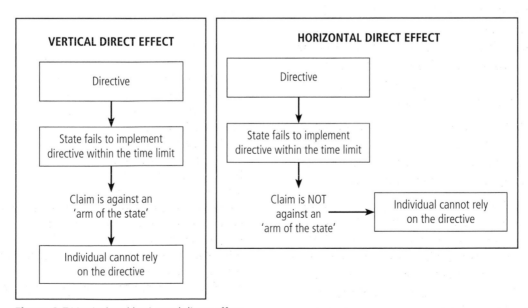

**Figure 8.5** Vertical and horizontal direct effect

**Figure 8.6** The effect of EU laws

| Type of law | Effect | Source/Case |
|---|---|---|
| **Treaties** | Directly applicable<br>Have direct effect (both vertically and horizontally) if give individual rights and are clear | Section 2(1) of the European Communities Act 1972<br>*Macarthys v Smith* |
| **Regulations** | Directly applicable<br>Have direct effect (both vertically and horizontally) if give individual rights and are clear | Article 288 TFEU<br>*Tachograph case* |
| **Directives** | NOT directly applicable<br>Have vertical direct effect if give individual rights and are clear<br>NO horizontal direct effect<br>BUT individual can claim against state for loss caused by failure to implement | Article 288 TFEU<br>*Marshall case*<br>*Duke v GEC Reliance*<br>*Francovitch v Italian Republic* |

## Activity

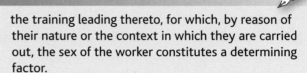

Source A contains extracts from Articles 1 and 2 of the Equal Treatment Directive 76/207. Read these and then apply them, giving reasons for your decision, to the facts set out in Source B.

### Source A

**Council Directive 76/207**

Article 1

1 The purpose of this Directive is to put into effect in the Member States the principle of equal treatment as regards access to employment, including promotion, and to vocational training and as regards working conditions ... This principle is hereinafter referred to as the 'principle of equal treatment'.

Article 2

1 For the purposes of the following provisions, the principle of equal treatment shall mean that there shall be no discrimination whatsoever on the grounds of sex either directly or indirectly by reference in particular to marital or family status.

2 This Directive shall be without prejudice to the right of Member States to exclude from its field of application those occupational activities and, where appropriate,

the training leading thereto, for which, by reason of their nature or the context in which they are carried out, the sex of the worker constitutes a determining factor.

3 This Directive shall be without prejudice to provisions concerning the protection of women, particularly as regards pregnancy and maternity.

4 This Directive shall be without prejudice to measures to promote equal opportunity for men and women, in particular by removing existing inequalities which affect women's opportunities in the areas referred to in Article 1(1).

### Source B

CASE FACTS: Amy Austin and Ben Bowen are employed by Green Gardens Ltd. There is a vacancy for a promotion to section manager, and both have applied for the post. Green Gardens have interviewed Amy and Ben and decided that both are equally qualified for the position. In this situation, if there are fewer women employed at the relevant level, Green Gardens have a policy of appointing the female applicant.

Ben complains that this is discriminatory and contrary to the Equal Treatment Directive.

**Figure 8.7** The effect of EU laws

| Case | Law |
| --- | --- |
| *Van Duyn v Home Office* (1974) | Individual entitled to rely on Treaty provision |
| *Macarthys Ltd v Smith* | Individual entitled to rely on Treaty provision even though national law is different |
| *Re Tachographs: Commission v United Kingdom* (1979) | Regulations are directly applicable in all Member States |
| *Marshall v Southampton and South West Hampshire Area Health Authority* (1986) | Directives have vertical direct effect<br>In an action against the state, individuals can rely on a directive which has not been implemented |
| *Francovich v Italian Republic* (1991) | Individuals can claim compensation from state for losses caused by failure to implement a directive |
| *Van Gend en Loos* (1963) | EU has right to decide whether EU law or national law prevails |
| *Costa v ENEL* (1964) | EU law takes precedence over national law |
| *Factortame case* (1990) | EU law takes precedence over national law even where the Member State has enacted it own law to the contrary |

## 8.5 The impact of European Union law on the law of England and Wales

European law takes precedence over national law. This was first established in *Van Gend en Loos* (1963) which involved a conflict of Dutch law and European law on customs duty. The Dutch government argued that the Court of Justice of the European Union had no jurisdiction to decide whether European law should prevail over Dutch law; that was a matter for the Dutch courts to decide. However, the European Court rejected this argument.

In *Costa v ENEL* (1964) the Court of Justice of the European Union held that even if there was a later national law it did not take precedence over the European law. This effect was seen clearly in *R v Secretary of State for Transport, ex parte Factortame* (1990) (usually referred to as the *Factortame case*) when the Court of Justice of the European Union decided that the UK could not enforce the Merchant Shipping Act 1988. This Act had been passed to protect British fishermen by allowing vessels to register only if 75 per cent of directors and shareholders were British nationals. It was held that this contravened the Treaty of Rome. The Act could not be enforced against EU nationals.

## 8.5.1 The effect of European law on the sovereignty of Parliament

From the cases given above it can be seen that Member States, including the uk, have definitely transferred sovereign rights to the European Union. None of the Member States can rely on their own law when it is in conflict with European Union law.

While the uk remains a member of the European Union it is therefore true to say that the sovereignty of Parliament has been affected and that, in the areas it operates, European law has supremacy over national law.

However, each Member State has the ultimate right to withdraw from the Union.

### Tip

The effect of regulations and directives is an important topic in EU law, but it is complicated. Make sure you have understood the differences.

## Check your understanding

1 Which one statement most accurately describes the effect of a European Union Treaty on the law of the UK?

  A It has horizontal direct effect

  B It automatically becomes part of the law of the UK

  C It only gives the state rights

  D It does not become law until the UK Parliament approves the Treaty

2 Which of the following is not an institution of the European Union?

  A The European Union Council of Ministers

  B The European Parliament

  C The European Court of Human Rights

  D The European Commission

3 Explain two forms of European Union law.

4 Consider the view that European Union law has had limited impact on UK law.

## Summary

- The institutions of the European Union are:
  - the Council of Ministers – responsible for broad policy decisions
  - the Commission with one Commissioner from each Member State
  - the European Parliament with MEPs directly elected by citizens in each Member State
  - the Court of Justice of the European Union with a judge from each Member State and to which cases can be referred by national courts in Member States.

- The sources of law of the European Union are:
  - treaties which become part of our law automatically under the European Communities Act 1972
  - regulations which are directly applicable
  - directives which have to be implemented by Member States – if not implemented they can be relied on against the state.

- European Union takes precedence over our national law even if a later Act is passed by Parliament to change the law.

- The sovereignty of Parliament is affected while we remain a member of the European Union.

# 9 The legal system: the civil courts

See Chapter 10 for details on other methods of dispute resolution.

After reading this chapter you should be able to:
- Have a basic understanding of civil courts
- Understand the track system used in the courts
- Explain the appeal system

## 9.1 Civil cases

As already stressed in Chapter 1, it is important to understand the differences between civil cases and criminal cases. Since civil cases cover a wide range there cannot be a very specific definition which will cover all of them, but a basic definition for **civil claims** is to say that these arise when an individual or a business believes that their rights have been infringed in some way. Some of the main areas of civil law are contract law, law of tort, family law, employment law and company law.

### Key term

Civil claims – claims made in the civil courts when an individual or a business believes that their rights have been infringed in some way.

As well as dealing with different areas of law, the types of dispute that can arise within these areas are equally varied. A company may be claiming that money is owed to them (contract law); this type of claim may be for a few pounds or for several million. An individual may be claiming compensation for injuries suffered in an accident (the tort of negligence), while in another tort case the claim might not be for money but for another remedy such as an injunction to prevent someone from building on disputed land. Other types of court orders include the winding up of a company which cannot pay its debts or a decree of divorce for a marriage that has failed. The list is almost endless.

When a dispute occurs, it is normal to try to resolve it by negotiating with the other person/business or by trying another method of dispute resolution. A case should only be started in the courts as a last resort.

The two courts in which civil cases are tried in are:
- the County Court
- the High Court.

The types of cases they deal with are explained below.

Royal Courts of Justice, London

## 9.2 Civil courts

### 9.2.1 County Court

There are about 200 County Courts, so that most major towns have a court. The County Court can try nearly all civil cases. The main areas of jurisdiction are:
- all contract and tort claims
- all cases for the recovery of land
- disputes over equitable matters such as trusts up to a value of £350,000.

Cases in the County Court are heard by a Circuit Judge or a District Judge. On very rare occasions it is possible for the judge to sit with a jury of eight. This will only happen for defamation cases or for the torts of malicious prosecution or false imprisonment.

### 9.2.2 High Court

The High Court is based in London but also has judges sitting in several towns and cities throughout England and Wales. It has the power to hear any civil case and has three divisions, each of which specialises in hearing certain types of case. These divisions are the Queen's Bench Division, the Chancery Division and the Family Division.

## Queen's Bench Division

This is the biggest of the three divisions. It deals with contract and tort cases where the amount claimed is over £100,000, though it can hear smaller claims where there is an important point of law.

Cases are normally tried by a single judge, but there is a right to jury trial for fraud, libel, slander, malicious prosecution and false imprisonment cases.

There are also specialist courts within the Queen's Bench Division. These include the Commercial Court which deals with insurance, banking and other commercial matters, the Admiralty Court dealing with matters related to shipping and the Administrative Court which supervises the lawfulness of the conduct of national and local government, of inferior courts and tribunals, and of other public bodies. This is done through a process called judicial review.

The Administrative Court can also hear appeals on the law from decisions by the Magistrates' Courts in criminal cases. See 11.3.2.

## Chancery Division

The main business of this division involves disputes concerned with such matters as:

- insolvency, both for companies and individuals
- the enforcement of mortgages
- disputes relating to trust property
- copyright and patents
- intellectual property matters
- contested probate actions.

There is also a special Companies Court in the division which deals mainly with winding up companies.

Cases are heard by a single judge. Juries are never used in the Chancery Division.

## Family Division

This division hears family cases where there is a dispute about which country's laws should apply and all international cases concerning family matters under the Hague Convention. In addition, it can hear cases which can be dealt with by the Family Court.

Cases are heard by a single judge and, although juries were once used to decide defended divorce cases, juries are not used in this division.

The Crime and Courts Act 2013 created a new separate Family Court. The majority of family matters previously dealt with in the Family Division are now dealt with by the Family Court. The Family Division can also deal with these cases, but are unlikely to unless the case is difficult or important.

# 9.3 Starting a court case

Most people who have been injured do not want to start a court case unless they have to. They will first of all try to negotiate an agreed settlement with the person who caused their injuries or damaged their property. Using a method other than going to court is known as Alternative Dispute Resolution (ADR) and is dealt with in Chapter 10. The vast majority of cases are settled and do not go to court.

## 9.3.1 Pre-action protocols

Parties are encouraged to give information to each other, in an attempt to prevent the need for so many court cases to be started. So before a claim is issued, especially in personal injury cases, a pre-action 'protocol' should be followed. This is a list of things to be done and if the parties do not follow the procedure and give the required information to the other party, they may be liable for certain costs if they then make a court claim.

## 9.3.2 Which court to use

If the other person denies liability or refuses to use ADR, then the only way to get compensation for the injuries will be to start a court case.

Once the decision is made to go to court, then the first problem is which court to use. The court to be used will depend on the amount that is being claimed. There are different limits depending on whether the claim is for personal injuries or for damage to property.

If the amount claimed is £100,000 or less the case must be started in the County Court. Where the claim is for less than £10,000 it is a small claim and will be dealt with on the small claims track. The exception is for personal injury cases – where the claim is for £50,000 or less, the case must be started in the County Court, and for less than £1,000 it is a small claim.

If the claim is for more than the above amounts (that is over £50,000 for personal injuries or over £100,000 for other claims), a claimant can choose whether to start the case in the County Court or the High Court. These limits are shown in Figure 9.1.

**Figure 9.1** Which court to start a claim in

| Claim | The court to start the claim in |
|---|---|
| Claim for £10,000 or less | Small claims track |
| Personal injury case claim for £1,000 or less | Small claims track |
| Claim for £100,000 or less | County Court |
| Personal injury case claim for £50,000 or less | County Court |
| Claim for over £100,000 | High Court or County Court |
| Personal injury case claim for over £50,000 | High Court or County Court |

### 9.3.3 Issuing a claim

If someone is using the county court, then they can choose to issue the claim in any of the 200 or so County Courts in the country. If they are using the High Court, then they can go to one of the 20 District Registries or the main court in London. They need a claim form called 'N1' (see Figure 9.2). The court office will give them notes explaining how to fill in the form.

The claim has to be filed at a court office and a fee will be charged for issuing the claim. This fee varies according to how much the claim is for. At the beginning of 2017, the fee for, a claim of up to £300 was £35. The more the claim is for, the higher the fee. At the top end of the scale the fee is £10,000 for claims of £200,000 or more.

---

**Look online**

Look up court forms such as N1 on the website https://hmctsformfinder.justice.gov.uk.

Also use that website to find guidance on starting cases in the County Court.

---

### 9.3.4 Defending a claim

When the defendant receives the claim form there are several routes which can be taken. The defendant may admit the claim and pay the full amount. Where this happens the case ends. The claimant has achieved what was wanted.

In other cases the defendant may dispute the claim. If the defendant wishes to defend the claim, he must send either an acknowledgement of service (Form N9) or a defence to the court within 14 days of receiving the claim.

If the defendant does not do either of these things, then the claimant can ask the court to make an order that the defendant pays the money and costs claimed.

Once a claim is defended the court will allocate the case to the most suitable 'track' or way of dealing with the case.

## 9.4 The three tracks

The decision on which track should be used is made by the District Judge in the County Court or the Master (a procedural judge) in the High Court. To help the judge consider to which track a claim should be allocated, both parties are sent an allocation questionnaire.

There are three tracks and these are:

1. The small claims track – for disputes under £10,000, except for personal injury cases where the limit is at the time of writing £1,000. NOTE there are proposals to increase this limit to £5,000.
2. The fast track – for straightforward disputes of £10,000 to £25,000.
3. The multi-track – for cases over £25,000 or for complex cases under this amount.

If it is thought necessary, especially where there is a complex point of law involved, the judge can allocate a case to a track that normally deals with claims of a higher value. Alternatively, if the parties agree, the judge can allocate a case to a lower value track.

### 9.4.1 Small claims

These cases are usually heard in private, but they can be heard in an ordinary court. The procedure allows the District Judge to be flexible in the way he hears the case. District Judges are given training in how to handle small claims cases, so that they will take an active part in the proceedings, asking questions and making sure that both parties explain all their important points. The parties are encouraged to represent themselves and they cannot claim the cost of using a lawyer from the other side, even if they win the case.

### 9.4.2 Fast track cases

In fast track cases the court will set down a very strict timetable for the pre-trial matters. This is aimed at preventing one or both sides from wasting time and running up unnecessary costs.

Once a case is set down for hearing, the aim is to have the case heard within 30 weeks, but in practice the

## Claim Form

**You may be able to issue your claim online which may save time and money. Go to www.moneyclaim.gov.uk to find out more.**

**In the**

| | |
|---|---|
| **Fee Account no.** | |
| **Help with Fees - Ref no.** (if applicable) | **H W F** – ☐☐☐ – ☐☐☐ |

*For court use only*

| | |
|---|---|
| **Claim no.** | |
| **Issue date** | |

Claimant(s) name(s) and address(es) including postcode

SEAL

Defendant(s) name and address(es) including postcode

Brief details of claim

Value

You must indicate your preferred County Court Hearing Centre for hearings here *(see notes for guidance)*

Defendant's name and address for service including postcode

| | £ |
|---|---|
| **Amount claimed** | |
| **Court fee** | |
| **Legal representative's costs** | |
| **Total amount** | |

For further details of the courts www.gov.uk/find-court-tribunal.
When corresponding with the Court, please address forms or letters to the Manager and always quote the claim number.

**N1** Claim form (CPR Part 7) (06.16)

© Crown Copyright 2016

**Figure 9.2a** Form N1 (front)

**Claim No.**

Does, or will, your claim include any issues under the Human Rights Act 1998?  ☐ Yes  ☐ No

Particulars of Claim (attached)(to follow)

**Statement of Truth**
*(I believe)(The Claimant believes) that the facts stated in these particulars of claim are true.
* I am duly authorised by the claimant to sign this statement

Full name _____

Name of claimant's legal representative's firm _____

signed _____ position or office held _____

*(Claimant)(Litigation friend)  (if signing on behalf of firm or company)
(Claimant's legal representative)  *delete as appropriate

Claimant's or claimant's legal representative's address to which documents or payments should be sent if different from overleaf including (if appropriate) details of DX, fax or e-mail.

▶ Print form  ▶ Reset form

**Figure 9.2b** Form N1 (continued)

wait is likely to be nearer 50 weeks. The actual trial will usually be heard by a Circuit Judge and take place in open court with a more formal procedure than for small claims. In order to speed up the trial itself, the hearing will be limited to a maximum of one day and the number of expert witnesses restricted, with usually only one expert being allowed.

### 9.4.3 Multi-track cases

Each case is tried by a judge who will also be expected to 'manage' the case from the moment it is allocated to the multi-track route. This includes:

■ identifying the issues at an early stage
■ encouraging the parties to use alternative dispute resolution if this is appropriate
■ dealing with any procedural steps without the need for the parties to attend court
■ fixing timetables by which the different stages of the case must be completed.

Case management is aimed at keeping the costs of the case as low as possible and making sure that it is heard reasonably quickly.

### Activity

Advise the people in the following situations:

1 Anika has bought a television set with a built-in DVD player costing £370 from a local electrical superstore. The DVD player has never worked properly, but the store has refused to replace it or to refund the purchase price to Anika. She wishes to claim against the store. Advise her as to which court to start the case in and how she should go about this. Also explain to her the way in which the case will be dealt with if the store defends its position and there is a court hearing.

2 Samuel has been badly injured at work and alleges that the injuries were the result of his employer's failure to take proper safety precautions. He has been advised that his claim is likely to be worth £300,000. Advise him as to which court or courts could hear his case.

## 9.5 Reform of the civil courts

The present system of civil justice started in 1999 and is based on the reforms recommended by Lord Woolf. He stated that a civil justice system should:

■ be just in the results it delivers
■ be fair in the way it treats litigants
■ offer appropriate procedures at a reasonable cost
■ deal with cases at a reasonable speed
■ be understandable to those who use it.

Lord Woolf found that virtually none of these points was being achieved in the civil courts, and criticised the system for being unequal, expensive, slow, uncertain and complicated. His reforms brought in the three-track system and gave judges more responsibility for managing cases.

The reforms also led to the simplifying of documents and procedures and having a single set of rules governing proceedings in both the High Court and the County Court. Lord Woolf also wanted more use of information technology and greater use of alternative dispute resolution.

### 9.5.1 The effect of the Woolf reforms

The main improvements to civil cases have been that the culture of litigation has changed for the better, so that there is more co-operation between the parties' lawyers. There have also been improvements in the delays between issuing a claim and the court hearing, but these are not as great as had been hoped. For example, there is still a wait of at least one year between issuing a fast track claim or multi-track claim and the trial of the case in court.

Another improvement has been in the number of cases that settle (that is the parties come to an agreement so that there is no need for the case to go to trial).

However, there are still many problems with the civil justice system. The main problems are:

■ alternative dispute resolution is not used enough
■ costs of cases have continued to increase – in particular, costs in fast track cases are often far greater than the amount claimed
■ the courts are still under-resourced – in particular the IT systems are very limited.

### 9.5.2 Further reforms

Since the Woolf Reforms, the civil case system has been reviewed and some more changes made. The financial limits for small claims and fast track cases have been increased to avoid expensive trials for lower value claims.

The Civil Procedure Rules have been amended to emphasise that the courts 'deal with cases justly and at a proportionate cost'. The winning party can only claim back costs where they are proportionate to the value of the claim.

The latest Review was by Lord Briggs in 2016. He put forward several proposals. Two main ones are:

**Figure 9.3** Civil courts

| Courts hearing civil cases | County Court<br>High Court |
| --- | --- |
| Three-track system | Up to £10,000 (£1,000 for personal injury cases) – small track<br>£10,000 to £25,000 – fast track<br>Over £25,000 – multi-track |
| Starting a court case | Parties should try to resolve case (can use ADR)<br>To start case must file Form N1<br>If case is defended, it will be allocated to most suitable track |
| Reform of civil justice system | **1999 Lord Woolf's reforms**<br>Brought in the three-track system, encouraged use of ADR, simplified terminology and tried to improve waiting times<br>**Post-Woolf reforms**<br>Emphasis on proportionate costs in cases<br>Increase in value the small claims and fast track cases can deal with<br>**Lords Briggs' proposals for the future**<br>Private mediation service in the County Court<br>Setting up of an Online Court |

1. that there should be an out-of-hours private mediation service in the County Court and
2. that an Online Court should be set up.

## Online Court

Lord Briggs has proposed that there should be an online court. In his interim report he said: 'There is a clear and pressing need to create an Online Court for claims of up to £25,000.'

He believes this court would give litigants effective access to justice without having to incur the disproportionate cost of using lawyers.

There would be three stages to the process:

**Stage 1** A largely automated, interactive online process for the identification of the issues and the provision of documentary evidence.

**Stage 2** Conciliation and case management carried out by case managers.

**Stage 3** If the case is not resolved by Stage 2, then there would be resolution by a judge. For this the Online Court would use documents on screen, telephone video or face-to-face meetings according to the needs of each case.

The intention is that cases would be dealt with more quickly and at lower cost. The hope is that the Online Court will be in operation by 2020.

**Tip**

It is important to understand the different courts that hear civil cases and the three-track system. These are the basis of the whole system.

# 9.6 Appeal routes in civil cases

Once a decision has been made in either the County Court or the High Court, there is always the possibility of appealing against that decision. There are different appeal routes from the County Court and the High Court. In addition, the value of the claim and the level of judge who heard the case affect which appeal route should be used.

## 9.6.1 Appeals from the County Court

For all claims the appeal route depends on the level of judge hearing the case. This means that:

- if the case was heard by a District Judge, then the appeal is to a Circuit Judge in the same County Court
- if the case was heard by a Circuit Judge, then the appeal is to a High Court Judge.

### Second appeals

There is the possibility of a second or further appeal. This appeal will always be to the Court of Appeal (Civil Division). However, such further appeals are only allowed in exceptional cases as set out in s 55 of the Access to Justice Act 1999 which states:

no appeal may be made to the Court of Appeal ... unless the Court of Appeal considers that–

a the appeal would raise an important point of principle or practice, or

b there is some other compelling reason for the Court of Appeal to hear it.

These appeal routes are shown in Figure 9.4.

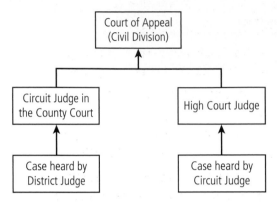

**Figure 9.4** Appeal routes from the County Court

## 9.6.2 Appeals from the High Court

From a decision in the High Court the appeal usually goes to the Court of Appeal (Civil Division).

In rare cases there may be a 'leap frog' appeal direct to the Supreme Court. Since 2015, such an appeal must involve an issue which is of national importance or raise issues of sufficient importance to warrant the leapfrog. In addition the Supreme Court has to give permission to appeal.

### Further appeals

From a decision of the Court of Appeal there is a further appeal to the Supreme Court but only if the Supreme Court or Court of Appeal give permission to appeal.

These appeal routes are shown in Figure 9.5.

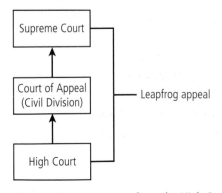

**Figure 9.5** Appeal routes from the High Court

# 9.7 Advantages and disadvantages of using the courts

## 9.7.1 Advantages of using the courts

The main advantages of using the courts to resolve a dispute are:

1 The process is fair in that everyone is treated alike. The judge is impartial.

2 The trial is conducted by a legal expert with the decision being made by a judge who is an experienced and qualified lawyer.

3 Enforcement of the court's decision is easier as any decision made by a court can be enforced through the courts.

4 There is an appeal process with specific appeal routes from decisions made in the courts, so, if the claimant is not happy with the decision, it is usually possible to appeal against it.

5 It may be possible to get **legal aid**, although legal aid for civil cases has been considerably reduced. There are still some types of case where it is available in the courts whereas legal aid is not usually available in tribunals or other methods of dispute resolution.

**Key term**

Legal aid – government help in funding a case.

## 9.7.2 Disadvantages of using the courts

The main problems in using the civil courts are:

1 Cost – the costs of taking a case to court are often more than the amount claimed. In the High Court, the cost can be hundreds of thousands of pounds. For smaller claims, the costs are often more than the amount claimed.

2 Delay – there are many preliminary stages to go through that add to the length of a case. Even after the case is set down for hearing at court there is still a long wait – usually about one year for larger claims before the case is heard in court. The total of all this can mean that some cases are not finished for years.

3 Complicated process – there may be compulsory steps to be taken before a case is started in court. For example, for some types of case, the parties must use set pre-action protocols and give the

other party certain information. When a case is started in court, there are forms to be filled in and set procedures to follow. These are all set out in the Civil Procedure Rules. All of this makes it complicated for an ordinary person to take a case without legal advice and help.

4 Uncertainty – there is no guarantee of winning a case. The person losing a case may have to pay the other side's costs. This makes it difficult to know how much a case is going to cost in advance. Delays in cases can also add to uncertainty and cost.

## Check your understanding

1 Which one of these case values are normally dealt with by the fast track procedure?

   A Under £10,000

   B Under £25,000

   C Under £100,000

   D Between £10,000 and £25,000

2 Which one of the following is not a part of case management in multi-track cases?

   A Encouraging the parties to use a form of alternative dispute resolution

   B Fixing the costs of the case

   C Fixing timetables by which the different stages of the case must be completed

   D Identifying the issues at an early stage hearing

3 Suggest why dealing with a claim using the small claims procedure may be beneficial.

4 Examine the problems involved in taking a claim for negligence through the civil courts and discuss the benefits of possible alternative approaches.

## Summary

- Civil cases are heard in the County Court or the High Court.
- Claims are started by filing a claim form N1 setting out what is claimed and why.
- If a case is defended it is allocated to one of three tracks:
  - small claims
  - fast track
  - multi-track.
- The Woolf reforms:
  - brought in the three-track system
  - gave judges more responsibility for managing cases
  - simplified documents and procedures
  - created a single set of rules.
- Future proposals for reform include:
  - a mediation service to be available in the County Court
  - an Online Court.
- Appeals from the County Court:
  - An appeal from a decision by a District Judge is heard by a Circuit Judge.
  - An appeal from a decision by a Circuit Judge is heard by a High Court Judge.
- Appeals from the High Court:
  - normally go to the Court of Appeal (Civil Division)
  - a 'leapfrog' appeal straight to the Supreme Court is possible where there is an issue of national importance or the case raises issues of sufficient importance.
- Advantages of using the courts are:
  - fair process
  - the judge is a legal expert
  - easier to enforce the decision
  - an appeal system is available
  - legal aid is available for some cases.
- Disadvantages of using the courts are:
  - cost
  - delay
  - complicated
  - uncertain.

# 10 Other forms of dispute resolution

After reading this chapter you should be able to:
- Have an outline understanding of the tribunal structure
- Understand the role of tribunals
- Understand the role of negotiation in resolving civil cases
- Understand the role of mediation in resolving civil cases

## 10.1 Tribunals

Tribunals operate alongside the court system and have become an important part of the legal system. Many tribunals were created in the second half of the twentieth century, with the development of the welfare state. They were created in order to give people a method of enforcing their entitlement to certain social rights. However, unlike alternative dispute resolution where the parties decide not to use the courts, the parties in tribunal cases cannot go to court to resolve their dispute. The tribunal must be used instead of court proceedings.

### Key term

Tribunals – forums used instead of a court for deciding certain types of disputes. They are less formal than courts.

### 10.1.1 Role of tribunals

Tribunals enforce rights which have been granted through social and welfare legislation. There are many different rights, such as:
- the right to a mobility allowance for those who are too disabled to walk more than a very short distance
- the right to a payment if one is made redundant from work
- the right not to be discriminated against because of one's sex, race, age or disability
- the right of immigrants to have a claim for political asylum heard.

These are just a few of the types of rights that tribunals deal with.

### 10.1.2 Organisation of tribunals

Tribunals were set up as the welfare state developed, so new developments resulted in the creation of a new tribunal. This led to more than 70 different types of tribunal. Each tribunal was separate and the various tribunals used different procedures. This made the system confused and complicated.

The whole system was reformed by the Tribunals, Courts and Enforcement Act 2007. This created a unified structure for tribunals, with a First-tier Tribunal to hear cases at first instance and an Upper Tribunal to hear appeals.

#### First-tier Tribunal

The First-tier Tribunal deals with about 600,000 cases each year and has nearly 200 judges and 3,600 lay members. It operates in seven Chambers (divisions). These are:
- Social Entitlement Chamber – this covers a wide range of matters such as Child Support, Criminal Injuries Compensation and Gender Recognition
- Health, Education and Social Care Chamber – this includes the former Mental Health Review Tribunal which dealt with appeals against the continued detention of those in mental hospitals – this Chamber also deals with Special Educational Needs issues
- War Pensions and Armed Forces Compensation Chamber
- General Regulatory Chamber
- Taxation Chamber
- Land, Property and Housing Chamber
- Asylum and Immigration Chamber.

As well as these, there is one tribunal which still operates separately from the First-tier Tribunal. This is the Employment Tribunal which hears claims for such matters as unfair dismissal, redundancy and discrimination.

#### Upper Tribunal

The Upper Tribunal is divided into four Chambers (divisions). These are:
- Administrative Appeals Chamber which hears appeals from Social Entitlement Chamber, Health, Education and Social Care Chamber and War Pensions and Armed Forces Compensation Chamber

- Tax and Chancery Chamber
- Lands Chamber
- Asylum and Immigration Chamber.

From the Upper Tribunal there is a further possible appeal route to the Court of Appeal and from here a final appeal to the Supreme Court.

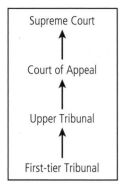

**Figure** 10.1 Appeal route in tribunal cases

## 10.1.3 Composition of tribunals

Cases in the First-tier Tribunal are heard by a tribunal judge. Also, for some types of case, two non-lawyers will sit with the judge to make the decision. These people will have expertise in the particular field of the tribunal. For example, the two non-lawyers in a hearing about a claim to mobility allowance would be medically qualified, while there would be surveyors sitting on the Lands Tribunal. In Employment Tribunals one person will usually be from an employers' organisation and the other from an employees' organisation. This gives them a very clear understanding of employment issues.

## 10.1.4 Procedure in tribunals

Both sides must be given an opportunity to put their case. In some tribunals, especially employment and asylum tribunals, this will be done in a formal way with witnesses giving evidence on oath and being cross-examined. Other tribunals will operate in a less formal way.

Funding for representation is only available in a few tribunals, so most applicants will not have a lawyer, but will present their own case. Where an applicant is putting his own case, the tribunal judge must try to make sure that the applicant puts the case fully.

The decision of the tribunal is binding.

## 10.1.5 Advantages of tribunals

Tribunals were set up to prevent the overloading of the courts with the extra cases that social and welfare rights claims generate.

For the applicant in tribunal cases, the advantages are that such cases are dealt with:

- more cheaply
- more quickly
- more informally
- by experts in the area.

### Cheapness

As applicants are encouraged to represent themselves and not use lawyers, tribunal hearings do not normally involve the costs associated with court hearings. It is also rare for an order for costs to be made by a tribunal, so that an applicant need not fear a large bill if he loses the case.

### Quick hearings

Most tribunal hearings are very short and can be dealt with in one day.

### Informality

The hearing is more informal than in court. Parties are encouraged to present their own case. In addition, most cases are heard in private.

### Expertise

In some tribunals two non-lawyers sit to hear the case with the tribunal judge. These members of the panel are experts in the type of case being heard. This gives them good knowledge and understanding of the issue in dispute.

## 10.1.6 Disadvantages of tribunals

### Lack of funding

Legal aid funding is not available for most tribunals, which may put an applicant at a disadvantage if the other side (often an employer or government department) uses a lawyer. Legal aid is available for cases where fundamental human rights are involved, such as in cases about whether an asylum seeker has the right to remain in the United Kingdom or whether a patient should remain in a secure mental hospital.

### More formal than ADR

A tribunal hearing is more formal than using ADR. The place is unfamiliar and the procedure can be confusing for individuals presenting their own cases. Where applicants are not represented the judge is expected to take an inquisitorial role and help to establish the points that the applicant wishes to make. But this ideal is not always achieved.

## Delay

Although the intention is that cases are dealt with quickly, the number of cases dealt with by tribunals means that there can be delays in getting a hearing. The use of non-lawyers as members of the panel can add to this problem as they sit part-time, usually one day a fortnight. If a case is complex lasting several days this can lead to proceedings being spread over a number of weeks or even months.

**Figure 10.2** Tribunals

| First-tier Tribunal | ■ Operates in seven Chambers (divisions)<br>■ Deals with about 300,000 cases a year<br>NB Employment Tribunal operates separately |
|---|---|
| Upper Tribunal | ■ Operates in four Chambers (divisions)<br>■ Hears appeals from the First-tier Tribunal<br>■ There is a further appeal to the Court of Appeal |
| Panel | ■ Case may be heard by a tribunal judge OR<br>■ By a tribunal judge sitting with two other members who have expertise in the area |
| Advantages | ■ Cheaper than courts<br>■ Quicker than courts<br>■ More informal than courts<br>■ Use of experts |
| Disadvantages | ■ Legal aid only available in a few cases<br>■ More formal than ADR<br>■ There can be delay |

# 10.2 Alternative dispute resolution (ADR)

Using the courts to resolve disputes can be costly, in terms of both money and time. It can also be traumatic for the individuals involved and may not lead to the most satisfactory outcome for the case. An additional problem is that court proceedings are usually open to the public and the press, so there is nothing to stop the details of the case being published in local or national newspapers. It is not surprising, therefore, that more and more people and businesses are seeking other methods of resolving their disputes. Alternative methods are referred to as 'ADR', which stands for 'alternative dispute resolution', and includes any method of resolving a dispute without resorting to using the courts. There are many different methods which can be used, ranging from very informal negotiations between the parties, to a comparatively formal commercial arbitration hearing.

## 10.2.1 Negotiation

Anyone who has a dispute with another person can always try to resolve it by **negotiating** directly with them. This has the advantage of being completely private, and is also the quickest and cheapest method of settling a dispute. If the parties cannot come to an agreement, they may decide to take the step of instructing solicitors, and those solicitors will usually try to negotiate a settlement.

In fact, even when court proceedings have been commenced, the lawyers for the parties will often continue to negotiate on behalf of their clients, and this is reflected in the high number of cases which are settled out of court. Once lawyers are involved, there will be a cost element – clearly, the longer negotiations go on, the higher the costs will be.

One of the worrying aspects is the number of cases that drag on for years, only to end in an agreed settlement literally 'at the door of the court' on the morning that the trial is due to start. It is this situation that alternative dispute resolution methods try to avoid.

### Key term

**Negotiation** – the process of trying to come to an agreement.

## 10.2.2 Mediation

This is where a neutral mediator helps the parties to reach a compromise solution. The role of a mediator is to consult with each party and see how much common ground there is between them. He will explore the position with each party, looking at their needs and carrying offers to and fro, while keeping confidentiality.

A mediator will not usually tell the parties his own views of the merits of the dispute; it is part of the job to act as a 'facilitator', so that an agreement is reached by the parties. However, a mediator can be asked for an opinion of the merits, and in this case the mediation becomes more of an evaluation exercise, which again aims at ending the dispute.

**Mediation** is only suitable if there is some hope that the parties can co-operate. Companies who are used to negotiating contracts with each other are most likely to benefit from this approach.

### Key term

**Mediation** – using a neutral person in a dispute to help the parties come to a compromise solution.

Mediation is also important in family cases. Parties in a family case must normally show that they have attended a Mediation Information and Assessment Meeting (MIAM) before starting any court proceedings in a family case. There are exceptions, such as where there has been domestic violence, where they do not need to attend a MIAM.

Mediation can also take different forms, and the parties will choose the exact method they want. The important point in mediation is that the parties are in control: they make the decisions.

An advantage of mediation is that the decision need not be a strictly legal one sticking to the letter of the law. It is more likely to be based on commercial common sense and compromise. The method will also make it easier for companies to continue to do business with each other in the future, and it may include agreements about the conduct of future business between the parties. This is something that cannot happen if the court gives judgment, as the court is only concerned with the present dispute. It avoids the adversarial conflict of the court room and the winner/loser result of court proceedings – it has been said that with mediation, everyone wins.

### Mediation services

There are a growing number of commercial mediation services. One of the main ones for business disputes is the Centre for Effective Dispute Resolution (CEDR) which was set up in London in 1991. It has many important companies as members, including almost all of the big London law firms. In 2016 CEDR reported in its audit of mediation services that over the previous 12 months 10,000 commercial mediations had taken place through various mediation services. These mediations involved £10.5 billion worth of commercial claims. They also estimated that using mediation to resolve these disputes had saved £2.8 billion in management time, relationships, productivity and legal fees.

The main disadvantage of using mediation services is that there is no guarantee the matter will be resolved, and it will then be necessary to go to court after the failed attempt at mediation. In such situations there is additional cost and delay through trying mediation. However the evidence is that a high number of cases will be resolved. In 2016 CEDR reported that its audit of mediation over the previous 12 months showed that 86 per cent of disputes were settled either at the mediation or shortly after.

There are also mediation services aimed at resolving smaller disputes, for example those between neighbours. An example of such a service is the West Sussex Mediation Service which offers mediation for disputes between neighbours to resolve disagreements arising from such matters as noise, car-parking, dogs or boundary fence disputes. The West Sussex Mediation Service also offers mediation for workplace disputes and for family disputes.

Other mediation services may offer mediation just for family issues. For example Kent Family Mediation Service offers mediation for family-based disputes on property, finances and children.

The latest idea is online dispute resolution. There are an increasing number of websites offering this, e.g. www.onlinemediators.com and www.mediate.com.

### Look online

Search the internet for mediation services in your area. Look to see what types of disputes they deal with and what the mediation service will cost.

# 10.3 Comparing courts and ADR

Using ADR is usually much cheaper than going to court. For small local disputes the parties are unlikely to use lawyers so saving legal fees. In commercial mediations lawyers may be involved but CEDR's audit in 2016 shows that very large savings are made by using arbitration.

Another advantage of most forms of ADR is that the parties are in control. In negotiation and mediation, the parties can choose to stop at any time. An agreement will only be reached if both sides accept it.

The fact that the parties come to an agreement has another advantage; it means they will be able to go on doing business with each other. Court proceedings are more adversarial, and will end with one party winning and one party losing. This is likely to make the parties very bitter about the dispute.

## Tip

Remember that tribunals and ADR are separate topics. Don't confuse them.

## Extension essay

Consider the need for alternative dispute resolution as opposed to court-based dispute resolution.

## Check your understanding

1 Which one is the correct term to use when the parties resolve a dispute by agreement?

   A Litigation

   B Negotiation

   C Mediation

   D Arbitration

2 To which of the following is an appeal from a decision of a first instance tribunal made?

   A County Court

   B Court of Appeal

   C Upper Tribunal

   D Supreme Court

3 Suggest why dealing with a case through a tribunal, rather than a civil court, may be beneficial.

4 Examine and discuss the benefits of using alternative dispute resolution methods as opposed to court-based resolution.

## Summary

- Tribunals enforce rights granted by social and welfare legislation.
- Cases are heard in the First-tier Tribunal by a tribunal judge sitting alone or with two non-lawyers as members of the panel.
- There is a right of appeal to the Upper Tribunal.
- Compared to going to court, tribunals:
  - are cheaper
  - are quicker
  - are more informal
  - use experts in the area.
- Disadvantages of using tribunals are:
  - lack of legal aid for applicants
  - more formal than ADR
  - delay in complex cases.

- Alternative dispute resolution (ADR) aims to resolve a dispute without the need to go to court.
- Negotiation is where the parties or their lawyers negotiate directly to see if they can find a resolution.
- Mediation is where an independent mediator helps the parties to reach a compromise solution.
- Mediation services are often used by businesses where they have a dispute with another business.
- The parties in family cases normally have to attend a Mediation Information and Assessment Meeting to see if mediation is possible in the case.
- ADR is cheap, flexible and can allow the parties to remain on good terms.

# 11 Criminal courts

After reading this chapter you should be able to:
- Understand the classification of offences and which offences are tried in which court
- Understand the work of the Magistrates' Court
- Understand the appeal system from the Magistrates' Court
- Understand the work of the Crown Court
- Understand the appeal system from the Crown Court

## 11.1 Classification of offences

The type of offence will make a difference as to where the case will be tried and who will try it. For trial purposes criminal offences are divided into three categories. These are:
- summary offences
- triable-either-way offences
- indictable offences.

### 11.1.1 Summary offences

Summary offences are the least serious offences, and are always tried in the Magistrates' Court. They include nearly all driving offences. They also include common assault, criminal damage which has caused less than £5,000 damage and shoplifting where the value of the goods is less than £200.

**Key term**

Summary offence – an offence that can only be tried in the Magistrates' Court.

### 11.1.2 Triable-either-way offences

These are the middle range of crimes. As the name implies, these cases can be tried in either the Magistrates' Court or the Crown Court. They include a wide range of offences such as theft and assault causing actual bodily harm.

In order to decide whether a **triable-either-way offence** will be tried in the Magistrates' Court or the Crown Court, the defendant is first asked whether he is pleading guilty or not guilty. If the defendant is pleading guilty the case is heard by the magistrates. Where the plea is not guilty the defendant then has

the right to ask for the case to be tried at the Crown Court by a jury.

The magistrates can also decide that the case is too serious for them and make the decision to send the case to the Crown Court.

**Key term**

Triable-either-way offence – an offence that can be tried in either the Magistrates' Court or the Crown Court.

### 11.1.3 Indictable offences

These are the most serious crimes and include murder, manslaughter and rape. The first preliminary hearing for such an offence will be at the Magistrates' Court, but then the case is transferred to the Crown Court. All **indictable offences** must be tried at the Crown Court by a judge and jury.

**Key term**

Indictable offence – an offence that has to be tried at the Crown Court.

**Figure 11.1** The three categories of offence

| Category of offence | Place of trial | Examples of offences |
| --- | --- | --- |
| Summary | Magistrates' Court | Driving without insurance Common assault Criminal damage under £5,000 |
| Triable-either-way | Magistrates' Court OR Crown Court | Theft Assault causing actual bodily harm |
| Indictable | Crown Court | Murder Manslaughter Rape Robbery |

## 11.2 Magistrates' Courts

There are about 280 Magistrates' Courts in England and Wales. They are local courts so there will be a Magistrates' Court in almost every town, while big cities will have several courts. Each court deals with cases that have a connection with its geographical area and they have jurisdiction over a variety of matters involving criminal cases.

Cases are heard by magistrates, who are either legally qualified District Judges or unqualified lay justices. There is also a legally qualified clerk attached to each court to assist the magistrates.

> See Chapter 13 for further details on magistrates.

Magistrates are limited in the sentences they can impose. The maximum prison sentence they can give is six months for one offence or twelve months for two offences. Magistrates can also impose fines. For the top end of the range of offences there is no limit on the amount magistrates can fine, but for other offences there are limits. Magistrates can also impose a range of other penalties such as community orders or a conditional discharge.

> See Chapter 12 for more detail on sentencing.

### 11.2.1 Jurisdiction of the Magistrates' Courts

In criminal cases the Magistrates' Courts deal with a variety of matters. They have a very large workload as they do the following:

- try all summary cases
- try any triable-either-way offences in which the magistrates are prepared to accept jurisdiction and where the defendant agrees to summary trial by the magistrates.

These two categories account for about 97 per cent of all criminal cases and about 1.5 million cases take place each year in Magistrates' Courts. As well as these, the magistrates also:

- deal with the preliminary hearings of any triable-either-way offence which is going to be tried in the Crown Court
- deal with the first preliminary hearing of all indictable offences
- deal with all the side matters connected to criminal cases, such as issuing warrants for arrest and deciding bail applications
- try cases in the Youth Court where the defendants are aged 10–17 inclusive.

Giving evidence in the Magistrates' Court

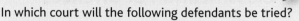

### Activity

In which court will the following defendants be tried?

1 Ali is charged with causing grievous bodily harm.
2 Gemma is charged with theft of £250 from her employer.
3 Daryl is charged with driving without insurance.
4 Nerinda is charged with theft from a shop of a pair of jeans worth £55.

## 11.3 Appeals from the Magistrates' Court

There are two different routes of appeal from the Magistrates' Court. The route used will depend on whether the appeal is only on a point of law or whether it is for other reasons. The two appeal routes are to the Crown Court or to the Administrative Court in the Queen's Bench Division.

### 11.3.1 Appeals to the Crown Court

This is the normal route of appeal from the Magistrates' Court. It is only available to the defence. If the defendant pleaded guilty at the Magistrates' Court, then he can only appeal against sentence. If the defendant pleaded not guilty and was convicted then the appeal can be against conviction and/ or sentence. In both cases the defendant has an automatic right to appeal and does not need to get leave (permission) to appeal.

At the Crown Court the case is completely reheard by a judge and two magistrates. They can come to the same decision as the magistrates and confirm the conviction or they can decide that the case is not proved and reverse the decision. In some cases it is possible for them to vary the decision and find the defendant guilty of a lesser offence.

Where the appeal is against sentence, the Crown Court can confirm the sentence or they can increase or decrease it. However, any increase can only be up to the magistrates' maximum powers for the case.

If it becomes apparent that there is a point of law to be decided, then the Crown Court can decide that point of law, but there is the possibility of a further appeal by way of case stated being made to the Administrative Court (see below).

## 11.3.2 Case stated appeals

A case stated appeal is an appeal on a point of law that goes to the Administrative Court. Both the prosecution and the defence can use this appeal route. The appeal can be made direct from the Magistrates' Court or following an appeal to the Crown Court as above.

This route is used by the defendant against a conviction or by the prosecution against an acquittal in situations where they claim the magistrates came to the wrong decision because they made a mistake about the law.

The magistrates (or the Crown Court) are asked to state the case by setting out their findings of fact and their decision. The appeal is then argued on the basis of what the law is on those facts; no witnesses are called. Although the appeal is made to the Administrative Court, the case can be sent to be heard by a panel of two High Court Judges. This court is then known as the Queen's Bench Divisional Court.

Where an appeal is made by way of case stated the decision can be confirmed, varied or reversed or the case can be sent back to the Magistrates' Court for the magistrates to implement the decision on the law.

## 11.3.3 Further appeals to the Supreme Court

From the decision of the Queen's Bench Divisional Court there is a possibility of a further appeal to the Supreme Court. Such an appeal can only be made if:

a the Divisional Court certifies that a point of law of general public importance is involved and

b the Divisional Court or the Supreme Court gives permission to appeal because the point is one

which ought to be considered by the Supreme Court.

A diagram setting out the appeal routes from the Magistrates' Court is shown in Figure 11.2.

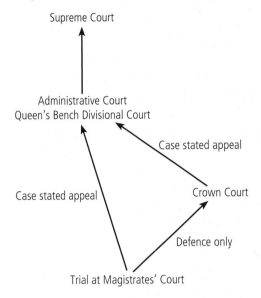

**Figure 11.2** Appeal routes from the Magistrates' Court

# 11.4 The Crown Court

The Crown Court currently sits in about 90 different centres throughout England and Wales. Each year the Crown Court deals with about 80,000 cases. They deal with:

■ triable-either-way offences where the defendant has elected to be tried in the Crown Court, or where the magistrates have decided the case is too serious for them and sent it to the Crown Court
■ all indictable offences
■ appeals from the Magistrates' Court.

For trials in the Crown Court the case is heard by a judge and a jury of 12. The judge decides the point of law and, if the defendant is found guilty, decides the appropriate sentence. The jury decide on the facts whether the defendant is guilty or not guilty.

> See Chapter 14 for information on juries.

For appeals to the Crown Court from the Magistrates Court, the case is heard by a judge sitting with two lay magistrates.

# 11.5 Appeals from the Crown Court

## 11.5.1 Appeals by the defendant

The defendant has the possibility of appealing against conviction and/or sentence to the Court of Appeal (Criminal Division). So, at the end of any trial in which a defendant has been found guilty, his lawyer should advise him on whether there should be an appeal.

### Leave to appeal

In all cases the defendant must get leave to appeal from the Court of Appeal or a certificate that the case is fit for appeal from the trial judge. The idea is that cases which are without merit are filtered out and the court's time saved.

The application for leave to appeal is considered by a single judge of the Court of Appeal in private, although if he refuses it is possible to apply to a full Court of Appeal for leave.

### Grounds for appeal

The Criminal Appeal Act 1995 simplified the grounds under which the court can allow an appeal. The Act states that the Court of Appeal:

a   shall allow an appeal against conviction if they think that the conviction is unsafe; and

b   shall dismiss such an appeal in any other case.

If the Court of Appeal decides that the conviction is unsafe, they can allow the defendant's appeal and quash the conviction. Alternatively they can vary the conviction to that of a lesser offence of which the jury could have convicted the defendant. If the appeal is against sentence, the court can decrease the sentence but cannot increase it on the defendant's appeal.

The Court of Appeal also has the power to order that there be a retrial of the case in front of a new jury. This power is only used in about 50 to 60 cases each year.

If the Court of Appeal decides that the conviction is safe, then they will dismiss the appeal.

## 11.5.2 Appeals by the prosecution

Originally the prosecution had no right to appeal against either the verdict or sentence passed in the Crown Court. Gradually, however, some limited rights of appeal have been given to them by Parliament.

### Against a judge's ruling

If the trial judge gives a ruling on a point of law which effectively stops the case against the defendant, the prosecution now have the right to appeal against that ruling. This right was given by the Criminal Justice Act 2003. It makes sure that an error of law by the judge does not lead to an acquittal.

### Against acquittal

There are only two limited situations in which the prosecution can appeal against an acquittal by a jury:

1   Where the acquittal was the result of the jury being 'nobbled'.

   This is where one or more jurors are bribed or threatened by associates of the defendant. In these circumstances, provided there has been an actual conviction for jury nobbling, the Criminal Procedure and Investigations Act 1996 allows the prosecution to appeal and the Court of Appeal can order a retrial. Once the acquittal is quashed, the prosecution could then start new proceedings for the same offence.

2   Where there is new and compelling evidence of the acquitted person's guilt and it is in the public interest for the defendant to be retried.

   This power is given by the Criminal Justice Act 2003 and it is only available for some 30 serious offences, including murder, manslaughter, rape and terrorism offences. It is known as double jeopardy, since the defendant is being tried twice for the same offence.

The Director of Public Prosecutions has to consent to the reopening of investigations in the case. Once the evidence has been found, then the prosecution have to apply to the Court of Appeal for the original acquittal to be quashed.

This power has been used in cases where new techniques of DNA testing now show that a defendant who is acquitted is in fact the offender. The first case in which this power was used is shown in the article on page 99.

Another case in which this power was used was in 2011 when two defendants who had been previously acquitted of the murder of black teenager, Stephen Lawrence, were retried and convicted some 19 years after his murder. Part of the new evidence was a DNA match with Stephen's blood found on the clothing of one of the defendants. This evidence became available due to improved DNA testing techniques.

## In the news

### Man admits murder in first UK double jeopardy case

Fifteen years after he was cleared of murder, the first person in Britain to face a retrial under new double jeopardy rules admitted today that he killed his victim.

Billy Dunlop, 43, pleaded guilty to murdering pizza delivery girl Julie Hogg, 22, in Billingham, Teeside, when he appeared at the Old Bailey today.

Dunlop stood trial twice in 1991 for her murder but each time a jury failed to reach a verdict. He was formally acquitted under the convention that the prosecution do not ask for a third trial in such circumstances.

But in April last year the double jeopardy rule – which prevented a defendant who had been acquitted from being tried again for the same offence – was changed under the Criminal Justice Act 2003.

The following November the Director of Public Prosecutions announced the legal process to retry Dunlop had begun. The case was sent to the Court of Appeal where his acquittal was quashed.

*Source: Daily Mail, 11 September 2006*

### Referring a point of law

Where the judge may have made an error in explaining the law to the jury, the prosecution have the right to refer a point of law to the Court of Appeal if the defendant is acquitted. This right is under s 36 of the Criminal Justice Act 1972 which allows the Attorney-General to refer the point of law to the Court of Appeal in order to get a ruling on the law. The decision by the Court of Appeal on that point of law does not affect the acquittal but it creates a precedent for any future case involving the same point of law.

### Against sentence

Under s 36 of the Criminal Justice Act 1988 the Attorney-General can apply for leave to refer an unduly lenient sentence to the Court of Appeal for re-sentencing. About 120 cases are referred each year and the sentence is increased in about 80 per cent of these cases.

Most increases are of an extra year or two being added to the sentence. However, there are some cases in which much greater increases are made. Examples of such increases include one defendant whose sentence for two offences of rape was increased from 3.5 years' imprisonment to 11 years' imprisonment and another defendant whose sentence for assault, conspiracy to kidnap and false imprisonment was increased from 3 years and 9 months to 9 years and 9 months.

### 11.5.3 Further appeals to the Supreme Court

Both the prosecution and the defence may appeal from the Court of Appeal to the Supreme Court, but it is necessary to have the case certified as involving a point of law of general public importance and to get permission to appeal, either from the Supreme Court or from the Court of Appeal. Only a few criminal appeals go to the Supreme Court each year.

### Tip

Appeal routes are complicated to remember. Try using the diagrams to help you identify the different appeal routes.

Figure 11.3 Appeal routes from the Crown Court

## Check your understanding

1 In which court will a summary offence be tried?

  A Crown Court

  B Supreme Court

  C Magistrates' Court

  D Administrative Court

2 An appeal from a guilty verdict by a jury in the Crown Court will be heard in which of the following courts?

  A Magistrates' Court

  B High Court

  C Court of Appeal

  D Administrative Court

3 Suggest why it may be beneficial for a defendant charged with an either-way offence, to have the trial heard in a Crown Court.

4 Consider the view that a defendant has greater rights of appeal than the prosecution in a criminal case.

## Summary

- There are three categories of offence:
  - summary offences
  - triable-either-way offences
  - indictable offences.
- The Magistrates' Court deals with summary offences and triable-either-way offences where the defendant elects trial there.
- Appeals from the Magistrates' Court normally go to the Crown Court but appeals on points of law go to the Administrative Court.
- The Crown Court deals with all indictable offences and with triable-either-way offences where the defendant has elected trial in the Crown Court or where the magistrates decide the case is too serious for them.

- Trial at the Crown Court is by judge and jury: the jury decide guilty or not guilty on the facts of the case.
- The defendant can appeal against conviction and/or sentence to the Court of Appeal.
- The prosecution has limited rights of appeal. They can only appeal to the Court of Appeal against an acquittal by a jury when:
  - the acquittal was the result of the jury being 'nobbled'
  - there is new and compelling evidence of the acquitted person's guilt and it is in the public interest for the defendant to be retried.

# 12 Sentencing

## 12.1 Aims of sentencing

When judges or magistrates have to pass a sentence they will not only look at the sentences available, they will also have to decide what they are trying to achieve by the punishment they give. Section 142 of the Criminal Justice Act 2003 sets out the purposes of sentencing for those aged 18 and over, saying that a court must have regard to:

- the punishment of offenders
- the reduction of crime (including its reduction by deterrence)
- the reform and rehabilitation of offenders
- the protection of the public and
- the making of reparation by offenders to persons affected by their offences.

Punishment is often referred to as retribution. In addition to the purposes of sentencing given in the 2003 Act, denunciation of crime is also recognised as an aim of sentencing. Each of the aims will now be examined in turn.

### 12.1.1 Retribution/punishment

**Retribution** is based on the idea of punishment. The offender deserves punishment for his acts. This aim of sentencing does not seek to reduce crime or alter the offender's future behaviour. A judge using this aim is only concerned with the offence that was committed and making sure that the sentence given is in proportion to that offence.

### Key term

**Retribution** – imposing a punishment because the offender deserves punishment.

The crudest form of retribution can be seen in the old saying, 'an eye for an eye and a tooth for a tooth and

a life for a life'. This was one of the factors used to justify the death penalty for the offence of murder.

### Tariff sentences

Retribution, today, is based more on the idea that each offence should have a certain tariff or level of sentencing. The Sentencing Council produces guidelines for all the main categories of offence. Judges have to take notice of these guidelines and should not normally give a lower sentence than the minimum set out in the guidelines.

**Figure 12.1** Sentencing Council's Guidelines (source: adapted from guidelines for assault occasioning actual bodily harm)

| STEP ONE Determining the offence category | |
|---|---|
| The court should determine the offence category using the table below | |
| Category 1 | Greater harm (serious injury must normally be present) **and** higher culpability |
| Category 2 | Greater harm (serious injury must normally be present) **and** lower culpability; **or** lesser harm **and** higher culpability |
| Category 3 | Lesser harm **and** lower culpability |
| The guidelines then give factors which indicate higher or lower culpability. They also give factors to help decide the level of harm. | |

| STEP TWO Starting point and category range | | |
|---|---|---|
| Having determined the category, the court should use the corresponding starting points to reach a sentence within the category range below. The starting point applies to all offenders irrespective of plea or previous convictions. A case of particular gravity, reflected by multiple features of culpability in step one, could merit upward adjustment from the starting point before further adjustment for aggravating or mitigating features, set out below. | | |
| **Offence category** | **Starting point (applicable to all offenders)** | **Category range (applicable to all offenders)** |
| Category 1 | 1 year 6 months' custody | 1–3 years' custody |
| Category 2 | 26 weeks' custody | Low level community order – 51 weeks' custody |
| Category 3 | Medium level community order | Band A – high level community order |

## 12.1.2 Deterrence

This can be individual **deterrence** or general deterrence. Individual deterrence is intended to ensure that the offender does not re-offend, through fear of future punishment. General deterrence is aimed at preventing other potential offenders from committing crimes. Both are aimed at reducing future levels of crime.

Winchester prison

> ### Key term
> **Deterrence** – giving a punishment aimed at putting off the defendant from re-offending because of fear of punishment or preventing other potential offenders from committing similar crimes.

### Individual deterrence

There are several penalties that can be imposed with the aim of deterring the individual offender from committing similar crimes in the future. These include a prison sentence, a suspended sentence or a heavy fine. However, prison does not appear to deter as about 55 per cent of adult prisoners re-offend within two years of release. With young offenders, custodial sentences have even less of a deterrent effect. Over 70 per cent of young offenders given a custodial sentence re-offend within two years.

### General deterrence

The value of this is even more doubtful as potential offenders are rarely deterred by severe sentences passed on others. However, the courts do occasionally resort to making an example of an offender in order to warn other potential offenders of the type of punishment they face.

Examples of deterrent sentencing were following rioting in the summer of 2011. Many offenders were given custodial sentences for relatively minor theft offences as these occurred during the looting of shops in the riots. This was sending a clear message to others that offenders committing offences during riots would be given severe sentences.

General deterrence is in direct conflict with the principle of retribution, since it involves sentencing an offender to a longer term than is deserved for the specific offence. It is probably the least effective and least fair principle of sentencing.

## 12.1.3 Reform/rehabilitation

The main aim of this penalty is to reform the offender and **rehabilitate** him into society. It is a forward-looking aim, with the hope that the offender's behaviour will be altered by the penalty imposed, so that he will not offend in the future (it aims to reduce crime in this way).

> ### Key term
> **Rehabilitate** – trying to alter the offender's behaviour so that he will conform to community norms and not offend in future.

**Reformation** is a very important element in the sentencing philosophy for young offenders, but it is also used for some adult offenders. The court will be given information about the defendant's background, usually through a pre-sentence report prepared by the probation service. Where relevant, the court will consider other factors, such as school reports, job prospects, or medical problems.

Offenders will usually be given a community order with various requirements aimed at rehabilitating them.

> ### Key term
> **Reformation** – trying to reform the offender's behaviour so that he will not offend in future.

## 12.1.4 Protection of the public

The public need to be protected from dangerous offenders. For this reason, life imprisonment or a long term of imprisonment are given to those who commit murder or other violent or serious sexual offences.

The Criminal Justice Act 2003 introduced a provision for serious offences that where the court is of the opinion that there is a significant risk to members of the public of serious harm being caused by the defendant in the future, the court must send the defendant to prison for the protection of the public.

For less serious offences there are other ways in which the public can be protected. For example, dangerous drivers are disqualified from driving. Another method is to include an exclusion order as a requirement in a community order. This will ban the offender from going to places where he is most likely to commit an offence.

A good example of this is where the defendant committed an affray in Manchester when attending a football match in which Oldham Athletic, the team he supported, was playing. The judge banned the defendant from going into Oldham town centre on home match days and also banned him from approaching within half a mile of any football stadium. Both bans were for a period of six years.

Another method of protecting the public is to impose a curfew order on the offender, ordering him to remain at home for certain times of the day or night. The curfew can be monitored by an electronic tag, which should trigger an alarm if the offender leaves his home address during a curfew period.

## 12.1.5 Reparation

This is aimed at compensating the victim of the crime usually by ordering the offender to pay a sum of money to the victim or to make restitution, for example by returning stolen property to its rightful owner. The courts are required to consider ordering compensation to the victim of a crime, in addition to any other penalty they may think appropriate. There are also projects to bring offenders and victims together, so that the offenders may make direct reparation.

The concept also includes making **reparation** to society as a whole. This can be seen mainly in the use of an unpaid work requirement where offenders are required to do so many hours' work on a community project under the supervision of the probation service.

**Key term**

Reparation – where an offender compensates the victim or society for the offending behaviour.

## 12.1.6 Denunciation

This is society expressing its disapproval of criminal activity. A sentence should indicate both to the offender and to other people that society condemns certain types of behaviour. It shows people that justice is being done.

**Denunciation** also reinforces the moral boundaries of acceptable conduct and can mould society's views on the criminality of particular conduct – for example, drink driving is now viewed by the majority of people as unacceptable behaviour. This is largely because of the changes in the law and the increasingly severe sentences that are imposed. By sending offenders to prison, banning them from driving and imposing heavy fines, society's opinion of drink driving has been changed.

**Key term**

Denunciation – expressing society's disapproval of an offender's behaviour.

**Figure 12.2** Aims of sentencing

| Theory | Aim of theory | Suitable punishment |
|---|---|---|
| Retribution/ Punishment | Punishment imposed only on ground that an offence has been committed | ■ Tariff sentences<br>■ Sentence must be proportionate to the crime |
| Deterrence | Individual – the offender is deterred through fear of further punishment<br>General – potential offenders warned as to likely punishment | ■ Prison sentence<br>■ Heavy fine<br>■ Long sentence as an example to others |
| Rehabilitation | Reform offender's behaviour | ■ Individualised sentence<br>■ Community order |
| Protection of the public | Offender is made incapable of committing further crime<br>Society is protected from crime | ■ Long prison sentences<br>■ Tagging<br>■ Banning orders |
| Reparation | Repayment/Reparation to victim or to community | ■ Compensation order<br>■ Unpaid work<br>■ Reparation schemes |
| Denunciation | Society expressing its disapproval<br>Reinforces moral boundaries | ■ Reflects blameworthiness of the offence |

# 12.2 Powers of the criminal courts

## 12.2.1 Custodial sentences

The Crown Court has unlimited powers in sentencing. It can pass a custodial sentence of any length up to the maximum for that particular offence. For example, the maximum sentence of an offence of occasioning actual bodily harm is five years' imprisonment. In practice the maximum sentence for lesser offences is very rarely given.

For very serious offences, such as manslaughter and rape, the maximum penalty available is life imprisonment and the Crown Court has the power to impose this sentence if it is suitable on the facts of the case.

The Magistrates' Courts only have the power to send a person to prison for six months for one offence or 12 months for two offences. They cannot impose any longer custodial sentence.

## 12.2.2 Fines

The Crown Court has unlimited power to pass a fine. There is no maximum limit to the amount they can fine someone. In practice, the biggest fines are usually on businesses for breaches of health and safety laws.

Summary offences in the Magistrates' Courts are set in five different levels with a maximum fine for each level. The current maximum fines are: level one: maximum £200, level two: £500, level three: £1,000, level four: £2,500 and level five: unlimited. So the magistrates have to stay within the limit for the particular offence.

## 12.2.3 Other powers

As well as being able to imprison offenders and/or fine them, the courts have other powers they can use when sentencing an offender. These include giving a conditional discharge, making a compensation order or disqualifying a person from driving.

# 12.3 Sentences available for adults

## 12.3.1 Custodial sentences

A custodial sentence is the most serious punishment that a court can impose. Custodial sentences range from a few weeks to life imprisonment. They include:

■ mandatory and discretionary life sentences
■ fixed-term sentences
■ suspended sentences.

Custodial sentences are meant to be used only for serious offences. The Criminal Justice Act 2003 says that the court must not pass a custodial sentence unless it is of the opinion that the offence (or combination of offences) 'was so serious that neither a fine alone nor a community sentence can be justified'.

## Mandatory life sentences

For murder, the only sentence a judge can impose is a life sentence. However, the judge is allowed to state the minimum number of years' imprisonment that the offender must serve before being eligible for release on licence. This minimum term is now governed by the Criminal Justice Act 2003. This gives judges clear starting points for the minimum period to be ordered. The starting points range from a full life term down to 12 years depending on the facts of the case.

## Discretionary life sentences

For other serious offences such as an offence under s 18 of the Offences Against the Person Act 1861 the maximum sentence is life imprisonment, but the judge does not have to impose it. The judge has discretion in sentencing and can give any lesser sentence where appropriate. For certain serious offences, a life sentence should be given for a second offence.

## Fixed-term sentences

For other crimes, the length of the sentence will depend on several factors, including the maximum sentence available for the particular crime, the seriousness of the crime and the defendant's previous record. Imprisonment for a set number of months or years is called a 'fixed-term' sentence.

Prisoners do not serve the whole of the sentence passed by the court. Anyone sent to prison is automatically released after they have served half of the sentence. Only offenders aged 21 and over can be given a sentence of imprisonment.

## Prison population

A problem is that prisons in England and Wales are overcrowded. There has been a big increase in the number of people in prison and there are not enough prison places. Figure 12.3 shows the increase in the prison population between 1951 and 2016.

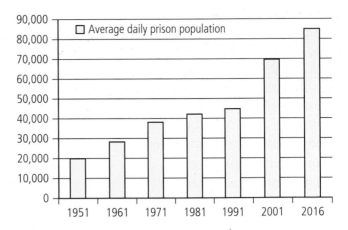

**Figure 12.3** Bar chart of average daily prison population for England and Wales 1951–2016

### Look online

Look up the current prison population on the internet. You should be able to find it by searching the term 'prison population'.

## Suspended prison sentences

An adult offender may be given a suspended prison sentence of up to two years (six months maximum in the Magistrates' Court). This means that the sentence does not take effect immediately. The court will fix a time during which the sentence is suspended; this can be for any period up to two years. If, during this time, the offender does not commit any further offences, the prison sentence will not be served. However, if the offender does commit another offence within the period of suspension, then the prison sentence is 'activated' and the offender will serve that sentence together with any sentence for the new offence.

A suspended sentence should only be given where the offence is so serious that an immediate custodial sentence would have been appropriate, but there are exceptional circumstances in the case that justify suspending the sentence.

## 12.3.2 Community orders

The Criminal Justice Act 2003 created one community order under which the court can combine any requirements they think are necessary. These requirements are listed below. The sentences can 'mix and match' requirements allowing them to fit the restrictions and rehabilitation to the offender's needs. The sentence is available for offenders aged

16 and over. The full list of requirements available to the courts is set out in s 177 of the Criminal Justice Act 2003. This states:

> 177(1) Where a person aged 16 or over is convicted of an offence, the court by or before which he is convicted may make an order imposing on him any one or more of the following requirements:

**a** an unpaid work requirement,

**b** an activity requirement,

**c** a programme requirement,

**d** a prohibited activity requirement,

**e** a curfew requirement,

**f** an exclusion requirement,

**g** a residence requirement,

**h** a mental health treatment requirement,

**i** a drug rehabilitation requirement,

**j** an alcohol treatment requirement,

**k** a supervision requirement, and

**l** in the case where the offender is aged under 25, an attendance centre requirement.

Each of these is defined within the Criminal Justice Act 2003. Most are self-explanatory from their name, such as drug rehabilitation and alcohol treatment. Much crime is linked to drug and alcohol abuse and the idea behind these two requirements is to tackle the causes of crime, and hopefully prevent further offences. Mental health treatment is also aimed at the cause of the offender's behaviour. The main other requirements are explained briefly below.

THIS IS THE GOVERNMENT'S LATEST IDEA FOR A COMMUNITY SENTENCE

## Unpaid work requirement

This requires the offender to work for between 40 and 300 hours on a suitable project organised by the probation service. The exact number of hours will be fixed by the court, and those hours are then usually worked in eight-hour sessions, often at weekends. The type of work involved will vary, depending on what schemes the local probation service have running. The offender may be required to paint school buildings, help build a play centre or work on conservation projects.

## Prohibited activity requirement

This requirement allows a wide variety of activities to be prohibited. The idea is to try to prevent the defendant from committing another crime of the type he has just been convicted of. Often the defendant is forbidden to go into a certain area where he has caused trouble. In some cases the defendant has been banned from wearing a 'hoodie'. In 2006, a defendant who was found guilty of criminal damage was banned from carrying paint, dye, ink or marker pens.

## Curfew requirement

Under these, an offender can be ordered to remain at a fixed address for between 2 and 16 hours in any 24-hour period. This order can last for up to six months and may be enforced by electronic tagging (where suitable). Courts can only make such an order if there is an arrangement for monitoring curfews in their area. Such monitoring can be done by spot-checks, with security firms sending someone to make sure that the offender is at home, or offenders may be electronically tagged. Satellite technology may be used to track those who are tagged.

## Supervision requirement

For this requirement the offender is placed under the supervision of a probation officer for a period of up to three years. During the period of supervision the offender must attend appointments with the supervising officer or with any other person decided by the supervising officer.

## Activity

Read the following facts taken from *Proven Re-offending Statistics Quarterly* October 2012 to September 2014, published in 2016, and answer the questions below.

- Adult offenders had a proven reoffending rate of 24.7 per cent.
- Around 356,000 proven offences were committed by adults over the one year follow-up period. Those that reoffended committed on average three reoffences each.
- Adult offenders with 11 or more previous offences have a higher reoffending rate than those with no previous offences – 45.6 per cent compared to 7.6 per cent.
- Adult offenders with an index offence of 'Theft' had the highest proven reoffending rate of 42.5 per cent. Those with the lowest rate had an index offence of 'Fraud' and reoffended at a rate of 10.3 per cent.
- The proven reoffending rate for adults starting a court order (community sentence or suspended sentence order) was 33.2 per cent.
- The proven reoffending rate for adult offenders released from custody was 45.5 per cent.
- The rate for those released from short custodial sentences has been consistently higher compared to those released from longer sentences. Adults who served sentences of less than 12 months reoffended at a rate of 59.7 per cent compared to 33.4 per cent for those who served determinate sentences of 12 months or more.

### Questions

1 What is the average re-offending rate for adults?
2 Which type of offence was associated with higher reoffending rates?
3 How many previous offences had been committed by those with the highest rate of reoffending?
4 What was the reoffending rate for those released from a custodial sentence? How does that compare with the reoffending rate for those given a community sentence or suspended sentence order?
5 How did the length of prison sentence served affect the reoffending rate?

## 12.3.3 Fines

This is the most common way of disposing of a case in the Magistrates' Court. In the Crown Court only a small percentage of offenders are dealt with by way of a fine. Usually the offender is ordered to pay the fine at a set rate each week.

## 12.3.4 Discharges

These may be either:

- a conditional discharge or
- an absolute discharge.

A conditional discharge means that the court discharges an offender on the condition that no further offence is committed during a set period of up to three years. It is intended to be used where it is thought that punishment is not necessary. If an offender re-offends within the time limit, the court can then impose another sentence in place of the conditional discharge, as well as imposing a penalty for the new offence. Conditional discharges are widely used by Magistrates' Courts for first-time minor offenders.

An absolute discharge means that, effectively, no penalty is imposed. Such a penalty is likely to be used where an offender is technically guilty but morally blameless. An absolute discharge is not often used.

## 12.3.5 Other powers of the court

The court has other orders it can make when sentencing an offender. These include:

- disqualifying the defendant from driving for a certain length of time – this is mostly used for motoring offences such as drink driving or dangerous driving but it can also be used for other offences such as theft of a car
- compensation order – the court can order the offender to pay a sum of money to the victim of the crime
- forfeiture order – this orders that certain property in the possession of the offender be taken from him, for example cans of spray paint (where a defendant is guilty of criminal damage involving the use of the paint).

### Victim surcharge

In addition when a court passes a sentence it must also order that the relevant surcharge is paid. The amount of the surcharge depends on the sentence and whether at the time the offence was committed the offender was an adult or a youth. Revenue raised from the victim surcharge is used to fund victim services through the Victim and Witness General Fund.

## 12.4 Factors in sentencing

When deciding what sentence to pass on a defendant, the courts consider the following matters:

- the offence
- sentencing guidelines
- the offender's background.

### 12.4.1 Aggravating factors in sentencing

In looking at the offence, the most important point to establish is how serious was it, of its type? This is now set out in s 143(1) of the Criminal Justice Act 2003 which states that:

> In considering the seriousness of the offence, the court must consider the offender's culpability in committing the offence and any harm which the offence caused, or was intended to cause or might reasonably forseeably have caused.

The Act goes on to give certain factors which are considered as aggravating factors making an offence more serious. These are:

- previous convictions for offences of a similar nature or relevant to the present offence
- the fact that the defendant was on bail when he committed the offence
- racial or religious hostility being involved in the offence
- hostility to disability or sexual orientation being involved in the offence.

As well as these points in the Criminal Justice Act 2003, there are also other factors which are regarded as aggravating features for specific offences. For example, where the defendant has committed an assault, aggravating features include:

- the offender being part of a group attacking the victim
- a particularly vulnerable victim, e.g. a young child or an elderly person
- a victim serving the public, e.g. an attack on a nurse in a hospital emergency unit
- the fact that the assault was premeditated.

Where there is an aggravating factor, the court will pass a more severe sentence than it would normally have given.

Magistrates and judges all have a copy of the guidelines issued by the Sentencing Council. These give a starting point for an offence, depending on certain factors, in particular whether the magistrates should be thinking of a custodial sentence or a community order. The guidelines also give a sentencing range.

### 12.4.2 Mitigating factors available in sentencing

A mitigating factor is one which allows the court to give a lighter sentence than would normally be given.

If the offender co-operates with the police, for example helping identify others involved in the crime, then the court can take this into account when deciding sentence.

Other factors taken into account in mitigation include:

- mental illness of the defendant
- physical illness of the defendant
- the fact that a defendant has no previous convictions
- evidence of genuine remorse.

### Reduction in sentence for a guilty plea

There will also be a reduction in sentence for a guilty plea, particularly where the defendant made that plea early in the proceedings. The Sentencing Council guidelines on this are that the reduction for a guilty plea at the first reasonable opportunity should attract a reduction of up to one-third, while a plea of guilty after the trial has started would only be given a one-tenth reduction. The amount of reduction is on a sliding scale as shown in Figure 12.4.

The only exception is where the evidence is overwhelming and the defendant's guilt is clear. In these circumstances, even if the defendant pleads guilty at the earliest possible opportunity, the judge need only give a 20 per cent discount for that plea of guilty.

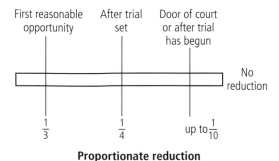

**Figure 12.4** Reduction in sentence for a guilty plea

## 12.4.3 Background of the offender

### Previous convictions

An important fact about the defendant is whether he has previous convictions or not. Where he has a previous conviction for the same or similar type of offence, then he is likely to receive a heavier sentence.

A defendant who has no previous convictions is usually treated more leniently.

### Reports

The courts will often have a report prepared by the probation service on the offender and his background. If the defendant is ill, then the court may also ask for a medical report. These reports will be considered with all other factors in deciding what sentence to impose on the defendant.

## Check your understanding

1. Which one of the following statements accurately describes the sentencing aim of retribution?

   A A punishment that protects society

   B A penalty proportionate to the offence

   C Deterring others from committing the same or similar offences

   D Making the offender pay compensation to the victim

2. Explain three aims of sentencing, suggesting a suitable sentence to achieve each aim.

3. Dan, aged 22, a single man, has been found guilty of stealing £10,000 from his employer. He has one previous conviction for assault. Advise Dan on the likelihood that a custodial sentence will be imposed on him.

## Summary

- The aims of sentencing are:
  - punishment of offenders
  - reduction of crime (including its reduction by deterrence)
  - reform and rehabilitation of offenders
  - protection of the public
  - making of reparation by offenders
  - denunciation of offending behaviour.
- Sentences for adult offenders include:
  - custodial sentences
  - community orders
  - fines
  - discharges.
- Other powers of the court include:
  - disqualification from driving
  - compensation order
  - forfeiture order.
- Factors taken into account when sentencing include:
  - aggravating factors
  - mitigating factors
  - plea of guilty
  - offender's background
  - reports on the offender.

# 13 Lay people: lay magistrates

After reading this chapter you should be able to:
- Understand the qualifications and training of lay magistrates
- Understand their role and powers in criminal cases
- Understand the advantages and disadvantages of using lay magistrates in the criminal courts

## 13.1 Lay magistrates

There are about 17,500 lay magistrates sitting as unpaid, part-time judges in the Magistrates' Courts; another name for lay magistrates is Justices of the Peace. They sit to hear cases as a bench of two or three magistrates. A single lay magistrate sitting on his own has very limited powers. They can, however, issue search warrants and warrants for arrest and conduct Early Administrative Hearings.

### Key term

Lay magistrates – these are unpaid, part-time judges who have no legal qualifications and hear cases in the Magistrates' Courts.

### 13.1.1 Qualifications

Lay magistrates do not have to have any qualifications in law. There are, however, some requirements as to their character. Candidates should have the following six key qualities:
- good character
- understanding and communication
- social awareness
- maturity and sound temperament
- sound judgment
- commitment and reliability.

They must have certain 'judicial' qualities – it is particularly important that they are able to assimilate factual information and make a reasoned decision upon it. They must also be able to take account of the reasoning of others and work as a team.

There are also formal requirements as to age and residence: lay magistrates must be aged between 18 and 65 on appointment and can sit as magistrates until they are 70. Not many younger people are appointed. However, since the age for appointment was reduced to 18 in 2003, a few more young magistrates have been appointed. However, the statistics for 2016 show that only 3 per cent of magistrates were under the age of 40.

### Activity

1 Put the list of the six key qualities for lay magistrates into order, with the one you think is the most important first and the least important last.
2 Compare your list with those of other people.
3 Explain what other qualities you think that magistrates might need.

### 13.1.2 Area

Up to 2003 it was necessary for lay magistrates to live within 15 miles of the commission area for the court which they sat in. In 2003 the Courts Act abolished commission areas. Instead there is now one commission area for the whole of England and Wales. However the country is divided into local justice areas. These areas are specified by the Lord Chancellor and lay magistrates are expected to live or work within or near to the local justice area to which they are allocated.

### 13.1.3 Commitment

The other requirement is that lay magistrates are prepared to commit themselves to sitting at least 26 half days each year. It is thought that this level of commitment deters many people from becoming lay magistrates. Lay magistrates are only paid expenses.

### 13.1.4 Restrictions on appointment

Some people are not eligible to be appointed. These include people with serious criminal convictions, though a conviction for a minor motoring offence will not automatically disqualify a candidate. Others who are disqualified include undischarged bankrupts, members of the forces and those whose work is incompatible with sitting as a magistrate, such as police officers and traffic wardens.

Relatives of those working in the local criminal justice system are not likely to be appointed as it would not appear 'just' if, for example, the wife or husband of a local police officer were to sit to decide cases. In addition people whose hearing is impaired, or who by reason of infirmity cannot carry out all the duties of a Justice of the Peace cannot be appointed. Close relatives will not be appointed to the same bench.

## 13.2 Appointment

About 700 new lay magistrates are appointed each year. Since 2013, appointments are made by the Lord Chief Justice, who can delegate these powers. The current Lord Chief Justice has delegated these powers to the Senior Presiding Judge. In order to decide who to appoint, the judge relies on recommendations made by the local advisory committees.

### 13.2.1 Local advisory committees

The membership of the committees must be published. The members tend to be current or ex-Justices of the Peace. About half the members have to retire in rotation every three years. The committees should have a maximum of 12 members and these should include a mixture of magistrates and non-magistrates.

Anyone can apply to become a magistrate. The process is explained online at www.gov.uk.

### 13.2.2 Recruitment of magistrates

Advertisements are used to try and encourage as wide a range of potential candidates as possible. Advertisements have been placed in local papers, or newspapers aimed at particular ethnic groups, and even on buses! People are also encouraged to go to open evenings at their local Magistrates' Court. All this is aimed at getting as wide a spectrum of potential candidates as possible. The intention is to create a panel that is representative of all aspects of society.

The aim is for membership to reflect a balance of occupations. The Lord Chancellor set down 11 broad categories of occupations, and advisory committees are recommended that they should not have more than 15 per cent of the bench coming from any one category.

#### Interview panels

There is usually a two-stage interview process. At the first interview the panel tries to find out more about the candidate's personal attributes, in particular looking to see if they have the six key qualities required. The interview panel will also explore the candidate's attitudes on various criminal justice issues such as youth crime or drink driving. The second interview is aimed at testing candidates' potential

judicial aptitude and this is done by a discussion of at least two case studies which are typical of those heard regularly in Magistrates' Courts. The discussion might, for example, focus on the type of sentence which should be imposed on specific case facts.

The advisory committees will then submit names of those they think are suitable to the Lord Chief Justice or his delegate, who will then appoint new magistrates from this list. Once appointed, magistrates may continue to sit until the age of 70.

Leeds Magistrates' Court

## 13.3 Composition of the bench today

The traditional image of lay justices is that they are 'middle-class, middle-aged and middle-minded'. However, in many respects the bench is well balanced. About 53 per cent of magistrates are women. This is a higher percentage than anywhere else in the judiciary. Only 22 per cent of judges in the High Court and above are women, though there are more at the lower levels. For example, about 32 per cent of District Judges in the Magistrates' Court are women.

Also, ethnic minorities are reasonably well represented in the magistracy. About 11 per cent of magistrates are from ethnic minorities. This compares very favourably to the professional judiciary where less than 5 per cent are from ethnic minority backgrounds.

The relatively high level of ethnic minority magistrates is largely a result of campaigns to attract a wider range of candidates. Adverts are placed in national newspapers and also in TV guides and women's magazines. In an effort to encourage those from ethnic minorities to apply, adverts have also appeared in such publications as the *Caribbean Times*, the *Asian Times* and *Muslim News*. This has led to an increase in the numbers of ethnic minority appointments.

Disabled people are encouraged to apply to become magistrates. This has included appointing blind persons as lay magistrates. About 4 per cent of magistrates have a disability.

### Look online

Look up the composition of the magistracy for your area. This is on www.judiciary.gov.uk but it may be easier to search for the term 'Magistrates in post'.

Find out:

1 how many male and female magistrates there are in your area

2 how many magistrates from an ethnic minority there are in your area.

## 13.4 The role and powers of magistrates

Magistrates have a very wide workload connected to criminal cases. They deal with all summary cases. They also deal with triable-either-way offences where the defendant chooses to be tried in the Magistrates' Court. These two categories account for about 94 per cent of all criminal cases. They deal with all the preliminary work in these cases. This includes Early Administrative Hearings, remand hearings and bail applications.

Where the defendant pleads not guilty the magistrates will hold a trial and decide whether the defendant is guilty or not guilty.

Where the defendant pleads guilty or is found guilty, the magistrates also decide the sentence. They have the power to imprison an offender for six months for one offence or twelve months for two offences. They also have other wide sentencing powers including making community orders, fining a defendant, ordering a conditional or absolute discharge and disqualifying a defendant from driving.

Lay magistrates also deal with the first hearing of indictable offences but then transfer these to the Crown Court for trial.

### 13.4.1 Youth Court

Specially nominated and trained justices from the Youth Court panel hear criminal charges against young offenders aged 10–17 years old. The panel must usually include at least one man and one woman.

### 13.4.2 Family Court

Specially trained lay magistrates sit in the Family Court to hear cases on family issues, such as maintenance and custody.

### 13.4.3 Appeals

Lay magistrates also sit at the Crown Court to hear appeals from the Magistrates' Court. In these cases two lay justices form a panel with a qualified judge.

## 13.5 Training of lay magistrates

The training of lay magistrates is supervised by the Magisterial Committee of the Judicial College. This Committee has drawn up a syllabus of the topics which lay magistrates should cover in their training. However, because of the large numbers of lay magistrates, the actual training is carried out in local areas, sometimes through the clerk of the court, sometimes through weekend courses organised by universities with magistrates from the region attending.

### 13.5.1 New magistrates

There is a syllabus for new magistrates which is divided into three parts:

1 Initial introductory training – this covers such matters as understanding the organisation of the bench and the administration of the court and the roles and responsibilities of those involved in the Magistrates' Court.

**Figure 13.1** Lay magistrates

| Qualifications | Between the ages of 18 and 65 on appointment<br>Have the six key qualities<br>Live or work near the area in which they sit<br>Be prepared to sit 26 half days a year |
|---|---|
| Appointment | Local advisory committee recommend for appointment<br>Appointment by Lord Chief Justice or anyone to whom the LCJ has delegated this power |
| Training | Supervised by the Magisterial Committee of the Judicial College<br>Most training delivered locally<br>Appraisal |
| Composition of bench | 17,500 lay magistrates: 47% men 53% women<br>Good representation of ethnic minorities<br>Only 3% are under the age of 40 |
| Role of magistrates | Deal with all summary offences<br>Deal with triable-either-way offences where defendant chooses trial in the Magistrates' Court<br>Deal with preliminary issues: remands and bail<br>Transfer indictable cases to the Crown Court<br>Youth Court<br>Family Court<br>Appeals in the Crown Court |

2 Core training – this provides the new magistrate with the opportunity to acquire and develop the key skills, knowledge and understanding required of a competent magistrate.

3 Activities – these will involve observations of court sittings and visits to establishments such as a prison or a probation office.

## 13.5.2 Training sessions

These are organised and carried out at local level within the 42 court areas. Much of the training is delivered locally by Justices' Clerks. However, some of the training of Youth Panel and Family Court Chairmen is delivered nationally.

After doing the core training and observing cases, a new magistrate will sit as a 'winger' to hear cases. This means that they will be one of a panel of three. The chairman (who sits in the middle) is a very experienced magistrate and the magistrates who sit on either side of the chairman are known as 'wingers'.

## 13.5.3 Appraisal

During the first two years of the new magistrate sitting in court, some of the sessions will be mentored. In the same period the magistrate is also expected to attend more training sessions. After two years, or whenever it is felt that the magistrate is ready, an appraisal will take place to check if he has acquired the competencies.

Any magistrate who cannot show that he has achieved the competencies will be given extra training. If he still cannot achieve the competencies, then the matter is referred to the local advisory committee, who may recommend to the Lord Chancellor that the magistrate is removed from sitting.

## 13.6 The magistrates' clerk

Every bench is assisted by a clerk, also known as a legal adviser. The senior clerk in each court has to be qualified as a barrister or solicitor for at least five years. The clerk's duty is to guide the magistrates on questions of law, practice and procedure. This is set out in s 28(3) of the Justices of the Peace Act 1979 which says:

> ❝ It is hereby declared that the functions of a justices' clerk include the giving to the justices ... of advice about law, practice or procedure on questions arising in connection with the discharge of their functions. ❞

The clerk is not meant to assist in the decision-making and should not normally retire with the magistrates when they go to make their decision.

Clerks deal with routine administrative matters. They can also issue warrants for arrest, extend police bail, adjourn criminal proceedings and deal with Early Administrative Hearings.

## Check your understanding

1 Select one of the following to show the maximum prison sentence that can be imposed by magistrates for a single conviction?

A 3 months

B 6 months

C 12 months

D 2 years

2 Explain three roles of magistrates in a criminal case involving an adult who pleads not guilty. Consider the view that trial by lay magistrates no longer represents trial by your peers.

## Summary

- Lay magistrates are not legally qualified but must have certain key qualities.
- They must be aged between 18 and 65 on appointment.
- Local advisory committees interview candidates and make recommendations for appointment.
- Lay magistrates are more representative of the community than professional judges with slightly more women than men and good representation of ethnic minorities.
- Magistrates deal with:
  - all summary cases
  - triable-either-way offences where the defendant chooses to be tried in the Magistrates' Court
  - all work connected to such cases, including bail applications and remands
  - first hearings of indictable offences which are then transferred to the Crown Court
  - youth cases for 10–17-year-olds
  - Family Court cases
  - appeals at the Crown Court.
- Where a defendant pleads not guilty, magistrates hear the case and decide if he is guilty or not guilty.
- When a defendant pleads guilty or is found guilty, the magistrates decide the sentence.
- Magistrates have to attend training courses and are appraised on their work.
- Magistrates are assisted on points of law by a legally qualified clerk.

# 14 Juries

After you have read this chapter you should be able to:
- Understand the qualifications for being a juror and how jurors are selected
- Describe the role of the jury in criminal courts
- Understand and be able to comment on the advantages and disadvantages of using juries in criminal courts

## 14.1 History of the jury system

Juries have been used in the legal system for over 1,000 years. There is evidence that they were used even before the Norman Conquest. However, in 1215 when trial by ordeal was condemned by the Church and (in the same year) the Magna Carta included the recognition of a person's right to trial by 'the lawful judgment of his peers', juries became the usual method of trying criminal cases. Originally they were used for providing local knowledge and information, and acted more as witnesses than decision makers. By the middle of the fifteenth century, juries had become independent assessors and assumed their modern role as deciders of fact.

### 14.1.1 The independence of the jury

The independence of the jury became even more firmly established following *Bushell's Case* (1670).

### Bushell's Case (1670)

Several jurors refused to convict Quaker activists of unlawful assembly. The trial judge would not accept the not guilty verdict, and ordered the jurors to resume their deliberations without food or drink. When the jurors persisted in their refusal to convict, the court fined them and committed them to prison until the fines were paid. On appeal, the Court of Common Pleas ordered the release of the jurors, holding that jurors could not be punished for their verdict.

This case established that the jury were the sole arbiters of fact and the judge could not challenge their decision. A more modern example, demonstrating that judges must respect the independence of the jury, is *R v McKenna* (1960).

### R v McKenna (1960)

The judge at the trial threatened the jury that if they did not return a verdict within another ten minutes they would be locked up all night. The jury then returned a verdict of guilty, but the defendant's conviction was quashed on appeal because of the judge's interference.

## 14.2 Juries in criminal courts

The most important use of juries today is in the Crown Court where they decide whether the defendant is guilty or not guilty. Jury trials, however, account for about 2 per cent of all criminal trials. This is because about 94 per cent of cases are dealt with in the Magistrates' Court, and of the cases that go to the Crown Court, about two out of every three defendants will plead guilty. A jury in the Crown Court has 12 members.

Certain basic qualifications are needed for a person to be eligible to be on a jury. There are also some people who are disqualified from being a juror.

### 14.2.1 Basic qualifications

The qualifications are set out in the Juries Act 1974 (as amended) so that to qualify for jury service a person must be:
- aged between 18 and 75 inclusive (age increased from 70 by the Criminal Justice and Courts Act 2015)
- registered as a parliamentary or local government elector
- ordinarily resident in the United Kingdom, the Channel Islands or the Isle of Man for at least five years since their thirteenth birthday.

However, certain people are not permitted to sit on a jury even though they are within these basic qualifications; these are people who are disqualified or mentally disordered.

### 14.2.2 Disqualification

Disqualified permanently from jury service are those who at any time have been sentenced to:
- imprisonment for life, detention for life or custody for life
- detention during Her Majesty's pleasure (prison) or during the pleasure of the Secretary of State (a young offenders' institute)

- imprisonment for public protection or detention for public protection
- an extended sentence
- a term of imprisonment of five years or more or a term of detention of five years or more.

Those in the following categories are disqualified for ten years:

- at any time in the last ten years served a sentence of imprisonment
- at any time in the last ten years had a suspended sentence passed on them
- at any time in the last ten years had a community order or other community sentence passed on them.

In addition anyone who is currently on bail in criminal proceedings is disqualified from sitting as a juror.

If a disqualified person fails to disclose that fact and turns up for jury service, he may be fined up to £5,000.

## 14.2.3 Mentally disordered persons

A mentally disordered person is defined in the Criminal Justice Act 2003 as:

1 A person who suffers or has suffered from mental illness, psychopathic disorder, mental handicap or severe mental handicap and on account of that condition either:
   a is resident in a hospital or similar institution, or
   b regularly attends for treatment by a medical practitioner.
2 A person for the time being under guardianship under section 7 of the Mental Health Act 1983.
3 A person who, under Part 7 of that Act, has been determined by a judge to be incapable of administering his property and affairs.

None of these are allowed to do jury service.

## 14.2.4 The right to be excused jury service

Prior to April 2004 people in certain essential occupations, such as doctors and pharmacists, had a right to be excused jury service if they did not want to do it. The Criminal Justice Act 2003 abolished this category. This means that doctors and other medical staff are no longer able to refuse

to do jury service, though they can apply for a discretionary excusal.

### Members of the forces

Full-time serving members of the forces will be excused from jury service if their commanding officer certifies their absence from duty (because of jury service) would be prejudicial to the efficiency of the service.

## 14.2.5 Discretionary excusals

Anyone who has problems which make it very difficult for them to do their jury service may ask to be excused or for their period of service to be put back to a later date. The court has discretion to grant such an excusal but will only do so if there is a sufficiently good reason. Such reasons include being too ill to attend court or suffering from a disability that makes it impossible for the person to sit as a juror, or being a mother with a small baby. Other reasons could include business appointments that cannot be undertaken by anyone else, examinations or holidays that have been booked.

In these situations the court is most likely to defer jury service to a more convenient date, rather than excuse the person completely. This is stated in the current guidance for summoning officers which is aimed at preventing the high number of discretionary excusals shown in the statistics in the Activity in section 14.3. The guidance states that:

> The normal expectation is that everyone summoned for jury service will serve at the time for which they are summoned. It is recognised that there will be occasions where it is not reasonable for a person summoned to serve at the time for which they are summoned. In such circumstances the summoning officer should use his/her discretion to defer the individual to a time more appropriate. Only in extreme circumstances, should a person be excused from jury service.

If a person is not excused from jury service he must attend on the date set or they may be fined up to £1,000 for non-attendance.

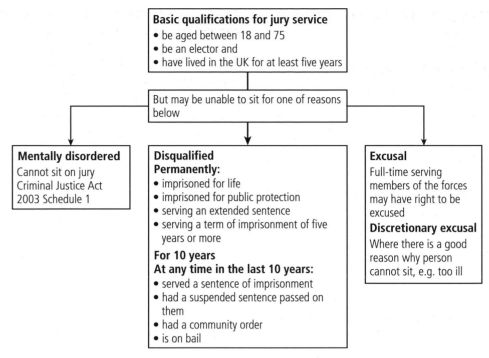

**Figure 14.1** Qualifications of jurors

## 14.2.6 Lawyers and police officers

There used to be a category of people who were ineligible for jury service. This included judges and others who had been involved in the administration of justice within the previous ten years. This category was abolished by the Criminal Justice Act 2003. This means that judges, lawyers, police, etc. are now eligible to serve on juries. Many people feel that this could lead to bias or to a legally well-qualified juror influencing the rest of the jury. This issue was considered in *R v Abdroikof, R v Green and R v Williamson* (2007).

### R v Abdroikof, R v Green and R v Williamson (2007)

The House of Lords considered appeals where a police officer or prosecutor had been one of the jury members.

They held that the fact that one of the members of the jury was a police officer did not of itself make a trial unfair. However, a majority of three of the five judges held that in the situation where a police officer on the jury had worked in the same station as a police officer giving evidence for the prosecution in the trial, then there was the risk of bias.

The House of Lords stated that the test to be applied in such cases was 'whether the fair-minded and informed observer, having considered the facts, would conclude that there was a real possibility that the tribunal was biased'.

The House of Lords also quoted from the decision in *R v Sussex Justices, ex parte McCarthy* (1924) where the judge stated that justice must not only be done, but must be seen to be done.

The same three judges in a majority decision also held that the presence of a juror who was a local Crown Prosecutor in the Crown Prosecution Service meant that justice was clearly not being seen to be done. Lord Bingham stated:

> 66 It is, in my opinion, clear that justice is not seen to be done if one discharging the very important neutral role of juror is a full-time, salaried, long-serving employee of the prosecutor. 99

The matter was also considered in *Hanif v United Kingdom* (2012).

### Hanif v United Kingdom (2012)

A police officer who was selected as a juror immediately alerted the court to the fact that he knew one of the prosecution police witnesses. It was particularly important as the evidence of this witness was crucial to the case against the defendant. However, the trial judge had ruled that this did not matter. The case continued with the police officer juror being the foreman of the jury. The defendant was convicted and appealed. The Court of Appeal, somewhat surprisingly, upheld the conviction.

The European Court of Human Rights ruled that having a police officer on the jury was a breach of Article 6(1) of the European Convention on Human Rights – the right to a fair trial.

This ruling by the trial judge and the Court of Appeal appears to be contrary to the judgment of the House of Lords in *Abdroikof*, as it would appear that a fair-minded person would conclude there was a real possible risk of bias.

## Judges on jury service

In June 2004 (just two months after the rules on jury service changed) a judge from the Court of Appeal, Lord Justice Dyson, was summoned to attend as a juror. This prompted the Lord Chief Justice, Lord Woolf, to issue observations to judges who are called for jury service. These point out that:

- a judge serves on a jury as part of his duty as a private citizen
- excusal from jury service will only be granted in extreme circumstances
- deferral of jury service to a later date should be sought where a judge has judicial commitments which make it particularly inconvenient for him to do jury service at the time he was called to do so
- at court if a judge knows the presiding judge or other person in the case, he should raise this with the jury bailiff or a member of the court staff if he considers it could interfere with his responsibilities as a juror
- it is a matter of discretion for an individual judge sitting as a juror as to whether he discloses the fact of his judicial office to the other members of the jury
- judges must follow the directions given to the jury by the trial judge on the law and should avoid the temptation to correct guidance which they believe to be inaccurate as this is outside their role as a juror.

### Activity

Discuss whether you think the following people should sit on a jury:

1 a woman who was fined for shoplifting a month ago
2 a man who was fined and disqualified from driving for taking cars without the consent of the owner
3 a doctor who works in general practice
4 a doctor who works in an accident and emergency unit of a busy city hospital
5 a Circuit Judge who frequently tries cases in the Crown Court.

## 14.2.7 Lack of capacity

A judge at the court may discharge a person from being a juror for lack of capacity to cope with the trial. This could be because the person does not understand English adequately or because of some disability which makes him unsuitable as a juror. This includes anyone who is blind, and who would be unable to see plans and photographs produced in evidence. Section 9B(2) of the Juries Act 1974 (which was added into the Act by the Criminal Justice and Public Order Act 1994, s 41) makes it clear that the mere fact of a disability does not prevent someone from acting as a juror. The judge can only discharge the juror if he is satisfied that the disability means that that juror is not capable of acting effectively as a juror.

## Deaf jurors

In June 1995 a deaf man was prevented from sitting on a jury at the Old Bailey despite wishing to serve and bringing with him a sign language interpreter. The judge pointed out that that would mean an extra person in the jury room and this was not allowed by law. He also said that the way in which witnesses gave evidence and the tone of their voice was important: 'a deaf juror may not be able to pick up these nuances and to properly judge their credibility.'

In November 1999 another deaf man challenged the ban on him sitting as a juror. The judge in this case felt that there was no practical reason why he should not sit, but the law only allowed the 12 jury members to be present in the jury room. It did not allow a thirteenth person – a sign-language interpreter – to be present. This made it impossible for the deaf man to be a juror.

# 14.3 Selecting a jury

At each Crown Court there is an official who is responsible for summonsing enough jurors to try the cases that will be heard in each two-week period. This official will arrange for names to be selected at random from the electoral registers, for the area which the court covers. This is done through a computer selection at a central office. It is necessary to summons more than 12 jurors as most courts have more than one courtroom and it will not be known how many of those summonsed are disqualified or may be excused. In fact, at the bigger courts up to 150 summonses may be sent out each fortnight.

Those summonsed must notify the court if there is any reason why they should not or cannot attend. All others are expected to attend for two weeks' jury service, though, of course, if the case they are trying goes on for more than two weeks they will have to stay until the trial is completed. Where it is known that a trial may be exceptionally long, such as a complicated fraud trial, potential jurors are asked if they will be able to serve for such a long period.

## Activity

Read the following extract from a Ministry of Justice report, 'Diversity and Fairness in the Jury System' (2007) and answer the questions below.

The Criminal Justice Act 2003 removed ineligibility and the right of excusal from jury service for a number of groups (those aged 65 to 69, MPs, clergy, medical professionals and those in the administration of justice). But summoned jurors may still be disqualified or excused from jury service (due to age, residency, mental disability, criminal charges, language, medical or other reasons).

■ The study found that the most significant factors predicating whether a summoned juror will serve or not are income and employment status, not ethnicity. Summoned jurors in the lower income brackets and those who are economically inactive are far less likely to serve than those in medium to high income brackets and those who are employed.

■ In 2005, of all those who replied to their summonses, 64 per cent of jurors served, 9 per cent were disqualified or ineligible, 27 per cent were excused. Of those excused, most were for medical reasons that prevented serving (34%) or childcare (15%) and work reasons (12%). Fifteen per cent of all the summonses in the survey were either returned as undeliverable or not responded to, which occurred most often in areas of high residential mobility.

■ The report established that most current thinking about who does and does not do jury service is based on myth, not reality.

Myth: Ethnic minorities are under-represented among those doing jury service.

Reality: Analysis showed that, in almost all courts (81 of the 84 surveyed), there was no significant difference between the proportion of black and ethnic minority jurors serving and the black and ethnic minority population levels in the local juror catchment area for each court.

Myth: Women and young people are under-represented among serving jurors, and the self-employed are virtually exempt from jury service.

Reality: The study establishes that jury pools at individual courts closely reflected the local population in terms of gender and age, and the self-employed are represented among serving jurors in direct proportion to their representation in the population.

### Questions

1 What are the current age limits for jury service?

2 What is the residency requirement to qualify for jury service?

3 What categories of people are disqualified from doing jury service?

4 What categories of people are less likely to serve on a jury?

5 What percentage failed to reply to their summons to do jury service?

6 For what types of reason were people excused from jury service?

7 What does the study show about the representative nature of juries?

## 14.3.1 Vetting

Once the list of potential jurors is known, both the prosecution and the defence have the right to see that list. In some cases it may be decided that this pool of potential jurors should be 'vetted', i.e. checked for suitability. There are two types of vetting:

■ police checks and
■ wider background check.

### Police checks

Routine police checks are made on prospective jurors to eliminate those disqualified. In *R v Crown Court at Sheffield, ex parte Brownlow* (1980) the defendant was a police officer and the defence sought permission to vet the jury panel for convictions. The judge gave permission but the Court of Appeal, while holding that they had no power to interfere, said that vetting was 'unconstitutional' and a 'serious invasion of privacy' and not sanctioned by the Juries Act 1974.

However, in *R v Mason* (1980) where it was revealed that the Chief Constable for Northamptonshire had been allowing widespread use of unauthorised vetting of criminal records, the Court of Appeal approved of this type of vetting. Lawton LJ pointed out that, since it is a criminal offence to serve on a jury while disqualified, the police were only doing their normal duty of preventing crime by checking for criminal records. Furthermore, the court said that, if in the course of looking at criminal records convictions were revealed which did not disqualify, there was no reason why these should not be passed on to prosecuting counsel, so that this information could be used in deciding to stand by individual jurors (see section 14.3.3 for information on the right of stand by).

### Juror's background

A wider check is made on a juror's background and political affiliations. This practice was brought to light by the 'ABC' trial in 1978 where two journalists and a soldier were charged with collecting secret information. It was discovered that the jury had been vetted for their loyalty. The trial was stopped and a new trial ordered before a fresh jury. Following this, the Attorney-General published guidelines in 1980 on when political vetting of jurors should take place. These guidelines state that:

a vetting should only be used in exceptional cases involving–
  – national security where part of the evidence is likely to be given in camera
  – terrorist cases
b vetting can only be carried out with the Attorney-General's express permission.

## 14.3.2 Selection at court

The jurors are usually divided into groups of 15 and allocated to a court. At the start of a trial the court clerk will select 12 out of these 15 at random.

## 14.3.3 Challenging

Once the court clerk has selected the panel of 12 jurors, these jurors come into the jury box to be sworn in as jurors. At this point, before the jury is sworn in, both the prosecution and defence have certain rights to challenge one or more of the jurors. These are:

■ to the array
■ for cause
■ prosecution right to stand by (put to one side) jurors.

### To the array

This right to challenge is given by s 5 of the Juries Act 1974 and it is a challenge to the whole jury on the basis that it has been chosen in an unrepresentative or biased way. This challenge was used successfully against the 'Romford' jury at the Old Bailey in 1993 when, out of a panel of 12 jurors, 9 came from Romford, with 2 of them living within 20 doors of each other in the same street. At the time jurors were chosen manually from the list of electors. Such a challenge is unlikely today as jurors are now selected at random by computer.

A **challenge to the array** was also used in *R v Fraser* (1987) where the defendant was of an ethnic minority background but all the jurors were white. The judge in that case agreed to empanel another jury. However, in *R v Ford* (1989) it was held that if the jury was chosen in a random manner then it could not be challenged simply because it was not multi-racial.

### Key term

Challenge to the array – a challenge to the whole jury on the basis that it has been chosen in an unrepresentative way.

### For cause

This involves challenging the right of an individual juror to sit on the jury. To be successful the challenge must point out a valid reason why that juror should not serve on the jury. An obvious reason is that the juror is disqualified, but a challenge for cause can also be made if the juror knows or is related to a witness or defendant. If such people are not removed from the jury there is a risk that any subsequent conviction could be quashed.

### Prosecution right to stand by jurors

This is a right that only the prosecution can exercise. It allows the juror who has been stood by to be put to the end of the list of potential jurors, so that he will not be used on the jury unless there are not enough other jurors. The prosecution does not have to give a reason for 'standing by', but the Attorney-General's guidelines make it clear that this power should be used sparingly.

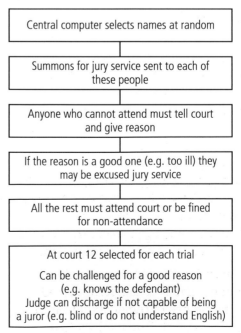

**Figure 14.2** Selecting a jury

## 14.4 The jury's role in criminal cases

The jury is used only at the Crown Court for cases where the defendant pleads not guilty. This means that a jury is used in about 30,000 cases each year.

### 14.4.1 Split function

The trial is presided over by a judge and the functions split between the judge and jury. The judge decides points of law and the jury decides the facts. At the end of the prosecution case, the judge has the power to direct the jury to acquit the defendant if he decides that, in law, the prosecution's evidence has not made out a case against the defendant. This is called a directed acquittal.

### Key term

Directed acquittal – where a judge decides there is insufficient prosecution evidence to allow the case to continue. The jury is directed to find the defendant not guilty.

Where the trial continues, the judge will sum up the case at the end to the jury and direct it on any law involved. The jury retires to a private room and makes the decision on the guilt or innocence of the accused in secret. Initially the jury must try to come to a unanimous verdict, i.e. one on which all the jurors are agreed. The judge must accept the jury verdict, even if he does not agree with it. This long established principle goes back to *Bushell's case* (1670). The jury does not give any reasons for its decision.

### 14.4.2 Majority verdicts

If, after at least two hours (longer where there are several defendants), the jury has not reached a verdict, the judge can call it back into the courtroom and direct it that he can now accept a majority verdict. Majority verdicts have been allowed since 1967. Where there is a full jury of 12, the verdict can be 10:2 or 11:1 either for guilty or for not guilty. If the jury has fallen below 12 for any reason (such as the death or illness of a juror during the trial) then only one can disagree with the verdict. That is, if there are 11 jurors, the verdict can be 10:1; if there are 10 jurors it can be 9:1. If there are only nine jurors the verdict must be unanimous. A jury cannot go below nine.

Majority verdicts were introduced because of the fear of jury 'nobbling', that is jurors being bribed or intimidated by associates of the defendant into voting for a not guilty verdict. When a jury had to be unanimous, only one member needed to be bribed to cause a 'stalemate' in which the jury was unable to reach a decision. It was also thought that the acquittal rates in jury trials were too high and majority decisions would result in more convictions.

Where the jury convicts a defendant on a majority verdict, the foreman of the jury must announce the numbers both agreeing and disagreeing with the verdict in open court. This provision is contained in s 17(3) of the Juries Act 1974 and is aimed at making sure the jury has come to a legal majority, and not one, for example of 8:4, which is not allowed. About 20 per cent of convictions by juries each year are by majority verdict.

**Figure 14.3** The use of juries in criminal cases

| Court | Crown Court |
|---|---|
| Qualifications | Age 18–75<br>Registered to vote<br>Resident in UK for at least five years since age 13 |
| Disqualified | Sentenced to five years' or more imprisonment – disqualified for life<br>Served a prison sentence OR suspended sentence OR a community service order – disqualified for ten years<br>Community order – disqualified for ten years<br>On bail – disqualified while on bail |
| Discretionary excuses | Ill, business commitments, or other 'good reason', but expectation is that nearly everyone will serve |
| Selection | A central office selects names from the lists of electors<br>Summons sent to these people<br>Must attend unless disqualified, ineligible or excused |
| Vetting | May be checked for criminal record – *R v Mason* (1980)<br>In cases of national security may be subject to a wider check on background subject to Attorney-General's guidelines |
| Challenges | Individual juror may be challenged for cause, e.g. knows defendant<br>Whole panel may be challenged for biased selection – but no right to a multi-racial jury (*R v Ford* (1989))<br>Prosecution may 'stand by' any juror |
| Function | Decide verdict – Guilty or Not guilty<br>Sole arbiters of fact but judge directs them on law |
| Verdict | Must try for a unanimous verdict<br>BUT if cannot reach a unanimous verdict then a majority verdict of 10:2 or 11:1 can be accepted |

### 14.4.3 Secrecy

The jury discussion takes place in secret and there can be no inquiry into how the jury reached its verdict. This used to be because disclosure of anything that happened in the jury room was a contempt of court. Now the Criminal Justice and Courts Act 2015 makes it a criminal offence to intentionally obtain, disclose or solicit any particulars of statements made, opinions expressed, arguments advanced or votes cast by members of a jury in the course of their deliberations in any legal proceedings. Disclosure is allowed in situations where it is in the interests of justice, such as reporting juror misconduct.

## 14.5 Advantages of jury trial

### 14.5.1 Public confidence

On the face of it, asking 12 strangers who have no legal knowledge and without any training to decide what may be complex and technical points is an absurd one. Yet the jury is considered one of the fundamentals of a democratic society. The right to be tried by one's peers is a bastion of liberty against the state and has been supported by eminent judges. For example, Lord Devlin said juries are 'the lamp that shows that freedom lives'. The tradition of trial by jury is very old and people seem to have confidence in the impartiality and fairness of a jury trial. This can be seen in the objection to withdrawing the right to jury trial from cases of 'minor' theft.

### 14.5.2 Jury equity

Since jurors are not legal experts, they are not bound to follow the precedent of past cases or even Acts of Parliament, and do not have to give reasons for their verdict. It is possible for them to decide cases on their idea of 'fairness'. This is sometimes referred to as jury equity. Several cases have shown the importance of this, in particular *Ponting's case* (1984).

#### Ponting's case (1984)

A civil servant was charged under the old wide-ranging s 2 of the Official Secrets Act 1911. He had leaked information on the sinking of the ship, The General Belgrano, in the Falklands war to an MP. At his trial he pleaded not guilty, claiming that his actions had been in the public interest. The jury refused to convict him even though the judge ruled there was no defence. The case also prompted the government to reconsider the law and to amend s 2.

More recently, a jury acquitted a mother of attempting to murder her daughter who had committed suicide. Her daughter was aged 31 and had been ill for 17 years. She had injected herself with an overdose of morphine. The mother had given her daughter some medication to ease her suffering in her final hours. She had pleaded guilty to assisting the daughter's suicide, but the prosecution had insisted on continuing to prosecute her for attempted murder. The jury found her not guilty.

### 14.5.3 Open system of justice

The use of a jury is viewed as making the legal system more open. Justice is seen to be done as members of the public are involved in a key role and the whole process is public. It also helps to keep the law clearer as points have to be explained to the jury, enabling the defendant to understand the case more easily.

Against this is the fact that the jury deliberates in private and that no one can inquire into what happened in the jury room. In addition, the jury does not have to give any reason for its verdict. When a judge gives a judgment he explains his reasoning and, if he has made an error, it is known and can be appealed against.

### 14.5.4 Secrecy of the jury room

This can be seen as an advantage, since the jury is free from pressure in its discussion. Jurors are protected from outside influences when deciding on the verdict. This allows juries to bring in verdicts that may be unpopular with the public as well as allowing jurors the freedom to ignore the strict letter of the law. It has been suggested that people would be less willing to serve on a jury if they knew that their discussions could be made public.

### 14.5.5 Impartiality

A jury should be impartial as it is not connected to anyone in the case. The process of random selection should result in a cross-section of society and this should also lead to an impartial jury, as jurors will have different prejudices and so should cancel out each others' biases. No one individual person is responsible for the decision. A jury is also not case-hardened since it sits for only two weeks and is unlikely to try more than three or four cases in that time.

# 14.6 Disadvantages of jury trial

## 14.6.1 Perverse decisions

In section 14.5.2 we looked at the idea of jury equity. That is the fact that the jury can ignore an unjust law. However, in some circumstances this type of decision can be seen as a perverse decision and one which was not justified. Juries have refused to convict in other clear-cut cases such as R v Randle and Pottle (1991).

### R v Randle and Pottle (1991)

The defendants were charged with helping the spy George Blake to escape from prison. Their prosecution did not occur until 25 years after the escape, when they wrote about what they had done and the jury acquitted them, possibly as a protest over the time lapse between the offence and the prosecution.

Another case where the evidence was clear, yet the jury acquitted the defendants was R v Kronlid and others (1996).

### R v Kronlid and others (1996)

The defendants admitted they had caused £1.5 million damage to a plane. They pleaded not guilty to charges of criminal damage on the basis that they were preventing the plane from being sent to Indonesia where it would have been used in attacks against the people of East Timor. The jury acquitted them.

## 14.6.2 Secrecy

Earlier we considered how the secrecy of the jury protects jurors from pressure. However, the secrecy of the jury room is also a disadvantage because, as no reasons have to be given for the verdict, there is no way of knowing if the jury understood the case and came to the decision for the right reasons.

In R v Mirza (2004) the House of Lords ruled that it could not inquire into discussions in a jury room. Two separate cases were considered in the appeal. These were R v Mirza and R v Connor and Rollock.

### R v Mirza (2004)

The defendant was a Pakistani who settled in the UK in 1988. He had an interpreter to help him in the trial and during the trial the jury sent notes asking why he needed an interpreter. He was convicted on a 10:2 majority. Six days after the jury verdict, one juror wrote to the defendant's counsel alleging that from the start of the trial there had been a 'theory' that the use of an interpreter was a 'ploy'. The juror also said that she had been shouted down when she objected and reminded her fellow jurors of the judge's directions.

### R v Connor and Rollock (2004)

A juror wrote to the Crown Court stating that while many jurors thought it was one or other of the defendants who had committed the stabbing, they should convict both to 'teach them a lesson'. This was five days after the verdict but before sentence was passed. As in Mirza there was a majority verdict of 10:2. The complaining juror said that, when she argued that the jury should consider which defendant was responsible, her co-jurors had refused to listen and remarked that if they did that they could be a week considering verdicts in the case.

The House of Lords held that s 8 of the Contempt of Court Act 1981 made it a contempt to disclose or obtain or solicit information about what had occurred in the jury room even for the purposes of an appeal. They also ruled that s 8 was compatible with Article 6 of the European Convention on Human Rights (the right to a fair trial). They pointed out that:

- confidentiality was essential to the proper functioning of the jury process
- there was merit in finality
- jurors had to be protected from harassment.

### Exceptions

There are two exceptions where the courts will inquire into the conduct of the jury in coming to their verdict. The first is where there has been a complete repudiation of the oath taken by the jurors to try the case according to the evidence. In other words, they have used another method to make their decision.

The best known example of this is the case of R v Young (Stephen) (1995).

### R v Young (Stephen) (1995)

The defendant was charged with the murder of two people. The jury had to stay in a hotel overnight as it had not reached a verdict by the end of the first day of deliberations. At the hotel, four of the jurors held a séance using a ouija board to try to contact the dead victims and ask them who had killed them. The next day, the jury returned a guilty verdict.

When the use of the ouija board became known, the Court of Appeal quashed the conviction and ordered a retrial. The Court also felt able to inquire into what had happened as it had occurred in a hotel and was not part of the jury room deliberations.

The second exception is where extraneous material has been introduced into the jury room. Examples have included telephone calls in and out of the jury room, papers mistakenly included in the set of papers given by the court to the jury and information from the internet. This happened in *R v Karakaya* (2005).

### R v Karakaya (2005)

The defendant was accused of rape. A juror did an internet search at home and brought into the jury room the printed-out results of the search. The jury convicted *Karakaya*, but this conviction was quashed because of the outside information that the jury had access to during its deliberations. A retrial was ordered and the defendant was acquitted by the jury in the second trial.

### Jurors and the internet

Judges direct jurors not to look at the internet for information. However, internet research by jurors has become more common. In Cheryl Thomas' research into various aspects of the use of juries, *Are Juries Fair?* (2010), she found that 12 per cent of jurors admitted they had looked on the internet for information about cases they were trying. Such information may be prejudicial to the defendant. For example, doing a search on a defendant's name may find newspaper reports of previous convictions, which the jury should not know about.

The Criminal Justice and Courts Act 2015 makes it a criminal offence for a juror to search the internet intentionally for information relevant to the case. The Act also makes it a criminal offence to disclose such information to another member of the jury.

### 14.6.3 Racial bias

Although jurors have no direct interest in a case, and despite the fact that there are 12 of them, they may still have prejudices which can affect the verdict. Some jurors may be biased against the police – this is one of the reasons that those with certain criminal convictions are disqualified from sitting on a jury.

In particular there is the worry that some jurors are racially prejudiced. One case that raised the problem of racial bias was *Sander v United Kingdom* (2000).

### Sander v United Kingdom (2000)

One juror had written a note to the judge raising concern over the fact that other jurors had been making openly racist remarks and jokes. The judge asked the jury to 'search their consciences'. The next day the judge received two letters, one signed by all the jurors in which they denied any racist attitudes and a second from one juror who admitted that he may have been the one making the jokes. Despite the discrepancies between these two letters the judge allowed the case to continue with the same jury. The European Court of Human Rights held that in these circumstances the judge should have discharged the jury as there was an obvious risk of racial bias and a breach of the right to a fair trial under Article 6 of the European Convention on Human Rights.

### 14.6.4 Media influence

Media coverage may influence jurors. This is especially true in high-profile cases, where there has been a lot of publicity about police investigations into a case. One case where media coverage was held to have influenced the jury was *R v Taylor and Taylor* (1993).

### R v Taylor and Taylor (1993)

Two sisters were charged with murder. Some newspapers published still photos taken from a video which gave a false impression of what was happening. After the jury had convicted the sisters, the judge gave leave to appeal because of the possible influence the picture could have had on the jury's verdict and the Court of Appeal quashed the convictions.

### 14.6.5 Lack of understanding

There are worries that jurors may not understand the case which they are trying.

Thomas' report *Are Juries Fair?* explored jurors' understanding of cases. In order to test understanding, a series of simulated trials was used. A total of 797 jurors in three different areas all saw the same simulated trial and heard exactly the same judicial directions on the law.

The jurors were first asked whether they thought they had understood the directions. In two of the areas, Blackfriars, London and Winchester, over two-thirds of the jurors felt they were able to understand the directions. In Nottingham, only just under half of the jurors felt they understood the directions.

The jurors' understanding of the directions was then tested. This discovered that only 31 per cent of the jurors had actually understood the directions fully in the legal terms used by the judge. When the jurors were given a written summary of the instructions, the number who fully understood increased to 48 per cent.

This study shows that, even with a written summary, less than half of jurors fully understood the judge's directions.

## 14.6.6 Fraud trials

Fraud trials with complex accounts being given in evidence can create special problems for jurors. Even jurors who can easily cope with other evidence may have difficulty understanding a fraud case. These cases are also often very long, so that the jurors have to be able to be away from their own work for months. A long fraud trial can place a great strain on jurors. Such cases also become very expensive, both for the prosecution and for the defendants.

In the Domestic Violence, Crime and Victims Act 2004, there is a special provision for cases where there is a large number of counts on the indictment. This allows a trial of sample counts with a jury and then, if the defendant is convicted on those, the remainder can be tried by a judge alone. This does help prevent long jury trials in very complex fraud cases.

## 14.6.7 Jury tampering

In a few cases, friends of the defendant may try to interfere with the jury. This may be by bribing jury members to bring in a not guilty verdict or by making threats against jury members so that they are too afraid to find the defendant guilty. In such cases, police may be used to try to protect the jurors, but this may not be effective and is also expensive and removes the police from their other work.

To combat this, s 44 of the Criminal Justice Act 2003 provides that where there has already been an effort to tamper with a jury in the case, the prosecution can apply for the trial to be heard by judge alone. The first trial without a jury was approved in *R v Twomey and others* (2009).

### *R v Twomey and others* (2009)

The defendants were charged with various offences connected to a large robbery from a warehouse at Heathrow. Three previous trials had collapsed and there had been a 'serious attempt at jury tampering' in the last of these. The prosecution applied to a single judge for the trial to take place without a jury. The judge refused, but the Court of Appeal overturned this decision, ordering that the trial should take place without a jury.

However, in other cases the Court of Appeal has not granted trial by judge alone. An example is *KS v R* (2010).

### *KS v R* (2010)

There had been several trials on various allegations of fraud committed by the defendant. It was not until the tenth trial that jury tampering occurred. It occurred because jurors and members of the public who wished to smoke during breaks were directed to the same area. During one of these breaks, a friend of the defendant approached a juror. The Court of Appeal refused an application for trial by judge alone. They pointed out that the casual arrangements at the Crown Court which had allowed the contact would not be repeated. Also the approach had been opportunistic rather than a deliberate targeting of jurors. For these reasons, there was no need to order trial by judge alone.

## 14.6.8 High acquittal rates

Juries are often criticised on the grounds that they acquit too many defendants. The figures usually quoted in support of this are that about 60 per cent of those who plead not guilty at the Crown Court are acquitted. However, this figure does not give a true picture of the workings of juries as it includes cases discharged by the judge and those in which the judge directed an acquittal.

The judicial statistics show that in most years more than half of acquittals are ordered by the judge without a jury even being sworn in to try the case. This happens where the prosecution drop the case at the last minute and offer no evidence against the defendant. Another 10 per cent of acquittals are by a jury but on the direction of a judge. This occurs where the judge rules that there is no case against

**Figure 14.4** Advantages and disadvantages of jury trial

| Advantages | Disadvantages |
|---|---|
| Public confidence | High acquittal rates undermine confidence in the criminal justice system |
| Considered to be a fundamental part of a democratic society | |
| New qualifications for jury service mean that almost everyone can serve on a jury | Doing jury service is unpopular |
| Jury equity:<br>*Ponting's case* | Perverse verdicts:<br>*Randle and Pottle*<br>*R v Kronlid* |
| Open system of justice | Media influence |
| Involves members of the public | Reporting may influence the decision:<br>*Taylor and Taylor* |
| Secrecy of the jury room protects jurors from pressure | Secrecy means that:<br>■ the reasons for the decision are not known<br>■ the jury's understanding of the case cannot be checked<br>Exception: *Young (Stephen)* |
| Impartiality | Bias |
| Having 12 members with no direct interest in the case should cancel out any bias | In some cases there has been racial bias:<br>*Sander v UK* |

the defendant; it might be because of a legal point or because the prosecution evidence is not sufficient in law to prove the case. When these decisions are excluded from the statistics it is found that juries actually acquit in less than 40 per cent of cases.

### 14.6.9 Other disadvantages

The compulsory nature of jury service is unpopular, so that some jurors may be against the whole system, while others may rush their verdict in order to leave as quickly as possible. Jury service can be a strain, especially where jurors have to listen to horrific evidence. Jurors in the Rosemary West case, where several young women and girls had been murdered by West and her husband, were offered counselling after the trial to help them cope with the evidence they had seen and heard.

## 14.7 Comparison of juries with lay magistrates

### 14.7.1 Cross-section of society

The use of both juries and lay magistrates involves members of the community in making decisions in

criminal cases. This means there is a wider cross-section of society than would be possible with the use of professional judges.

There is a better balance of men and women. Although individual juries may not have a 50:50 balance, overall the numbers of men and women should be fairly even. For lay magistrates 53 per cent are women. Also, there is considerable involvement of ethnic minorities in both juries and lay magistrates.

However, lay magistrates are often perceived as being middle-aged and middle class. Their average age is over 50 and they are often from professional backgrounds. Juries will be from a wide age-range and backgrounds.

### 14.7.2 Local knowledge

Jurors are chosen from the local community. Lay magistrates are also expected to live or work near the court. This means that both jurors and lay magistrates should have local knowledge of particular problems in the area.

However, as most magistrates come from the professional and managerial classes, it is unlikely that they live in, or have any real knowledge of, the

**Figure 14.5** Cases on juries

| Case | Facts | Law |
|------|-------|-----|
| *Bushell's Case* (1670) | A jury refused to convict Quaker activists<br>They were fined and imprisoned<br>They were released after an appeal | The jury makes the decision on the facts<br>The judge must not challenge that decision |
| *R v Abdroikof, R v Green and R v Williamson* (2007) | The jury in each case had a police officer or a prosecutor as a member | Having a police officer who had no contact with the case on a jury did not make the trial unfair<br>Where the police officer knew the officers giving evidence in the case OR having a prosecutor who was a local prosecutor were both situations where there was possible bias<br>Justice must be seen to be done |
| *Ponting's case* (1984) | A civil servant leaked information to an MP<br>The jury refused to convict him even though the judge ruled he had no defence | A jury is independent and if it decides cases on the basis of fairness, its decision cannot be challenged |
| *R v Mirza* (2004) | One juror complained that the other members of the jury had shown racial bias in coming to their decision | Discussions in the jury room are secret and the court will not normally inquire into them |
| *R v Young (Stephen)* (1995) | Four jurors held a séance to try to contact two murder victims and find out who had murdered them | The court was able to inquire into what had happened as it was at a hotel where the jurors were staying and not in the jury room discussions |
| *R v Karakaya* (2005) | A juror did an internet search on the defendant and brought the printed out results into the jury room | The court could inquire into this as outside information had been used in the jury room |
| *R v Twomey and others* (2009) | There was a serious attempt at interfering with the jury and three previous trials had collapsed | Section 44 of the Criminal Justice Act 2003 applied and a retrial was ordered by judge alone |
| *KS v R* (2010) | There was an effort to interfere with the jury, but it had only occurred because jurors and members of the public were taking breaks in the same area | An application under s 44 of the Criminal Justice Act 2003 for trial without a jury was refused<br>The approach was opportunistic rather than a deliberate targeting of jurors |

problems in the poorer areas. Jurors will be from a much broader cross-section of the local society and, therefore, more likely to have an awareness of social problems in the area.

## 14.7.3 Cost

The use of unpaid lay magistrates is cheap. The cost of replacing them with paid judges has been estimated at £100 million a year (there would also be the problem of recruiting sufficient qualified lawyers). The cost of a trial in the Magistrates' Court is also much cheaper than in the Crown Court.

However, for juries there is also a judge present at the trial, so there is no saving of costs. Indeed, it is probable that having a jury adds to the length of a case and therefore to the costs.

## 14.7.4 Training

Lay magistrates have training and so are not complete 'amateurs'. The majority of decisions made by them require common sense rather than professional training.

Jurors do not have any training and may often have to consider quite complicated directions from the judge about points of law in the case. As seen earlier in this chapter, research has shown that jurors often do not understand such directions.

## 14.8 Alternatives to jury trial

Despite all the problems of using juries in criminal cases, there is still a strong feeling that they are the best method available. However, if juries are not thought suitable to try serious criminal cases, what alternative form of trial could be used?

### 14.8.1 Trial by a single judge

This is the method of trial in the majority of civil cases which is generally regarded as producing a fairer and more predictable result. Trial by a single judge was used for some criminal trials in Northern Ireland until 2007. These were called the Diplock courts and were brought in on the recommendation of Lord Diplock to replace jury trial because of the special problems of threats and jury nobbling that existed between the different sectarian parties.

However, there appears to be less public confidence in the use of judges to decide all serious criminal cases. The arguments against this form of trial are that judges become case-hardened and prosecution-minded. They are also from a very elite group and would have little understanding of the background and problems of defendants. Individual prejudices are more likely than in a jury where the different personalities should go some way to eliminating bias. But, on the other hand, judges are trained to evaluate cases and they are now being given training in racial awareness. This may make them better arbiters of fact than an untrained jury.

### 14.8.2 A panel of judges

In some continental countries cases are heard by a panel of three or five judges sitting together. This allows for a balance of views, instead of the verdict of a single person. However, it still leaves the problems of judges becoming case-hardened, prosecution-minded and coming from an elite background. The other difficulty is that there are not sufficient judges and our system of legal training and appointment would need a radical overhaul to implement this proposal. It would also be expensive.

### 14.8.3 A judge plus lay assessors

Under this system the judge and two lay people would make the decision together. This method is used in the Scandinavian countries. It provides the legal expertise of the judge, together with lay participation in the legal system by ordinary members of the public. The lay people could either be drawn from the general public, using the same method as is used for selecting juries at present or a special panel of assessors could be drawn up as in tribunal cases. This latter suggestion would be particularly suitable for fraud cases.

### 14.8.4 A mini-jury

Finally, if the jury is to remain, then it might be possible to have a smaller number of jurors. In many continental countries when a jury is used there are nine members. For example, in Spain, which reintroduced the use of juries in certain criminal cases in 1996, there is a jury of nine. Alternatively a jury of six could be used for less serious criminal cases that at the moment have a full jury trial, as occurs in some American states.

**Tip**

Some questions may ask for information or comment on both juries and lay magistrates. It is important to know both.

## Check your understanding

1 Which one of the following age limits accurately shows eligibility for jury service?

   A 21–75        C 21–70

   B 18–70        D 18–75

2 Which one of the following potential jurors cannot serve?

   A A man, currently on bail, who intends pleading not guilty to an offence of shoplifting

   B An 18-year-old student who is still at school

   C A woman, aged 32, who has recently been fined for driving without a valid licence

   D A police officer

3 Explain what is meant by a unanimous verdict of a jury in a criminal trial and explain when a jury has to reach a unanimous verdict.

Consider the view that trial by jury still represents trial by your peers.

## Summary

- Juries have been used for over 1,000 years in the English legal system.
- The jury is the sole decider of fact in a case and is independent in its decision making (*Bushell's case, R v McKenna*).
- Juries are used at the Crown Court in criminal cases.
- Jurors must be:
  - aged between 18 and 75 inclusive
  - registered as a parliamentary or local elector
  - ordinarily resident in the UK for at least five years since their thirteenth birthday.
- Those who have at any time been sentenced to a prison sentence of at least five years are disqualified for life from jury service.
- Also disqualified are those who have at any time in the last ten years:
  - served a sentence of imprisonment
  - had a suspended sentence
  - been given a community order.
- People on bail are also disqualified from being a juror.
- The court can give a discretionary excusal to anyone chosen for jury service but there must be a very good reason.
- Jurors are selected at random from the registers of electors.
- Jurors can be vetted by a police check or, in exceptional cases, by a wider background check.
- The jury decides the verdict of guilty or not guilty in cases at the Crown Court where the defendant pleads not guilty.
- The verdict can be a majority one of 10:2.
- Advantages of jury trial are:
  - public confidence
  - jury equity
  - open system of justice
  - decision made in secret
  - impartiality.
- Disadvantages of jury trial are:
  - perverse decisions
  - secrecy of the decision
  - racial bias
  - media influence
  - lack of understanding of jurors, especially in fraud trials
  - the possibility of jury tampering
  - high acquittal rates
  - jury service is unpopular and can be a strain.
- Alternatives to the current system of jury trial are trial by:
  - a single judge
  - a panel of judges
  - a judge plus lay assessors
  - a mini-jury.

# 15 Legal personnel

After reading this chapter you should be able to:
- Understand the roles of barristers, solicitors and legal executives
- Explain the differences in these roles
- Understand in outline the regulation of legal personnel

## 15.1 Types of legal personnel

In England and Wales there are two types of lawyers (barristers and solicitors), jointly referred to as the legal profession. Most countries do not have this clear-cut division among lawyers: a person will qualify simply as a lawyer, although, after qualifying, it will be possible for him to specialise as an advocate, or in a particular area of law.

There are also legal executives who work in solicitors' firms, who have qualifications in law but are not fully qualified as solicitors.

## 15.2 Barristers

There are about 12,700 barristers who are self-employed in independent practice in England and Wales. In addition there are about 3,000 barristers employed by organisations such as the Crown Prosecution Service, independent businesses, local government and the Civil Service.

Collectively barristers are referred to as 'the Bar' and they are controlled by their own professional body – the General Council of the Bar. All barristers must also be a member of one of the four Inns of Court: Lincoln's Inn, Inner Temple, Middle Temple and Gray's Inn, all of which are situated near the Royal Courts of Justice in London.

A barrister

## 15.2.1 Training

Entry to the Bar is normally degree-based. If the degree is not in law, it is necessary to take the Graduate Diploma in Law (GDL) or the Common Professional Examination (CPE) in order to go on to qualify as a barrister.

All student barristers also have to pass the Bar Professional Training Course. On this course students study:
- case preparation legal research
- written skills
- opinion writing (giving written advice)
- drafting documents such as claim forms
- conference skills (interviewing clients)
- negotiation
- **advocacy**.

### Key term

**Advocacy** – the art of speaking in court on behalf of another; conducting a case in court as the legal representative of another person.

Once a student has passed the Bar Professional Training Course, he is then 'called to the Bar'. This means that he is officially qualified as a barrister. However, there is still a practical stage to his training which must be completed. This is called pupillage.

### Pupillage

After the student has passed the Bar Professional Training Course there is 'on the job' training where the trainee barrister becomes a pupil to a qualified barrister. This effectively involves 'work shadowing' that barrister, and can be with the same barrister for 12 months or with two different pupil masters for six months each.

## 15.2.2 Role of barristers

Barristers practising at the Bar are self-employed, but usually work from a set of chambers where they can share administrative expenses with other barristers. Most sets of chambers are fairly small, with about 15–20 barristers. They will employ a clerk as a practice administrator – booking in cases and negotiating fees – and they will have other support staff.

The majority of barristers will concentrate on advocacy. Advocacy is presenting cases in court. Barristers have full **rights of audience**. This means they can present cases in any court in England and Wales. However, there are some barristers who specialise in areas such as tax and company law, and will rarely appear in court. Even those who specialise in advocacy will do a certain amount of paperwork, writing opinions on cases, giving advice and drafting documents for use in court.

> ### Key term
>
> Rights of audience – the right to present a case in court on behalf of another person.

### Direct access

Originally it was necessary for anybody who wished to instruct a barrister to go to a solicitor first. The solicitor would then brief the barrister. This was thought to create unnecessary expense for clients, as it meant they had to use two lawyers instead of one. It is no longer necessary to go to a solicitor in order to instruct a barrister for civil cases, although in the majority of cases this will still happen. Direct access is still not allowed for criminal cases or family work. To do direct access work, a barrister must do additional training.

### Employed barristers

Barristers can be employed by government organisations, the Civil Service, local government and businesses. In particular the Crown Prosecution Service employs a large number to prosecute cases in the criminal courts. Employed barristers have the same rights of audience (i.e. the right to present cases in court) as self-employed barristers.

## 15.3 Solicitors

There are about 130,000 solicitors practising in England and Wales and they are controlled by their own professional body, the Law Society. Of 130,000, about 90,000 are in private practice and the remainder are in employed work, such as for local government, the Civil Service, the Crown Prosecution Service or private businesses.

### 15.3.1 Training

To become a solicitor it is usual to have a law degree, although those with a degree in a subject other than law can take the Common Professional Examination (CPE) or Graduate Diploma in Law (GDL). The next stage is the Legal Practice Course (LPC). This includes training in skills such as client interviewing, negotiation, advocacy, drafting documents and legal research. There is also an emphasis on business management, for example keeping accounts and then

### Training contract

Even when this course has been passed, the student is still not a qualified solicitor. He must next obtain a training contract under which he works in a solicitors' firm for two years, getting practical experience. This training period can also be undertaken in certain other legal organisations such as the Crown Prosecution Service, or the legal department of a local authority. Once the trainee has completed his training contract he will be admitted as a solicitor by the Law Society.

A solicitor meeting with clients

### 15.3.2 Role of solicitors

The majority of those who succeed in qualifying as a solicitor will then work in private practice in a solicitors' firm. However, there are other careers available, and some newly qualified solicitors may go on to work in the Crown Prosecution Service or for a local authority or government department. Others will become legal advisers in commercial or industrial businesses. About 40,000 solicitors are employed.

A solicitor in private practice may work as a sole practitioner or in a partnership. There are some 9,500 firms of solicitors, ranging from the small 'high street' practice to the big city firms. The number of partners is not limited, and some of the biggest firms will have over a hundred partners as well as employing assistant solicitors.

The type of work done by a solicitor will largely depend on the type of firm he is working in. A small high street firm will probably be a general practice advising clients on a whole range of topics such as consumer problems, housing and business matters and family problems. A solicitor working in such a practice is likely to spend some of his time interviewing clients in his office and negotiating on their behalf, and a large amount of time dealing with paperwork. This will include:

■ writing letters on behalf of clients
■ drafting contracts, leases or other legal documents
■ drawing up wills
■ dealing with conveyancing (the legal side of buying and selling flats, houses, office buildings and land).

The solicitor may also, if he wishes, act for some of his clients in court. Standing up in court, putting the client's case and questioning witnesses is known as advocacy. Some solicitors will specialise in this and spend much of their time in court.

## Specialising

Although some solicitors may be general practitioners handling a variety of work, it is not unusual, even in small firms, for a solicitor to specialise in one particular field. The firm itself may handle only certain types of cases (perhaps only civil actions) and not do any criminal cases, or a firm may specialise in matrimonial cases. Even within the firm the solicitors are likely to have their own field of expertise.

In large firms there will be an even greater degree of specialisation, with departments dealing with one aspect of the law. The large city firms usually concentrate on business and commercial law.

## Conveyancing

Prior to 1985, solicitors had a monopoly on conveyancing: this meant that only solicitors could deal with the legal side of transferring houses and other buildings and land. This was changed by the Administration of Justice Act 1985 which allowed people other than solicitors to become licensed conveyancers. As a result of the increased competition in this area, solicitors had to reduce their fees, but even so they lost a large proportion of the work. This led to a demand for wider rights of advocacy.

## Briefing barristers

Where it is necessary to go to court, the solicitor may decide to brief a barrister to do the case. A solicitor may also go to a barrister for an opinion on a complex case.

## Rights of advocacy

All solicitors have always been able to act as advocates in the Magistrates' Courts and the County Courts, but their rights of audience in the higher courts used to be very limited. This was changed by the Courts and Legal Services Act 1990. Solicitors in private practice now have the right to apply for a certificate of advocacy which enables them to appear in the higher courts. Such a certificate is granted if the solicitor already has experience of advocacy in the Magistrates' Court and the County Court, takes a short training course and passes examinations on the rules of evidence.

Solicitors with an advocacy qualification are also eligible to be appointed as Queen's Counsel (see section 15.5).

# 15.4 Overlap of roles of barristers and solicitors

Until the end of the last century the roles of barristers and solicitors were to a large degree quite different. Barristers specialised in presenting cases in courts and could appear in any court. Solicitors generally did office-based work and only had limited rights to present cases in court. Solicitors can now apply for rights of audience in all courts.

However, there are only about 6,500 solicitors with higher rights. This is only one in every 200 solicitors. So, although the rules allow barristers and solicitors to carry out the same advocacy work, in practice there is still a difference in the work they do.

Another difference was that barristers could not be briefed directly. Clients had to go to a solicitor first and the solicitor would decide whether a barrister was needed. If so, then the solicitor had to brief the barrister. This meant that the client had two lawyers, a solicitor and a barrister, and had to pay the fees for both. Since 2004 a person with a civil dispute can go direct to a barrister. This means the barrister will then do the preparatory work in the case, such as interviewing the client, writing letters to the other side and negotiating, which previously only solicitors could do.

This has created some overlap in the work done by barristers and solicitors. However, direct access applies only in civil cases. There is no direct access to a barrister in criminal cases or family work.

## 15.4.1 Alternative Business Structures (ABS)

Changes in the rules about the types of business structures allowed in the legal profession have also brought some overlap in the roles of barristers and solicitors. The Legal Services Act 2007 allows:

- legal businesses to include lawyers and non-lawyers
- legal businesses to include barristers and solicitors
- non-lawyers to own legal businesses
- legal businesses to operate as companies.

In order to set up an ABS, a licence must be applied for from the Legal Services Board. The first three licences under the Act were given in April 2012. Two of these were to 'high street' solicitors who wished to bring in a non-lawyer practice manager to their practices. The third was to the Co-operative Society, a big business with shops nationwide.

As more ABSs are set up, the style of legal advice and services is likely to change considerably. Traditional solicitors' firms will face competition from commercial firms such as the Co-operative Society.

# 15.5 Queen's Counsel

After at least ten years as a barrister or as a solicitor with an advocacy qualification, it is possible to apply to become a Queen's Counsel (QC). About 10 per cent of the barristers practising at the Bar are Queen's Counsel. Becoming a Queen's Counsel is known as 'taking silk'. QCs usually take on more complicated and high-profile cases than junior barristers (all barristers who are not Queen's Counsel are known as 'juniors'), and they can command higher fees for their recognised expertise. Often a QC will have a junior barrister to assist with the case.

# 15.6 Legal executives

Legal executives work in solicitors' firms as assistants. They are qualified lawyers who have passed the Institute of Legal Executives' Professional Qualification in Law. They specialise in a particular area of law. There are over 20,000 legal executives practising.

## 15.6.1 Training

To become a legal executive it is necessary to pass the Professional Diploma in Law and the Professional Higher Diploma in Law. As well as passing the PHDL examinations, it is also necessary to have worked in a solicitors' firm (or other legal organisation such as the Crown Prosecution Service or local government) for at least five years. When all the qualifications have been achieved the person becomes a Fellow of the Chartered Institute of Legal Executives.

A Fellow of the Chartered Institute of Legal Executives can go on to become a solicitor. In order to do this they will have to pass the Law Society's Legal Practice Course, but they may be given exemption from the two-year training contract.

## 15.6.2 Role of legal executives

Legal executives specialise in a particular area of law. Within that area of law their day-to-day work is similar to that of a solicitor, though they tend to deal with the more straightforward matters. For example, they can:

- handle various legal aspects of a property transfer
- assist in the formation of a company
- draft wills
- advise people with matrimonial problems
- advise clients accused of serious or petty crime.

They also have some rights of audience. They can appear to make applications where the case is not defended in family matters and civil cases in the County Court.

Since 2008 legal executives have been able to do a course on advocacy and obtain wider rights of audience. There are three different practising certificates: a Civil Proceedings Certificate, a Criminal Proceedings Certificate and a Family Proceedings Certificate. These allow legal executives to do such matters as make an application for bail or deal with cases in the Youth Court or the Family Court of the Magistrates' Courts.

Legal executives are fee earners. This means that where a legal executive works for a firm of solicitors in private practice, that legal executive's work is charged at an hourly rate directly to clients. In this way a legal executive makes a direct contribution to the income of the law firm. The partners of the firm are responsible for the legal executive's work.

**Figure 15.1** Comparing barristers, solicitors and legal executives

| | Barristers | Solicitors | Legal executives |
|---|---|---|---|
| **Training** | Degree: if not in law then must pass CPE or GDL<br>Bar Professional Training Course<br>Pupillage | Degree: if not in law then must pass CPE or GDL<br>Legal Practice Course<br>Training contract | Professional Higher Diploma in Law<br>Work for at least five years |
| **Role** | Self-employed in chambers OR employed<br>Mostly court work<br>Also write opinions and draft documents<br>Briefed by solicitors<br>Direct access by clients in civil cases | Private practice in solicitors' firm OR employed<br>Wide variety of work mostly office-based<br>Contracts, leases, wills, conveyancing<br>Direct access by clients<br>May brief a barrister where it is necessary to go to court | Work in a solicitors' firm OR in other legal organisation<br>Similar work to solicitors<br>Deal with more straightforward matters |
| **Advocacy** | Full rights of audience in all courts | Automatic rights of audience in Magistrates' Court or County Court<br>Can get advocacy qualification to do cases in higher courts | Very limited rights of audience: applications in undefended cases<br>Can obtain advocacy certificate to make some applications in Magistrates' Court or County Court |
| **Queen's Counsel** | Can apply to become a QC after at least ten years in practice<br>Will then do more complicated cases | If have an advocacy qualification can apply to become a QC after at least ten years in practice<br>Will then do more complicated cases | |

## 15.7 Regulation of legal personnel

Barristers, solicitors and legal executives all have their own regulatory bodies. All of these bodies are overseen by the Legal Services Board.

### 15.7.1 The General Council of the Bar

The General Council of the Bar represents barristers in England and Wales. It promotes the Bar's high-quality specialist advocacy and advisory services. It fulfils the function of what might be called a 'trade union', representing the interests of the Bar. It makes the Bar's view on issues, such as legal aid payment rates, known to the appropriate government department.

The Council also promotes fair access to justice for all, the highest standards of ethics, equality and diversity across the profession, and the development of business opportunities for barristers at home and abroad.

The Council also used to be responsible for disciplining barristers who breached the Code of Practice. This was seen as creating a conflict in its roles, so the independent Bar Standards Board was created to deal with disciplinary matters and also oversee training and education requirements.

### 15.7.2 Bar Standards Board

This is the body which regulates the profession of barristers. It sets training and entry standards. It also sets out a Code of Conduct which barristers should comply with.

The Board investigates any alleged breach of the Code of Conduct. It can discipline any barrister who is in breach of the Code. If the matter is serious it will be referred to a Disciplinary Tribunal arranged by an independent Bar Tribunals and Adjudication service. A tribunal has several sanctions it can impose including:

- reprimand the barrister (that is, formally warn them about their behaviour)
- make the barrister complete further professional development training

- order the barrister to pay a fine of up to £50,000
- suspend the barrister for up to 12 months
- disbar (strike off) the barrister: this can only be done in extreme cases.

If the complainant is unhappy with the decision of the Bar Standards Board, he may take the matter to the Legal Ombudsman (see section 15.7.7 below)

## 15.7.3 The Law Society

The Law Society is the governing body of solicitors. All practising solicitors must be members of the Law Society. On its website the Law Society states that it 'exists to support, promote and represent all solicitors so they can help their clients. We also work to ensure no one is above the law and to protect everyone's right to have access to justice.'

It has supported the interests of solicitors in England and Wales for almost 200 years. It leads the debate on issues affecting solicitors throughout England and Wales. In particular it speaks to government, parliament and the public on a range of legal issues and works to influence policy and legislation to make sure that it protects its members, the public and the justice system.

The Law Society makes sure the profession's voice is heard by the right people – government, industry and in international jurisdictions. It helps raise the profile of the profession through campaigns and networking and promotes the UK legal sector locally and globally.

The Law Society used to be responsible for hearing complaints about solicitors and disciplining those who breach the Code of Conduct. This meant there was a conflict in its roles, as it was both representing solicitors and also trying to help clients who complained about solicitors. There were also problems with delays and inefficiencies in its complaints procedure. So the independent Solicitors Regulatory Authority was set up to deal with complaints.

## 15.7.4 Solicitors Regulatory Authority

This deals with complaints about professional misconduct of solicitors. The Authority will investigate the matter. It there is evidence of serious professional misconduct, it can put the case before

the Solicitors' Disciplinary Tribunal. If the tribunal upholds the complaint, it can fine or reprimand the solicitor or, in more serious cases, it can suspend a solicitor from the Roll, so that he cannot practise for a certain time. In very serious cases, the tribunal can strike off a solicitor from the Roll so that he is prevented from practising as a solicitor.

If the complainant is unhappy with the decision of the Solicitors Regulatory Authority, he may take the matter to the Legal Ombudsman (see section 15.7.7 below).

## 15.7.5 Chartered Institute of Legal Executives

All legal executives are members of the Chartered Institute of Legal Executives (CILEx). This organisation provides education, training and development of skills for legal executives. It also protects the status and interests of legal executives. Another aim is to 'promote and secure professional standards of conduct amongst Fellows and those who are registered with the Institute'.

CILEx publishes a code of conduct and guides to good practice but regulation of members is done by the CILEx Regulation Board.

## 15.7.6 CILEx Regulation Board

The CILEx Regulation Board is the independent regulator of members of CILEx and investigates complaints about legal executives.

When an investigation is complete a summary of the issues is prepared and the matter is put to the Professional Conduct Panel for consideration. The Panel will decide if there has been misconduct. If there has not it will reject the complaint. If there has been misconduct it may reprimand or warn a member. It will refer serious matters to the Disciplinary Tribunal.

The Disciplinary Tribunal has the power to:

- exclude a person from membership
- reprimand or warn the member.

In addition the tribunal can order the legal executive to pay a fine up to £3,000 and costs.

**Figure 15.2** Regulation of legal personnel

|  | Barristers | Solicitors | Legal executives |
|---|---|---|---|
| **Representative body** | General Council of the Bar | Law Society | Chartered Institute of Legal Executives (CILEx) |
| **Regulatory body** | Bar Standards Board | Solicitors Regulatory Authority | CILEx Regulation Board |
| **Complaints** | Complaints about decisions of the regulatory bodies go to the Legal Ombudsman | | |

## 15.7.7 The Legal Ombudsman

The Legal Ombudsman's office was set up by the Office for Legal Complaints to deal with complaints against the legal profession. It deals with complaints against the handling of complaints by the Bar Standards Board, the Solicitors Regulatory Authority and CILEx Regulatory Board. It can order the legal professional who was complained about to:

■ apologise to the client
■ give back any documents the client might need
■ put things right if more work can correct what went wrong

■ refund or reduce the legal fees or
■ pay compensation of up to £30,000.

The main complaints made include excessive costs, deficient information on costs, delay, failure to follow instructions and failure to keep informed.

### Look online

Look at the Legal Ombudsman's website www.legalombudsman.org.uk and find a case study of a complaint. You could use this as the basis of a presentation to your class.

---

### Check your understanding

1  Which one body deals with client's complaints about the service provided by their legal professional?

   A  Legal Services Board

   B  Legal Ombudsman

   C  Legal Complaints Board

   D  Legal Services Agency

2  Suggest why it may be preferable for an accused to have legal representation in a criminal court case.

3  Explain the different sources of legal advice available to someone who is owed £50,000 and if the case goes to court, suggest which legal professional could be instructed for the court case.

## Summary

- Barristers:
  - can be self-employed or work for an organisation: they must be a member of one of the four Inns of Court
  - have to pass the Bar Professional Training Course and do pupillage before they can practise
  - (most) do court work: they have full rights of audience
  - are represented by the General Council of the Bar: their regulatory body is the Bar Standards Board.
- Solicitors:
  - can work in a solicitors' firm or for an organisation: they must belong to the Law Society
  - have to pass the Legal Training Course and do a two-year training contract
  - do mostly office-based work, but can present cases in the Magistrates' Court and County Court; they can also qualify for rights of audience in higher courts
  - are represented by the Law Society: their regulatory body is the Solicitors Regulatory Authority.
- Legal executives:
  - work in a solicitors' firm or other legal organisation
  - have to pass the Professional Higher Diploma in Law and work for at least five years
  - do the more straightforward matters: they have very limited rights of audience
  - are represented by CILEx: their regulatory body is the CILEx Regulation Board.
- Queen's Counsel:
  - are barristers of ten years' standing; solicitors with higher rights of advocacy can apply to become a Queen's Counsel
  - do more complex cases.
- Legal Ombudsman:
  - hears complaints about the regulatory bodies' failure to deal properly with clients' complaints
  - can order an apology, putting things right, a refund or reduction in legal fees, compensation.

# 16 The judiciary

After reading this chapter you should be able to:
- Understand the different types of judge
- Understand the role of judges in civil and criminal courts
- Understand how the independence of the judiciary is ensured
- Comment on the reasons for and the advantages of judicial independence
- Understand the methods by which judicial independence is achieved.

British Circuit Judges walk to the Houses of Parliament

## 16.1 Introduction

When speaking of judges as a group, we refer to them as the judiciary. There are many different levels of judges, but their basic function is the same. Their main role is to make decisions in respect of disputes. This they must do in a fair, unbiased way, applying the law and the legal rules of England and Wales.

The judiciary is divided into what are known as 'superior' judges (those in the High Court and above) and 'inferior' judges (those in the lower courts). This distinction affects training, work and, in particular, the terms on which they hold office. So it is important to start by understanding which judges sit in which court.

## 16.2 Types of judges

### 16.2.1 Superior judges

Superior judges are those in the Supreme Court, the Court of Appeal and the High Court. They are:
- the Justices of the Supreme Court
- the Lord Justices of Appeal in the Court of Appeal
- High Court Judges (also known as puisne (pronounced 'pew-nay') judges) who sit in the three divisions of the High Court; judges in the Queen's Bench Division of the High Court also sit to hear serious cases in the Crown Court.

The head of the judiciary is the Lord Chief Justice.

### 16.2.2 Inferior judges

The inferior judges include:
- Circuit Judges who sit in both the Crown Court and the County Court
- recorders who are part-time judges who usually sit in the Crown Court, though some hear cases in the County Court
- District Judges who hear small claims and other matters in the County Court
- District Judges (Magistrates' Courts) who sit in Magistrates' Courts in London and other major towns and cities
- tribunal judges.

## 16.3 Qualifications, selection and appointment

### 16.3.1 Qualifications

The relevant qualifications for the different judicial posts are set out in the Courts and Legal Services Act 1990 as amended by the Tribunals, Courts and Enforcement Act 2007. Qualifications to become a judge are based on legal qualifications plus relevant legal experience for a number of years.

### 16.3.2 Selection

Up to 2005, selection of superior judges was done by the Lord Chancellor. The system was secretive. In addition, the Lord Chancellor is a political appointment. This meant selection of judges was not independent from political influence.

The system was changed by the Constitutional Reform Act 2005 which established the Judicial Appointments Commission to deal with the selection of judges. This Commission advertises vacancies for judicial posts, interviews applicants and recommends to the Lord Chancellor who should be appointed.

### 16.3.3 Appointment

Once a candidate has been selected, the appointment is made by the Queen. This keeps selection and appointment separate from the government.

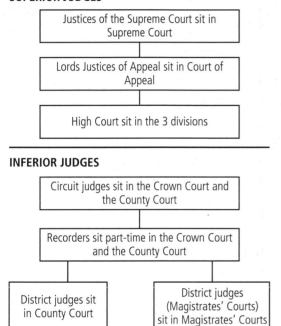

**SUPERIOR JUDGES**

| Justices of the Supreme Court sit in Supreme Court |
| --- |
| Lords Justices of Appeal sit in Court of Appeal |
| High Court sit in the 3 divisions |

**INFERIOR JUDGES**

| Circuit judges sit in the Crown Court and the County Court |
| --- |
| Recorders sit part-time in the Crown Court and the County Court |

| District judges sit in County Court | District judges (Magistrates' Courts) sit in Magistrates' Courts |
| --- | --- |

**Figure 16.1** The hierarchy of judges

## 16.4 Role of judges

### 16.4.1 Justices of the Supreme Court

Judges in the Supreme Court hear about 100 cases each year. These are appeals. They can be in civil or criminal cases. However, the majority of cases are civil appeals. A case can only be appealed to the Supreme Court if there is a point of law involved. Often civil cases involve complicated and technical areas of law such as planning law or tax law.

The Justices of the Supreme Court must sit as an uneven number panel (minimum three judges) to hear a case.

Any decision the Supreme Court makes on a point of law becomes a precedent for all lower courts to follow. You can find reports of cases decided by the Supreme Court at www.supremecourt.uk.

The Supreme Court

### 16.4.2 Lords Justices of Appeal

All their work is concerned with appeals. The Lords Justices of Appeal sit in both the civil and criminal divisions of the Court of Appeal, so they deal with both civil and criminal cases. Their workload is much heavier than the Supreme Court.

On the criminal side they will hear over 7,000 applications for leave to appeal against sentence or conviction. These are dealt with by one judge. Only about a quarter of these get leave to appeal, so the full court then has about 1,800 criminal appeals to hear. In addition, they hear over 3,000 civil appeals. These may be appeals against the finding of liability or an appeal about the remedy awarded, e.g. the amount of money given as damages.

Court of Appeal judges usually sit as a panel of three to hear cases. On rare occasions in important cases, there may be a panel of five. Decisions by the Court of Appeal on points of law become precedents which lower courts must follow.

### 16.4.3 High Court Judges

The main function of High Court Judges is to try cases. These are known as cases at first instance because it is the first time the case has been heard by a court. They will hear evidence from witnesses, decide what the law is and make the decision as to which side has won the case. If the claim is for damages (an amount of money) the judge decides how much should be awarded to the winning claimant.

When hearing first instance cases, judges sit on their own.

High Court Judges also hear some appeals. These are mainly from civil cases tried in the County Court.

**Figure 16.2** The role of judges

| In appellate courts | Hear appeals for the decision of the court below<br>The reasons for the decision can form a precedent which has to be followed in later cases |
|---|---|
| In civil courts | Sit alone to decide facts and law, make decision of which party wins case, award damages |
| In criminal courts | **Crown Court**<br>Sit with a jury of 12. Judge decides law: jury decides facts and verdict: if defendant is guilty, the judge decides the sentence<br>**Magistrates' Court**<br>District Judge sits on own and makes decisions about law and facts: decides if defendant is guilty or not guilty; decides sentence where defendant is guilty |

The judges in the Queen's Bench Division also hear criminal appeals from the Magistrates' Courts by a special case stated method. These are appeals on law only. When sitting to hear appeals, there will be a panel of two judges.

Judges from the Queen's Bench Division also sit in the Crown Court to hear criminal trials. When they do this they sit with a jury. The jury decides the facts and the judge decides the law. Where a defendant pleads guilty or is found guilty by a jury, the judge then has to decide on the sentence.

### 16.4.4 Inferior judges

Circuit Judges sit in the County Court to hear civil cases and also in the Crown Court to try criminal cases. They decide the law and the facts. They make the decision on who has won the case.

In criminal cases they sit with a jury. The jury decides the facts and the judge decides the law. Where a defendant pleads guilty or is found guilty by a jury, the judge then has to decide on the sentence.

Recorders are part-time judges who are appointed for a period of five years. They are used mainly in the Crown Court to try criminal cases, but some sit in the County Court to decide civil cases.

District Judges sit in the County Court to deal with small claims cases (under £10,000) and can also hear other cases for larger amounts.

District Judges (Magistrates' Courts) try criminal cases in the magistrates' courts. They sit on their own and decide facts and law. When a defendant pleads guilty or is found guilty, they also have to decide on the sentence.

# 16.5 Independence of the judiciary

Judges in the English system can be thought of as being independent in a number of ways.

## 16.5.1 Security of tenure of superior judges

Superior judges have security of tenure in that they cannot be dismissed by the government. This right originated in the Act of Settlement 1701 which allowed them to hold office while of good behaviour. Before 1700 the monarch could dismiss judges at will. The same provision is now contained in the Senior Courts Act 1981 for High Court Judges and Lords Justices of Appeal, and in the Constitutional Reform Act 2005 for the Justices of the Supreme Court.

As a result they can only be removed by the monarch following a petition presented to her by both Houses of Parliament. This gives superior judges protection from political whims and allows them to be independent in their judgments.

This power to remove a superior judge has never been used for an English judge, though it was used in 1830 to remove an Irish judge, Jonah Barrington, who had misappropriated £700 from court funds.

## 16.5.2 Tenure of inferior judges

These do not have the same security of tenure of office as superior judges. The Lord Chancellor, with the consent of the Lord Chief Justice, has the power to dismiss inferior judges for incapacity or misbehaviour.

A criminal conviction for dishonesty is obviously misbehaviour and would lead to the dismissal of the judge concerned. This has happened in the 1970s in the case of Bruce Campbell, a Circuit Judge, who was convicted of evading customs duty on cigarettes and whisky. It also happened in 2014 in the case of Constance Briscoe, a Recorder, who was convicted and imprisoned for perverting the course of justice. She had lied and then altered her witness statement regarding her involvement in a case where a Cabinet Minister and his wife had 'swapped driving points'.

## Complaints

Complaints against judges are investigated by the Judicial Conduct Investigations Office. If they find the complaint to be true, the matter is reported to the Lord Chancellor and the Lord Chief Justice. The offending judge can be warned or reprimanded about his conduct or in serious cases the judge can be removed from office. Judges have been removed from office for being an undischarged bankrupt or for failing to pay child maintenance and as result have been given a suspended committal to prison order.

The fact that complaints are investigated by an independent office helps to maintain judicial independence.

## 16.5.3 Immunity from suit

Judges are given immunity from prosecution for any acts they carry out in performance of their judicial function.

They also have immunity from being sued in a civil case for actions taken or decisions made in the course of their judicial duties. This was confirmed in *Sirros v Moore* (1975) and is a key factor in ensuring judicial independence in decision making.

### *Sirros v Moore* (1975)

In a case in the Crown Court, the judge wrongly ordered someone's detention. That person started a claim for false imprisonment against the judge.

The Court of Appeal held that, although the detention had been unlawful, no action could be taken against the judge as he had acted in good faith, believing he had the power to imprison.

Judges also benefit from immunity from being sued for defamation for the things they say about parties or witnesses in the course of hearing cases. Immunity from suit allows a judge to perform his duties without fear of repercussions. It gives judges complete independence. A judge would only be liable if he was not acting in a judicial capacity or if he knew that he had no jurisdiction to do what he did.

## 16.5.4 Independence from the executive

Superior judges cannot be dismissed by the government, and in this way they can truly be said to be independent of the government. They can make decisions which may displease the government without the threat of dismissal.

Judicial independence is now guaranteed under s 3 of the Constitutional Reform Act 2005. This states that the Lord Chancellor, other ministers in the government and anyone with responsibility for matters relating to the judiciary or the administration of justice must uphold the continued independence of the judiciary.

The section also specifically states that the Lord Chancellor and other ministers must not seek to influence particular judicial decisions.

The fact that judges are now recommended for appointment by the Judicial Appointments Commission also helps to keep judges independent from the executive.

## Independence from the legislature

Judges generally are not involved in the law making functions of Parliament. Full-time judges are not allowed to be members of the House of Commons, although the rule is not as strict for part-time judges so that recorders and assistant recorders can be Members of Parliament. There used to be judges in the House of Lords when the Appellate Committee of the House of Lords was the final court of appeal. The main reason for the creation of the Supreme Court in 2009 was to separate the judiciary from the legislature.

## 16.5.5 Independence from case

Judges must not try any case where they have any interest in the issue involved. The *Pinochet* case in 1998 reinforced this rule. In that case the House of Lords judges heard an appeal by Augusto Pinochet, the former head of the state of Chile. There was a claim to extradite him to Chile to face possible trial for crimes involving torture and deaths which had occurred there while he was head of state.

Amnesty International, the human rights movement, had been granted leave to participate in the case.

**Figure 16.3** Judicial independence

| Way in which independence is protected | Facts | Comment |
|---|---|---|
| **Security of tenure** | Superior judges can only be removed by the monarch following a petition presented to her by both Houses of Parliament<br>Inferior judges can be removed by the Lord Chancellor and Lord Chief Justice for misbehaviour or incapacity | Allows judges to make decisions against the government without fear of being dismissed |
| **Immunity from suit** | Cannot be sued for decisions they make in cases, even if they make a mistake | Allows a judge to perform his duties without fear of repercussions |
| **Independence from the executive** | Judicial independence is guaranteed under s 3 of the Constitutional Reform Act 2005 | The Lord Chancellor and other ministers must not seek to influence particular judicial decisions |
| **Independence from case** | Must not try any case where they have any interest in the issue involved | Judges must be completely impartial when making decisions |

After the House of Lords ruled that Pinochet could be extradited, it was discovered that one of the judges, Lord Hoffmann, was an unpaid director of Amnesty International Charitable Trust. Pinochet's lawyers asked for the decision to be set aside and to have the case re-heard by a completely independent panel of judges.

The Law Lords decided that their original decision could not be allowed to stand. Judges had to be seen to be completely unbiased. The fact that Lord Hoffmann was connected with Amnesty meant that he might be considered not to be completely impartial. The case was retried with a new panel of judges.

# 16.6 Reasons for judicial independence

An independent judiciary is seen as important in protecting the liberty of the individual from abuse of power by the executive. If the government could make judges decide the way the government wanted, this could lead to opponents of the government being imprisoned without reasonable cause. An independent judiciary is vital in a democracy.

In 2016 following the referendum in which the people voted to leave the European Union, the government announced that in 2017 it would start the process for leaving. There was then a challenge as to whether the executive could do this without consulting Parliament.

This challenge was heard in the courts and it was held that the government could not start the process for leaving without consulting Parliament. This decision was attacked by some people who felt that the judiciary should not interfere. However, the Prime Minister, Theresa May, publicly upheld the right of the judiciary to be independent.

In particular it is important that the government cannot force a judge to resign if that judge makes a decision with which the government of the day disagrees. In judicial review cases, judges often have to decide if an act or decision by a government department is reasonable. It is important that the judges can carry out this function without fear of repercussions.

It is also important that judges should be impartial in their decisions. It is vital that each judge is able to decide cases solely on the evidence presented in court by the parties and in accordance with the law.

Judges must be free to exercise their judicial powers without interference from litigants, the state, the media or powerful individuals or entities, such as large companies.

Judicial independence is important whether the judge is dealing with a civil or a criminal case. Individuals involved in any kind of case before the courts need to be sure that the judge dealing with their case cannot be influenced by an outside party or by the judge's own personal interests.

## 16.7 Advantages of judicial independence

Because judges are independent, decisions are made only on the basis of the facts of the case and law. This ensures fairness in all cases and is an important advantage of judicial independence.

Another important advantage is that the judiciary are able to protect citizens against unlawful acts of government. There can be an impartial judicial review of acts or decisions by the government.

Also the public have confidence in our judicial system. They know that their cases will be decided fairly and in accordance with the law.

### Check your understanding

1 Which one of these judges does not sit in the Crown Court?

A High Court Judge

B Lord Justice of Appeal

C Recorder

D Circuit Judge

2 Explain the role of a judge in a civil claim for negligence.

3 Examine the main ways in which judicial independence is maintained and discuss why it is important that we have a system of judicial independence.

### Summary

- There are different types of judge in each level of the courts.
- Judges are selected by the Judicial Appointments Commission which makes recommendations to the Lord Chancellor.
- The role of judges varies according to the court they are sitting in:
  - appellate courts – judges hear appeals which can involve points of law, and decisions may create precedents
  - civil courts at first instance – judge decides facts, law and awards appropriate remedy
  - criminal courts:
    - Crown Court – judge decides law, jury decides verdict, judge passes sentence
    - Magistrates' Court – judge decides law, verdict and passes sentence.

- For independence of the judiciary it is important that judges
  - have security of tenure
  - are immune from suit
  - are independent from the executive
  - are impartial in all cases.
- Judicial independence is needed to protect the liberty of the individual and for judges to be able to act without pressure and without fear of repercussions.
- The advantages of judicial independence are:
  - ensures fairness in all cases
  - protects citizens against unlawful acts of government
  - public confidence.

# 17 Access to justice and funding

After reading this chapter you should be able to:
- Have a basic understanding of the different sources of legal advice available
- Have a basic understanding of the ways of privately funding a case
- Have a basic understanding of public funding available in civil cases
- Have a basic understanding of public funding available in criminal cases

## 17.1 Access to justice

Where a person cannot get the help he needs, he is being denied access to justice. Access to justice involves both an open system of justice and also being able to fund the costs of a case.

However, the problem of cost still remains a major hurdle. The cost of civil cases in the High Court may run into hundreds of thousands of pounds. Even in the cheaper County Court, the cost will possibly be more than the amount of money recovered in damages. There is the additional risk in all civil cases that the loser has to pay the winner's costs.

In criminal cases, a person's liberty may be at risk and it is essential that he should be able to defend himself properly.

For these reasons there are many sources of free legal advice available.

## 17.2 Sources of legal advice

When someone has a legal problem it is important that he should be able to get help and advice about it.

A number of different advice schemes are available. Some of these are by telephone or on a website. Others also provide face-to-face advice. Important sources of advice include Citizens Advice Bureau and law centres.

In addition, there are other agencies which offer specialist advice on certain topics, for example trade unions will help members with legal problems, particularly in work-related matters. There are also charities, such as Shelter which offers advice to people with housing problems.

### 17.2.1 Help lines

Civil Legal Advice (CLA) is a government-funded scheme for providing advice. It is possible to get telephone help from CLA for problems such as:
- debt, if your home is at risk
- housing, e.g. if you are homeless or at risk of being evicted
- domestic abuse
- family issues, e.g. family mediation or if your child is being taken into care
- special education needs
- discrimination.

In the 12 months from July 2015 to June 2016, nearly 160,000 people rang the CLA telephone service.

### 17.2.2 Citizens Advice Bureaux

These were first set up in 1939 and today they give advice in over 2,500 locations throughout the country, with a bureau existing in most towns. They give general advice free to anyone on a variety of issues mostly connected to social welfare problems and debt, but they also advise on some legal matters. They can provide information on which local solicitors do legal aid work or give cheap or free initial interviews. Many have arrangements under which solicitors may attend at the bureau once a week or fortnight to give more qualified advice on legal matters.

The Citizens Advice Bureaux (CABx) is very important in providing legal advice. In 2014–15 they provided advice to 2.5 million people. Forty-eight per cent were by face-to-face contact, 45 per cent on the telephone and 7 per cent by email or webchat.

The main areas that Citizens Advice Bureau help with are:
- entitlement to benefits
- debt problems
- consumer issues
- housing issues
- employment issues.

### 17.2.3 Law centres

These offer a free, non-means-tested legal service to people in their area. The first law centre opened in North Kensington in 1970. This stated its aims as providing:

> " a first class solicitor's service to the people … a service which is easily accessible, not intimidating, to which they can turn for guidance as they would to their family doctor, or as someone who can afford it would turn to his family solicitor. "

Their aim is to provide free legal advice (and sometimes representation) in areas where there are few solicitors. Many of their clients are disadvantaged. In 2016 there were 44 law centres in operation.

### Funding

Law centres have always struggled to secure enough funding. Cuts by local authorities in their budgets have meant the withdrawal or reduction of funding from this source. As a result, some law centres have had to close. They also receive some funding from central government, but cuts have also been made to this funding. Some centres have received funds from the National Lottery fund where the law centre is part of a community project.

### Look online

Look at the website of the Law Centres Federation at www.lawcentres.org.uk. Find out the present number of law centres, and collect more information about the work they do.

### 17.2.4 Trade unions

Trade unions usually offer their members free legal advice for all work-related problems. Many trade unions also offer free legal advice for other legal problems such as personal injury cases. This help may be available even where the injury was not connected to work. Unite, the biggest trade union in the country, gives its members free legal advice and also free legal representation for any personal injury case.

### 17.2.5 Schemes run by lawyers

Some solicitors offer a free half-hour first interview. Local CABx will have a list of solicitors who offer this service.

#### Bar Pro Bono Unit

Since 1996, volunteer barristers have staffed the Bar Pro Bono Unit. This unit, situated in London, gives free advice to those who cannot afford to pay and who cannot get legal aid. They will give advice on any area of law and will also, where necessary, represent the client in court proceedings.

### 17.2.6 Advice in criminal cases

Anyone held as a suspect at a police station has the right to free legal advice. There is a duty solicitor scheme available 24 hours a day. This is government funded. In 2016 advice was given to over 650,000 suspects at police stations. The advice may be by telephone or face to face.

**Figure 17.1** Where to get advice in civil cases

| Source | Fact | Comment |
| --- | --- | --- |
| **Help line** | Civil Legal Advice – government run | Nearly 160,000 calls in year |
| **Citizens Advice Bureaux** | Operate in about 2,500 locations throughout the country | Provide advice to about 2.5 million people a year |
| **Law centres** | Funding cuts have reduced numbers | Operate in disadvantaged areas |
| **Trade unions** | Offer members free legal advice | Usually only for work-related issues, but may also include personal injury cases |
| **Schemes run by lawyers** | Solicitors may offer a free half-hour interview<br>Bar Pro Bono Unit | London-based but will advise on any area of law |

# 17.3 Private funding of cases

## 17.3.1 Own resources

Anyone who can afford it can pay for a solicitor and/ or a barrister to deal with a legal matter.

There are firms of solicitors in most towns. However, some solicitors specialise in certain types of work. If your legal problem is in an unusual area of law, then it may be necessary to travel to another town to find a solicitor who can deal with it.

The bigger firms of solicitors work in the major cities, in particular London. They often specialise in commercial law and the majority of their clients are businesses.

Consulting a solicitor can be expensive. The average cost of a solicitor outside London is about £150 an hour. For a big London firm of solicitors, the charges are usually at least £600 an hour and can be as much as £1,000 an hour.

On issues of civil law, it is also possible to consult a barrister directly, without going to a solicitor first. This can be cheaper than using a solicitor because barristers do not have such high business expenses as solicitors.

## 17.3.2 Insurance

Another way of funding a court case is by legal insurance. Most motor insurance policies offer cover (for an additional small amount) for help with legal fees in cases arising from road accidents. Policies for home insurance will offer cover for any legal claims arising such as a visitor being injured on the premises.

There are also policies purely for insurance against legal costs. These can be 'before the event', that is when there is no known legal claim. There is also 'after the event' insurance, which is often used alongside a conditional fee agreement. See section 17.3.3 below.

### Activity

Advise where it might be possible for each of the following people to get legal advice:

1 Aylmer has been arrested and taken to a police station to be questioned about a robbery the police suspect him of being involved in.

2 Benjamin has a dispute with his employers regarding his employment contract.

3 Charity has been injured when a car in which she was passenger overturned because the driver was driving too fast.

4 Denzil has a dispute with his landlord. Denzil is unemployed.

## 17.3.3 Conditional fee agreements

One of the main problems of taking a case to court is that it is difficult to estimate how long it will last or how much it will cost. If a person is funding his own case, this is a major problem for him. Also, if he loses the case, he may have to pay the costs of the other party. The combined costs of the case can be many thousands of pounds. In order to overcome these problems, a conditional fee agreement (CFA) can be used in all civil cases except family cases.

CFAs cannot be used in criminal cases.

### How conditional fees work

The solicitor and client agree on the fee that would normally be charged for such a case. The agreement will also set out what the solicitor's success fee will be if he wins the case.

Many conditional fee agreements will be made on the basis that if the case is lost, the client pays nothing. Because of this sort of agreement, the scheme is often referred to as 'no win, no fee'. However, some solicitors may prefer to charge a lower level fee, for example half the normal fee, even if the case is lost.

If the case is won, the client has to pay the normal fee plus the success fee.

### Success fee

The success fee could be up to 100 per cent of the normal fee. However, there is a 'cap' on the success fee in personal injuries cases which prevents it from being more than 25 per cent of the damages (amount of money) that the client wins as compensation. This protects the client from having to pay more than he won as compensation. Even so, it can mean that the client is left with very little of his damages. This is easier to understand by looking at the examples given in Figure 17.2.

A winning claimant cannot claim the success fee back from the losing defendant.

### Insurance premiums

Although the client will often not have to pay anything to his own lawyer if the case is lost, he will usually have to pay the costs of the other side. This can leave the client with a very large bill to pay. To help protect against this, it is possible to insure against the risk. This type of insurance is known as 'after-the-event' insurance. So, if the case is lost, the insurers will pay the other side's costs.

**Figure 17.2** Illustration of conditional fees

| Agreement | |
|---|---|
| Normal fee | £4,000 |
| Fee if case is lost | NIL |
| Success fee | £2,000 |
| Cap on success fee | 25% of damages |
| **Possible results of case** | **Client pays** |
| Case is lost | Nothing |
| Case is won: client gets £50,000 damages | £6,000 (£4,000 + £2,000) |
| Case is won: client gets £6,000 damages | £5,500 (£4,000 + £1,500*) |

*This £1,500 is because the success fee cannot be more than 25% of the damages

# 17.4 Public funding in civil cases

The funding for legal aid comes from the government's budget. This means that a set amount is made available each year. Also the amount set has to be considered against all the other claims on the budget, such as hospitals and health care and education. As a result, the government cannot afford to make legal aid available to everyone. In order to qualify, there is a strict means test.

## 17.4.1 Availability of legal aid

Under previous legal aid systems, aid was available for all cases except those specifically excluded. There always were certain types of case excluded, for example small claims.

Since 2013, the starting point is that legal aid is not available for civil cases unless it is in a category specifically mentioned in the Act or other regulations. The types of cases for which legal aid is allowed include those involving children's rights and those involving liberty of the individual. This includes cases being heard at Mental Health Tribunals as these are about whether a person should continue to be detained in a mental hospital and cases involving claims for asylum.

Breach of contract cases cannot get public funding, nor can claims in tort, such as claims for personal injury and trespass to the person, land or property.

## 17.4.2 Means testing

A person applying for government-funded advice or representation must show that he does not have enough money to pay for his own lawyer. In order to decide if the applicant is poor enough to qualify for government-funded help, his income and capital are considered.

People receiving Income Support or Income-Based Job Seekers' Allowance automatically qualify, assuming their disposable capital is below the set level. For all other applicants, their gross income is considered first. If a person's gross income is above a set amount per month, then they do not qualify.

### Disposable income

If the person's gross income is below the set amount per month, then their disposable income has to be calculated by starting with their gross income and taking away:

- tax and National Insurance
- housing costs
- childcare costs or maintenance paid for children
- an allowance for themselves and for each dependant.

If the amount left after making all deductions is below a minimum level, the applicant does not have to pay any contribution towards his funding. If the amount left is above a maximum level, the person will not qualify for any of the schemes provided by the Legal Aid Agency.

Where the disposable income is between the minimum level and the maximum level, the person applying for legal help has to pay a monthly contribution. The more in excess of the minimum, the greater the amount of the contribution. This idea of minimum and maximum levels is shown in Figure 17.3.

## Look online

The figures for the limits on income are increased slightly each year. You will be able to find the current figures on the Ministry of Justice's website: www.justice.gov.uk.

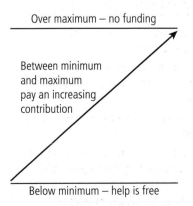

Over maximum – no funding

Between minimum and maximum pay an increasing contribution

Below minimum – help is free

**Figure 17.3** Increasing contributions for legal aid

## Disposable capital

Disposable capital means the assets of the person, such as money in a bank or savings account, stocks and shares, or expensive jewellery. In order to qualify for funding to take a court case, there is a maximum limit for disposable capital of £8,000.

If the assets are over £8,000, he must use his own money to fund any legal case, although once he has spent the money in excess of £8,000 he can become eligible for funding. Even where the disposable capital is below £8,000, he can be asked to pay a contribution towards his case.

Where a person owns a home, the value of that home is taken into account in deciding the disposable capital. This is so even though the person may have a large mortgage. Only the first £100,000 of any mortgage is deducted from the value of the home. This rule means that any person can be regarded as having too much disposable capital because of the value of their house, although in reality they might have no spare money.

# 17.5 Public funding in criminal cases

Since 2013, criminal legal aid services have been under the Legal Aid Agency in the Ministry of Justice. The agency makes contracts with law firms to provide legal services to people charged with criminal offences. Most service providers are solicitors.

In order to get representation at court for a criminal case, the defendant has to qualify under the 'interests of justice' test. There is also a means test.

## 17.5.1 Interests of justice

A defendant will only get help with legal funding for representation in court if he can show that he comes within at least one of the five 'interests of justice' factors. These factors are:

1   Whether, if any matter arising in the proceedings is decided against him, the individual would be likely to lose his liberty or livelihood or suffer serious damage to his reputation.
2   The case will involve consideration of a point of law.
3   The individual is unable to understand the proceedings in court or to state his own case.

4   The case may involve the tracing, interviewing or expert cross-examination of witnesses.
5   It is in the interests of another person that the individual be represented (such as in a rape case).

## 17.5.2 Magistrates' Court means testing

As well as having to qualify under the 'interests of justice' test, there is a strict means test in the Magistrates' Court. It is often described as the 'in or out' scheme, where applicants are either:

■   eligible for legal aid (because they pass the initial or full means test) or
■   ineligible (because they fail the initial or full means test) and are therefore expected to pay for legal representation privately.

Those who are on Income Support, defendants under the age of 16 and those under 18 in full-time education automatically pass the means test. For everyone else, the test starts with a first-stage simple means test which is calculated on gross annual income. If his income is too high on this test, the defendant does not qualify for legal aid. If a defendant's income is below a certain level, he qualifies. For those in the middle bracket, they are further means tested to calculate their disposable income and if they are above the set limit, they will not get legal aid.

The levels allowed are very low. This means that about three-quarters of adults do not qualify for legal aid in criminal cases in the Magistrates' Courts.

## 17.5.3 Crown Court means testing

The main difference from the Magistrates' Courts is that there is no upper limit on disposable income. Most defendants can receive legal aid. It is free for those on low incomes. Those on higher incomes (but below £37,500 disposable income) have to pay towards their legal aid. Those whose disposable income is above £37,500 (figure in 2016) are ineligible for legal aid and will have to pay privately for representation in court.

Where a defendant has to pay, then the higher his income, the higher the contribution he will have to pay towards the case. The maximum amount he has to pay through contributions from his income is set by the type of case. If a defendant is found guilty, he may also have to pay extra from his capital.

If a defendant is found not guilty, any contributions paid will normally be refunded.

## Tip

Read questions carefully. The question may ask only about civil legal help or only about criminal legal help. Make sure you write about the one asked for.

## Check your understanding

1 Which one of the following statements correctly describes conditional fee agreements?

   A It is a publicly funded method of taking a case to court

   B It can be used for representation in the Crown Court

   C If the claimant does not win his case, he does not have to pay his lawyer's costs

   D It can only be used if it is in the interests of justice

2 Explain two ways in which a person could fund legal advice for a civil law claim.

3 Gary, who is currently unemployed, has been charged with robbery and will be tried at Crown Court. Explain to him the different ways to pay for a lawyer to represent him in court and advise him whether he is likely to get public funding.

## Summary

- Legal advice is available from:
  - helplines
  - Citizens Advice Bureaux
  - law centres
  - trade unions
  - schemes run by lawyers (free half-hour offered by solicitors and Bar Pro Bono Unit).
- Advice in criminal cases is available under the government scheme for those being questioned at a police station.
- Legal advice and representation can be paid for privately through the person's own resources.
- Insurance can help pay for the costs of a case, especially in cases arising from road accidents.

- Conditional fee agreements can be used to fund a case – these often operate on a 'no win, no fee' basis.
- Public funding for representation in civil cases is limited:
  - it is only available for a few categories of case
  - it is means tested.
- Public finding for representation in criminal cases is also limited:
  - it must be in the interest of justice
  - it is means tested.

# Criminal law

# 18 Rules of criminal law

After reading this chapter you should be able to:

■ Understand the definition of a crime
■ Understand the rules and principles of criminal liability including:
  – the concept of the elements of *actus reus* and *mens rea* in crimes
  – the standard of proof in criminal cases
  – the burden of proof in criminal cases

## 18.1 Defining a crime

### 'Murder' 'Robbery' 'Theft'

Virtually everyone can identify these as criminal offences. But how many others can you name? There are thousands of different offences. They vary from the most serious, such as murder and manslaughter, to minor breaches of regulations, such as selling a lottery ticket to someone who is under the age of 16.

With such a wide range of criminal offences, it is difficult to have a general definition covering all offences. The only way in which it is possible to define a crime is to say that it is conduct:

■ forbidden by the state
■ for which there is a punishment.

Lord Atkin supported this definition when, in the case of *Proprietary Articles Trade Association v Attorney-General for Canada* (1931), he said:

> 66 The criminal quality of an act cannot be discerned by intuition (made out by 'gut feeling'); nor can it be discovered by reference to any standard but one: is the act prohibited with penal consequences? 99

This is the only definition which covers all crimes. However, there have been other definitions. An American legal writer, Herbert Packer, thought that, to be a crime:

■ the conduct must be wrongful and
■ it must be necessary to condemn or prevent such conduct.

However, what is considered criminal will change over time. This can be caused, for example, by changing views in society, or changes in technology which lead to the need for new offences to cover new situations.

Changing views on what is criminal can be demonstrated by the changes in the law on consenting homosexual acts. In 1885 the Criminal Law Amendment Act made consenting homosexual acts criminal even if they were in private. This remained as the law until 1967 when the Sexual Offences Act 1967 decriminalised such behaviour between those aged 21 and over. The age was reduced to 18 in 1994 and finally, in 2000, it was further reduced to 16. This age brings the law into line with consenting sexual acts between heterosexuals.

New technology can lead to new areas of criminal law. For example, the invention of the motor car over a hundred years ago led to new road traffic laws. These have been added to over the years so that we now have such offences as driving without a licence, driving while over the legal limit of alcohol, having tyres which do not have the right level of tread and causing death by dangerous driving.

Computers and the internet have led to new offences being created, to protect people from internet fraud and to prevent pornographic material from being viewed or downloaded.

## 18.1.1 The role of the state

The criminal law is mainly set down by the state. This can be by passing an Act of Parliament such as the Theft Act 1968 or by the issuing of regulations.

A breach of criminal law can lead to a penalty, such as imprisonment or a fine, being imposed on the defendant in the name of the state. Therefore, bringing a prosecution for a criminal offence is usually seen as part of the role of the state. Indeed, the majority of criminal prosecutions are conducted by the Crown Prosecution Service (CPS) which is the state agency for criminal prosecutions.

However, it is also possible for a private organisation to start a prosecution. For example, the RSCPA regularly brings prosecutions against people for offences of cruelty towards or neglect of animals.

## 18.1.2 Conduct criminalised by the judges

Although in the vast majority of offences the state decides what conduct is considered to be criminal, some conduct is criminalised by judges rather than the state. This occurs where judges create new criminal offences through case law. In modern times this only happens on rare occasions because nearly all law is made by Parliament. An example of conduct criminalised by judges is the offence of conspiracy to corrupt public morals. This offence has never been enacted by Parliament. However, the judges recognised that it existed in *Shaw v DPP* (1962).

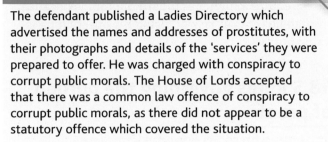

### Shaw v DPP (1962)

The defendant published a Ladies Directory which advertised the names and addresses of prostitutes, with their photographs and details of the 'services' they were prepared to offer. He was charged with conspiracy to corrupt public morals. The House of Lords accepted that there was a common law offence of conspiracy to corrupt public morals, as there did not appear to be a statutory offence which covered the situation.

Another offence which has been created by the judges in modern times is marital rape. This was declared a crime in *R v R* (1991). Before that case, the law held that a husband could not be guilty of raping his wife, as she was assumed, by the fact of marriage, to consent to sexual intercourse with him. When the House of Lords decided the case of *R v R* they pointed out that society's views on the position of women had changed. The House of Lords said:

> ** The status of women and the status of a married woman in our law have changed quite dramatically. A husband and wife are now for all practical purposes equal partners in marriage. **

The House of Lords ruled that if a wife did not consent to intercourse, then the husband could be guilty of raping her.

## 18.2 Elements of a crime

There are many offences aimed at different 'wrong' behaviour. For AQA AS you have to study non-fatal offences against the person. For A-level you will also have to study murder, manslaughter, theft and robbery. However, there are general principles which apply to all offences.

The most important principle is that for all crimes, except crimes of strict liability, there are two elements which must be proved by the prosecution. These are:

- *actus reus* and
- *mens rea*.

These terms come from a Latin maxim (*actus non facit reum nisi mens sit rea*) which means 'the act itself does not constitute guilt unless done with a guilty mind'. Both an act (or omission) and a guilty mind must be proved for most criminal offences.

### 18.2.1 *Actus reus*

'*Actus reus*' has a wider meaning than 'an act', as it can cover omissions or a state of affairs. The term '*actus reus*' has been criticised as misleading. Lord Diplock in *Miller* (1983) preferred the term 'prohibited conduct', while the Law Commission in the Draft Criminal Code (1989) used the term 'external element'.

The conduct must be voluntary and the *actus reus* includes any required consequences caused by the prohibited conduct.

> See Chapter 19 for a detailed look at the concept of *actus reus*.

### Key term

*Actus reus* – this is an act, an omission or a state of affairs that is the voluntary prohibited conduct together with any required consequences caused by the prohibited conduct of an offence.

### 18.2.2 *Mens rea*

'*Mens rea*' translates as 'guilty mind' but this is also misleading. The Law Commission in the Draft Criminal Code (1989) used the term 'fault element'. The levels of 'guilty mind' required for different offences vary from the highest level, which is specific intention for some crimes, to much lower levels, such as negligence or knowledge of a certain fact, for less serious offences.

> The levels of *mens rea* are explained in detail in Chapter 20.

### Key term

*Mens rea* – the mental element (guilty mind) or the fault element in an offence.

**Figure 18.1** The elements of an offence

## Examples

The *actus reus* and *mens rea* will be different for different crimes. For example, in murder the *actus reus* is the killing of a human being, and the *mens rea* is causing the death 'with malice aforethought' which means that the killer must have intended to kill or to cause grievous bodily harm. For theft, the *actus reus* is the appropriation of property belonging to another, while the *mens rea* is doing this dishonestly and with the intention permanently to deprive the other of the property.

The *actus reus* and the *mens rea* must be present together, but if there is an ongoing act, then the existence of the necessary *mens rea* at any point during that act is sufficient. This is explained fully in Chapter 20. However, even where the *actus reus* and *mens rea* are present, the defendant may be not guilty if he has a defence (see section 18.3).

### 18.2.3 Strict liability offences

There are some crimes which are an exception to the general rule that there must be both *actus reus* and *mens rea*. These are crimes of strict liability, where the prosecution need prove only the *actus reus*; no mental element is needed for guilt.

> See Chapter 21 for discussion on crimes of strict liability.

## 18.3 Rules of defence

Although the defendant may have done the required act, there are a number of general defences that may be available which will lead to a 'not guilty' verdict.

You do not need to study defences for AS. For A-level, you have to study general defences of self-defence/prevention of crime, duress and duress of circumstances and mental capacity defences of insanity, automatism and intoxication. These topics are covered in Book 2.

## 18.4 Rules governing the standard of proof

The prosecution has to prove the case against the defendant. There are rules on the level to which the case has to be proved. This is referred to as the 'standard of proof'. The standard of proof in criminal cases is 'beyond reasonable doubt'. This is usually explained by the judge telling the jury that it should only convict if it is satisfied on the evidence, so that it is sure of the defendant's guilt.

This is a higher standard than the one used in civil cases. Civil cases have to be proved only 'on the balance of probabilities'. The reason that criminal cases require a higher standard of proof is because the defendant is at risk of losing his liberty if he is found guilty.

## 18.5 Rules governing the burden of proof

An accused person is presumed innocent until proven guilty. The burden of proof is on the prosecution. This means that the prosecution must prove both the required *actus reus* and the required *mens rea*. An important case on these principles is *Woolmington* (1935).

### *Woolmington v DPP* (1935)

D's wife had left him and gone to live with her mother. D went to the mother's house and shot his wife dead. He claimed that he had decided to ask his wife to come back to him and, if she refused, that he would commit suicide. For this reason he was carrying under his coat a loaded sawn-off shotgun. When his wife indicated that she would not return to him, he threatened to shoot himself and brought the gun out to show her he meant it. As he brought it out, it somehow went off, killing his wife. He claimed that this was a pure accident.

The judge at the trial told the jury that the prosecution had to prove beyond reasonable doubt that the defendant killed his wife. He then went on to tell them that, if the prosecution satisfied them of that, the defendant had to show that there were circumstances which made that killing pure accident. This put the burden of proof on the defendant to prove the defence. In the House of Lords it was held that this was not correct.

The decision in this case made several important points which the House of Lords regarded as fixed matters on English law. These were:

- the prosecution must prove the case
- this rule applies to all criminal cases
- the rule must be applied in any court where there is a criminal trial (currently the Magistrates' Court and the Crown Court)

- guilt must be proved beyond reasonable doubt and
- a reasonable doubt can be raised by evidence from either the prosecution or the defence.

## Tip

*The rules and principles set out in this chapter apply to all of the offences you will learn about.*

## Check your understanding

1 Which one statement accurately describes the concept of actus reus?

   A The mental element of an offence

   B The fault element of an offence

   C An offence where there is no need to prove a guilty mind

   D An act or omission which is prohibited conduct

2 Which one statement accurately describes the concept of mens rea?

   A The mental element of an offence

   B A prohibited act

   C A prohibited omission

   D An offence where there is no need to prove a guilty mind

3 Explain the standard of proof required in a criminal case and on whom the burden of proof lies.

## Summary

- A crime can be defined as conduct which is forbidden by the state and for which there is a punishment.
- Ideas of what conduct is criminal can change over time.
- Criminal law is mainly set down by the state, though some conduct is criminalised by judges.

- The two elements of any offence are *actus reus* and *mens rea*.
- The standard of proof is beyond reasonable doubt.
- The burden of proving guilt is on the prosecution: the defendant is presumed innocent until proven guilty.

# 19 Actus reus

After reading this chapter you should be able to:
- Understand the concept of *actus reus* including
  - when criminal liability can be imposed for a failure to act (omission)
  - the need for voluntariness
  - the legal rules on causation and consequences
- Analyse and evaluate the law on omission and causation
- Apply the law to factual situations

## 19.1 What is *actus reus*?

As already stated in Chapter 18, the *actus reus* is the physical element or the prohibited conduct of a crime. It can be an act, a failure to act (an omission) or a 'state of affairs'.

The prohibited conduct must be voluntary and where a consequence is required for the offence to be completed, the prohibited conduct must cause that consequence.

In most cases the prohibited conduct of the *actus reus* will be something the defendant does, but there are situations in which a failure to act is sufficient for the *actus reus*. These are set out at section 19.2. 'State of affairs' cases are considered at section 19.1.3.

### 19.1.1 Conduct crimes

For many crimes, it is not necessary for any consequence to be proved These are known as 'conduct' crimes. An example is theft where the prohibited conduct to be proved is that the defendant appropriated property belonging to another. It is not necessary to prove any consequence.

### 19.1.2 Consequence crimes

For some crimes the prohibited conduct must also result in a consequence. This means that the *actus reus* is only committed where, as well as the defendant doing (or failing to do) something, there is also a particular prohibited consequence caused by the defendant's conduct.

This can be seen in the offence of assault occasioning actual bodily harm (s 47 of the Offences Against

the Person Act 1861). There must be an application or threat of unlawful force but there must also be a consequence of 'actual bodily harm' – in other words, some injury to the victim. This could be a bruise, a broken nose or broken arm. It could even be psychiatric injury. But without the consequence of 'actual bodily harm' there cannot be a s 47 offence. The *actus reus* for s 47 is not complete.

### 19.1.3 'State of affairs' crimes

In other crimes the *actus reus* can be a state of affairs for which the defendant is responsible. An example is having an offensive weapon in a public place (s 1 of the Prevention of Crime Act 1953). The defendant does not have to do anything with the weapon, nor does it have to be visible. It is enough that he has it with him in a public place.

Another example is being in possession of a controlled drug (s 5 of the Misuse of Drugs Act 1971). It does not matter whether the defendant is going to use the drug himself or is going to hand it over to someone else. The fact that he is in possession of it is sufficient for the *actus reus* of the offence.

### 19.1.4 Voluntary nature of *actus reus*

The act or omission must be voluntary on the part of the defendant. If the defendant has no control over his actions then he has not committed the *actus reus*. In *Hill v Baxter* (1958) the court gave examples of where a driver of a vehicle could not be said to be doing the act of driving voluntarily. These included where a driver lost control of his vehicle because he was stung by a swarm of bees, or if he was struck on the head by a stone or had a heart attack while driving.

Other examples of an involuntary act include where the defendant hits another person because of a reflex action or a muscle spasm. Yet another is where one person pushes a second person, causing him to bump into a third person. In this situation the act of the second person who has been pushed is involuntary. Even though he has hit the third person, he has not committed the *actus reus* for any assault offence. Of course, the original 'pusher' can be liable. This was shown in the case of R v Mitchell (1983).

### R v Mitchell (1983)

D tried to push his way into a queue at the post office. A 72-year-old man told him off for this. D punched this man, causing him to stagger backwards into an

89-year-old woman. The woman was knocked over and injured, and a few days later died of her injuries. D was convicted of unlawful act manslaughter. The man who had been punched and fallen against the woman was not liable for any criminal act.

This also illustrates that the criminal law is concerned with fault on the part of the defendant. Where there is an absence of fault, then the defendant is usually not liable.

### 19.1.5 'Involuntariness'

There are some rare instances in which the defendant has been convicted even though he did not act voluntarily. These situations involve a 'state of affairs', but not one that the defendant entered into voluntarily. An example of this is the case of *R v Larsonneur* (1933).

---

#### *R v Larsonneur* (1933)

The defendant had been ordered to leave the United Kingdom. She decided to go to Eire, but the Irish police deported her and took her back to the UK. She did not wish to go back and was certainly not doing this voluntarily. When she landed in the UK she was immediately arrested and charged that being 'an alien to whom leave to land in the UK had been refused', she had been found in the UK. She was convicted because she was an alien who had been refused leave to land and she had been 'found in the UK'. It did not matter that she had been brought back by the Irish police against her will.

---

#### Tip

*Actus reus* is one of the essential elements needed to prove an offence. It is important to understand the basic concepts as you will need to show understanding of it and/or apply these rules in criminal law questions.

---

## 19.2 Omissions as *actus reus*

The normal rule is that an omission cannot make a person guilty of an offence. This was explained by Stephen J, a nineteenth-century judge, in the following way:

> 66 A sees B drowning and is able to save him by holding out his hand. A abstains from doing so in order that B may be drowned. A has committed no offence. 99

---

#### Activity

Read the following scenario and disc [...]
think Zoe should be guilty of an offe [...]

Zoe is sitting by a swimming pool in th [...]
Jason is swimming in the pool. He is th [...]
water and there are no other people ne [...]
gets out of the pool and while walking around it slips and falls into the water. He is knocked unconscious. Zoe sees this happen but she does nothing. Jason drowns.

**Question:**

Would it make any difference to your answer if Zoe could not swim?

---

### A 'Good Samaritan' law?

Some other countries have a law which is known as a 'Good Samaritan' law. It makes a person responsible for helping other people in an 'emergency situation', even though they are complete strangers. French law has this and an example was seen when Princess Diana's car crashed in Paris in 1997. Journalists who had been following her car took photographs of her, injured, in the car. They did not try to help her, even though she was critically injured. The French authorities threatened to charge these journalists under the French 'Good Samaritan' law.

There are problems in enforcing such a law. What if a 'rogue' pretends to be seriously hurt in order to lure a stranger to his assistance, so that the rogue can then rob the stranger? There is also the risk that an untrained person, by intervening, could do more harm to an injured person. Also, what is an 'emergency situation'? Who decides that there is an emergency so that the 'Good Samaritan' law is operating?

A problem would also arise if several people witnessed the incident. Do all of them have to help? Or is it enough if one of them helps? If one person helps, are the others still under a duty to help?

Finally, there is the question of whether would-be rescuers have to put themselves at risk in order to help. It seems unlikely that the law would require this. In the case of *Miller* (1983) (see section 19.2.1) the House of Lords thought that a defendant who has created the risk would only be expected to take reasonable steps. He would not be expected to put himself at risk. If this is the situation for the person who has caused the problem, then surely the same would have to apply to innocent passers-by?

157

## Exceptions to the rule

There are exceptions to the rule that an omission cannot make a person guilty of an offence. In some cases it is possible for a failure to act (an omission) to be the *actus reus*.

An omission is only sufficient for the *actus reus* where there is a duty to act. There are six ways in which such a duty can exist:

- a statutory duty
- a contractual duty
- a duty because of a relationship
- a duty which has been taken on voluntarily
- a duty through one's official position
- a duty which arises because the defendant has set in motion a chain of events.

### A statutory duty

An Act of Parliament can create liability for an omission. Examples include the offences of failing to stop or report a road traffic accident (s 170 of the Road Traffic Act 1988) and of failing to provide a specimen of breath (s 6 of the Road Traffic Act 1988). In fact, these offences can only be committed by failing to do something.

Another example where an Act of Parliament creates a duty is in s 1 of the Children and Young Persons Act 1933. This section puts parents who are legally responsible for a child under a duty for providing food, clothing, medical aid and lodging for their children. If a parent fails (omits) to do this, he can be guilty of the offence of wilful neglect.

A more recent example is the offence of allowing the death of a child or vulnerable adult under s 5 of the Domestic Violence, Crime and Victims Act 2004. This applies where a person in the same household fails to take such steps as he reasonably could have been expected to take to protect the victim.

### A contractual duty

In *R v Pittwood* (1902) a railway-crossing keeper omitted to shut the gates, with the result that a person crossing the line was struck and killed by a train. The keeper was guilty of manslaughter. A more modern example would be of a lifeguard at a pool who leaves his post unattended. His failure to do his duty could make him guilty of an offence if a swimmer were injured or drowned.

### A duty because of a relationship

This is usually a parent–child relationship as a parent has a duty to care for young children. A duty can also exist the opposite way round, where a grown-up child is caring for his elderly parent. A case involving a parent–child duty is R v *Gibbins and Proctor* (1918).

> ### *R v Gibbins and Proctor* (1918)
>
> The father of a seven-year-old girl lived with a partner. The father had several children from an earlier marriage. He and his partner kept the girl separate from the father's other children and deliberately starved her to death. They were both convicted of murder.
>
> The father had a duty to feed her because he was her parent, and the mistress was held to have undertaken to look after the children, including the girl, so she was also under a duty to feed the child. The omission or failure to feed her was deliberate with the intention of killing or causing serious harm to her. In these circumstances they were guilty of murder. The failure to feed the girl was enough for the *actus reus* of murder.

### A duty which has been undertaken voluntarily

In the above case of *Gibbins v Proctor* (1918) the partner had voluntarily undertaken to look after the girl. She therefore had a duty towards the child. When she failed to feed the child she was guilty of murder because of that omission.

Another example of where a duty had been undertaken voluntarily is R v *Stone and Dobinson* (1977).

> ### *R v Stone and Dobinson* (1977)
>
> Stone's elderly sister, Fanny, came to live with the defendants. Fanny was eccentric and often stayed in her room for several days. She also failed to eat. She eventually became bedridden and incapable of caring for herself. On at least one occasion Dobinson, Stone's partner, helped to wash Fanny and also occasionally prepared food for her. Fanny died from malnutrition. Both defendants were found guilty of her manslaughter.
>
> As Fanny was Stone's sister, he owed a duty of care to her. Dobinson had undertaken some care of Fanny and so also owed her a duty of care. The duty was either to help her themselves or to summon help from other sources. Their failure to do either of these meant that they were in breach of their duty.

A more recent case where a mother was guilty of manslaughter through her failure to act is R v *Evans* (2009).

## R v Evans (2009)

The victim (V), aged 16 and a heroin addict, lived with her mother and her older half-sister. The half-sister (D) bought some heroin and gave it to V who self-injected. Later it became obvious that V had overdosed. Neither the mother nor the half-sister tried to get medical help. Instead they put V to bed and hoped she would recover. V died.

Both the mother and D were convicted of gross negligence manslaughter. The mother clearly owed a duty of care to V as she was her daughter. D appealed, claiming that she did not owe a duty of care to a sister. The Court of Appeal upheld the conviction on the basis that D had created a state of affairs which she knew or ought reasonably to have known was threatening the life of V and therefore owed her a duty.

## A duty through one's official position

This is very rare but did happen in *R v Dytham* (1979).

## R v Dytham (1979)

D was a police officer who was on duty. He saw a man (V) being thrown out of a nightclub about 30 yards from where he was standing. Following the throwing out, there was a fight in which three men kicked V to death. D took no steps to intervene or to summon help. When the fight was over, D told a bystander that he was going off-duty and left the scene. He was convicted of misconduct in a public office.

Because Dytham was a police officer, he was guilty of wilfully and without reasonable excuse neglecting to perform his duty.

## A duty which arises because the defendant set in motion a chain of events

This concept of owing a duty and being liable through omission was created in the case of *R v Miller* (1983) where a squatter had accidentally started a fire.

## R v Miller (1983)

D was living in a squat. He fell asleep while smoking a cigarette. He awoke to find his mattress on fire. He did not attempt to put out the fire or to summon help but went into another room and went back to sleep. The house caught fire. He was convicted of arson.

In this case it was not the setting of the mattress on fire which made D guilty. Instead, it was the fact that he had failed to take reasonable steps to deal with the fire when he discovered that his mattress was on fire. This failure or omission meant that he had committed the *actus reus* for arson. The House of Lords pointed out that D was only expected to take reasonable steps. He did not have to put himself at risk. So, if, when he woke and found the fire, it was very small and could easily be put

out then he was expected to do that. However, if it was too dangerous for him to deal with it personally then his duty was to summon the fire brigade.

Another case where the defendant knew that there was a dangerous situation but failed to take any steps is *DPP v Santa-Bermudez* (2003).

## DPP v Santa-Bermudez (2003)

A policewoman, before searching the defendant's pockets, asked him if he had any needles or other sharp objects on him. The defendant said 'no', but when the police officer put her hand in his pocket she was injured by a needle which caused bleeding. The defendant was convicted of assault occasioning actual bodily harm under s 47 of the Offences Against the Person Act 1861.

In this case it was the failure to tell the police officer of the needle which made the defendant liable. He knew that there was danger to the police officer but failed to warn her about it. This failure was enough for the *actus reus* for the purposes of an assault causing actual bodily harm.

The case of *Evans* (2009) also illustrates the principle of a defendant being liable for failing to act after creating a state of affairs. Supplying heroin had created a state of affairs which she knew or ought reasonably to have known was threatening the life of V, but she did nothing about it. She could easily have called for medical assistance for V. The failure to do so made her liable for V's death.

**Figure 19.1** When omissions can be *actus reus*

| Source | Examples |
| --- | --- |
| Statutory duty | Failing to provide a specimen of breath (s 6 of the Road Traffic Act 1988). Wilful neglect (s 1 of the Children and Young Persons Act 1933) |
| Under a contract, especially of employment | *Pittwood* (1902) |
| Because of a relationship such as parent and child | *Gibbins and Proctor* (1918) *Evans* (2009) |
| A duty voluntarily undertaken, e.g. care of an elderly relative | *Stone and Dobinson* (1977) |
| Because of a public office, e.g. police officer | *Dytham* (1979) |
| As a result of a dangerous situation created by the defendant | *Miller* (1983) *Santa-Bermudez* (2003) *Evans* (2009) |

## 19.2.2 The duty of doctors

There can be cases where doctors decide to stop treating a patient. If this discontinuance of treatment is in the best interests of the patient then it is not an omission which can form the *actus reus*. This was decided in *Airedale NHS Trust v Bland* (1993).

### Airedale NHS Trust v Bland (1993)

Bland was a young man who had been crushed by the crowd at the Hillsborough football stadium tragedy in 1989. This had stopped oxygen getting to his brain and left him with severe brain damage. He was in a persistent vegetative state (PVS), unable to do anything for himself and unaware of what was happening around him. He was fed artificially through tubes. He had been in this state for three years and the doctors caring for him asked the court for a ruling that they could stop feeding him.

The court ruled that the doctors could stop artificially feeding Bland even though it was known that he would die as a result. This was held to be in his best interests.

## 19.2.3 Comment on the law of omissions

The first point is that the Latin phrase *actus reus* is not an accurate description of conduct which can be sufficient to make a person liable for an offence. *Actus reus* means an act: yet the law clearly recognises that a failure to act can be sufficient for liability. The Law Commission in its Draft Criminal Code (1989) preferred the phrase 'external element' and this is a more accurate description.

There are several other issues. These include:

- whether there should be wider liability for omissions such as the Good Samaritan law (discussed in section 19.2)
- the problems of deciding when a duty should be imposed so that an omission is sufficient for the *actus reus* of an offence
- whether a person should be liable for failure to act when they assume a duty
- omissions in medical treatment
- the justification for statutory imposition of liability for an omission.

### Good Samaritan law

As already pointed out, other countries have a law that places people under a duty to help. Although there are problems in having such a law (see section 19.2) it can be argued that the modern view of moral responsibility is in favour of such a duty.

What about the situation where it is clear that a child is going very near the edge of a cliff? The child's parents or guardians would be liable for failure to act if they did not warn the child and try to remove him from the danger. However, a stranger would not be liable. In today's society is this acceptable?

There are also objections to making people criminally liable for failure to act. Should ordinary people be forced to act as 'rescuers'? In a developed country, the state provides well-trained and well-equipped professionals such as the police, fire-brigade and ambulance crews to deal with emergency situations. These services are paid for through taxes, so it can be argued that every taxpayer is already doing his bit.

As already discussed in section 19.2 there is the risk that an untrained person might do more harm than good if he attempted to 'rescue' someone. Alternatively the rescuer might put his own life at risk, thereby causing more work for the emergency services and possibly leading to the loss of two lives.

A practical problem is the possibility that many people could be liable for one incident. What is the position if a commuter falls on to a railway line in the rush hour when the platform is full of people waiting for trains? Are all the people who see the person fall liable if they do not try to rescue him (if it is safe to do so) or alert station staff about it (if it is not safe to take more direct action)? It would be impractical to prosecute large numbers.

## Problems of deciding when a duty exists

It is not completely certain when a duty to act will exist. The existence of a duty is a matter of law for the judge to determine. The normal way of deciding this is, first, the judge at the trial will determine whether there is evidence capable of establishing a duty in law. The judge will then direct the jury that if they decide certain facts are proved, then a duty existed. Finally, the jury make the decision as to whether those facts are proved in the case and whether the duty has been broken.

This means that the law is capable of expanding to cover more situations. This was stated in *R v Khan and Khan* (1998).

### *R v Khan and Khan* (1998)

The defendants had supplied heroin to a new user who took it in their presence and then collapsed. They left her alone and by the time they returned to the flat she had died. Their conviction for unlawful act manslaughter was quashed but the Court of Appeal thought there could be a duty to summon medical assistance in certain circumstances, so that a defendant could be liable for failing to do so.

This point was also made in *R v Evans* (2009); see section 19.2.1.

The Court of Appeal stated *obiter* in *Khan and Khan* that duty situations could be extended to other areas. However, this could be argued to make the law too uncertain. In what new situations will it be decided that a failure to act can be sufficient for the *mens rea* of an offence?

## Assuming a duty

It can seem harsh that someone who accepts an adult into his home can be held to have assumed a duty towards that adult. This was the situation in *Stone and Dobinson* (1977), although there was also a blood relationship to the victim in that case. The victim was also a vulnerable person who had become incapable of looking after herself.

An adult is normally held to be responsible for his own life. In fact a mentally capable adult can refuse medical treatment even though this is likely to cause his death.

If the adult is vulnerable, then the argument for imposing a duty is that the person assuming the duty is in the best position to ensure that potential harm is avoided. He will know of the vulnerability of the victim when others do not. This is the reason for placing such a person under a duty to act and making him liable for failure to do anything.

There is also the question of what the defendant needs to do to discharge or fulfil his duty. Usually, such a duty can be fulfilled by summoning help. It is not necessary for the person to do more than that. In *Stone and Dobinson* the defendants were found guilty because they did not summon help.

## Medical treatment

One area where the law seems contradictory is in the duty of doctors. If doctors decide it is in the patient's best interests to withdraw feeding from that patient, then they are not liable for any offence in respect of the patient's death. This was the effect of the judgment in *Airedale NHS Trust v Bland* (1993). Even though by withdrawing feeding from an unconscious patient, the medical staff are aware that this will cause the patient to die, they are not liable for the omission, the key issue being that such a failure to feed has to be in the patient's best interests.

However, the House of Lords in *Bland* emphasised that euthanasia by a positive act terminating the patient's life would remain unlawful.

## Statutory duties

Statutes impose duties in a wide variety of situations and make it an offence to fail to do something. Many of these are connected with vehicles and/or driving. Laws in this area often also impose strict liability. This means that not only is the defendant liable because he has failed do to something but, in addition, the prosecution do not have to prove that he had any *mens rea*.

The justification for this is the greater good of society. If a driver fails to get insurance to drive, those injured by him will have difficulty getting compensation for their injuries. The defendant himself is unlikely to be able to pay.

Some of the statutory duties have been imposed because of the difficulty of proving an offence. This was the reason for the introduction of the offence of causing or allowing the death of a child or vulnerable adult under the Domestic Violence, Crime and Victims Act 2004.

Prior to this Act, where a child had died as a result of physical abuse in the home the prosecution used to have difficulty in discovering which member of the household had actually caused the death. For example, if both the mother and the father were charged with murder of the child then each would blame the other so that it could not be proved which one had done it.

Under the 2004 Act all members of the household are liable for failure to protect the child. This makes it much easier to succeed in a prosecution. This is important as the law should provide children and vulnerable adults with as much protection as possible. The law may have the effect of persuading other family members to report the abuse.

# 19.3 Causation

Where a consequence must be proved, then the prosecution has to show that:

- the defendant's conduct was the factual cause of that consequence and
- it was the legal cause of that consequence

## 19.3.1 Factual cause

The defendant can only be guilty if the consequence would not have happened 'but for' the defendant's conduct. This 'but for' test can be seen in operation in the case of R v Pagett (1983).

### R v Pagett (1983)

The defendant (D) took his pregnant girlfriend from her home by force. He then held the girl hostage. Police called on him to surrender. D came out, holding the girl in front of him and firing at the police. The police returned fire and the girl was killed by police bullets. D was convicted of manslaughter.

Pagett was guilty because the girl would not have died 'but for' him using her as a shield in the shoot-out.

The opposite situation was seen in White (1910) where the defendant put cyanide in his mother's drink, intending to kill her. She died of a heart attack before she could drink it. The defendant was not the factual cause of her death. So, he was not guilty of murder, although he was guilty of attempted murder.

In R v Hughes (2013) the Supreme Court held that factual causation is not necessarily enough on its own for liability. It distinguished between 'cause' in the 'but for' sense without which a consequence would not have occurred, and 'cause' in the sense of something which was a legally effective cause of that consequence.

### R v Hughes (2013)

D was driving his camper van. His driving was faultless. As he rounded a right-hand bend on his correct side of the road a car came towards him swerving all over the road and crossing on to D's side of the road. The car smashed into D's camper van and tipped it over. The other driver, who was found to be under the influence of heroin, suffered fatal injuries as a result.

D was not insured and did not have a full driving licence. He was charged under s 3ZB of the Road Traffic Safety Act 1988 with causing death by driving without a licence and while uninsured, and convicted. The Supreme Court quashed the conviction on the ground that although D was the 'cause' of the other driver's death in the sense that but for D's camper van being on the road there would have been no collision, this was not enough to be a legal effective cause. It was the merest chance that what the other driver hit was the van that D was driving.

There had to be something about the driving that was open to criticism and which contributed in some more than minimal way to the death, even if it would not have amounted to the fault element in 'careless' driving.

## 19.3.2 Legal cause

There may be more than one act contributing to the consequence. Some of these acts may be made by people other than the defendant. The rule is that the defendant can be guilty if his conduct was more than a 'minimal' cause of the consequence. But the defendant's conduct need not be a substantial cause. In some cases they have stated that the conduct must be more than de minimis. In R v Kimsey (1996) the Court of Appeal held that instead of using this Latin phrase 'de minimis' it was acceptable to tell the jury it must be 'more than a slight or trifling link'.

### R v Kimsey (1996)

D was involved in a high-speed car chase with a friend. She lost control of her car and the other driver was killed in the crash. The evidence about what happened immediately before D lost control was not very clear. The trial judge directed the jury that D's driving did not have to be 'the principal, or a substantial cause of the death, as long as you are sure that it was a cause and that there must be something more than a slight or trifling link'. The Court of Appeal upheld D's conviction for causing death by dangerous driving.

In *R v Hughes* (2013) the Supreme Court further explained the minimum threshold requirement for legal causation as follows:

> 66 Where there are multiple legally effective causes, it suffices if the act or omission under consideration is a significant (or substantial) cause, in the sense that it is not *de minimis* or minimal. It need not be the only or the principle cause. It must, however, be a cause which is more than *de minimis*, more than minimal. 99

### Multiple causes

There may be more than one person whose act contributed to the death. The defendant can be guilty even though his conduct was not the only cause of the death. In *Kimsey* both drivers were driving at high speed, but Kimsey could be found guilty.

### The 'thin-skull' rule

The defendant must also take the victim as he finds him. This is known as the 'thin-skull' rule. It means that if the victim has something unusual about his physical or mental state which makes an injury more serious, then the defendant is liable for the more serious injury. So, if the victim has an unusually thin skull which means that a blow to his head gives him a serious injury, then the defendant is liable for that injury. This is so even though that blow would have only caused bruising in a 'normal' person. If the person has a mental state, whether mental illness or a state of mind such as a belief, then the defendant has to take them as he finds them. An example is the case of *R v Blaue* (1975).

#### R v Blaue (1975)

A young woman was stabbed by the defendant. She was told that she needed a blood transfusion to save her life but she refused to have one as she was a Jehovah's Witness and her religion forbade blood transfusions. She died and the defendant was convicted of her manslaughter.

The fact that the victim was a Jehovah's Witness made the wound fatal, but the defendant was still guilty because he had to take his victim as he found her.

### 19.3.3 Intervening acts

There must be a direct link from the defendant's conduct to the consequence. This is known as the chain of causation. In some situations something else happens after the defendant's act or omission and, if this is sufficiently separate from the defendant's conduct, it may break the chain of causation.

An example would be where the defendant has stabbed the victim who needs to be taken to hospital for treatment. On the way to hospital, the ambulance carrying the victim is involved in an accident and crashes, causing fatal head injuries to the victim. In this example there is causation in fact but no causation in law.

**Figure 19.2** Breaking the chain of causation

Under the 'but for' test it could be argued that the victim would not have been in the ambulance but for the defendant's act in stabbing him. However, the accident is such a major intervening act that the defendant would not be liable for the death of the victim.

The chain of causation can be broken by:

- an act of a third party or
- the victim's own act or
- a natural but unpredictable event.

In order to break the chain of causation so that the defendant is not responsible for the consequence, the intervening act must be sufficiently independent of the defendant's conduct and sufficiently serious.

Where the defendant's conduct causes a foreseeable action by a third party, then the defendant is likely to be held to have caused the consequence. This principle was applied in *Pagett* (1983) where his girlfriend was shot when he held her as a shield against police bullets (see section 19.3.1).

### 19.3.4 Medical treatment

Medical treatment is unlikely to break the chain of causation unless it is so independent of the defendant's acts and 'in itself so potent in causing death' that the defendant's acts are insignificant. The following three cases show this.

### R v Smith (1959)

Two soldiers had a fight and one was stabbed in the lung by the other. The victim was carried to a medical centre by other soldiers, but was dropped on the way. At the medical centre the staff gave him artificial respiration by pressing on his chest. This made the injury worse and he died. The poor treatment probably affected his chances of recovery by as much as 75 per cent. However, the original attacker was still guilty of his murder.

In this case it was held that a defendant would be guilty, provided that the injury caused by D was still an 'operating' and 'substantial' cause of death. Smith was guilty because the stab wound to the lung was still 'operating' (it obviously had not healed up) and it was a substantial cause of V's death.

### R v Cheshire (1991)

D shot the victim in the thigh and the stomach. V needed major surgery. He developed breathing problems and was given a tracheotomy (i.e. a tube was inserted in his throat to help him breathe). Some two months after the shooting, V died from rare complications left by the tracheotomy. These complications were not diagnosed by the doctors. By the time V died, the original wounds had virtually healed and were no longer life-threatening. The defendant was still held to be liable for V's death.

In this case the Court of Appeal held that even though treatment for injuries was 'short of the standard expected of a competent medical practitioner', D could still be criminally responsible for the death. The prosecution had only to prove that D's acts contributed to the death. D's acts need not be the sole cause or even the main cause of death, provided that his acts contributed significantly to the death.

### R v Jordan (1956)

The victim had been stabbed in the stomach. He was treated in hospital and the wounds were healing well. He was given an antibiotic but suffered an allergic reaction to it. One doctor stopped the use of the antibiotic but the next day another doctor ordered that a large dose of it be given. The victim died from the allergic reaction to the drug. In this case the actions of the doctor were held to be an intervening act which caused the death. The defendant was not guilty of murder.

In the first two cases the doctors were carrying out treatment for the injuries in an attempt to save the victim's life. The victims would not have needed treatment if they had not been seriously injured by the defendant. In such situations the attacker is still liable even though the medical treatment was not very good. This was pointed out in *R v Cheshire* (1991) by Beldam LJ:

> **❝** Even though negligence in the treatment of the victim was the immediate cause of death, the jury should not regard it as excluding the responsibility of the accused unless the negligent treatment was so independent of his acts, and in itself so potent in causing death, that they regard the contribution made by his acts as insignificant. **❞**

In the third case of *Jordan* (1956), the fact that the victim was given a large amount of a drug when the doctors knew he was allergic to it was a sufficiently independent act to break the chain of causation. However, if a normal dose of a drug is given as part of emergency treatment and the doctors do not know that the victim is allergic to it, then the giving of the drug would not break the chain of causation.

## Life-support machines

Switching off a life-support machine by a doctor when it has been decided that the victim is brain-dead does not break the chain of causation. This was decided in R v *Malcherek* (1981).

### R v Malcherek (1981)

D stabbed his wife in the stomach. In hospital she was put on a life-support machine. After a number of tests showed that she was brain dead, the machine was switched off. D was charged with her murder. The trial judge refused to allow the issue of causation to go to the jury. D was convicted and the Court of Appeal upheld his conviction.

**Figure 19.3** Medical intervention and causation

| Case | Facts | Law |
|---|---|---|
| *Smith* (1959) | Soldier stabbed another soldier<br>V's medical treatment very poor and affected chances of recovery | D liable if the injuries he caused are still an operating and substantial cause |
| *Cheshire* (1991) | D shot V<br>V needed a tracheotomy<br>V died because of complications from the tracheotomy<br>His wounds were virtually healed | Medical treatment would only break the chain of causation if it is 'so independent' of D's acts and 'in itself so potent in causing death' |
| *Jordan* (1956) | V was stabbed<br>When his wounds were almost healed he was given a large dose of a drug to which it was known he was allergic | The chain of causation was broken in this case |
| *Malcherek* (1981) | D stabbed his wife<br>She was put on a lifesupport machine but when tests showed she was brain dead, the machine was switched off | Switching off a life-support machine does not break the chain of causation |

## 19.3.5 Victim's own act

If the defendant causes the victim to react in a reasonably foreseeable way, then any injury to the victim will be considered to have been caused by the defendant. This occurred in *R v Roberts* (1971).

### R v Roberts (1972)

A girl jumped from a car in order to escape from Roberts' sexual advances. The car was travelling at between 20 and 40 mph and the girl was injured by jumping from it. The defendant was held to be liable for her injuries.

The Court of Appeal upheld D's conviction for assault causing actual bodily harm under s 47 of the Offences Against the Person Act 1861. They held that the test to be applied is:

'was [the reaction of V] the natural result of what [D] said and did, in the sense that it was something that could reasonably have been foreseen as the consequence of what [D] was saying or doing? ...

If, of course [V] does something so "daft" ... or so unexpected ... that no reasonable man could be expected to foresee it, then it is only in a very remote and unreal sense a consequence of [D's] assault. It is really occasioned by a voluntary act on the part of [V] which could not reasonably be foreseen and which breaks the chain of causation between the assault and harm or injury.'

Another case in which it was held that D was liable if V's action were reasonably foreseeable was *R v Marjoram* (2000).

### R v Marjoram (2000)

Several people, including D, shouted abuse and kicked the door of V's hostel room. They eventually forced the door open. V then fell (or possibly jumped) from the window of the room and suffered serious injuries. D's conviction for inflicting grievous bodily harm was upheld by the Court of Appeal.

In this situation it was reasonably foreseeable that V would fear that the group was going to use violence against him, and that the only escape route for him was the window.

V's action was also reasonably foreseeable in *Bristow, Dunn and Delay* (2012) where the owner of a motor repair business in remote farm buildings tried to stop robbers and was run over and killed by them.

### Unreasonable reaction

However, if the victim's reaction is unreasonable, then this may break the chain of causation. In *R v Williams and Davis* (1992) a hitch-hiker jumped from Williams' car and died from head injuries caused by his head hitting the road. The car was travelling at about 30 mph. The prosecution alleged that there had been an attempt to steal the victim's wallet and that was the reason for his jumping from the car. The Court of Appeal said that the victim's act had to be reasonably foreseeable and also had to be in proportion to the threat. The question to be asked was whether the victim's conduct was 'within the ambit of reasonableness and not so daft as to make his own voluntary act one which amounted to a *novus actus interveniens* (a new intervening act) and consequently broke the chain of causation'.

This makes it necessary to consider the surrounding circumstances in deciding whether the victim's conduct has broken the chain of causation. Where the threats to the victim are serious, then it is more likely for it to be reasonable for him to jump out of a moving car (or out of a window or into a river, etc.). Where the threat is very minor and the victim takes drastic action, it is more likely that the courts will hold that it broke the chain of causation.

The main rules on causation are shown in a flowchart in Figure 19.4.

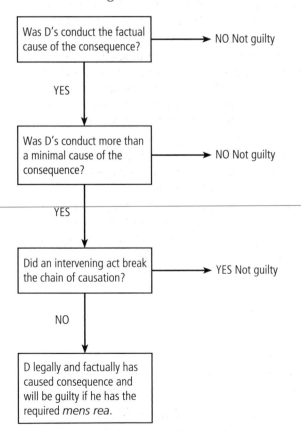

**Figure 19.4** Flowchart of rules on causation

## 19.3.6 Comment on the law on causation

A major problem in the law on causation is: what is meant by more than a 'slight and trifling link'? This is vague and difficult to define. As a result, it could lead to juries applying different standards in different cases.

### Taking your victim as you find him

Where V has a medical condition which makes the injury more serious, should D be liable for the more serious injury? It can be seen as being unjust where D does not know about the medical condition. For example, if a victim has an exceptionally thin skull, so that a blow kills him, is it justifiable that D should be liable for murder when the blow would not have killed a normal person. D did not intend to kill but if he intended to cause really serious injury then D is guilty of murder.

This is also a criticism of the *mens rea* for murder – see Chapter 20 for more on this.

### V refusing treatment

Also, should D be liable when V refuses treatment? This was probably justified when medical treatment was very primitive, especially when operations had to be carried out without anaesthetic. In *R v Holland* (1841), D deliberately cut V's finger. The cut became infected and V was advised that he should have the finger amputated. He refused to have the amputation until it was too late, and he died from the infection. D was liable for his death. In 1841 surgery was very primitive and this decision can be justified, but should D be liable in the same scenario today? D is in any event guilty of an assault causing actual bodily harm, but should he be liable for the death?

In *Blaue* (1975) the victim refused a blood transfusion because of her religious beliefs. Her life could have been saved had she had a transfusion. It can be argued that D should not be liable for her death. He could have been charged with wounding with intent to do so (s 18 of the Offences Against the Person Act 1961). This offence has a maximum penalty of life imprisonment, so a suitable punishment could have been imposed on D. On the other hand, it is clear that the stab wound was the cause of V's death, so on this basis it can be argued that he should be liable for her death.

What if a victim refused a blood transfusion because of a fear of becoming HIV positive through the transfusion? Is this any different from the situation in *Blaue*? Surely the rule must apply in the same way, regardless of the reason for refusing medical treatment? An even more extreme case is *R v Dear* (1996).

### R v Dear (1996)

D slashed V several times with a Stanley knife, severing an artery. V did not bother to have the wounds attended to and, possibly, even opened the wounds further, making the bleeding worse. V died from loss of blood. D's conviction for murder was upheld by the Court of Appeal.

The court held that, provided the wounds were an operating and significant cause, the jury was entitled to convict D. Even if V had effectively decided to commit suicide by allowing the wounds to continue to bleed, the wounds were still the cause of death.

If V really had opened up the wounds further, should this be regarded as an intervening act which broke the chain of causation? Or is the court's view justifiable that as the wounds were the cause of death, then D was liable for the death?

## Negligent medical treatment

In *Smith* (1959) the court used the test of 'operating and substantial cause'. However, this test might not have led to a conviction in *Cheshire* (1991). In *Cheshire*, V's wounds were virtually healed. Were they an 'operating and substantial cause' of V's death? Probably not.

Yet, V would not have had to have a tracheotomy if he had not been shot by D. So, the medical negligence in failing to notice the complications from the tracheotomy was not 'so independent of' D's acts. D's acts were a significant factor in V's death. The test developed in *Cheshire* was more suited to the situation in that case. The tracheotomy was part of the initial treatment which was presumably justified because of the injuries D had caused to V. The tracheotomy was performed correctly without any negligence by the

doctors. The complication which arose was equally not the fault of the doctors. Consequently there was no possible break in the chain of consequences from the shooting to the complication, from which V died.

### Tip

The law on causation is complex. Make sure you have understood the section and then do the activity below to test your ability to apply the law.

### Activity

Read the following situations and explain whether causation would be proved.

1 Aled has been threatened by Ben in the past. When Aled sees Ben approaching him in the street, Aled runs across the road without looking and is knocked down and injured by a car. Would Ben be liable for Aled's injuries?

2 Toyah stabs Steve in the arm. His injury is not serious but he needs stitches, so a neighbour takes Steve to hospital in his car. On the way to the hospital, the car crashes and Steve sustains serious head injuries. Would Toyah be liable for the head injuries?

3 Lewis has broken into Katie's third-floor flat. He threatens to rape her and in order to escape from him she jumps from the window and is seriously injured. Would Lewis be liable for her injuries?

4 Ross stabs Panjit in the chest. Panjit is taken to hospital where he is given an emergency blood transfusion. Unfortunately, he is given the wrong type of blood and he dies. Would Ross be liable for Panjit's death?

## Check your understanding

1 Which one of the following statements accurately describes an 'intervening act' in the chain of causation?

  A An act which breaks the direct link from D's conduct to the consequence

  B An act done after D's act

  C Medical treatment

  D An act done by the victim

2 Explain three situations where the chain of causation has not been broken by the victim's action.

3 Examine the law of criminal liability for failure to act and discuss whether it is satisfactory.

## Summary

- *Actus reus* is the physical element of a crime and it can include conduct, circumstances or consequences.
- *Actus reus* can be a failure to act (an omission) – this usually occurs where D is under a duty to act. There is no general duty to act in English law but specific duties have been recognised; these are:
  - statutory
  - under a contract
  - by a relationship
  - a duty voluntarily undertaken
  - because of an official position
  - through the creation of a dangerous situation.

- In consequence crimes, the act or omission by D must have caused consequence:
  - there must be factual and legal causation
  - D need not be the only cause or even the main cause, but it must be more than a minimal cause
  - D is not liable if the chain of causation is broken
  - medical treatment does not normally break the chain of causation.

# 20 Mens rea

After reading this chapter you should be able to:

■ Understand the law of intention, both direct and oblique
■ Understand the law of recklessness
■ Understand the principle of transferred malice
■ Understand the need for coincidence of *actus reus* and *mens rea*
■ Evaluate the law on intention and recklessness

## 20.1 Levels of *mens rea*

*Mens rea* is the mental element of an offence. Each offence has its own *mens rea* or mental element. The only exceptions are offences of strict liability. These offences do not require proof of a mental element in respect of at least part of the *actus reus*. In criminal cases it is for the prosecution to prove the required *mens rea*.

There are different levels of *mens rea*. To be guilty, the accused must have at least the minimum level of *mens rea* required for the offence.

The highest level of *mens rea* is intention. This is also referred to as 'specific intention'. The other main types of *mens rea* are knowledge and recklessness. Sometimes, negligence is described as *mens rea* though it is tested objectively, as a failure to meet a required standard of conduct.

## 20.2 Intention (specific intent)

In the case of *Mohan* (1975) the court defined 'intention' as:

❝ a decision to bring about, in so far as it lies within the accused's power, [the prohibited consequence], no matter whether the accused desired that consequence of his act or not. ❞

### Key term 🔑

**Intention:** a decision to bring about, in so far as it lies within the accused's power, [the prohibited consequence], no matter whether the accused desired that consequence of his act or not.

This makes it clear that the defendant's motive or reason for doing the act is not relevant. The important point is that the defendant decided to bring about the prohibited consequence.

This can be illustrated by looking at the offence set out in s 18 of the Offences Against the Person Act 1861. For this offence, the defendant must wound or cause grievous bodily harm. The *mens rea* is that the defendant must intend to cause grievous bodily harm or intend to resist arrest. If the defendant did not intend either of these then he cannot be guilty of this offence. For example, if a person opens a door very suddenly and hits and seriously injures someone on the other side of the door whom he did not know was there, then he does not intend to 'bring about' the prohibited consequence.

### Motive

*Mohan* (1975) also makes it clear that motive is not the same as intention and is not relevant in deciding whether the defendant had intention. For example, a person may feel very strongly that the banking system in the Western world is causing poverty in poorer nations. That person then steals millions of pounds from a bank so that he can give it to people in poorer nations. His motive is to make sure that the poor receive money. This is irrelevant in deciding whether the defendant has the *mens rea* required for theft.

## 20.2.1 Direct and oblique intent

In the majority of cases the defendant has what is known as direct intent. This means that he intends the specific consequence to occur. For example, D decides to kill V. He aims a gun directly at V's head and pulls the trigger. Here D has the direct intent to kill V.

However, there can be situations where the defendant does not necessarily desire an outcome. It is not his aim or purpose. His aim or purpose is something different. This is known as oblique intent or indirect intent.

An example of this is where the defendant intends to frighten someone so as to stop him going to work, as occurred in the case of *Hancock and Shankland* (1986). See 20.2.2. The actual consequence in that case was that the driver of the car taking the person to work was killed through D's actions The outcome of the driver's death was not the direct intent of D. This is shown in diagram form in Figure 20.1.

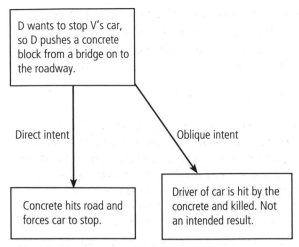

**Figure 20.1** Direct intent/oblique intent

## 20.2.2 Foresight of consequences

The main problem with proving intention is in cases where the defendant's main aim was not the prohibited consequences. He intended something else. If, in achieving the other thing, the defendant foresaw that he would also cause those consequences, then he may be found guilty. This idea is referred to as 'foresight of consequences'.

An example of this type of situation is where the defendant decides to set fire to his shop in order to claim insurance. His main aim is damaging the shop and getting the insurance. Unfortunately, he starts the fire when members of staff are still in the shop and some of them are seriously injured. Has the defendant the intention for the s 18 offence of causing grievous bodily harm?

The starting point for foresight of consequences is s 8 of the Criminal Justice Act 1967 which states that:

> A court or jury, in determining whether a person has committed an offence–
>
> a shall not be bound in law to infer that he intended or foresaw a result of his actions by reason only of its being a natural and probable consequence of those actions; but
> b shall decide whether he did intend or foresee that result by reference to all the evidence, drawing such inferences from the evidence as appear proper in the circumstances.

This wording has been the subject of several cases over the last 30 years or so. These are mainly cases where defendants have been charged with murder. The important point is that the defendant must intend or foresee a result. In a murder case this means that the defendant must foresee that death or really serious injury will be caused. The leading case on this is now *Woollin* (1998), but to understand the law and the problems it is necessary to look at cases which came before *Woollin*. The first of these was *Moloney* (1985).

### *Moloney* (1985)

D and his step-father had drunk a considerable amount of alcohol at a family party. After the party, they were heard talking and laughing. Then there was a shot. D phoned the police, saying that he had just murdered his step-father. D said that they had being seeing who was the faster at loading and firing a shotgun. He had loaded his gun faster than his step-father. His step-father then said that D hadn't got 'the guts' to pull the trigger. D said 'I didn't aim the gun. I just pulled the trigger and he was dead'. D was convicted of murder but this conviction was quashed on appeal.

In this case the House of Lords ruled that foresight of consequences is only evidence of intention. It is not intention in itself. This part of the House of Lords' judgment is still law.

However, other parts of this judgment have been overruled by later cases. This was because Lord Bridge stated that jurors should be told to consider two questions:

- Was death or really serious injury a natural consequence of the defendant's act?
- Did the defendant foresee that consequence as being a natural result of his act?

The problem with these questions (which are often referred to as the Moloney guidelines) is that the word 'probable' is not mentioned.

If you look back to s 8 of the Criminal Justice Act 1967, you will see that the section uses the phrase 'natural and probable consequence'. Lord Bridge referred only to a 'natural' result. This omission of the word 'probable' was held in *Hancock and Shankland* (1986) (see below) to make the guidelines defective. The guidelines are therefore no longer law.

### *Hancock and Shankland* (1986)

Ds were miners who were on strike. They tried to prevent another miner from going to work by pushing a concrete block from a bridge on to the road along which he was being driven to work in a taxi. The block struck the windscreen of the taxi and killed the driver. The trial judge used the

Moloney guidelines to direct the jury, and Ds were convicted of murder. On appeal, the Court of Appeal quashed their convictions. This was upheld by the House of Lords.

The problem with *Moloney* (1985) was explained by Lord Scarman who stated that the guidelines in that case were unsafe and misleading. He said:

> " In my judgment, therefore, the Moloney guidelines as they stand are unsafe and misleading. They require a reference to probability. They also require an explanation that the greater the probability of a consequence the more likely it is that the consequence was foreseen and that if that consequence was foreseen the greater the probability is that that consequence was also intended. "

The next case was *Nedrick* (1986) where the Court of Appeal thought that the judgments in the two earlier cases of *Moloney* (1985) and *Hancock and Shankland* (1986) needed to be made clearer.

## Nedrick (1986)

D had a grudge against a woman. He poured paraffin through the letter box of her house and set it alight. A child died in the fire. D was convicted of murder but the Court of Appeal quashed the conviction and substituted one of manslaughter.

To make the law decided in *Moloney*, *Hancock* and *Nedrick* easier for jurors to understand and apply in murder trials, the Court of Appeal said that it was helpful for a jury to ask themselves two questions:

- How probable was the consequence which resulted from D's voluntary act?
- Did D foresee that consequence?

It was necessary for the consequence to be a virtual certainty and for D to have realised that. If this was so then there was evidence from which the jury could infer that D had the necessary intention. Lord Lane CJ put it this way:

> " The jury should be directed that they are not entitled to infer the necessary intention unless they feel sure that death or serious bodily harm was a virtual certainty (barring some unforeseen intervention) as a result of the defendant's actions and that the defendant appreciated that such was the case. "

This remained the law until 1998 and the case of *Woollin* (1998). This went to the House of Lords who felt that the Court of Appeal's views in *Nedrick* (1986) were not helpful.

## Woollin (1998)

D threw his three-month-old baby towards his pram which was against a wall some three or four feet away. The baby suffered head injuries and died. The court ruled that the consequence must have been a virtual certainty and the defendant must have realised this. Where the jury was satisfied on both these two points, then there was evidence on which the jury could find intention.

The Law Lords thought that the two questions in *Nedrick* were not helpful. They held that the model direction from *Nedrick* should be used, but that the word 'find' should be used rather than the word 'infer'. So the model direction to be given to a jury considering foresight of consequences should now be:

> " the jury should be directed that they are not entitled to find the necessary intention unless they feel sure that death or serious bodily harm was a virtual certainty (barring some unforeseen intervention) as a result of the defendant's actions and that the defendant appreciated that such was the case. "

### Problems with the decision in *Woollin*

The decision in *Woollin* causes some problems. First of all, the word 'infer' is used in s 8 of the Criminal Justice Act 1967 and this is presumably why it was used in *Nedrick*. Does the substitution of the word 'find' improve the clarity of the direction to the jury? Another problem is whether the use of the word 'find' means that foresight of consequence is intention and not merely evidence of it.

In his judgment Lord Steyn also went on to say that the effect of the direction is that 'a result foreseen as virtually certain is an intended result'. He also pointed out that in *Moloney* the House of Lords had said that if a person foresees the probability of a consequence as little short of overwhelming, this 'will suffice to establish the necessary intent'. Lord Steyn emphasised the word 'establish'. This seems to suggest that the House of Lords in *Woollin* regarded foresight of consequences as the same as intention, when *Moloney* had clearly stated that it was not.

In later cases there have been conflicting decisions on this point. In the civil case of *Re A* (2000), doctors asked the courts whether they could operate to separate conjoined twins when they foresaw that this would kill the weaker twin. The Court of Appeal (Civil Division) clearly thought that *Woollin* laid down the rule that foresight of consequences is intention.

In the criminal case of *Matthews and Alleyne* (2003) the Court of Appeal held that the judgment in *Woollin* meant that foresight of consequences is not intention: it is a rule of evidence. If a jury decides that the defendant foresaw the virtual certainty of death or serious injury, they are entitled to find intention but do not have to do so.

## Matthews and Alleyne (2003)

The defendants dropped the victim 25 feet from a bridge, into the middle of a deep river. The victim had told them that he could not swim. They watched him 'dog paddle' towards the bank but left before seeing whether he reached safety. The victim drowned.

The trial judge had directed the jury that the defendants' intention to kill could be proved either by direct intention to kill or by the defendants' appreciation that V's death was a virtual certainty (barring an attempt to save him) together with the fact that the defendants did not intend to save the victim.

The Court of Appeal stated that the trial judge had been wrong to say that an appreciation of a virtual certainty constituted intention.

However, they upheld the convictions because, if the jury were sure that the defendants appreciated the virtual certainty of death if they did not attempt to save V and that at the time of throwing V off the bridge they had no intention of saving him, then it was impossible to see how the jury could not have found that the defendants intended V to die.

A chart of the cases on foresight of consequences is included to help keep the cases clear.

**Figure 20.2** Case chart on foresight of consequences

| Case | Brief facts | Law |
|---|---|---|
| *Moloney* (1985) | D shot step-father in 'quick on the draw' incident. | Foresight of consequences is *not* intention; it is evidence of intention. |
| *Hancock and Shankland* (1986) | Miner dropped lumps of concrete onto road, killing taxi driver. | The greater the probability of a consequence, the more likely it is that the consequence was foreseen and if that consequence was foreseen, the greater the probability that that consequence was also intended. |
| *Nedrick* (1986) | Poured paraffin through letter box, causing fire in the house in which a child died. | Jury not entitled to infer the necessary intention unless sure that death or serious bodily harm was a virtual certainty and that the defendant appreciated this. |
| *Woollin* (1998) | Threw baby at pram, causing its death. | The direction in *Nedrick* should not use the word 'infer'. Instead, the jury should be told they are entitled to *find* intention. |
| *Re A* (2000) | Doctors wanted to operate on conjoined twins, but knew this would cause one of them to die. | Court thought that *Woollin* made it law that foresight of consequences *is* intention. |
| *Matthews and Alleyne* (2003) | Threw V into river, where he drowned. | *Woollin* meant that foresight of consequences is *not* intention. It is a rule of evidence. If a jury decides that the defendant foresaw the virtual certainty of death or serious injury, then they are entitled to find intention but they do not have to do so. |

## Activity

In each of the following situations, explain whether the defendant has the required intention for murder. The *mens rea* for murder is an intention to kill or an intention to cause grievous bodily harm.

1 Geraint dislikes Victor and decides to attack him. Geraint uses an iron bar to hit Victor on the head. Victor dies as a result.

2 Inderpal throws a large stone into a river to see how much of a splash it will make. Jake is swimming in the river and is hit on the head by the stone and killed.

3 Kylie throws a large stone from a bridge, onto the motorway below. It is rush hour and there is a lot of traffic on the motorway. The stone smashes through the windscreen of Ashley's car and kills his passenger.

## 20.2.3 Comment on foresight of consequences as intention

It can be seen from the above that the courts have struggled with the concept of intention where foresight of consequences is involved. For example:

- natural and probable consequence
- difficulty for jurors in applying the tests after the cases of *Moloney* and *Hancock and Shankland*
- the change in Woollin from inferring intention to finding intention
- the fact that there are still two interpretations of the judgment in *Woollin*.

### Natural and probable consequences

It is necessary to include both words in the test for intention. This is because something can be a natural consequence without being a probable consequence. For example, a natural consequence of sexual intercourse is that the girl becomes pregnant. However, it is not a probable consequence. Pregnancy only occurs in a small percentage of cases.

### The difficulty for jurors applying the law

Following the cases of *Moloney* and *Hancock and Shankland* where jurors had to be directed on the level of probability, the law was left in a state which made it difficult for judges to explain it to jurors and for jurors to apply the law. The difficulties it caused were emphasised when the Court of Appeal in *Nedrick* thought it necessary to try to make the law easier for jurors to understand and apply.

### Infer or find

The use of the two question test from *Nedrick* operated for some 12 years until the case of *Woollin*.

Then the House of Lords said that they thought the two questions from *Nedrick* were not helpful. They also held that the direction to the jury should use the word find instead of infer. As already discussed in the previous section, the decision in *Woollin* appears to create more problems than it solved.

### Two interpretations of *Woollin*

There are still problems in the law on intention as shown by the fact that the Court of Appeal in two separate cases has interpreted the decision of the House of Lords in *Woollin* in different ways.

In *Re A* (2001) the Court of Appeal thought that *Woollin* meant that foresight of consequences is intention, whereas in *Matthews and Alleyne* they stated that foresight of consequences is only evidence of intention.

It can be seen from this that the law on intention is still not in a satisfactory state.

## 20.2.4 Reform of the law on intention

'Intention' is not defined in any statute.

The Law Commission has in the past suggested definitions for 'intention'. The first of these was in the Draft Criminal Code in 1989. The definition in clause 18(b) was that a person acts:
"intentionally" with respect to–

i a circumstance when he hopes or knows that it exists or will exist:

ii a result when he acts either in order to bring it about or being aware that it will occur in the ordinary course of events;

### Criticisms of this definition

This definition was criticised by Professor Sir John Smith as having three major shortcomings. He pointed out that using the phrase 'being aware' risked blurring 'intention' with 'recklessness'. Recklessness requires that D knows there is a risk of a result. It is a lower level of *mens rea* than intention. So it is important that there is a clear distinction between them.

Another problem was the requirement that D had to be aware that a result 'will occur in the ordinary course of events'. This did not cater for situations in which D is not sure that his main purpose will be achieved and so cannot be aware that the secondary result will in the ordinary course of events follow.

An example of this is where D places a bomb on a plane intending to destroy the cargo so that he can claim on insurance. However, he knows that this type of bomb does not always go off. In fact it is likely to be successfully detonated only 50 per cent of the time. So, it cannot be said that D is aware that the deaths of the crew of the plane will happen 'in the ordinary course of events'. There is a 50 per cent chance that it will not happen. Yet, surely this situation is one that should be covered by the definition of intention.

The third criticism was that a person could be held to have intended a result that it was his purpose to avoid. Lord Goff expanded on this problem in a debate in the House of Lords and gave the following example:

> A house is on fire. A father is trapped in the attic floor with his two little girls. He comes to the conclusion that unless they jump they will all be burned alive. But he also realises that if they jump they are all likely to suffer serious personal harm. The children are too frightened to jump and, so in attempt to save their lives, he throws one out of the window to the crowd waiting below and jumps with the other one in his arms. All are seriously injured, and the little girl he threw out of the window dies of her injuries.

As a result of these criticisms, the Law Commission came up with a different definition in 1993. In its report Offences Against the Person and General Principles, it proposed that 'intentionally' should be defined as follows:

A person acts intentionally with respect to a result when:

i  it is his purpose to cause it; or

ii although it is not his purpose to cause it, he knows that it would occur in the ordinary course of events if he were to succeed in his purpose of causing some other result.

However, even this definition could cause problems. What is meant by 'in the ordinary course of events'? The meaning of this phrase appears broader than the test of 'virtual certainty' used in *Nedrick/Woollin*. This could mean that such a change in the law would lead to more people being convicted of offences which they did not directly intend to commit.

## Law Commission Reports

In 2003, the Law Commission proposed yet another definition of intention. This was in its Consultation Paper No. 177, A New Homicide Act for England and Wales. However, following consultation, the Law Commission decided that the present law had the flexibility to deal with situations at both ends of the spectrum, such as the example of the bomb where it may only go off 50 per cent of the time and the example of the father trying to save the lives of his children.

So in its report Murder, Manslaughter and Infanticide, No. 304 (2006), the Law Commission recommended the following definition:

1  A person should be taken to intend a result if he or she acts in order to bring it about.

2  In cases where the judge believes that justice may not be done unless an expanded understanding of intention is given, the jury should be directed as follows: an intention to bring about a result may be found if it is shown that the defendant thought that the result was a virtually certain consequence of his or her action.

The recommended reforms on murder have never been implemented, so this definition has not been made part of statutory law. The definition in *Woollin* is still the law on intention.

**Tip**

Foresight of consequences is a difficult topic. It is important to understand it and the sequence of cases which have created the law.

# 20.3 Subjective recklessness

This is a lower level of *mens rea* than intention. Recklessness is where the defendant knows there is a risk of the consequence happening but takes that risk.

## 20.3.1 The case of *Cunningham*

The explanation of recklessness comes from the case of *Cunningham* (1957).

## Cunningham (1957)

D tore a gas meter from the wall of an empty house in order to steal the money in it. This caused gas to seep into the house next door, where a woman was affected by it. Cunningham was charged with an offence under s 23 of the Offences Against the Person Act 1861, of maliciously administering a noxious thing. It was held that he was not guilty since he did not realise the risk of gas escaping into the next-door house. He had not intended to cause the harm, nor had he taken a risk he knew about.

The offence involved in *Cunningham* uses the word 'maliciously' to indicate the *mens rea* required. The court held that this word meant that to have the necessary *mens rea* the defendant must either intend the consequence or realise that there was a risk of the consequence happening and decide to take that risk. Knowing about a risk and taking it can also be referred to as '**subjective recklessness**'. It is subjective because the defendant himself realised the risk.

The case of *Savage* (1992) confirmed that the same principle applies to all offences where the definition in an Act of Parliament uses the word 'maliciously'. The Law Lords said that 'maliciously' was a term of legal art. In other words, it has a special meaning when used in an Act of Parliament, not its normal dictionary definition. It means doing something intentionally or being subjectively reckless about the risk involved.

Do not forget that if the defendant has the higher level of intention he will, of course, be guilty. For example, if the defendant intends to punch the victim in the face, that defendant has the higher level of intention and is guilty of a battery. It is only when the defendant does not have the higher level that recklessness has to be considered.

Offences for which recklessness is sufficient for the *mens rea* include:

- assault and battery
- assault occasioning actual bodily harm (s 47 of the Offences Against the Person Act 1861)
- malicious wounding (s 20 of the Offences Against the Person Act 1861).

## Key term

Subjective recklessness – where the defendant knows there is a risk of the consequence happening but takes that risk.

## 20.3.2 Past problems in the law

There used to be two levels of recklessness. These were:

- subjective, where the defendant realised the risk, but decided to take it
- objective, where an ordinary prudent person would have realised the risk: the defendant was guilty even if he did not realise the risk.

The first type of recklessness is the only recklessness that the law now recognises as being sufficient to prove a defendant guilty where recklessness is required for the *mens rea* of an offence. However, during the period from 1982 to 2003, it was accepted that a defendant could be guilty of certain offences even though he had not realised that there was a risk. This was decided in the case of *Metropolitan Police Commissioner v Caldwell* (1981).

## Metropolitan Police Commissioner v Caldwell (1981)

D had a grievance against the owner of a hotel. He got very drunk and decided to set fire to the hotel. The fire was put out quickly, without serious damage to the hotel. D was charged with arson under s 1(2) of the Criminal Damage Act 1971. This requires that D intended endangerment to life or was reckless as to whether life was endangered. D claimed that he was so drunk he had not realised people's lives might be endangered. His conviction was upheld.

In *Caldwell* the House of Lords held that recklessness covered two situations. The first is where D had realised the risk and the second is where D had not thought about the possibility of any risk.

This second meaning of 'reckless' caused problems in cases where D was not capable of appreciating the risk involved in his conduct, even though a reasonable person would have realised there was a risk. This occurred in *Elliott v C* (1983) where D was a 14-year-old girl with learning difficulties. She did not appreciate the risk that her act might set a shed on fire. But she was found guilty because ordinary adults would have realised the risk.

This seemed very unfair. The girl was not blameworthy. If she had been judged by the standard of a 14-year-old with learning difficulties then she would not have been convicted. It was absurd to judge her against the standard of ordinary adults. This problem was eventually resolved when the House of Lords overruled *Caldwell* in the case of *G and another* (2003).

## G and another (2003)

The defendants were two boys, aged 11 and 12 years, who set fire to some bundles of newspapers in a shop yard. They threw them under a large wheelie bin and left. They thought that the fire would go out by itself. In fact, the bin caught fire and this spread to the shop and other buildings, causing about £1 million worth of damage. The judge directed the jury that they had to decide whether ordinary adults would have realised the risk. The boys were convicted under both ss 1 and 3 of the Criminal Damage Act 1971. On appeal, the House of Lords quashed their conviction.

The House of Lords held that a defendant could not be guilty unless he had realised the risk and decided to take it. The House of Lords overruled the decision in *Caldwell*, holding that in that case the Law Lords had adopted an interpretation of s 1 of the Criminal Damage Act 1971 which was 'beyond the range of feasible meanings'.

In *G and another*, the House of Lords approved of the definition of recklessness set out in the draft Criminal Code which states that a person acts:

**“** recklessly with respect to:

   i   a circumstance when he is aware of a risk that it exists or will exist;

   ii  a result when he is aware of a risk that it will occur;

and it is, in the circumstances known to him, unreasonable to take the risk. **”**

The reasons for the defendant taking the risk are not relevant. It does not matter whether it was done because the defendant was in a temper or he chose to disregard the risk or simply did not care about the risk.

The important point is that the defendant must be aware of the risk. This is the subjective aspect of recklessness.

### General application of law on recklessness

Initially it was thought that this decision in *G and another* only affected the law on recklessness in relation to criminal damage. However, the *G and another* version of recklessness has since been applied by the Court of Appeal to other areas of law. So now the law is clear. Where recklessness is sufficient for the *mens rea* of an offence, it must be subjective recklessness. The prosecution must prove that the defendant realised the risk and decided to take it.

## 20.3.3 Comment on subjective recklessness

Following the decision in *G and another* (2003), recklessness is now firmly based on a subjective test. It focuses on whether D realised the risk (the subjective test). This makes it clear that D is at fault. It makes people take responsibility where they are aware there is a risk of the consequence occurring.

It no longer makes defendants liable when they did not realise the risk. This is fair on the defendant. He is only guilty if he realises the risk. This is an improvement on the law before the case of *G and another* (2003) where even a 14-year-old with learning difficulties, as in *Elliott v C* (1983), was liable because the 'reasonable' adult would have seen the risk.

### Problems

Although the law is fairer to defendants now, it can be argued that the law is not so fair on innocent victims and their families. Someone may have been seriously injured or even killed yet the attacker may be not guilty if he was not subjectively reckless. It can be argued that the law does not give sufficient protection to innocent members of the public.

There is conflict between public policy and legal principles. Public policy is based on public protection and the encouragement of good behaviour. Legal principles impose liability where there is fault. It was recognised in *G and another* (2003) that D must be shown to be aware of the risk (the mental fault element). It is often not possible to balance public protection with fairness to the defendant.

It has also been suggested that having a subjective test for recklessness means that a defendant can too easily avoid liability. The prosecution have to prove that D was aware of the risk. It can be difficult to prove what was in D's mind.

Another problem in the law on recklessness is that it allows D's characteristics to be taken into account in deciding whether D realised the risk. Other areas of criminal law, such as the defence of loss of control and the defence of duress, do not allow all of D's characteristics to be taken into account. This means that there are conflicting legal principles in the different areas of law.

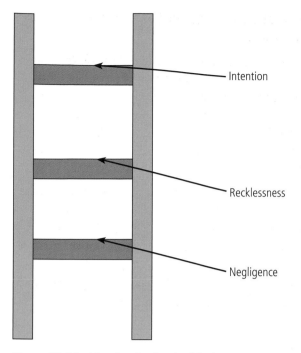

**Figure 20.3** Ladder showing levels of fault

# 20.4 Negligence

A person is negligent if he fails to meet the standards of the reasonable man. This may be enough to make a person liable in civil law (see Chapter 23) but is not usually sufficient to make a person criminally liable. This is because Negligence has a much lower level of fault to intention and recklessness, that we have already looked at. What the defendant intended is not relevant.

There are two exceptions to this general rule:

- Negligence can occur in some statutory offences, for example s 3 of the Road Traffic Act 1988 makes it an offence to drive without due care and attention; and

- One form of manslaughter can be committed by 'gross negligence'. This means there has to be a very high degree of negligence, more than just civil negligence. The leading case on this is R v Adomako (1994). This case and the rules on gross negligence manslaughter are explained in more detail in Book 2.

# 20.5 Transferred malice

This is the principle that the defendant can be guilty if he intended to commit a similar crime but against a different victim. An example is aiming a blow at one person with the necessary *mens rea* for an assault causing actual bodily harm, but actually hitting another person. This occurred in *Latimer* (1886).

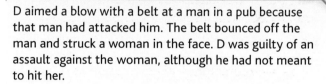

### *Latimer* (1886)

D aimed a blow with a belt at a man in a pub because that man had attacked him. The belt bounced off the man and struck a woman in the face. D was guilty of an assault against the woman, although he had not meant to hit her.

However, where the *mens rea* is for a completely different type of offence, then the defendant may not be guilty. This was the situation in *Pembliton* (1874), where the defendant threw a stone, intending it to hit people with whom he had been fighting. The stone hit and broke a window. The intention to hit people could not be transferred to the window.

**Figure 20.4** Key facts table on levels of fault

| Level of fault | | Explanation | Case/example |
|---|---|---|---|
| *mens rea* | **Intention (specific intent)** | 'A decision to bring about, in so far as it lies within the accused's power, [the prohibited consequence], no matter whether the accused desired that consequence of his act or not.' | *Mohan* (1975) |
| | **Recklessness (basic intent)** | The defendant must realise that there is a risk of the consequences occurring and decide to take that risk. | *Cunningham* (1957) |
| **Negligence** | | A failure to meet the standards of the reasonable man. | *Adomako* (1994) |

A more recent case on transferred malice is *Gnango* (2011).

### Gnango (2011)

Gnango and another man, known only as 'Bandana Man', shot at each other. Bandana Man hit an innocent passerby and killed her. Gnango was tried and convicted of her murder. The Court of Appeal quashed the conviction but it was reinstated by the Supreme Court. They held he was guilty of the murder of the passerby as, by agreeing to the shoot-out with Bandana Man, he was attempting to murder Bandana Man and also aiding and abetting Bandana Man's attempt to murder him. Bandana Man would have been guilty of the murder of the passerby under the doctrine of transferred malice. This meant that Gnango, because of his participation in the attempted murder of himself, was also guilty of the murder of the passerby under the principle of transferred malice.

## 20.5.1 General malice

In some cases, the defendant may not have a specific victim in mind: for example, a terrorist who plants a bomb in a pub, intending to kill or injure anyone who happens to be there. In this case the defendant's *mens rea* is held to apply to the actual victim.

## 20.6 Coincidence of *actus reus* and *mens rea*

In order for an offence to take place, both the *actus reus* and the *mens rea* must be present at the same time. For example, if you decide to go round to your next-door neighbour, intending to assault him, but when you get to his house you change your mind and do not actually assault him, you cannot be guilty of an assault even though you had the *mens rea*.

If, two hours later, you are driving your car out of your driveway and knock down your neighbour because you did not see him, you have now done what could be the *actus reus* for an assault. However, you are not guilty of any criminal offence since at the moment you hit your neighbour you did not have the necessary *mens rea*. The *mens rea* and the *actus reus* were not present at the same time.

In *Thabo Meli v R* (1954) the court had to decide whether the *actus reus* and *mens rea* were present together.

### Thabo Meli v R (1954)

Ds attacked a man and believed they had killed him. They then pushed his body over a low cliff. In fact, the man had survived the attack but died of exposure when unconscious at the foot of the cliff. It was held that Ds were guilty of murder.

The defendants in this case were guilty as the required *mens rea* and *actus reus* were combined in a series of acts. A similar situation occurred in *Church* (1965).

### Church (1965)

D had a fight with a woman and knocked her out. He tried, unsuccessfully, for about half an hour to bring her round. He thought she was dead and he put her in the river. She drowned. His conviction for manslaughter was upheld.

## 20.6.1 Continuing act

Where there is a continuing act for the *actus reus* and at some point while that act is still going on the defendant has the necessary *mens rea*, then the two do coincide and the defendant will be guilty. This is illustrated by the case of *Fagan v Metropolitan Police Commissioner* (1986).

### Fagan v Metropolitan Police Commissioner (1986)

**Fagan v Metropolitan Police Commissioner (1986)**

Fagan was told by a police officer to park by a kerb. In doing this Fagan drove on to the policeman's foot, without realising he had done so. Initially, Fagan refused to move the car. When the policeman pointed out what had happened, he asked Fagan several times to move the car off his foot. Eventually, Fagan did move the car. Fagan was convicted of assaulting the police officer in the execution of his duty.

The Court of Appeal held that once Fagan knew the car was on the police officer's foot he had the required *mens rea*. As the *actus reus* (the car putting force on the foot) was still continuing, the two elements were then present together. The *actus reus* in this case was a continuing act as, so long as the defendant developed the *mens rea* at some time while the act was continuing, then he could be guilty.

## Activity

Explain in the following situations whether *actus reus* and *mens rea* are present. (Do not forget that there may be transferred malice.)

1 Bart has had an argument with Cara. He aims a punch at her head, but Cara dodges out of the way and Bart hits Homer who was standing behind Cara.

2 Desmond is sitting in a lecture. He pushes his chair back, but does not realise that one of the chair legs is pressing on to Mark's foot. Mark asks Desmond to move the chair, but Desmond thinks what has happened is funny and does not move but sits there laughing for several minutes.

3 Sian throws a stone at a cat. Her aim is very poor and the stone hits Ratinder who is standing several feet away.

## Check your understanding

1 Which one of the following statements accurately describes recklessness in criminal law?

A Failing to meet the standards of the reasonable man

B A reasonable man would realise the risk

C D realises the risk and decides to take it

D Being capable of realising the risk

2 Which one of the following statements accurately describes foresight of consequences in criminal law?

A Intention to commit the offence charged

B Foreseeing that the consequence is a natural result of the act

C Evidence from which intention can be found

D Realising the risk and taking it

3 Explain the concept in criminal law of coincidence of *actus reus* and *mens rea*.

## Summary

- Different crimes require different levels of *mens rea*
- Intention is the highest form of *mens rea*
  - this may be direct intent where D's aim or purpose of desire is to bring about the consequence; or
  - it may be oblique where D does not desire the consequence but foresees it as virtually certain
  - foresight of consequences is not the same as intention but it is evidence from which a jury may 'find' intention

- Recklessness requires proof that D, knowing of the risk, took that risk: this is subjective recklessness
- Negligence is where D fails to meet the standards of the reasonable man
- Transferred malice is where D intends to commit a crime against one person, but inadvertently commits against another person
- There must be coincidence of *actus reus* and *mens rea*: this can be through a continuing act

# 21 No fault and strict liability

After reading this chapter you should be able to:
- Understand the concept of no fault and strict liability in criminal law
- Understand the tests the courts use to decide whether an offence is one of strict liability or not
- Understand the role of policy in the creation of strict liability offences

## 21.1 The concept of strict liability

The previous chapter explained the different types of *mens rea*. This chapter considers those offences where *mens rea* is not required in respect of at least one aspect of the *actus reus*. Such offences are known as **strict liability offences**.

### Key term

**Strict liability offences** – offences where *mens rea* is not required in respect of at least one aspect of the *actus reus*.

An example demonstrating strict liability is *Pharmaceutical Society of Great Britain v Storkwain Ltd* (1986).

### *Pharmaceutical Society of Great Britain v Storkwain Ltd* (1986)

D was charged under s 58(2) of the Medicines Act 1968 which states that no one shall supply certain drugs without a doctor's prescription. D had supplied drugs on prescriptions, but the prescriptions were later found to be forged. There was no finding that D had acted dishonestly, improperly or even negligently. The forgery was sufficient to deceive the pharmacists. Despite this, the House of Lords held that the Divisional Court was right to direct the magistrates to convict D. The pharmacists had supplied the drugs without a genuine prescription and this was enough to make them guilty of the offence.

### 21.1.1 Requirement of *actus reus*

For nearly all strict liability offences, it must be proved that the defendant did the relevant *actus reus*. For *Storkwain*, this meant proving that the chemist had supplied drugs without a genuine prescription. It also has to be proved that the doing of the *actus reus* was voluntary. If the chemist had been forced at gun-point to provide the drug, then the act would not have been voluntary.

However, there are a few rare cases where the defendant has been found guilty even though he did not do the *actus reus* voluntarily. These are known as crimes of absolute liability.

## 21.2 Absolute liability

Absolute liability means that no *mens rea* at all is required for the offence nor does the the *actus reus* have to be voluntary. Absolute liability involves 'status offences', offences where the *actus reus* is a 'state of affairs'. The defendant is liable because they have 'been found' in a certain situation. Such offences are very rare. To be an absolute liability offence, the following conditions must apply:
- the offence does not require any *mens rea* and
- there is no need to prove that the defendant's *actus reus* was voluntary.

The following two cases demonstrate this.

### *R v Larsonneur* (1933)

The defendant, who was from a foreign country (and was therefore termed an 'alien', in the language of the time), had been ordered to leave the United Kingdom. She decided to go to Eire, but the Irish police deported her and took her in police custody back to the UK, where she was put in a cell in Holyhead police station. She did not want to return to the UK. She had no *mens rea*. Her act in returning was not voluntary. She was taken back to the UK. Despite this, she was found guilty under the Aliens Order 1920 of being 'an alien to whom leave to land in the United Kingdom has been refused ... found in the United Kingdom'.

The other case is *Winzar v Chief Constable of Kent* (1983).

### *Winzar v Chief Constable of Kent* (1983)

D was taken to hospital on a stretcher, but when he was examined by doctors they found that he was not ill but was drunk. D was told to leave the hospital, but was later found slumped on a seat in a corridor. The police were called and they took D to the roadway outside the hospital. They formed the opinion that he was drunk so they put him in the police car, drove him to the police station and charged him with being found drunk in a highway, contrary to s 12 of the Licensing Act 1872. The Divisional Court upheld his conviction.

As in *Larsonneur*, the defendant had not acted voluntarily. He had been taken to the highway by the police. In the Divisional Court Goff LJ justified the conviction, pointing out that the particular offence was designed to deal with the nuisance which can be caused by persons who are drunk in a public place.

It is not known how Winzar came to be taken to the hospital on a stretcher but it is possible that there may have been an element of fault in his conduct. He had become drunk (presumably voluntarily) and must have either been in a public place when the ambulance collected him and took him to hospital, or he must have summoned medical assistance when he was not ill but only drunk. However, it does not matter whether there was any prior fault. The defendant was guilty simply because he had been found drunk in a public place.

## 21.3 Strict liability

For all offences there is a presumption that *mens rea* is required. The courts will always start with this presumption, but if they decide that the offence does not require *mens rea* for at least part of the *actus reus* then the offence is one of strict liability. This idea of not requiring *mens rea* for part of the offence is illustrated by two cases: *R v Prince* (1875) and *R v Hibbert* (1869). In both these cases the charge against the defendant was that he had taken an unmarried girl under the age of 16 out of the possession of her father, against his will, contrary to s 55 of the Offences Against the Person Act 1861.

In both cases the girls willingly went with the respective defendants and both were under 16. The issue was whether *mens rea* was required in respect of two points: first, whether the defendant had to know the girl was under 16 and second, whether the defendant had to know he was taking the girl from the 'possession' of her father.

### *R v Prince* (1875)

Prince knew that the girl he 'took' was in the possession of her father but believed, on reasonable grounds, that she was aged 18. He was convicted as he had the intention to remove the girl from the possession of her father. *Mens rea* was required for this part of the *actus reus* and he had the necessary intention. However, the court held that knowledge of her age was not required. On this aspect of the offence there was strict liability.

### *R v Hibbert* (1869)

The defendant met a girl aged 14 on the street. He took her to another place where they had sexual intercourse. He was acquitted of the offence as it was not proved that he knew the girl was in the custody of her father. Even though the age aspect of the offence was one of strict liability, *mens rea* was required for the removal aspect and, in this case, the necessary intention was not proved.

These cases were, of course, in Victorian times when the law was very different to what it is today. However, they illustrate that *mens rea* may be required for one part of an offence, but that another element of the offence is one of strict liability.

### 21.3.1 No fault

As already stated, the *actus reus* must be proved and the defendant's conduct in doing the *actus reus* must be voluntary. However, a defendant can be convicted if his voluntary act inadvertently caused a prohibited consequence. This is so even though the defendant was totally blameless in respect of the consequence. An example was the case of *Callow v Tillstone* (1900).

### Callow v Tillstone (1900)

A butcher asked a vet to examine a carcass to see if it was fit for human consumption. The vet assured him that it was all right to eat and so the butcher offered it for sale. In fact, it was unfit and the butcher was convicted of the offence of exposing unsound meat for sale.

Because it was a strict liability offence the butcher was guilty, even though he had taken reasonable care not to commit the offence. The butcher was not at fault in any way.

## 21.3.2 No 'due diligence' defence

For some offences the statute provides a defence of 'due diligence'. In other words, the defendant will not be liable if he can show that he did all that was within his power not to commit the offence.

### Key term

Due diligence – where the defendant has done all that was within his power not to commit an offence.

However, there does not seem to be any sensible pattern for when Parliament decides to include a 'due diligence' defence and when it does not. It can be argued that such a defence should always be available for strict liability offences. If it was a defence, then the butcher in *Callow v Tillstone* would not have been guilty. By asking a vet to check the meat, he had clearly done all that he could to make sure that he did not commit the offence.

Another example of where the defendants took all reasonable steps to prevent the offence but were still guilty because there was no 'due diligence' defence available is *Harrow LBC v Shah and Shah* (1999).

### Harrow LBC v Shah and Shah (1999)

The defendants owned a newsagents business where lottery tickets were sold. They had told their staff not to sell tickets to anyone under 16 years old. They frequently reminded their staff that if there was any doubt about a customer's age, the staff should ask for proof of age, and if still in doubt should refer the matter to the defendants. One of their staff sold a lottery ticket to a 13-year-old boy, without asking for proof of age. The salesman mistakenly believed the boy was over 16 years old. D1 was in a back room of the premises at the time: D2 was

not on the premises. The defendants were charged with selling a lottery ticket to a person under 16, contrary to s 13(1)(c) of the National Lottery Act 1993. The magistrates dismissed the charges, but the prosecution appealed to the Divisional Court which held that the offence was one of strict liability. This meant that the defendants were guilty.

The Divisional Court held that the offence did not require any *mens rea*. The act of selling the ticket to someone who was actually under 16 was enough to make the defendants guilty, even though they had done their best to prevent this happening in their shop.

## 21.3.3 No defence of mistake

Another feature of strict liability offences is that the defence of mistake is not available. This is important as, if the defence of mistake is available, the defendant will be acquitted when he made an honest mistake. Two cases which illustrate the difference in liability are *Cundy v Le Cocq* (1884) and *Sherras v De Rutzen* (1895). Both of these involved offences under the Licensing Act 1872.

### Cundy v Le Cocq (1884)

D was charged with selling intoxicating liquor to a drunken person. The magistrate trying the case found as a fact that the defendant and his employees had not noticed that the person was drunk. The magistrate also found that while the person was on the licensed premises he had been 'quiet in his demeanour and had done nothing to indicate insobriety; and that there were no apparent indications of intoxication'. However, the magistrate held that the offence was complete on proof that a sale had taken place and that the person served was drunk, and convicted the defendant. The defendant appealed against this but the Divisional Court upheld the conviction.

### Sherras v De Rutzen (1895)

D was convicted of supplying alcohol to a constable on duty. Local police, when on duty, wore an armband on their uniform. An on-duty police officer removed his armband before entering the defendant's public house. The officer was served by D's daughter in the presence of D. D thought that the constable was off duty because he was not wearing his armband. D was convicted but the Divisional Court quashed the conviction. It held that the offence was not one of strict liability and accordingly a genuine mistake provided the defendant with a defence.

**Figure 21.1** Strict liability

| Levels of liability | Law | Cases |
|---|---|---|
| **Absolute liability** | These offences do not need proof of *mens rea* or voluntary *actus reus* | *Larsonneur* (1933) <br> *Winzar* (1993) |
| **Strict liability** | *Mens rea* need not be proved <br> Proof will not be required for one aspect of *mens rea* <br> BUT may be required for another aspect of *mens rea* | *Storkwain* (1986) <br> *Prince* (1875) <br> *Hibbert* (1869) |
| **No fault liability** | D is liable if he voluntarily did the *actus reus* (e.g. 'sells') even though he is not blameworthy | *Callow v Tillstone* (1900) |
| **No 'due diligence' defence** | If the Act of Parliament does not allow a 'due diligence' defence, then D will be guilty even though he took all possible care | *Harrow LBC v Shah and Shah* (1999) |
| **No defence of mistake** | D will still be guilty even though he made a genuine mistake | *Cundy v le Cocq* (1884) |

The judge pointed out that there was nothing the publican could do to prevent the commission of the crime. Even if the publican asked the officer, it would be as easy for the constable to deny that he was on duty as for him to remove his armband before entering the public house. This explains the different decisions in the two cases. The fact of a person being drunk is an observable fact, so the publican should be put on alert and could avoid committing the offence.

### 21.3.4 Summary of strict liability

So, where an offence is held to be one of strict liability, the following points apply:

- The defendant must be proved to have done the *actus reus*.
- This must be a voluntary act on his part.
- There is no need to prove *mens rea* for at least part of the *actus reus*.
- No 'due diligence' defence will be available.
- The defence of mistake is not available.

These factors are well established. The problem lies in deciding which offences are ones of strict liability. For this, the courts will start with presuming that *mens rea* should apply. This is so for both common-law and statutory offences

## 21.4 Strict liability at common law

Nearly all strict liability offences have been created by statute. Strict liability is very rare in common-law offences. Only three existing common-law offences are ones of strict liability. These are:

- public nuisance
- criminal libel
- outraging public decency.

Public nuisance and criminal libel probably do not require *mens rea*, but there are no modern cases. Outraging public decency was held to be a strict liability offence in *Gibson and Sylveire* (1991).

### *Gibson and Sylveire* (1991)

Gibson had created an art exhibit of a model head with earrings which were made out of freeze-dried real human foetuses. He wanted to highlight how casually abortions were thought of. The model was put on display in Sylveire's art gallery. Both men were convicted of outraging public decency. It was a strict liability offence as it did not have to be proved either that D intended to outrage public decency, or that D was reckless as to whether his conduct would have the effect of outraging public decency.

## 21.5 Strict liability in statute law

The surprising fact is that over half of all statutory offences are ones of strict liability. This amounts to over 3,500 offences. Most strict liability offences are regulatory in nature. This may involve such matters as regulating the sale of food, alcohol and gaming tickets, the prevention of pollution and the safe use of vehicles.

Strict liability offences created by an Act of Parliament will not contain any words requiring *mens rea* in their definition. However, the courts will still look at a number of factors before deciding that a statutory offence is one of strict liability.

# 21.6 Interpretation by the courts

Statutory interpretation of Acts of Parliament is an important role of the courts. You will have studied the different rules and approaches to interpretation. Strict liability is an area of law where the courts will use statutory interpretation. The starting point is one of the presumptions of statutory interpretation – the presumption of *mens rea*.

## 21.6.1 Presumption of *mens rea*

In order to decide whether an offence is one of strict liability, the courts start by assuming that *mens rea* is required, but they are prepared to interpret the offence as one of strict liability if Parliament has expressly or by implication indicated this in the relevant statute.

The judges often have difficulty in deciding whether an offence is one of strict liability or not. The first rule is that where an Act of Parliament includes words indicating *mens rea* (e.g. 'knowingly', 'intentionally', 'maliciously' or 'permitting'), the offence requires *mens rea* and is not one of strict liability. However, if an Act of Parliament makes it clear that *mens rea* is not required, the offence will be one of strict liability.

However, in many instances a section in an Act of Parliament is silent about the need for *mens rea*. Parliament is criticised for this. If it made clear in all sections which create a criminal offence whether *mens rea* was required or not, then there would be no problem. As it is, where there are no express words indicating *mens rea* or strict liability, the courts have to decide which offences are ones of strict liability.

## 21.6.2 Principle in *Sweet v Parsley*

Where an Act of Parliament does not include any words indicating *mens rea*, the judges will start by presuming that all criminal offences require *mens rea*. This was made clear in the case of *Sweet v Parsley* (1969).

### Sweet v Parsley (1969)

D rented a farmhouse and let it out to students. The police found cannabis at the farmhouse and D was charged with 'being concerned in the management of premises used for the purpose of smoking cannabis resin'. D did not know that cannabis was being smoked there. It was decided that she was not guilty as the court presumed that the offence required *mens rea*.

In giving judgment, Lord Reid said:

> There has for centuries been a presumption that Parliament did not intend to make criminals of persons who were in no way blameworthy in what they did. That means that whenever a section is silent as to *mens rea* there is a presumption that ... we must read in words appropriate to require *mens rea*.

Although the courts start with the presumption that *mens rea* is required, they look at a variety of points to decide whether the presumption should stand or should be displaced and the offence made one of strict liability.

## 21.6.3 The *Gammon* tests

In *Gammon (Hong Kong) Ltd v Attorney-General of Hong Kong* (1984) the appellants had been charged with deviating from building work in a material way from the approved plan, contrary to the Hong Kong Building Ordinances. It was necessary to decide whether it had to be proved that they knew that their deviation was material or whether the offence was one of strict liability on this point.

The Privy Council started with the presumption that *mens rea* is required before a person can be held guilty of a criminal offence and that this presumption of *mens rea* applies to statutory offences.

They went on to give four other factors to be considered. These were that:

- The presumption can only be displaced if this is clearly or by necessary implication the effect of the words of the statute.
- The presumption is particularly strong where the offence is 'truly criminal' in character.
- The presumption can only be displaced if the statute is concerned with an issue of social concern such as public safety.
- Strict liability should only apply if it will help enforce the law by encouraging greater vigilance to prevent the commission of the prohibited act.

## 21.6.4 Looking at the wording of an Act

As already stated, where words indicating *mens rea* are used, the offence is not one of strict liability. If the particular section is silent on the point then the courts will look at other sections in the Act. Where the particular offence has no words of intention, but other sections in the Act do, then it is likely that this offence is a strict liability offence.

In *Storkwain* (1986) (see section 21.1) the relevant section, s 58(2) of the Medicines Act 1968, was silent on *mens rea*. The court looked at other sections in the Act and decided that, as there were express provisions for *mens rea* in other sections, Parliament had intended s 58(2) to be one of strict liability.

Where other sections allow for a defence of 'due diligence' but another section does not, then this is another possible indicator from within the statute that the offence is meant to be one of strict liability.

In *Harrow LBC v Shah and Shah* (1999) the defendants were charged under s 13(1)(c) of the National Lottery Act 1993. This subsection does not include any words indicating either that *mens rea* is required or not, nor does it contain any provision for a defence of 'due diligence'. However, another subsection, s 13(1)(a), clearly allows a defence of 'due diligence'. The inclusion of a 'due diligence' defence in subsection (1)(a) of s 13 but not in the subsection under which the defendants were charged, was an important point in the Divisional Court coming to the decision that s 13(1)(c) was an offence of strict liability.

## 21.6.5 Quasi-criminal offences

In *Gammon* (1984) the Privy Council stated that the presumption that *mens rea* is required is particularly strong where the offence is 'truly criminal' in character. Offences which are regulatory in nature are not thought of as being truly criminal matters and are, therefore, more likely to be interpreted as being of strict liability.

Regulatory offences are also referred to as 'quasi-crimes'. They affect large areas of everyday life. They include offences such as breaches of regulations in a variety of fields such as:

- selling food, as in *Callow v Tillstone* (1900)
- the selling of alcohol, as in *Cundy v le Cocq* (1884)
- building regulations, as in occurred in *Gammon* (1984)
- sales of lottery tickets to an under-age child, as in *Harrow LBC v Shah and Shah* (1999) and
- regulations preventing pollution from being caused, as in *Alphacell Ltd v Woodward* (1972).

### Alphacell Ltd v Woodward (1972)

The company was charged with causing polluted matter to enter a river, contrary to s 2(1)(a) of the Rivers (Prevention of Pollution) Act 1951, when pumps which they had installed failed, causing polluted effluent to overflow into a river. There was no evidence either that the company knew of the pollution or that it had been negligent. The offence was held by the House of Lords to be one of strict liability and the company was found guilty because it was of the 'utmost public importance' that rivers should not be polluted.

## 21.6.6 Penalty of imprisonment

Where an offence carries a penalty of imprisonment, it is more likely to be considered 'truly criminal' and so less likely to be interpreted as an offence of strict liability. This was an important factor in *B v DPP* (2000).

### B v DPP (2000)

D, a 15-year-old boy, asked a 13-year-old girl on a bus to give him a 'shiner' (i.e. have oral sex with him). He believed she was over the age of 14. He was charged with inciting a child under the age of 14 to commit an act of gross indecency, under s 1(1) of the Indecency with Children Act 1960. The House of Lords quashed his conviction, as *mens rea* was required for the offence.

The offence, inciting a child under the age of 14 to commit an act of gross indecency, carried a maximum penalty of two years' imprisonment. Lord Nicholls pointed out that this was a serious offence and that:

> the more serious the offence, the greater was the weight to be attached to the presumption [of *mens rea*], because the more severe was the punishment and the graver the stigma that accompanied a conviction.

However, some offences carrying imprisonment have been made strict liability offences. For example in *Storkwain* (1986) (see section 21.1) the offence carried a maximum sentence of two years' imprisonment. Despite this, the House of Lords still held that the offence was one of strict liability.

It appears unjust that an individual should be liable to imprisonment even though the offence does not require proof of any fault by the defendant.

## 21.6.7 Issues of social concern

The type of crime and whether it is 'truly criminal' are linked to another condition laid down by the case of *Gammon* (1984): that is the question of whether the crime involves an issue of social concern. The Privy Council ruled that the only situation in which the presumption of *mens rea* can be displaced is where the statute is concerned with an issue of social concern.

This allows strict liability to be justified in a wide range of offences, as issues of social concern can be seen to cover any activity which is a 'potential danger to public health, safety or morals'.

Regulations covering health and safety matters in relation to food, drink, pollution, building and road use are obviously issues of social concern, but other issues such as possession of guns are also regarded as matters of public safety.

Even transmitting an unlicensed broadcast has been held to be a matter of social concern. This was decided in R v Blake (1997).

### R v Blake (1997)

D was a disc jockey who was convicted of using a station for wireless telegraphy without a licence, contrary to s 1(1) of the Wireless Telegraphy Act 1949. His defence was that he believed he was making a demonstration tape and did not know he was transmitting. He was convicted on the basis that the offence was one of strict liability. He appealed to the Court of Appeal but his appeal was dismissed.

## 21.6.8 Promoting enforcement of the law

In *Gammon* (1984) the final point in considering whether strict liability should be imposed, even where the statute is concerned with an issue of social concern, was whether it would be effective to promote the objects of the statute by encouraging greater vigilance to prevent the commission of the prohibited act. If the imposition of strict liability will not make the law more effective then there is no reason to make the offence one of strict liability.

In *Lim Chin Aik v The Queen* (1963) the appellant had been convicted under s 6(2) of the Immigration Ordinance of Singapore of remaining in (having entered) Singapore when he had been prohibited from entering by an order made by the Minister under s 9 of the same Ordinance.

The Ordinance was aimed at preventing illegal immigration. However, the appellant had no knowledge of the prohibition and there was no evidence that the authorities had even tried to bring it to his attention. The Privy Council thought that it was not enough to be sure that the statute dealt with a grave social evil in order to infer strict liability. It was also important to consider whether the imposition of strict liability would assist in the enforcement of the regulations. If it did not, then the offence should not be one of strict liability.

**Figure 21.2** How the courts decide whether strict liability applies

| | Law | Cases |
|---|---|---|
| **Presumption of *mens rea*** | Unless the words make it clear that *mens rea* is not required, the courts will always start with the presumption that *mens rea* is required | *Sweet v Parsley* (1969) |
| **Looking at the rest of the Act** | If other subsections state that *mens rea* is required but the section being considered does not state this, it is likely that the offence will be held to be one of strict liability | *Storkwain* (1986) |
| **Quasi-criminal offences** | Regulatory crimes (not truly criminal) are more likely to be held to be strict liability offences | *Harrow LBC v Shah and Shah* (1999) |
| **Penalty of imprisonment** | Where an offence is punishable by imprisonment, it is less likely that it will be held to be one of strict liability | *B v DPP* (2000) |
| **Issue of social concern** | Where the offence involves potential danger to public health, safety or morals then it is more likely to be held to be a strict liability offence | *Blake* (1997) |
| **Would strict liability promote enforcement of the law?** | If making the offence one of strict liability would not help law enforcement then there is no reason to make the offence a strict liability one | *Lim Chin Aik v The Queen* (1963) |

# 21.7 Justification for strict liability

## 21.7.1 Policy issues

Many statutory offences created by Parliament are aimed at preventing danger or other problems to the public. The risks of such danger are thought to outweigh the defendant's individual rights. It is more important to protect the public, even though this may in some cases mean that defendants who have taken every possible care will be convicted of an offence.

For example, many statutory offences are connected with cars and other transport. It is important that all vehicles are in a safe condition and operated safely. If they are not, then there are obvious risks of causing death or injury. It is thought that by having offences of strict liability, people who operate vehicles will take greater care to carry out regular safety checks.

Roscoe Pound, an American academic of the early twentieth century, explained it in this way:

> **"** Such statutes are not meant to punish the vicious but to put pressure upon the thoughtless and inefficient to do their whole duty in the interests of public health or safety. **"**

## 21.7.2 Social utility

The main justification for strict liability offences is their usefulness to the public as a whole. Strict liability offences help protect society by regulating activities 'involving potential danger to public health, safety or morals'. Making an offence one of strict liability promotes greater care over these matters by encouraging higher standards in such matters as hygiene in processing and selling food, or in obeying building or transport regulations. It makes sure that businesses are run properly.

As failure to comply with high standards may cause risk to the life and health of large numbers of the general public, there is good reason to support this point of view. However, some opponents of strict liability argue that there is no evidence that strict liability leads to businesses taking a higher standard of care. Some even argue that strict liability may be counter-productive. If people realise that they could be prosecuted even though they have taken every possible care, they may be tempted not to take any precautions.

## 21.7.3 Other justifications

Other justifications for the imposition of strict liability include the following:

- It is easier to enforce as there is no need to prove *mens rea*.
- It saves court time as people are more likely to plead guilty.
- Parliament can provide a 'due diligence' defence where this is thought to be appropriate.
- Lack of blameworthiness can be taken into account when sentencing.

As there is no need to prove *mens rea*, it is clear that enforcement of the law is more straightforward. In addition, rather than prosecute for minor regulatory breaches, the Health and Safety Executive and local Trading Standards officers are more likely to serve improvement notices or prohibition notices in the first instance. This can help to ensure that the law is complied with, without the need for a court hearing. When a case is taken to court, the fact that only the act has to be proved saves time and also leads to many 'guilty' pleas.

The use of a 'due diligence' defence (or a 'no negligence' defence) can soften the law on strict liability. In many instances Parliament provides such a defence in the statute creating the offence. If the inclusion of such defences was done in a consistent way, then many of the objectors to the imposition of strict liability would be satisfied.

However, the use of 'due diligence' clauses in Acts often seems haphazard. For example, in *Harrow LBC v Shah and Shah* (1999) the relevant section allowed a 'due diligence' defence for promoters of the lottery but not for those managing a business in which lottery tickets were sold (see section 21.3.2).

The final justification for strict liability is that allowances for levels of blameworthiness can be made in sentencing. A judge can pass a very lenient sentence where he feels that the defendant's level of blameworthiness was low.

# 21.8 Arguments against strict liability

Although there are sound justifications for imposing strict liability, there are equally persuasive arguments against its use. The arguments against strict liability include:

- It imposes liability on people who are not blameworthy.
- Those who are unaware of risks may be guilty.
- There is no evidence that it improves standards.

- The imposition of strict liability is contrary to human rights.
- Some strict liability offences carry a social stigma.

## 21.8.1 Liable even though not blameworthy

The main argument against strict liability is that it imposes guilt on people who are not blameworthy in any way. Even those who have taken all possible care will be found guilty and can be punished.

This happened in the case of *Harrow LBC v Shah and Shah* (1999) where the defendants had done their best to prevent sales of lottery tickets to anyone under the age of 16. Another case where all possible care had been taken was *Callow v Tillstone* (1900). In this case even the use of an expert (a vet) was insufficient to avoid liability.

## 21.8.2 Guilty even though unaware of risk

Strict liability may be imposed even though the defendant was unaware of any risks.

In *Environment Agency v Empress Car Co (Abertillery) Ltd* (1998) the House of Lords considered the word 'cause' in an Act where there was strict liability. They held that a defendant could only escape liability if he could show that the occurrence arising from the operations of his business was 'abnormal and extraordinary' rather than a normal fact of life.

At first sight this seems to allow a defence for defendants who had no knowledge of the possibility that the event might happen. However, the Law Lords went on to say that even though it was not foreseeable that it would happen to the particular defendant or take the particular form, a defendant would be liable if the matter was one of ordinary occurrence.

So defendants can be guilty of a happening caused by a risk of which they were unaware. An example of this was seen in *Environment Agency v Brock plc* (1998).

### Environment Agency v Brock plc (1998)

A leakage was caused by a hidden defect in a seal. The leak caused pollution. It was pointed out that defects in valves are a rare but ordinary fact of life. The company was liable for the leak.

## 21.8.3 Does not improve standards

Although an important reason for imposition of strict liability is the maintenance of high standards so that health and safety are not put in jeopardy, there is,

as mentioned earlier, no evidence that it improves standards. In fact, if the precautions against a very small risk are too expensive, then company managers may decide not to pay for the precautions, but to take the risk. This is the idea of 'profit from risk'. The company's profits are more important than spending large sums of money on protecting against a small risk. The cost of the precautions may even be far greater than any fine that will be imposed on the company for breaking the law.

## 21.8.4 Contrary to human rights

Another argument against the imposition of strict liability where an offence is punishable by imprisonment is that it is contrary to the principles of human rights. This point was raised in *R v G* (2008).

### R v G (2008)

G was a 15-year-old boy who had consensual sex with a girl he thought was aged 15. In fact she was only aged 12, but agreed that she had told him she was 15. G was prosecuted under s 5 of the Sexual Offences Act 2003 for the offence of rape of a child under 13. He was advised that this was a strict liability offence and his belief that she was 15 was irrelevant. He, therefore, pleaded guilty. The case was referred to the House of Lords on two points. The first was whether the fact that the offence was one of strict liability violated Article 6(1) (entitlement to a fair hearing) and/or 6(2) (presumption of innocence) of the European Convention on Human Rights.

The Law Lords unanimously decided that there was no breach of either part of Article 6. Article 6(1) only guaranteed fair procedure: it was not concerned with the content of the law. Article 6(2) required a defendant to be presumed innocent of the offence, but did not say anything about what the mental or other elements of the offence should be.

So, in the case of G, the defendant was guilty of a very serious offence, even though he genuinely (and on reasonable grounds) believed that the girl was the same age as himself.

## 21.8.5 Social stigma

The case of *R v G* also shows that strict liability can be imposed even where it creates serious social stigma. As a result of his conviction, G was put on the register of sex offenders. This was a particularly serious consequence for G. This is a strong argument against the imposition of strict liability in crimes which do lead to serious social stigma.

This is not an issue in regulatory quasi-criminal offences as these carry little or no social stigma.

**Figure 21.3** Strict liability

| Case | Facts | Law/Comment |
|------|-------|-------------|
| *Pharmaceutical Society of Great Britain v Storkwain Ltd* (1986) | Pharmacists did not realise that a prescription was a forgery | Supplying the drugs without a genuine prescription made them guilty of the offence, even though the forgery was very difficult to spot<br>An example of strict liability |
| *R v Larsonneur* (1933) | D, having left the UK, was sent back in police custody | Even though her return was not voluntary she was guilty of being 'found in the UK'<br>An example of absolute liability |
| *Callow v Tillstone* (1900) | A butcher sold meat that had been passed fit to sell by a vet<br>The meat was found to be unfit | The butcher was guilty even though he was not at fault in any way<br>No defence of no fault |
| *Harrow LBC v Shah and Shah* (1999) | Ds had told their staff to ask for proof of age<br>Despite this a lottery ticket was sold to an underage boy<br>Ds were guilty | The offence was one of strict liability<br>Ds were guilty even though they had done their best to prevent such an offence happening |
| *Sweet v Parsley* (1969) | Tenants in a farmhouse owned by D smoked cannabis there<br>The landlord did not know | D was not guilty as there was a presumption that *mens rea* was required |
| *Alphacell Ltd v Woodward* (1972) | Pumps at Ds' factory failed, causing polluted effluent to overflow into a river<br>There was no evidence either that the company knew of the pollution or that it had been negligent | Ds were guilty because the offence was one of strict liability<br>It was important to protect against pollution |
| *B v DPP* (2000) | The conviction of D, a 15-year-old boy for inciting a child under the age of 14 to commit an act of gross indecency was quashed | *Mens rea* was required for the offence as it carried a maximum penalty of two years' imprisonment |
| *R v G* (2008) | D, 15-year-old boy had consensual sex with a girl he thought was aged 15 but was actually 12<br>He was held guilty of rape (a 12-year-old not being old enough to consent) | The offence was one of strict liability even though it could lead to a custodial sentence<br>Also it was not contrary to human rights to make it an offence of strict liability |

# 21.9 Proposals for reform of strict liability

The main problem is that there is no way of knowing whether Parliament has deliberately decided to make an offence one of strict liability, or whether it did not realise that that was the effect of the wording of the Act.

It has, therefore, been suggested that Parliament should always state expressly whether an offence is meant to be one of strict liability or not. This would mean that there would be no need for the courts to use complicated rules of interpretation in order to decide if an offence is one of strict liability or not. It would be clear to everybody.

The Draft Criminal Code suggested this could be done by including the presumption of *mens rea* in the Code. Clause 20 of the draft Code states: 'Every offence requires a fault element of recklessness with respect to each of its elements other than fault elements, unless otherwise provided.'

Another way of reforming strict liability could be by requiring each offence to have a defence of due diligence. This would avoid the injustice of those who have taken all possible care being guilty of an offence. This would be in line with the law in Australia and Canada where judges have developed a general 'no-negligence' defence.

Yet another way of reforming the law on strict liability could be to have a rule that no offence carrying the penalty of imprisonment could be an offence of strict liability. This reform is not so wide-ranging as the two ideas above, but it still promotes justice as it would ensure that no one could be imprisoned for a breach of strict liability.

Finally, an alternative way of reforming strict liability law might be by removing regulatory offences from the criminal system. These could instead be treated as administrative issues.

However, this type of reform could not be applied to mainstream criminal offences of strict liability, such as those in the Sexual Offences Act 2003. These would have to remain in the criminal law with the risk of injustice to those convicted of such offences as in the case of R v G.

## Tip

This area of law can be confusing as there are contradictory cases. It is important to understand the cases and can use them to support your answer.

## Check your understanding

1  Suggest why strict liability is justified in criminal law

2  Stuart is setting up a new business which involves the making and selling of coffee and cakes.

Explain the principle of 'strict liability' in criminal law and advise Stuart how it could affect his business.

## Summary

- Strict liability is where *mens rea* is not required for at least one part of the *actus reus*.

- Absolute liability is where there is no requirement for *mens rea* at all AND it is not necessary to prove D's *actus reus* was voluntary – these cases are very rare.

- For strict liability offences D can be convicted even if blameless:
  - there is no defence of due diligence
  - there is no defence of mistake.

- The only common law offences of strict liability are:
  - public nuisance
  - criminal libel
  - outraging public decency.

- More than half of all statutory offences are ones of strict liability.

- To decide if a statutory offence is one of strict liability the courts use the *Gammon* tests. These are:
  - there is a presumption that *mens rea* is required
  - this presumption is particularly strong where the offence is 'truly criminal'

  - the presumption can only be displaced if the statute is concerned with an issue of social concern such as public safety
  - strict liability should only apply if it will help enforce the law by encouraging greater vigilance to prevent the commission of the prohibited act.

- Strict liability is justified because:
  - it protects the public
  - it promotes greater care
  - it is easier to enforce
  - it saves court time
  - lack of blameworthiness can be taken into consideration when sentencing.

- Arguments against strict liability are:
  - liability should not be imposed on people who are blameless
  - those who have taken all possible care should not be penalised
  - there is no evidence that it improves standards
  - it is contrary to the principles of human rights.

# 22 Non-fatal offences against the person

After reading this chapter you should be able to:

■ Understand the offences of assault and battery
■ Understand assault occasioning actual bodily harm – s 47 OAPA 1861
■ Understand malicious wounding or inflicting grievous bodily harm – s 20 OAPA 1861
■ Understand wounding or causing grievous bodily harm with intent – s 18 OAPA 1861
■ Analyse and evaluate the law on these offences

## 22.1 Common assault

There are two ways of committing this:

■ assault
■ battery.

Assault and battery are common-law offences. There is no statutory definition for either assault or for battery. However, statute law recognises their existence as both of these offences are charged under s 39 Criminal Justice Act 1988 which sets out that the maximum punishment for them is six months' imprisonment or a fine of £5,000, or both.

The act involved is different for assault and battery. For assault, there is no touching, only causing the fear of immediate, unlawful force. For battery, there must be actual force. There are often situations in which both occur. For example, where the defendant approaches the victim shouting that he is going to 'get him', then punches the victim in the face. The approaching, shouting and raising his arm prior to the punch constitute an assault, while the punch is the battery. As the act is different for each it is easier to consider assault and battery separately.

### 22.1.1 Definition of assault

An **assault** is an act which causes the victim to apprehend the infliction of immediate, unlawful force with either an intention to cause another to fear immediate unlawful personal violence or recklessness as to whether such fear is caused.

In *R v Nelson* (2013) the Court of Appeal stated that 'What is required for common assault is for [D] to have done something of a physical kind which causes someone else to apprehend that they are about to be struck'.

**Key term**

**Assault** – an act which causes the victim to apprehend the infliction of immediate, unlawful force with either an intention to cause another to fear immediate unlawful personal violence or recklessness as to whether such fear is caused.

### 22.1.2 *Actus reus* of assault

An assault is also known as a technical assault or a psychic assault. There must be:

■ an act
■ which causes the victim to apprehend the infliction of immediate, unlawful force.

#### An 'act'

An assault requires some act or words. An omission is not sufficient to constitute an assault. However, words are sufficient for an assault. These can be verbal or written. In *R v Constanza* (1997) the Court of Appeal held that letters could be an assault. The defendant had written 800 letters and made a number of phone calls to the victim. The victim interpreted the last two letters as clear threats. The Court of Appeal said there was an assault as there was a 'fear of violence at some time, not excluding the immediate future'.

In *R v Ireland* (1997) it was held that even silent telephone calls can be an assault. It depends on the facts of the case.

#### 'Apprehend immediate unlawful force'

The important point is that the act or words must cause the victim to apprehend that immediate force is going to be used against him. There is no assault if the situation is such that it is obvious that the defendant cannot actually use force. For example, where the defendant shouts threats from a passing train there is no possibility that he can carry out the threats in the immediate future.

It was decided in *R v Lamb* (1967) that pointing an unloaded gun at someone who knows that it is unloaded cannot be an assault. This is because the other person does not fear immediate force. However, if the other person thought the gun was loaded then this could be an assault.

Fear of immediate force is necessary; 'immediate' does not mean instantaneous, but imminent, so an assault can be through a closed window, as in *Smith v Chief Superintendent of Woking Police Station* (1983).

### Smith v Chief Superintendent of Woking Police Station (1983)

D broke into a garden and looked through V's bedroom window on the ground floor at about 11 p.m. one evening. V was terrified and thought that D was about to enter the room. Although D was outside the house and no attack could be made at that immediate moment, the court held that V was frightened by his conduct. The basis of the fear was that she did not know what he was going to do next, but that it was likely to be of a violent nature. Fear of what he might do next was sufficiently immediate for the purposes of the offence.

Words indicating that there will be no violence may prevent an act from being an assault. This is a principle which comes from the old case of *Tuberville v Savage* (1669) where the defendant placed one hand on his sword and said, 'If it were not assize time, I would not take such language from you'. This was held not to be an assault, because what he said showed he was not going to do anything.

However, it will depend on all the circumstances. For example, in *R v Light* (1857) the defendant raised a sword above the head of his wife and said, 'Were it not for the bloody policeman outside, I would split your head open.' It was held that this was an assault. The wife feared that force was going to be used on her and the words in the circumstances were not enough to negate that fear.

Fear of any unwanted touching is sufficient: the force or unlawful personal violence which is feared need not be serious.

There are many examples of assault:

- raising a fist as though about to hit the victim
- throwing a stone at the victim which just misses
- pointing a loaded gun at someone within range
- making a threat by saying 'I am going to hit you'.

### Unlawfulness of the force

The force which is threatened must be unlawful. If it is lawful, there is no offence of common assault.

Whether force is lawful or unlawful is discussed in detail under the *actus reus* of battery in the next section.

### 22.1.3 Definition of battery

**Battery** is the application of unlawful force to another person intending either to apply unlawful physical force to another or recklessness as to whether unlawful force is applied.

### Key term

**Battery** – the application of unlawful force to another person intending either to apply unlawful physical force to another or recklessness as to whether unlawful force is applied.

### 22.1.4 *Actus reus* of battery

The *actus reus* of battery is the application of unlawful force to another person. Force is a slightly misleading word as it can include the slightest touching, as shown by the case of *Collins v Wilcock* (1984).

### Collins v Wilcock (1984)

Two police officers saw two women apparently soliciting for the purposes of prostitution. They asked the appellant to get into the police car for questioning but she refused and walked away.

As she was not known to the police, one of the officers walked after her to try to find out her identity. She refused to speak to the officer and again walked away. The officer then took hold of her by the arm to prevent her leaving. She became abusive and scratched the officer's arm. She was convicted of assaulting a police officer in the execution of his duty. She appealed against that conviction on the basis that the officer was not acting in the execution of his duty, but was acting unlawfully by holding her arm as the officer was not arresting her. The court held that the officer had committed a battery and the defendant was entitled to free herself.

In this case, the court pointed out that touching a person to get his attention was acceptable, provided that no greater degree of physical contact was used than was necessary. However, physical restraint was not acceptable.

A similar point arose in *Wood v DPP* (2008) where a police officer took hold of Wood's arm to check his identity.

## Wood (Fraser) v DPP (2008)

The police had received a report that a man named Fraser had thrown an ashtray at another person in a public house. The ashtray had missed the person but had been smashed. Three police officers went to the scene. They saw a man (the appellant, W) who fitted the description of 'Fraser' leave the public house. One of the police officers took hold of W by the arm and asked if he was Fraser. W denied this and struggled, trying to pull away. At that point another officer took hold of W's other arm. W was charged with assaulting two of the police officers while they were acting in the execution of their duty.

The police officer who had first caught hold of W's arm said that he had done this in order to detain W, but was not at that point arresting him. It was held that as the officer had not arrested W, then there was a technical assault (battery) by the police officers. This meant that W was entitled to struggle and was not guilty of any offence of assault against the police.

Even touching the victim's clothing can be sufficient to form a battery. In *R v Thomas* (1985) the defendant touched the bottom of a woman's skirt and rubbed it. The Court of Appeal said, *obiter*, 'There could be no dispute that if you touch a person's clothes while he is wearing them that is equivalent to touching him'.

## Continuing act

A battery may be committed through a continuing act, as in *Fagan v Metropolitan Police Commissioner* (1968) where the defendant parked his car with one of the tyres on a police officer's foot. When he parked he was unaware that he had done this, but when the police officer asked him to remove it, he refused to do so for several minutes. The court said that at the start there was an act which could be a battery but the full offence of battery was not committed at that point because there was no element of intention. However, it became an offence of battery the moment the intention was formed to leave the wheel on the officer's foot.

## Indirect act

A battery can also be through an indirect act such as a booby trap. In this situation the defendant causes force to be applied, even though he does not personally touch the victim. This occurred in *R v Martin* (1881) where the defendant placed an iron bar across the doorway of a theatre. He then switched off the lights. In the panic which followed several of the audience were injured when they were trapped and unable to open the door. Martin was convicted of an offence under s 20 of the Offences Against the Person Act (OAPA) 1861.

A more modern example is *DPP v K* (1990).

## DPP v K (1990)

D was a 15-year-old schoolboy who took sulphuric acid without permission from his science lesson, to try its reaction on some toilet paper. While he was in the toilet he heard footsteps in the corridor, panicked and put the acid into a hot-air hand drier to hide it. He returned to his class intending to remove the acid later. Before he could do so another pupil used the drier and was sprayed by the acid. D was charged with assault occasioning actual bodily harm (s 47). The magistrates acquitted him because he said he had not intended to hurt anyone (see section 22.2.2 for the *mens rea* of s 47). The prosecution appealed, by way of case stated, to the Queen's Bench Divisional Court which held that a common assault (which includes both an assault and a battery) could be committed by an indirect act.

How can it be assault, I didn't touch her?

Another example of indirect force occurred in *Haystead v Chief Constable of Derbyshire* (2000) where the defendant caused a small child to fall to the floor by punching the woman holding the child. The defendant was found guilty because he was reckless as to whether or not his acts would injure the child. It is worth noting that, in this case, the conviction could also be justified by the principle of transferred malice.

## Omissions

Criminal liability can arise by way of an omission, but only if the defendant is under a duty to act. Such a duty can arise out of a contract, a relationship, from the assumption of care for another or from the creation of a dangerous situation. As the *actus reus* of battery is the application of unlawful force it is difficult to think how examples could arise under these duty situations, but there has been one reported case, *DPP v Santa-Bermudez* (2003).

### DPP v Santa-Bermudez (2003)

In this case a policewoman, before searching D's pockets, asked him if he had any needles or other sharp objects on him. D said 'no', but when the police officer put her hand in his pocket she was injured by a needle which caused bleeding. The Divisional Court held that the defendant's failure to tell her of the needle could amount to the *actus reus* for the purposes of an assault causing actual bodily harm.

Other scenarios which could make a defendant liable by way of omission are where the defendant has created a dangerous situation which may lead to force being applied to the victim. This can be seen by analogy with *R v Miller* (1983) where D accidentally set fire to his mattress but failed to do anything to prevent damage to the building in which he was sleeping. He was convicted of arson.

No other person was involved, but if there had been someone else asleep in the room and Miller had failed to wake them and warn them of the danger, then he could have been liable for a battery if there had been any problem. For example, if the person was hit by plaster falling from the ceiling as a result of the fire, then there appears to be no reason why Miller could not have been charged with battery of that person.

## Unlawful force

For a battery to be committed, the force must be unlawful. If the victim gives genuine consent to it then the force may be lawful. Force may also be lawful where it is used in self-defence or prevention of crime. This can only be so if the force used is

reasonable in the situation as the defendant believed it to be. If the force is lawful, then the person using the force is not guilty of a battery.

Another situation where force may be lawful is in the correction of a child by a parent. English law recognises that moderate and reasonable physical chastisement of a child is lawful. However, in *A v UK* (1998) where a jury had acquitted a father who had beaten his son with a garden cane, the European Court of Human Rights ruled that a law allowing force to be used on children offends Article 3 of the European Convention on Human Rights. This article prohibits torture and inhuman or degrading treatment or punishment.

However, the Children Act 2004 now provides that a battery committed on a child is unlawful if it results in any injury.

## Battery without an assault

It is possible for there to be a battery even though there is no assault. This can occur where the victim is unaware that unlawful force is about to be used on him, such as where the attacker comes up unseen behind the victim's back. The first thing the victim knows is when he is struck; there has been a battery but no assault.

### Activity

Explain whether there is an assault and/or battery in the following situations:

1 At a party Tanya sneaks up behind Wilhelm, whom she knows well, and slaps him on the back.

2 Vince throws a stone at Delyth, but misses. He picks up another stone and this time hits the edge of Delyth's coat.

3 Imram turns round quickly without realising that Harry is standing just behind him, and bumps into Harry. Harry shouts at him, 'If you were not wearing glasses, I would hit you in the face'.

4 Ramsey and Sue are having an argument. During the argument, Ramsey says, 'If you don't shut up, I'll thump you'. Sue is so annoyed at this that she gets out a penknife and waves it in front of Ramsey's face. Ramsay pushes her away.

## 22.1.5 *Mens rea* of assault and battery

The *mens rea* for an assault is either an intention to cause another to fear immediate unlawful personal violence, or recklessness as to whether such fear is caused. The *mens rea* for battery is either an intention to apply unlawful physical force to another or recklessness as to whether unlawful force is applied. So intention or recklessness is sufficient for both assault and battery.

The test for recklessness is subjective. For an assault, the defendant must realise there is a risk that his acts/words could cause another to fear unlawful personal violence. For a battery the defendant must realise there is a risk that his act (or omission) could cause unlawful force to be applied to another.

Assault and battery are classed as offences of basic intent. This means that if the defendant is intoxicated when he does the relevant *actus reus* he is considered as doing it recklessly. This was stated by the House of Lords in *DPP v Majewski* (1976).

---

### DPP v Majewski (1976)

D had consumed large quantities of alcohol and drugs and then attacked the landlord of the public house where he was drinking. The landlord called the police and D also attacked the police officers who tried to arrest him. The Law Lords held that becoming intoxicated by drink and drugs was a reckless course of conduct, and recklessness is enough to constitute the necessary *mens rea* in assault cases.

---

This ruling can be criticised, as the point at which the drink or drugs are taken is a quite separate time to the point when the *actus reus* for the offence is committed. It is difficult to see how there is coincidence of the two. It is reasonable to say that the defendant is reckless when he takes drink or other intoxicating substances, but this does not necessarily mean that when he commits an assault or battery three or four hours later he is reckless for the purposes of the offence. The decision can be viewed as a public policy decision.

## 22.2 Section 47 OAPA 1861: assault occasioning actual bodily harm

We now look at assaults where an injury is caused. The lowest level of injury is referred to in the Offences Against the Person Act 1861 as 'actual bodily harm' under s 47. It is a triable-either-way

**Figure 22.1** Assault and battery

| Case | Facts | Law |
|---|---|---|
| *Constanza* (1997) | D wrote 800 letters and made phone calls to V | Written words can be an assault if they cause V to fear immediate violence |
| *Smith v Chief Superintendent (Woking)* (1983) | D looked through V's bedroom window late at night | Fear of what D would do next was sufficient for the *actus reus* of assault |
| *Tuberville v Savage* (1669) | D put hand on sword and said 'Were it not assize time, I would not take such language from you' | Words can prevent an act from being an assault, but it depends on the circumstances |
| *Collins v Wilcock* (1984) | A police officer held a woman's arm to prevent her walking away | Any touching may be a battery, and always is if there was physical restraint |
| *Wood (Fraser) v DPP* (2008) | An officer took hold of W's arm to check his identity | This was a battery by the police and W was entitled to struggle to release himself |
| *Fagan v MPC* (1968) | D, unknowingly, stopped his car with a wheel on a policeman's foot and refused to move when requested | The *actus reus* of battery can be an on-going act so that the complete offence is committed when D forms the *mens rea* |
| *DPP v K* (1990) | D put acid in a hand drier – the next person to use it was sprayed with acid | An indirect act can be the *actus reus* of battery |
| *DPP v Santa-Bermudez* (2003) | D failed to tell a policewoman that he had a needle in his pocket – she was injured when she searched him | An omission is sufficient for the *actus reus* of battery |
| *DPP v Majewski* (1976) | D, who had taken drink and drugs, attacked the landlord of a pub and police officers | Getting drunk is a reckless course of conduct and is sufficient for the *mens rea* of battery |

offence. The section states: 'Whosoever shall be convicted of any assault occasioning actual bodily harm shall be liable ... to imprisonment for five years.'

As can be seen from this very brief section, there is no definition of 'assault' or 'actual bodily harm'. Nor is there any reference to the level of *mens rea* required. For all these points it is necessary to look at case law.

## 22.2.1 *Actus reus* of s 47

It is necessary to prove that there was an assault or battery and that this caused actual bodily harm. An assault is sufficient even though the defendant does not touch the victim, provided the assault has caused actual bodily harm. This can occur in situations where V tries to escape from apprehended force by D and injures himself through doing this. Alternatively the apprehension of force may cause psychiatric injury to V.

### Actual bodily harm

In *Miller* (1954) it was said that actual bodily harm is 'any hurt or injury calculated to interfere with the health or comfort of the victim'. In *R v Chan Fook* (1994) the trial judge directed the jury that a nervous and hysterical condition could be actual bodily harm. On appeal the Court of Appeal disagreed with this. They held that 'actual' meant not so trivial as to be wholly insignificant. 'Harm' was injury which goes beyond interference with the health and comfort of the victim.

They also went on to say that 'bodily' is not limited to harm to skin, flesh and bones but includes injury to the nervous system and brain such as recognised and identifiable psychiatric harm.

In *T v DPP* (2003) loss of consciousness, even momentarily, was held to be actual bodily harm.

### T v DPP (2003)

D and a group of other youths chased V. V fell to the ground and saw D coming towards him. V covered his head with his arms and was kicked. He momentarily lost consciousness and remembered nothing until being woken by a police officer. D was convicted of assault occasioning actual bodily harm.

So, s 47 can be charged where there is any injury. Bruising, grazes and scratches all come within this offence. As we have seen in *T v DPP* (2003) it was held that loss of consciousness, even for a very short time, could be actual bodily harm. In *DPP v Smith (Michael)* (2006) it was held that cutting the victim's hair can amount to actual bodily harm.

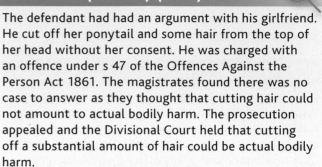

### DPP v Smith (Michael) (2006)

The defendant had had an argument with his girlfriend. He cut off her ponytail and some hair from the top of her head without her consent. He was charged with an offence under s 47 of the Offences Against the Person Act 1861. The magistrates found there was no case to answer as they thought that cutting hair could not amount to actual bodily harm. The prosecution appealed and the Divisional Court held that cutting off a substantial amount of hair could be actual bodily harm.

In *Smith* the court held that physical pain was not a necessary ingredient of actual bodily harm. Hair is attached to the head and this makes it a part of the body so that harm to the hair comes within the meaning of 'actual bodily harm'. However, the court did stress that a substantial amount of hair has to be cut off for the harm to be 'actual' as opposed to trivial or insignificant harm.

As already stated earlier in this section, psychiatric injury is also classed as 'actual bodily harm'. This was decided by the Court of Appeal in *R v Chan Fook* (1994). However, the Court of Appeal pointed out that actual bodily harm does not include 'mere emotions such as fear, distress or panic' nor does it include 'states of mind that are not themselves evidence of some identifiable clinical condition'.

This decision was approved by the House of Lords in *R v Burstow* (1997) where it was said that 'bodily harm' in ss 18, 20 and 47 OAPA 1861 must be interpreted so as to include recognisable psychiatric illness.

## 22.2.2 *Mens rea* of s 47

The section in the Act makes no reference to *mens rea* but, as the essential element is a common assault, the courts have held that the *mens rea* for a common assault is sufficient for the *mens rea* of a s 47 offence.

This means the defendant must intend or be subjectively reckless as to whether the victim fears or is subjected to unlawful force. This is the same *mens rea* as for an assault or a battery. It is important to note that there is no need for the defendant to intend or be reckless as to whether actual bodily harm is caused. This is demonstrated by the case of *R v Roberts* (1971).

### R v Roberts (1971)

D, who was driving a car, made advances to the girl in the passenger seat and tried to take her coat off. She feared that he was going to commit a more serious assault and jumped from the car while it was travelling at about 30 miles per hour. As a result of this she was slightly injured. D was found guilty of assault occasioning actual bodily harm even though he had not intended any injury or realised there was a risk of injury. He had intended to apply unlawful force when he touched her as he tried to take her coat off. This satisfied the *mens rea* for a common assault and so he was guilty of an offence under s 47.

This decision was confirmed by the House of Lords in the combined appeals of *R v Savage* (1991) and *R v Parmenter* (1991).

### R v Savage (1991)

D threw beer over another woman in a pub. In doing this the glass slipped from D's hand and V's hand was cut by the glass. D said that she had only intended to throw beer over the woman. D had not intended her to be injured, nor had she realised that there was a risk of injury. She was convicted of a s 20 offence but the Court of Appeal quashed that and substituted a conviction under s 47 (assault occasioning actual bodily harm). She appealed against this to the House of Lords. The Law Lords dismissed her appeal.

The fact that she intended to throw the beer over the other woman meant she had the intention to apply unlawful force and this was sufficient for the *mens rea* of the s 47 offence.

From all these cases, we can now get a definition for an assault occasioning actual bodily harm, which is given below.

### Key term

**Assault occasioning actual bodily harm** – an assault or battery which causes actual bodily harm to V and D intends or is subjectively reckless as to whether the victim fears unlawful force or is actually subjected to unlawful force.

**Figure 22.2** Assault, battery and s 47

| Offence | Actus reus | Consequence (injury) required | Mens rea |
|---|---|---|---|
| **Assault** | Causing V to fear immediate unlawful violence Requires an act but can be by silent telephone calls: *Ireland* (1997), or letters: *Constanza* (1997) | None needed | Intention of, or subjective recklessness as to, causing V to fear immediate unlawful violence |
| **Battery** | Application of unlawful violence, even the slightest touching: Collins v Wilcock (1984). | None needed | Intention of, or subjective recklessness as to, applying unlawful force: *DPP v Majewski* (1976 |
| NB Assault and battery are both charged under s 39 of the Criminal Justice Act 1988 and are known as common assault | | | |
| **Assault occasioning actual bodily harm s 47 OAPA 1861** | Assault, i.e. an assault or battery | Actual bodily harm (e.g. bruising) This includes: ■ momentary loss of consciousness: *R(T) v DPP* (2003) ■ psychiatric harm: *Chan Fook* (1994) | Intention or subjective recklessness as to causing fear of unlawful violence or of applying unlawful force, i.e. the *mens rea* for an assault or battery |

## 22.3 Section 20 OAPA 1861: malicious wounding/inflicting grievous bodily harm

This is the next offence in seriousness. It is an offence under s 20 OAPA 1861 which states:

> " Whosoever shall unlawfully and maliciously wound or inflict any grievous bodily harm upon any other person, either with or without a weapon or instrument, shall be guilty of an offence and shall be liable ... to imprisonment for not more than five years. "

The offence is commonly known as 'malicious wounding'. It is triable either way and the maximum sentence is five years. This is the same maximum sentence as for a s 47 offence, despite the fact that s 20 is seen as a more serious offence and requires both a higher degree of injury and *mens rea* as to an injury.

For the offence to be proved it must be shown that the defendant:

- wounded OR
- inflicted grievous bodily harm

and that he did this:

- intending some injury (but not serious injury) be caused OR
- being reckless as to whether any injury was inflicted.

### 22.3.1 Wound

'Wound' means a cut or a break in the continuity of the whole skin. A cut of internal skin, such as in the cheek, is sufficient, but internal bleeding where there is no cut of the skin is not sufficient. In *JJC v Eisenhower* (1983) the victim was hit in the eye by a shotgun pellet. This did not penetrate the eye but did cause severe bleeding under the surface. As there was no cut, it was held that this was not a wound. The cut must be of the whole skin, so that a scratch is not considered a wound.

Even a broken bone is not considered a wound, unless the skin is broken as well. In the old case of *R v Wood* (1830) the victim's collar bone was broken but, as the skin was intact, it was held there was no wound.

### 22.3.2 Grievous bodily harm

It was held in *DPP v Smith* (1961) that grievous bodily harm means 'really serious harm'. The harm does not have to be life-threatening and in *Saunders* (1985) it was held that it was permissible to direct a jury that there need be 'serious harm' not including the word 'really'.

In *R v Bollom* (2004) it was held that the severity of the injuries should be assessed according to the victim's age and health.

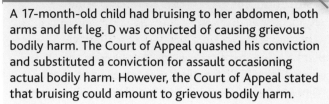

### R v Bollom (2004)

A 17-month-old child had bruising to her abdomen, both arms and left leg. D was convicted of causing grievous bodily harm. The Court of Appeal quashed his conviction and substituted a conviction for assault occasioning actual bodily harm. However, the Court of Appeal stated that bruising could amount to grievous bodily harm.

However, bruising of this severity would be less serious on an adult in full health, than on a very young child.

In *R v Burstow* (1997) where the victim of a stalker suffered a severe depressive illness as a result of his conduct, it was decided that serious psychiatric injury can be grievous bodily harm.

In *R v Dica* (2004) there was the first ever conviction for causing grievous bodily harm through infecting victims with the HIV virus.

### R v Dica (2004)

The defendant had had unprotected sex with two women without telling them he was HIV-positive. Both women became infected as a result. Although on appeal the defendant's conviction was quashed on the question of consent and the case sent for re-trial, there was no doubt that infecting someone with HIV was inflicting grievous bodily harm. At his retrial the defendant was convicted.

### 22.3.3 Inflicting grievous bodily harm

Section 20 uses the word 'inflict'. Originally, this was taken as meaning that there had to be a technical assault or battery. Even so it allowed the section to be interpreted quite widely, as shown in *R v Lewis* (1974) where D shouted threats at his wife through a closed door in a second-floor flat and tried to break his way through the door. The wife was so frightened that she jumped from the window and broke both her legs. D was convicted of a s 20 offence. The threats could be considered as a technical assault.

In *R v Burstow* (1997) it was decided that 'inflict' does not require a technical assault or a battery.

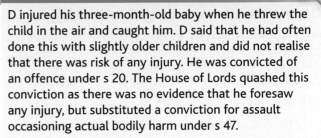

**R v Burstow (1997)**

D carried out an eight-month campaign of harassment against a woman with whom he had had a brief relationship some three years earlier. The harassment consisted of both silent and abusive telephone calls, hate mail and stalking. This caused V to suffer from severe depression. D's conviction under s 20 OAPA 1861 was upheld by the House of Lords.

**R v Parmenter (1991)**

D injured his three-month-old baby when he threw the child in the air and caught him. D said that he had often done this with slightly older children and did not realise that there was risk of any injury. He was convicted of an offence under s 20. The House of Lords quashed this conviction as there was no evidence that he foresaw any injury, but substituted a conviction for assault occasioning actual bodily harm under s 47.

This means that it need only be shown that the defendant's actions have led to the consequence of the victim suffering grievous bodily harm. The decision also means that there now appears to be little, if any, difference in the *actus reus* of the offences under s 20 and s 18 which uses the word 'cause'. In fact, in R v Burstow (1997) Lord Hope said that for all practical purposes there was no difference between the two words.

### 22.3.4 *Mens rea* of s 20

The word used in the section is 'maliciously'. In *Cunningham* (1957) it was held that 'maliciously' did not require any ill will towards the person injured. It simply meant either:

- an intention to do the particular kind of harm that was in fact done or
- recklessness as to whether such harm should occur or not (i.e. the accused has foreseen that the particular kind of harm might be done, and yet gone on to take the risk of it).

> See section 20.3.1 for full details on the *Cunningham* case.

In R v Parmenter (1991) the House of Lords confirmed that the *Cunningham* meaning of recklessness applies to all offences in which the statutory definition uses the word 'maliciously'. So, for the *mens rea* of s 20 the prosecution can prove either that the defendant intended to cause another person some harm or that he was subjectively reckless as to whether another person suffered some harm.

This left another point which the courts had to resolve. What was meant by the particular kind of harm? Does the defendant need to realise the risk of a wound or grievous bodily harm? It was decided by the House of Lords in *Parmenter* that, although the *actus reus* of s 20 requires a wound or grievous bodily harm, there is no need for the defendant to foresee this level of serious injury.

This decision means that, although there are four offences which appear to be on a ladder in terms of seriousness, there is overlap in terms of the *mens rea*.

## 22.4 Section 18 OAPA 1861: wounding or causing grievous bodily harm with intent

This offence under s 18 OAPA 1861 is often referred to as 'wounding with intent'. In fact, it covers a much wider range of offences than this implies.

It is considered a much more serious offence than s 20, as can be seen from the difference in the maximum punishments. Section 20 has a maximum of five years' imprisonment whereas the maximum for s 18 is life imprisonment. Also, s 20 is triable either way but s 18 must be tried on indictment at the Crown Court. The definition in s 18 OAPA 1861 states:

> 66 Whosoever shall unlawfully and maliciously by any means whatsoever wound or cause any grievous bodily harm to any person, with intent to do some grievous bodily harm to any person, or with intent to resist or prevent the lawful apprehension or detainer of any person, shall be guilty of ... an offence. 99

### 22.4.1 *Actus reus* of s 18

This can be committed in two ways:

- wounding or
- causing grievous bodily harm.

The meanings of 'wound' and 'grievous bodily harm' are the same as for s 20. The word 'cause' is very wide so that it is only necessary to prove that the defendant's act was a substantial cause of the wound or grievous bodily harm.

**Figure 22.3** Sections 20 and 18

| Offence | *Actus reus* | Consequence (injury) required | *Mens rea* |
|---|---|---|---|
| **Maliciously wounding or inflicting grievous bodily harm s 20 OAPA 1861** | A direct or indirect act or omission: *Martin* (1881) No need to prove an assault: *Burstow* (1998) | Either a wound – a cutting of the whole skin: *JJC v Eisenhower* (1984) OR Grievous bodily harm (really serious harm) which includes psychiatric harm: *Burstow* (1998) | Intention or subjective recklessness as to causing some injury (though not serious): *Parmenter* (1991) |
| **Wounding or causing grievous bodily harm with intent s 18 OAPA 1861** | A direct or indirect act or omission which causes V's injury | A wound or grievous bodily harm (as above) | Specific intention to cause grievous bodily harm, OR Specific intention to resist or prevent arrest plus recklessness as to causing injury: *Morrison* (1989) |

## 22.4.2 *Mens rea* of s 18

This is a specific intent offence. The defendant must be proved to have intended to:

- do some grievous bodily harm or
- resist or prevent the lawful apprehension or detainer of any person.

Note that an intention to wound is not enough for the *mens rea* of s 18. This was clearly stated in R *v Taylor* (2009).

### R v Taylor (2009)

V was found with scratches across his face and a stab wound in his back. Photographs of the scratches showed no more than surface scratches and it was impossible to tell the depth of the wound. The medical evidence did not help in showing whether D had intended to cause really serious injury. The judge directed that the jury must be sure that the prosecution had proved that D had intended to cause grievous bodily harm or to wound. D was convicted of a s 18 offence. On appeal, the Court of Appeal quashed the conviction on the basis that the judge had misdirected the jury. An intention to wound was not sufficient for the *mens rea* of s 18. Instead the Court of Appeal substituted a conviction for s 20.

### Intent to do some grievous bodily harm

Although the word 'maliciously' appears in s 18, it has been held that this adds nothing to the *mens rea* of this section where grievous bodily harm is intended. The important point is that s 18 is a specific intent crime. Intention must be proved; recklessness is not enough for the *mens rea* of s 18. 'Intention' has the same meaning as shown in the leading cases on murder.

So, as decided in *Moloney* (1985), foresight of consequences is not intention; it is only evidence from which intention can be inferred or found. Following the cases of *Nedrick* (1986) and *Woollin* (1998), intention cannot be found unless the harm caused was a virtual certainty as a result of the defendant's actions and the defendant realised that this was so.

> See section 20.2.2 for a fuller discussion on these cases and the meaning of 'intention'.

Where the defendant is trying to resist or prevent arrest or detention then the level of intention regarding the injury is lower. The prosecution must prove that he had specific intention to resist or prevent arrest, but so far as the injury they need only prove that he was reckless as to whether his actions would cause a wound or injury. This was decided in R *v Morrison* (1989).

### R v Morrison (1989)

A police officer seized hold of D and told him that she was arresting him. He dived through a window, dragging her with him as far as the window so that her face was badly cut by the glass. The Court of Appeal held that as the word 'maliciously' is used in respect of this part of the section it must have the same meaning as in *Cunningham* (1957). This means that the prosecution must prove that the defendant either intended injury or realised there was a risk of injury and took that risk.

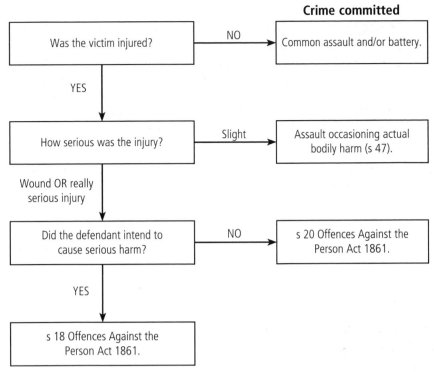

**Figure 22.4** Flowchart on offences against the person

## Activity

Explain in each of the situations below, what type of offence may have been committed.

1 In a football match Billy is kicked by Rio as Rio tries to get control of the ball. This causes bruising to Billy's leg. Billy is annoyed at this and punches Rio in the face causing a cut to his lip.

2 Anish is walking along a canal bank. Carol is in a hurry and pushes past him, knocking him into the canal. Anish hits his head on the side and suffers a fractured skull.

3 A police officer sees Jason damaging a parked car. The officer puts his hand on Jason's shoulder and says 'I am arresting you for criminal damage'. Jason punches the officer hard in the face breaking his jaw. Jason then runs off.

4 Karl waves a knife at Lily, saying 'I am going to cut that silly smile off'. Lily is very frightened and faints. She falls against Mary, who is knocked to the ground and suffers bruising.

## 22.5 Evaluation of the need for reform of the law on assault

In the 1980s and 1990s many reports on this area of law were published. All of these emphasised the need for reform. They included:

- Criminal Law Revision Committee, Fourteenth Report, Offences against the Person (1980)
- Legislating the Criminal Code: Offences against the Person and General Principles, Law Commission Report (1993)
- Violence: Reforming the Offences against the Person Act 1861. Home Office Consultation Paper with draft Bill (1998)
- Reform of Offences Against the Person, Law Commission, (2015) (Law Com No. 361).

### 22.5.1 Out of date

The 1861 Act is over 150 years old. This has caused a number of problems. For example, when it was created people did not have the understanding of mental health problems that we have today. So the Act only referred to 'bodily' harm in the offences and did not mention any mental harm.

As a result, for some time it was not sure that the offences could include those where the victim had suffered mental harm. To fill this gap in the law, the courts in *Chan Fook* (1994) and *Burstow* (1997) held that the meaning of 'bodily harm' did include injury to mental health. Since then defendants causing such injury can be convicted of offences under the 1861 Act.

Another area which has created problems is whether inflicting bodily harm could cover the situation of infecting another person with a disease. In 1861 there was only limited understanding of how some diseases were transmitted from person to person. The idea that a criminal offence could be committed by infecting someone with a disease was certainly not thought of then. Again the courts filled this gap by ruling in *Dica* (2004) that infecting someone with HIV did come within the wording of inflicting grievous bodily harm.

## 22.5.2 Inconsistency between offences

There are inconsistencies in the Act, especially with regard to the *mens rea* required for each offence. In particular, s 47 has the same *mens rea* as for an assault or battery. It does not require the defendant to intend or even realise that there is a risk of any injury. This appears unjust as s 47 carries a maximum sentence of five years' imprisonment while assault and battery only carry a maximum of six months' imprisonment.

It is also unjust that a person who causes a small cut can be charged with the more serious offence of s 20 instead of the offence of 'occasioning actual bodily harm' under s 47. This is because s 20 refers to 'wound or grievous bodily harm'. Yet clearly there are different levels of wound, and many of them do not equate with grievous bodily harm.

Another inconsistency is that the maximum sentence for both s 47 and s 20 offences is the same (five years' imprisonment). Yet the s 20 offence is clearly more serious than s 47 as it requires more serious injury. It also requires that D intends or is reckless as to causing V some harm whereas for s 47 it is not necessary to prove that D intended or was reckless as to whether he would cause some harm to V. It seems unjust that these two offences carry the same maximum penalty when the levels of blameworthiness are so different.

The 2015 Report points out that the above problems mean there is no clear hierarchy of offences.

Yet another inconsistency in the 1861 Act is that a defendant who intends or foresees the risk of minor injury can be convicted of the very serious offence of s 18 if serious injury occurs when he intends to resist arrest. This is the effect of the decision in *Morrison* (1989) (see section 22.4.2). Is it right that by intending to resist arrest, the defendant becomes liable for the same offence as someone who has intended to cause very serious injuries?

### Correspondence principle

The 2015 Report also points out that the offences in the Act do not conform to the 'correspondence principle'. Under this principle the results which D must intend or foresee should match the results which actually occur. D should not be held liable for a given kind and level of harm unless he meant to do it or at least knowingly ran the risk of it.

Under the 1861 Act a defendant can be guilty of a s 20 offence without intending or being reckless as to causing serious harm. Equally a defendant can be guilty of a s 47 offence without intending or being reckless as to causing any harm. Both these are clear breaches of the correspondence principle.

## 22.5.3 Need for modern, simplified language

Section 20 uses the word 'maliciously'. In modern language today, the word 'maliciously' suggests acting deliberately and with ill-will to the victim. Yet the meaning of the word in the 1861 Act has been held to be that D either intended to do the type of harm that was done or was reckless as to whether that type of harm occurred (see *Cunningham* (1957)). The Law Commission has recommended that the word 'reckless' should be used.

The Act is not consistent in that for s 20 the word 'inflict' is used, yet for s 18 the word 'cause' is used. This led to considerable debate as to whether the word 'inflict' in s 20 meant that a technical assault had to take place. This was finally resolved by the case of *Burstow* (1997) (see section 22.3.3) in which the House of Lords ruled that it did not.

## 22.5.4 The 1998 draft Bill

In 1998 the Home Office issued a Consultation Document, 'Violence: Reforming the Offences Against the Person Act 1861'. This included a draft Bill which set out four main offences. These were intended to replace ss 18, 20, 47 and assault and battery. In order, the clauses of the draft Bill, starting with the most serious are:

### Clause 1

Intentional serious injury: where a person would be guilty if he intentionally caused serious injury to another.

## Clause 2

Reckless serious injury: where a person would be guilty if he recklessly caused serious injury to another.

## Clause 3

Intentional or reckless injury: where a person would be guilty if he intentionally or recklessly caused injury to another.

## Clause 4

Assault: a person would be guilty if he intentionally or recklessly:

a applied force to or caused an impact on the body of another or

b caused the other to believe that any such force or impact is imminent.

In each of these the level of injury and the required *mens rea* are made clear by the wording. In addition, the draft Bill also defined the word 'injury', making it clear that both physical and mental injury were included.

## 22.5.5 Law Commission Report 2015

This Report set out several recommendations. The first one is that OAPA 1861 should be replaced by a 'comprehensive modern statute'.

Any new statute should respect the following principles:

- It should provide a clear hierarchy of offences from the most serious to the least. The place of each offence in the hierarchy should reflect:
  - the harm caused
  - the culpability of the defendant and
  - the maximum penalty should be in proportion.
- Each offence should provide a clear and accurate label for the conduct in question and should be defined in language that is easy to understand.
- Each ingredient of an offence, whether an external element or a mental element, should be set out explicitly.

The Report also recommended that any new statute on crimes of violence should follow the scheme of the 1998 draft Bill, though it has also suggested some additions and modifications.

### Draft Bill clauses 1–3

**Clause 1** above would become the definition of the most serious non-fatal offence against the person replacing the present s 18 offence. The word 'wounding' is not used so that it would only be included if the wound caused a serious injury. The offence would carry a maximum sentence of life imprisonment.

**Clause 2** would replace the existing s 20 offence. Under it the normal principles of recklessness would apply. So a defendant would only be guilty if he was aware, in the circumstances as he knew or believed them to be, that there was a risk of serious injury. This is a higher level of *mens rea* required than under the present s 20 where the defendant can be guilty if he is reckless about any injury (including minor injury) occurring. The recommendation is that this offence should carry a maximum sentence of seven years' imprisonment (an increase on the present five years). This is justified because of the higher level of *mens rea* required by Clause 2.

**Clause 3** would replace the existing s 47 offence. The defendant would be guilty if he intentionally or recklessly caused an injury to another person. The injury need not be serious. This offence would carry a maximum sentence of five years' imprisonment (the same as the present s 47).

For all of these three offences, injury would include both physical and mental illness. Mental injury should have the same limits as the existing law, namely recognised psychiatric conditions. Disease would still be considered a physical injury as in the case of *Dica* (2004) (see section 22.3.2). So a defendant who recklessly transmitted HIV could be charged with the offence in Clause 2, while a defendant who recklessly transmitted a less serious sexual disease could be charged under Clause 3.

### Aggravated assault

The 2015 Report also recommended that there should be another offence where low-level injuries are involved. This would be 'aggravated assault'. The intention is that it should cover injuries such as superficial cuts, scratches, minor bruising, grazes and swellings. Although these are technically 'actual bodily harm' in the present law, the Crown Prosecution Service charging standards recommend that they should currently be charged as common assault.

The proposed new offence recognises that victims who have suffered a low-level injury can feel aggrieved when their case is only charged as a common assault. The *mens rea* would be the same as for the current common assault: that is that D must intend or be reckless as to whether V is put in fear of unlawful force or is subjected to unlawful force.

The Report recommends that this offence should have a maximum of 12 months' imprisonment.

### Physical assault

The 2015 Report recommends that there should be an offence of physical assault to replace the common-law battery. This should not be used for low-level injury, as happens at present. These would come under the aggravated assault offence. It would be where there is unwanted and unjustifiable touching of the victim, either direct physical contact between D and V or by D causing some object to come into contact with V such as throwing a stone or setting a trap.

The *mens rea* would be the same as for the current offence of common assault: that is that D must intend or be reckless as to whether V is put in fear of unlawful force or is subjected to unlawful force. The Report recommends that this offence should have a maximum of six months' imprisonment, the same as for the current offence of battery.

### Threatened assault

The 2015 Report recommends that there should be an offence of threatened assault to replace the common law offence of assault. It would cover the same conduct as the present offence of assault and would be subject to the same penalty of a maximum of six months' imprisonment. The *mens rea* required would be the same as for the current offence of common assault: that is that D must intend or be reckless as to whether V is put in fear of unlawful force or is subjected to unlawful force.

### Causing serious harm intending to resist arrest

At the moment this offence is included in s 18. This means that it is subject to a maximum sentence of life imprisonment even though D need not intend or foresee serious injury. The 1998 draft Bill proposed a separate offence where D caused serious harm intending to resist arrest, prevent or terminate the lawful arrest or detention of himself or a third party. It was also thought that there should be a lower maximum penalty. This would recognise the fact that the *mens rea* required is lower than for s 18.

### Assault intending to resist arrest

The draft Bill also included a lower level of assault where D intends to resist arrest, prevent or terminate the lawful arrest or detention of himself or a third party. This would be charged where no serious harm was caused and it was proposed that the maximum penalty should be two years' imprisonment. The 2015 Report supports this proposal.

## 22.5.6 Comment on the 2015 Report

The recommendations in the Report would provide a more coherent set of offences than exists at present. There would be no overlap or inconsistency between the offences.

The *actus reus* and the *mens rea* for each proposed new offence are clearly set out. The offences conform to the 'correspondence principle' and defendants would only be held liable for a given kind and level of harm where they either meant to do it or knowingly ran the risk of it.

The law would be strengthened if the recommendation for a higher maximum penalty of seven years' imprisonment for Clause 2 is implemented. Also the proposed new offence of aggravated assault would carry a higher maximum penalty than common assault. This would give victims greater protection.

### Look online

For further reading on this topic, look at the Law Commission's Report, Reform of Offences against the Person (Law Com No. 361). This can be found on the Law Commission's website: www.lawcom.gov.uk. Chapter 3 of the Report on the need for reform and Chapter 9 Recommendations are particularly useful.

### Tip

When applying the law to a scenario-based question, it is helpful to look to see what injury, if any, has occurred. If there is no injury then the offence can only be an assault or a battery. If there is slight injury, then you need to consider s 47 OAPA. If the injury is more serious, it is necessary to look at ss 20 and 18. Don't forget to discuss whether the necessary *mens rea* exists.

## Check your understanding

1 Which one of the following statements most accurately describes what is meant by 'a wound' in non-fatal offences against the person?

   A Any bleeding including internal bleeding

   B A graze or a scratch

   C A cut of the whole skin

   D A cut causing serious injury

2 Which one of the following statements most accurately describes the actus reus of a battery in non-fatal offences against the person?

   A Intending to apply unlawful force to another person

   B Causing a minor injury to another person

   C The application of unlawful force to another person

   D Threatening to apply unlawful force to another person

3 Aimee and Bryonie are hockey players. During a match, Aimee tries to hit Bryonie's stick to get the ball away from her but instead she hits Bryonie's leg causing bruising. Later in the match, Aimee is annoyed when Bryonie scores a goal, and shouts at her 'I'll get you after the match'. Bryonie retaliates by hitting Aimee on her arm with her stick, breaking the arm.

Advise Aimee as to her potential liability for a non-fatal offence.

Advise Bryonie as to her potential liability for a non-fatal offence.

## Summary

- The present law on non-fatal offences against the person is mainly set out in the Offences Against the Person Act 1861.

- Common assault can be either an assault or battery.

- An assault is an act which intentionally or recklessly causes another to fear immediate and unlawful violence.

- Battery is the application, intentionally or recklessly, of unlawful force to another person.

- Assault occasioning actual bodily harm (s 47 OAPA 1861) is assault or battery which causes actual bodily harm. 'Actual bodily harm' is 'any hurt or injury calculated to interfere with the health or comfort' of the victim. It includes psychiatric injury.

- Unlawfully and maliciously wounding or inflicting grievous bodily harm upon another person (s 20 OAPA 1861) D must intend to cause another person some harm or be subjectively reckless as to whether he suffers some harm. There is no need for the defendant to foresee serious injury.

- Wounding or causing grievous bodily harm with intent to do so (s 18 OAPA 1861) is a specific intent offence. D must be proved to have intended to:
   - do some grievous bodily harm or
   - resist or prevent the lawful apprehension or detainer of any person.

- Where D intends to resist or prevent lawful apprehension or detainer there is no need for him to intend to cause grievous bodily harm. Recklessness as to injury is sufficient.

- For ss 20 and 18, grievous bodily harm means 'really serious harm' but this does not have to be life-threatening: wound means a cut or a break in the continuity of the whole skin.

- The law is in need of reform: the wording is old fashioned and unclear; there are major inconsistencies between the offences.

- The Law Commission's Report (2015) proposes a new statute to replace the 1861 Act with a clearer hierarchy of offences.

# Tort

# 23 The rules of tort law

After reading this chapter you should be able to:
■ Understand the rules and principles concerning liability and fault in actions for negligence and occupiers' liability, and associated remedies.

## 23.1 The principles of liability and fault in tort

Virtually everyone can identify and name some criminal offences. But how many civil actions can you identify and name?

There are many different types of civil actions but they generally receive less publicity than criminal offences and the public generally are less aware of them. For AS, you only have to learn about the actions of negligence and occupiers' liability. Both of these actions will come about when personal injury or damage to property has been caused. For A-level you also have to learn the rules of other civil actions such as nuisance, negligent misstatement and where the victim has suffered psychiatric injury; you will also learn about vicarious liability, where someone other than the person who committed the wrong can be **liable**. Finally, for A-level, you will learn about the defences available in civil actions. For both AS and A-level you need to understand the general principles of fault and strict liability in civil actions.

### Key term

**Liable** – the judge's decision that the case against the defendant is proved and that the defendant should pay compensation.

**Civil law** is concerned with settling disputes between individuals, between individuals and a business, or between a business and another business. The key difference between civil and criminal law is that civil law is mainly intended to settle disputes, not to punish wrongdoing. There are many different areas of civil law including:

■ **tort** law, which allows a person to claim compensation when he has been injured or his property has been damaged

■ contract law, which operates when goods or services are bought and sold
■ family law, which sets out rules governing family relationships
■ employment law, which sets out rules operating between an employer and an employee.

### Key terms

**Civil law** – the law concerned with the relationship between individuals.

**Tort** – a tort is a civil wrong, and tort law compensates a person who has been injured or whose property is damaged. The word 'tort' comes from the French word for 'wrong'.

In tort law, a civil case is started by the person who has suffered the loss or injury. The loss may be damage to property or simply loss of money. Injury will often be some form of physical injury but could include mental injury. The injury may be minor or severe involving lifelong care. He is called the **claimant**. The action will be taken against the individual or business that has caused the loss and they will be called the **defendant**.

The state is not usually concerned with tort law as the action is between the persons involved in the accident.

### Key terms

**Claimant** – the person who has suffered loss or damage and is bringing a claim for compensation.
**Defendant** – the person who has caused the loss or damage.

If the claimant is successful in proving their case they will be asking the court to award a remedy. Usually in a tort case this remedy will be **damages** but in some torts, such as nuisance, the claimant will be looking to the court to award an **injunction** to stop the action being complained of.

### Key terms

**Damages** – the payment of money by way of compensation. The aim of damages in tort is to put the claimant back in the position he was in before the tort, so far as money can do so.

**Injunction** – an order of the court to stop doing something, e.g. to stop making noise after 10 p.m. Failure to follow the court order can lead to further sanctions, including possibly imprisonment. An injunction can order a positive action, e.g. to move a muck heap to avoid causing a smell nuisance.

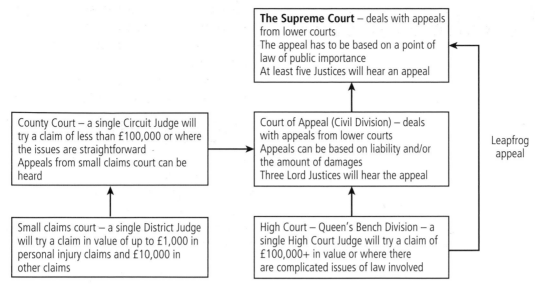

**Figure 23.1** The civil court system and appeal routes for dealing with tort claims

## 23.1.1 The courts

Civil and criminal laws are dealt with separately, and there are separate court systems to deal with civil and criminal cases. The claimant will have to prepare his claim and the initial evidence to show that he has a case. He will also have to suggest the amount of damages he is intending to claim, in order to issue the claim in the correct court and to follow the correct tracking procedure.

In civil trial courts a judge will sit alone to decide:

- the liability – whether the claimant or defendant has proved the case
- how much damages should be paid
- if the winning party is entitled to the payment of his legal costs by the losing party.

In civil cases the general rule is that the loser pays the winner's legal costs in addition to his own costs.

One of the parties can appeal against the decision of the judge, either:

- against liability – the decision who wins the case, but on the grounds that the judge misdirected himself on the relevant law or
- against the amount of damages awarded – that they were excessive or insufficient.

## 23.1.2 Burden of proof

The burden of proof is the obligation on a party in a court case to establish the evidence to a required degree. In civil cases, the burden of proving that the defendant is liable is on the claimant.

There are rules on the level to which the case has to be proved. This is referred to as the 'standard of proof'. The standard of proof in civil cases is 'the balance of probabilities'. This means that it is more likely than not that the judge believes the claimant. This is a lower standard than the one used in criminal cases. Civil cases have to be proved only 'on the balance of probabilities'. The reason that civil cases require a lower standard of proof is because the defendant is not being punished and is not at risk of losing his liberty if the case is proved. The claimant is merely proving that the defendant was at fault for the accident and responsible for the damage and injuries.

## 23.1.3 Fault

Many civil torts, particularly those based on negligence, require the claimant to prove that the defendant was at fault. Fault in this sense means that there is some wrongdoing by the defendant. The claimant will have to prove this fault with evidence. In an accident claim based on negligence, this evidence will have to show how and why the accident happened and that it was due to the wrongdoing of the defendant. As will be seen later, this is known as a breach of duty by the defendant. This proving of fault is often difficult for the claimant as expert evidence may have to be paid for and produced. Torts that require fault to be proved in this specification are:

- negligence
- occupiers' liability
- psychiatric injury and
- economic loss, particularly caused by negligent misstatement.

If the claimant cannot present sufficient evidence to prove the fault he will be left without compensation, even if he is suffering physical injury or damage to his property.

### 23.1.4 Strict liability

Some torts do not require fault to be proved, and they are known as **strict liability** actions. They will usually be cheaper and simpler for the claimant to prove as they do not require evidence to be produced to show how and why the accident happened. In this specification strict liability torts are:

- nuisance – an action to stop unreasonable use of neighbouring land
- *Rylands v Fletcher* – an action for damage to land caused by material escaping from neighbouring land and
- vicarious liability – where an employee commits a tort in the course of his employment.

All these torts and actions will be covered in detail in Book 2.

### Key term

**Strict liability** – a civil action where fault of the defendant does not need to be proved.

### 23.1.5 Defences

There are fewer defences available to a defendant in civil law than in criminal law, but the defendant can dispute the claimant's case and, in some cases, suggest that the claimant wholly or partly caused his own injury. These defences are called consent and contributory negligence and will be considered in Chapter 24.

See section 24.5.1 for more information on contributory negligence, and section 24.5.2 for information on consent (*volenti*).

## 23.2 The rules and principles of liability in negligence and occupiers' liability

### 23.2.1 Negligence

**Negligence** can apply in a wide variety of situations where a person is injured, or his property is damaged, as a result of an accident. One of the most common accidents is a car crash in which the vehicles are damaged and the drivers and passengers injured. When this happens, the injured person will want to claim compensation for his injuries and for damage to his vehicle or other property. He may also want to claim for a hire car while his own vehicle is being repaired. Other common accidents include people being injured at work or through medical negligence. In all these types of situation, the tort of negligence is used as the basis of the claim. Negligence needs proof of fault on the part of the person who caused the accident.

Negligence was defined in the case of *Blythe v Birmingham Waterworks Co.* (1856) by Baron Alderson as 'failing to do something which the reasonable person would do or doing something which the reasonable person would not do'. From this definition it can be seen that negligence can result from either an act or an omission.

### Key term

**Negligence** – an act or a failure to act due to the fault of the defendant which causes injury or damage to another person or his property.

Negligence is a common-law tort – in other words, the rules have developed as a result of decisions of judges in court. The main remedy for a successful claim of negligence is compensation for the injuries or damage suffered.

Many negligence claims are settled out of court if the defendant admits liability or blame for the accident. However the case may go to court if the defendant disputes the amount of damages or, as in the news example below, the claimant is a child, when the court has to approve the amount of compensation. The newspaper article shows a claim which has been made in negligence for personal injuries suffered in an accident.

### In the news

Agnes Collier was left paralysed in all four limbs at the age of 13 when a car pulled out of a side road, forcing the Colliers' car into the path of a lorry. Agnes's brother was also badly hurt and their mother was killed in the accident.

She sued the other driver who caused the crash. His insurers admitted liability, and Agnes has now been awarded the biggest payout ever achieved in a personal injury case in England and Wales.

A High Court Judge awarded a £7.25 million lump sum payout to Agnes, now 17, praising her academic achievements and determination to go on to university despite her injuries.

In addition, Agnes will receive index-linked, tax-free payments of £270,000 a year. This money will cover the costs of her care for the rest of her life. The total payout is expected to reach £23 million.

*Source: Adapted from The Daily Telegraph, 19 November 2012*

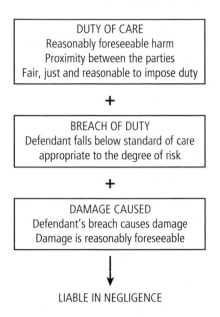

**Figure 23.2** What has to be proved in a negligence claim

## 23.2.2 Occupiers' liability

Occupiers' liability is a branch of negligence when the claimant suffers personal injury while on the occupier's premises. While negligence is a common-law tort created by judges, occupiers' liability has been created by statute. There are two separate actions:

The Occupiers' Liability Act 1957 provides that an occupier of premises owes a duty of care to lawful visitors. A lawful visitor is someone who is on the premises with the permission of the occupier. The duty that is owed is called the common duty of care. If that duty is broken and the visitor is injured, he is entitled to receive compensation. The visitor can also claim compensation for any property damages – for example, clothing.

The Occupiers' Liability Act 1984 allows claims by trespassers who are injured on the occupier's property. A trespasser is someone who does not have the occupier's permission to be on the premises. A trespasser is also owed a duty of care,

though a different duty from a lawful visitor, and suffers injury due to a danger on the premises. If a trespasser is successful he will be able to claim compensation for personal injury only.

In both types of claim, the breach of duty by the occupier shows fault on the part of the occupier.

**Figure 23.3** The difference between claims for negligence and occupier's liability

| Negligence | Occupier's liability |
|---|---|
| Injury happens on road or other public place, but may also occur on private property | Accident happens on occupier's property |
| Defendant owes claimant a duty of care | Defendant owes claimant the common duty of care |
| Defendant breaches duty of care causing accident | Defendant breaches duty of care causing accident |
| Clamant suffers loss or injury | Clamant suffers loss or injury |
| If defendant is liable he is ordered to pay compensation | If defendant is liable he is ordered to pay compensation |

## 23.3 The rules underpinning remedies for these torts

If the claimant successfully proves his tort claim, he will be entitled to a remedy. In a tort claim the court can award a successful claimant compensation for the injuries he has suffered or damage to his property. This award is known as damages, as we discussed in section 23.1.

### Key term

**Remedy** – the way in which a court will enforce or satisfy a claim when injury or damage has been suffered and proved. In tort law the remedy will usually be damages or occasionally an injunction.

Damages can place the claimant in the same position as if the tort had not been committed where the claim is for damage to property. However, if the claimant has suffered disabling personal injury, this is not possible.

Damages are divided into special and general damages:

■ Special damages cover the period up to the trial and cover claims that can be specifically calculated. For a personal injury claim, these include the cost of treatment or loss of wages.

- General damages cover the period after trial and include the pain and suffering as a result of the accident, future loss of earnings, future medical costs and any loss of amenity.

In many personal injury claims where the injuries are severe and the amount of damages is large, the claimant will be hoping that the defendant was insured and will aim to recover compensation from the defendant's insurance company.

In a claim for damaged property, such as a *Rylands v Fletcher* claim, the amount of damages is likely to be smaller than a personal injury claim. The amount of compensation claimed will be what is required to replace or repair the damaged property.

In a claim for nuisance, the claimant will often be trying to stop the nuisance continuing and will be seeking an injunction from the court ordering the problem to stop. If the defendant does not observe the order then the court can impose further sanctions such as a fine or, at worst, imprisonment.

## Activity

Scott was a keen home-brewer of beer. He invited his neighbour Peter into his house to taste some bottles from his latest brew. He put some bottles on the cooker hob before opening them. Unfortunately, Scott forgot that the hob was still warm from cooking lunch. Several bottles exploded, which injured Peter. He lost four weeks' wages and was unable to ride his bicycle competitively for six months. His expensive shirt and trousers were damaged.

Assume that Scott was negligent and caused Peter's injuries. Outline the damages that Peter could claim from Scott.

## Tip

You will not have to calculate exactly how much money in the form of damages the claimant will be awarded as, in a court action, this will be a job for the judge. You should suggest what specific and general damages can be claimed – for example, medical expenses to pay for physiotherapy.

## Check your understanding

1 Which one of the following most accurately describes fault in a tort claim?

A How the accident happened

B The legal blameworthiness for the accident

C Something wrong with the claimant

D A defect in the defendant's car

2 Explain the standard of proof required in a civil case and on whom the burden of proof lies.

## Summary

- A tort is a civil wrong; the case will usually be between an individual and another individual or an individual and a business.
- The state is not usually involved in a tort claim.
- The aim of taking a tort action is usually to claim compensation.
- The standard of proof in a tort claim is 'the balance of probabilities'.
- The burden of proving the case is on the claimant.

- Negligence is the breach of a duty of care leading to the claimant suffering injury, loss or damage to his property.
- An occupier's liability claim arises when a visitor is injured while on the occupier's property.
- The aim of the award of damages in negligence and occupiers' liability is to put the claimant back in the position he was in before the accident, so far as money can do so.

# 24 Liability in negligence: personal injury and damage to property

After reading this chapter you should be able to:
- Understand the concept of duty of care and when it is owed
- Understand the need to prove breach of duty
- Understand the legal rules on damage: factual causation and legal causation (remoteness of damage)
- Understand defences available in this tort: contributory negligence and consent (*volenti non fit injuria*).

## 24.1 Duty of care

The idea of a duty of care in the tort of negligence is to establish a legal relationship between the claimant and the defendant. The modern law of negligence originated in the famous case of *Donoghue v Stevenson* (1932). This established for the first time the broad principle of when a duty of care was owed – **the neighbour principle** – and of general liability in negligence.

### Donoghue v Stevenson (1932)

Mrs Donoghue went to a cafe with a friend. The friend bought her a drink of ginger beer and ice cream. The bottle of ginger beer had dark glass so that its contents could not be seen. After drinking some of it, Mrs Donoghue poured the rest out and then saw that it contained a dead (and decomposing) snail. Because of the impurities in the drink she suffered both physical and psychological injuries.

She wanted to claim for her injuries. As she had not bought the drink she could not use the law of contract to sue the café or the manufacturer. She sued the manufacturer in negligence, claiming that they were at fault in the manufacturing process and that they owed her a duty of care.

In the House of Lords Lord Atkin set the test for when a person would owe a duty to another. He said: 'You must take reasonable care to avoid acts or omissions which

you can reasonably foresee would be likely to injure your neighbour.' He went on to explain this by saying:

> Who then, in law, is my neighbour? Persons who are so closely and directly affected by my act that I ought reasonably to have them in my contemplation as being affected when I am directing my mind to the acts or omissions in question.

### Key term

**Neighbour principle** – the person who is owed a duty of care by the defendant. It is not the person living next door. According to Lord Atkin it is anyone you ought to have in mind who might potentially be injured by your act or omission.

This 'neighbour' principle was used by judges for a number of years but it became clear over time that it was not sufficient to deal with new situations that came before the courts. In a new situation judges would only find a duty of care existed if the neighbour test was satisfied and there were policy reasons for finding a duty. This meant that judges would consider whether society would benefit from finding a duty of care existed. This rather piecemeal approach was replaced by a **three-part test** set out by the House of Lords in the case of *Caparo v Dickman* (1990):

- Was damage or harm reasonably foreseeable?
- Is there a sufficiently proximate (close) relationship between the claimant and the defendant?
- Is it fair, just and reasonable to impose a duty?

This three-part test sets guidelines to help a court decide whether to extend liability into 'new' areas. Using this approach liability will be extended to 'new' areas step-by-step and comparing the 'new' area with existing areas of liability.

### Caparo v Dickman (1990)

The claimant company wanted to take over another company – Fidelity Limited. They looked at the statutory accounts prepared for Fidelity by the defendant, which showed a profit. Based on these books they decided to take over Fidelity. After completing the purchase they looked at the detailed books which showed a loss. They sued the defendant for their loss.

The House of Lords set the three-stage test for owing a duty of care. They decided that the defendant did not owe the claimants a duty of care as the accounts were prepared for Fidelity and for statutory reasons.

AQA Law 1

## Key term

The three-part test – an update of the neighbour test to show who is owed a duty of care in negligence. All three parts have to be satisfied in order that this test is satisfied.

## 24.1.1 Damage or harm reasonably foreseeable?

This is where a reasonable person could foresee that damage or injury could be caused to another person by his actions or omissions. Whether the injury or damage is reasonably foreseeable depends on the facts of the case. An example of this is the case of *Kent v Griffiths* (2000).

### Kent v Griffiths (2000)

An ambulance was called to take the claimant, who was suffering an asthma attack, to hospital. Despite repeated assurances by the control centre, and for no obvious reason, the ambulance failed to arrive within a reasonable time. As a result the claimant suffered a respiratory arrest.

The court decided it was 'reasonably foreseeable' that the claimant would suffer further illness if the ambulance did not arrive promptly.

## 24.1.2 Proximity of relationship

Even if the harm is reasonably foreseeable, a duty of care will only exist if the relationship between the claimant and the defendant is sufficiently close or proximate. This can be considered as the previous 'neighbour test'. An example of how this test was applied was in the case of *Bourhill v Young* (1943).

### Bourhill v Young (1943)

A pregnant woman heard the sound of an accident as she got off a tram. The accident was caused by a motor cyclist who died in the accident. After a short while she approached the scene of the accident and saw blood on the road. She suffered such shock from what she saw that she later gave birth to a stillborn baby. She sued the relatives of the dead motor cyclist. Under the 'neighbour' test at the time she had to prove that she was proximate, or close to, the motorcyclist so that she was owed a duty of care. The House of Lords decided that the motorcyclist could not anticipate that, if he was involved in an accident, it would cause mental injury to a bystander. He was not proximate to Mrs Bourhill and she was not owed a duty of care.

One reason for the decision in this case could have been that Mrs Bourhill was not related to the victim and, if she was allowed to sue, it would open the floodgates to many claims by unrelated strangers. A different result was achieved in *McLoughlin v O'Brien* (1982).

### McLoughlin v O'Brien (1982)

In this case, while she was at home, the claimant's husband and children were involved in a serious road accident. The accident was caused by the negligence of the defendant lorry driver. One of the children was killed at the scene and the other family members were taken to hospital. The claimant was told of the accident and went to the hospital. She saw her family before they had been treated. As a result she suffered severe shock, organic depression and a personality change. She claimed against the defendant for the psychiatric injury she suffered. The House of Lords decided that the lorry driver owed her a duty of care and extended the class of persons who would be considered proximate to the event to those who came within the immediate aftermath of the event (in this case, two hours after the accident).

The court may have accepted Mrs McLoughlin's claim because there could only be a limited number of people who could claim – they had to be related to the victim and suffer the injury within a limited time. These restrictions could not open the floodgates to unlimited numbers of claims.

## 24.1.3 Fair, just and reasonable to impose a duty

The third part of the *Caparo* test allows the courts to consider if, the law ought to impose a duty of care on the defendant when both the foreseeability and proximity tests are satisfied. Using this test the courts are considering what is best for society as a whole. Equally they have to consider whether, by allowing a claim, they will be 'opening the floodgates' to many future claims.

The courts are often reluctant to find that it is 'fair, just and reasonable' to impose a duty of care on public authorities such as the police. In the case of *Hill v Chief Constable of West Yorkshire* (1990) it was pointed out that imposing a duty of care on police (and allowing them to be sued) could lead to policing being carried out in a defensive way. This might divert their resources and attention away from the prevention and detection of crime, and could likely lead to lower standards of policing, not higher ones.

214

### Hill v Chief Constable of West Yorkshire (1990)

In this case a serial killer, the Yorkshire Ripper, had been attacking and murdering women in Yorkshire and across the north of England. The claimant's daughter was the killer's last victim before he was caught. By the time of her death the police already had enough information to arrest the killer, but had failed to do so. The mother claimed that the police owed a duty of care to her daughter. It was decided by the House of Lords that the relationship between the victim and the police was not sufficiently close (proximate) for the police to be under a duty of care and that it was not fair, just or reasonable for the police to owe a duty of care to the general public. The police knew that the killer might strike again but they had no way of knowing who the victim might be.

**Figure 24.1** Duty of care tests

**Figure 24.2** Duty of care

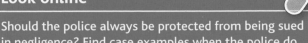

### Look online

Should the police always be protected from being sued in negligence? Find case examples when the police do owe a duty of care and have been successfully sued.

### Activity

It is well-established law that certain categories of persons owe a duty of care to others. For example, drivers owe a duty of care to other road users, manufacturers owe a duty of care to consumers and doctors owe a duty of care to their patients. Discuss in small groups whether teachers owe a duty of care to their students in the following situations:

- on a school trip
- when teaching students in a practical lesson
- when preparing them for an exam.

### Extension activity

What about other emergency services? Will they owe a duty of care? For example:

- Do the coastguards owe a duty of care to a yachtsman whose boat is sinking?
- Do the fire brigade owe a duty of care to a house owner to put out a fire?
- Does a lifeguard owe a duty of care to a swimmer in difficulties in a supervised swimming pool?
- Does an off-duty lifeguard owe a duty of care to a swimmer in difficulties in the sea?

How do the courts decide in novel situations whether a duty of care is owed?

| Principle | Case | Judgment |
|---|---|---|
| Duty of care | *Donoghue v Stevenson* (1932) | Neighbour principle:<br>■ You must take reasonable care not to injure your neighbour |
| General principles | *Caparo v Dickman* (1990) | Three-part test:<br>■ Injury or damage has to be reasonably foreseeable<br>■ There must be proximity of relationship<br>■ It must be fair, just and reasonable to owe a duty of care |
| Reasonably foreseeable | *Kent v Griffiths* (2000) | Ambulance took unreasonable time to arrive and take patient to hospital – duty of care owed |
| Proximity of relationship | *Bourhill v Young* (1943) | Woman heard accident and suffered shock when saw blood on road – but no duty of care owed |
| | *McLoughlin v O'Brian* (1982) | Mother suffered shock when saw injured family in hospital – duty of care owed |
| Fair just and reasonable to owe a duty | *Hill v Chief Constable of West Yorkshire* (1990) | Not fair, just or reasonable for police to owe a duty to member of public not known to them |

Ryan had just collected his car from Sam's garage, where Sam had been working on the brakes. Sam told Ryan that the work was complete, but, in fact, Sam had forgotten to tighten the handbrake cable. Ryan parked his car on a hill, applied the handbrake and got out. The handbrake failed to hold the car which rolled down the hill and crushed Tanya, who was loading shopping into the back of her van. As a result of the collision, both Ryan's car and Tanya's van were slightly damaged.

Discuss whether Sam owed a duty of care to Tanya.

# 24.2 Breach of duty: the objective standard of care

Once it has been shown that a duty of care is owed, the claimant has to prove that the duty of care has been broken by failing to reach the required standard of care. The standard is objective – that of the 'reasonable person'.

## 24.2.1 The reasonable person

This **reasonable person** is the ordinary person performing the task competently. It could be the reasonable driver, the reasonable doctor or the reasonable manufacturer.

There are a number of variations of the 'reasonable person', and the court may have to consider whether the defendant has a special characteristic. For example, is he an inexperienced learner, is he a professional, or is he a child? If any of these apply, how should he be judged?

**Key term**

The **reasonable person** – this used to be said to be 'the man on the Clapham omnibus'. Now it is considered to be the ordinary person in the street or doing a task.

Professionals are judged by the standard of the profession as a whole. The case to illustrate this is *Bolam v Friern Barnet Hospital Management Committee* (1957).

**Bolam v Friern Barnet Hospital Management Committee (1957)**

In this case the claimant was suffering from a mental illness and the treatment at the time was to be given a type of electric shock (ECT). He signed a consent form but was not told of the risk of broken bones while receiving the shocks and was not given relaxant drugs. He suffered a broken pelvis while receiving the treatment.

There were two opinions within the medical profession when using ECT. One opinion favoured the use of relaxant drugs in every case. The other was that drugs should only be used if there was a reason to do so, which was not present in Bolam's case. The court decided that as the hospital had followed one of these courses of action it had not breached its duty of care.

The principle from this case for deciding whether professionals such as doctors, lawyers and accountants have breached their duty of care is to ask the following questions:

- does the defendant's conduct fall below the standard of the ordinary, competent, member of that profession?
- is there a substantial body of opinion within the profession that would support the course of action taken by the defendant?

If the answer to the first question is 'No' and to the second question 'Yes', then the correct standard has been reached and the defendant professional has not broken his duty of care. So, for example, if a surgeon has carried out an operation under a known and accepted procedure, but a patient has still suffered injury, he will not have broken his duty of care.

Learners are judged at the standard of the competent, more experienced person. This principle was set by the case of *Nettleship v Weston* (1971).

**Nettleship v Weston (1971)**

Mrs Weston arranged with Mr Nettleship for him to give her driving lessons. She was on her third lesson and failed to straighten up after turning a corner. She hit a lamppost which fell on to the car, injuring Mr Nettleship. The court decided that Mrs Weston should be judged at the standard of the competent driver, not at the standard of the inexperienced learner driver, and she had breached her duty of care to Mr Nettleship.

Although the decision seems unfair on the face of it, it is logical as Mrs Weston was covered by an insurance policy, and it would be unjust on an injured claimant if the defence was put forward as 'I am only on my third lesson and you cannot expect me to be as good a driver as someone who has been driving for some time'.

For children and young people, the standard is that of a reasonable person of the defendant's age at the time of the accident. This is shown by the case of *Mullin v Richards* (1998).

### Mullin v Richards (1998)

Two girls, aged 15, were play-fighting with plastic rulers in class at school. One of the rulers snapped and fragments entered Teresa Mullin's eye, resulting in her losing all useful sight in that eye. The court decided that the other girl, Heidi Richards, had to meet the standard of a 15-year-old schoolgirl, and not that of a reasonable adult. As she had reached the required standard, she had not breached her duty of care.

## 24.2.2 Risk factors

When the court considers whether there has been a breach of duty, it will take into account certain factors to consider whether the standard of care should be raised or lowered. The question will be asked: would the reasonable person take more or fewer risks in the same situation? Any of the following risk factors may be considered:

- Has the claimant any special characteristics which should be taken account of?
- What is the size of the risk?
- Have all appropriate precautions been taken?
- Were the risks known about at the time of the accident?
- Is there a public benefit to taking the risk?

### Special characteristics

This is shown in the case of *Paris v Stepney Borough Council* (1951).

### Paris v Stepney Borough Council (1951)

Mr Paris was known to his employers to be blind in one eye. He was given work to do which involved a small risk of injury to the eyes. He was not given any protective goggles. While doing this work, his good eye was damaged by a small piece of metal and he became totally blind. His employers were held to have broken their duty of care to him.

The employers knew that the consequences of an injury to his good eye would be very serious. They should have taken greater care because of this and provided him with goggles, even though at that time it was not thought necessary to provide goggles for other workers. Also, the cost and effort of providing goggles was very small compared with the consequences of the risk.

### Size of the risk

Where a risk is small, it is unlikely that there is a breach of duty. This is shown in *Bolton v Stone* (1951).

### Bolton v Stone (1951)

A cricket ball hit a lady passer-by in the street outside a cricket ground. The evidence was that there was a 17-foot-high fence around the ground and the wicket was a long way from this fence. There was also evidence that cricket balls had only been hit out of the ground six times in the 30 years before the incident.

Because of the number of times balls had been hit out of the ground, it was found that the cricket club had done everything it needed to do in view of the low risk, and it had not breached its duty of care.

The principle that applies here is that the higher the risk of injury, the greater the precautions that need to be taken to prevent injury. As in this case, the lower the risk, the fewer precautions that need to be taken.

On the other hand, if there is a higher risk of injury, the standard of care is higher. This was shown by the case of *Haley v London Electricity Board* (1965).

### Haley v London Electricity Board (1965)

The electricity board dug a trench for its cables and, following its standard practice, it only put out warning signs; it did not put any barriers around the trench. The claimant was blind and was injured when he fell into the trench. As it was known that that particular road was used by a number of blind people, greater precautions should have been taken and the defendant had breached its duty of care.

### Appropriate precautions

The courts will consider the balance of the risk involved against the cost and effort of taking adequate precautions to eliminate the risk. A case to illustrate this is *Latimer v AEC Ltd* (1953).

### Latimer v AEC Ltd (1953)

A factory became flooded and, as the floor was very slippery with a mixture of the water and oil, the workers were evacuated. Sawdust was spread over the floor to minimise the risk of slipping and the workers were required to go back in. Despite the spreading of sawdust one worker slipped and was injured. The court held that there was no breach of the duty of care.

It was found that the only way to completely prevent injury would have been to close the factory for a period of time. It was unreasonable to expect the owners to do this. They had taken sufficient steps at the time to prevent injury.

It is quite likely that if this situation occurred today, higher standards of health and safety would mean that the factory owners would have to do more to protect their workers than merely spread sawdust.

Also, if the risk had been much more serious, for example, if there was a risk of an explosion, then there would have been a higher standard of care on the owners. It would have been reasonable to expect them to close the factory until the problem had been dealt with.

## Unknown risks

If the risk of harm is not known, there can be no breach. This is illustrated by the case of *Roe v Minister of Health* (1954).

### Roe v Minister of Health (1954)

In a hospital, anaesthetic was kept in glass tubes which were sterilised by cleaning solution after each use. At the time it was not known that invisible cracks could occur in the glass and allow the anaesthetic to become contaminated by the cleaning solution. The claimant was paralysed by some contaminated anaesthetic. As the risk of contamination was not known at the time, there was no breach and he could not claim compensation.

## Public benefit

If there is an emergency then greater risks can be taken and a lower standard of care can be accepted. This is consistent with the third part of establishing a duty of care (the fair, just and reasonable

requirement). Also, the courts take a realistic view of dealing with emergencies. They accept, in hindsight, that the situation could have been dealt with differently but accept that speedy action was taken without the benefit of hindsight. This can be illustrated by the case of *Watt v Hertfordshire County Council* (1954).

### Watt v Hertfordshire County Council (1954)

The claimant was a fireman. There had been a road accident a short distance from the fire station and the fire service was called to release a trapped woman from underneath a lorry. A jack was needed to release the injured woman but the normal vehicle for carrying the jack was not available. A flatbed truck was found but there was no means of securing the jack to the lorry. The claimant was injured when the jack slipped and fell on him on the way to the accident. The court decided that the fire service had not breached its duty of care to the claimant because of the emergency situation and the utility of saving a life outweighed the need to take precautions.

A later example is *Day v High Performance Sports* (2003).

### Day v High Performance Sports (2003)

The claimant, an experienced climber, fell from an indoor climbing wall and suffered serious injuries. She had to be rescued from the wall by the duty manager at a height of 9 metres (30 feet) when she became 'frozen' in her position. The way the manager rescued her was inappropriate, causing her fall. The court decided that the manager, and the centre, had not breached their duty of care in view of the emergency situation.

## Activity

Assume that a duty of care is owed in each of the following situations. Has the duty been broken?

1 Harry is texting on his phone while driving his car at speed. He loses control and the car mounts the pavement, hitting Jamie, who suffers a broken leg.

2 Katie, a childminder, is looking after Leo, a child aged six. She takes him to a park and while he plays she reads a magazine. She does not notice Leo leave the play area which is close to a busy road. Leo runs out into the road and is knocked down by a motorbike.

3 Peter fell off his bicycle and suffered a fractured skull. He needed an operation to remove a blood clot in his brain. During the operation the surgeon used an innovative procedure that had not been fully approved. Unfortunately, due to complications during the operation, Peter is paralysed.

4 Mavis, an 80-year-old partially sighted woman, was shopping in her local supermarket. She was injured when she slipped and fell on some yoghurt which had been spilt on the floor. She could not see the warning sign which had been placed by the spillage.

**Figure 24.3** Breach of duty

| Person or risk factor | Case | Judgment |
|---|---|---|
| Professionals/Experts | *Bolam v Friern Barnet Hospital Management* (1957) | Professionals judged according to standards in profession |
| Learners | *Nettleship v Weston* (1971) | Learners judged at the standard of the competent, more experienced person |
| Children and young persons | *Mullin v Richards* (1998) | Judged at standard of the defendant's age at the time of the accident |
| Vulnerable victim | *Paris v Stepney Borough Council* (1951) | Has claimant any special characteristics to be taken account of? |
| Size of risk | *Bolton v Stone* (1951) | Greater care to be taken if higher chance of injury |
| Cost of precautions | *Latimer v AEC* (1954) | Risk involved is balanced against the cost and effort of taking precautions |
| Knowledge of danger | *Roe v Minister of Health* (1954) <br> *Haley v LEB* (1965) | If risk not known at the time of accident, can be no breach <br> If high risk of injury, the standard of care is higher |
| Public benefit (utility) | *Watt v Hertfordshire* (1954) | Greater risks can be taken in emergency situations |
| | *Day v High Performance Sports* (2003) | Duty of care not breached in view of emergency |

## 24.3 Damage

The third part of any negligence claim is for the claimant to prove that the damage suffered was caused by the breach of duty, and that the loss or damage is not too remote. This is referred to as **damage** and should be distinguished from **damages** which is the payment of compensation.

There are two parts to damage: causation and remoteness of damage. Causation is the idea that the breach of duty has caused the injury or damage being claimed for. This is called factual causation. Causation in law decides if the injury or damage suffered was reasonably foreseeable. Both elements have to be proved for a negligence claim to succeed.

### Key term

**Damage** – this is a legal concept. It asks the question, has the defendant's breach of duty led to the injury or property damage suffered by the claimant?

### 24.3.1 Causation

Factual **causation** is the starting point – if factual causation cannot be proved, there is no need to consider legal causation.

Factual causation is decided by the 'but for' test: but for the defendant's act or omission, the injury or damage would not have occurred.

This is illustrated by the case of *Barnett v Chelsea and Kensington Hospital Management Committee* (1969).

### *Barnett v Chelsea and Kensington Hospital Management Committee* (1969)

Three night watchmen went to a hospital A & E department complaining of sickness after drinking tea made by a fourth man. A nurse telephoned the duty doctor, who did not come to examine the men but, instead, recommended that they go home and see their own doctors. One of the men went home and died a few hours later from poisoning by arsenic.

His widow sued the hospital, claiming that the doctor was negligent in not examining her husband and had caused his death. She was able to prove that the doctor owed a duty of care to her husband and that by not examining him, the doctor had broken that duty of care. However, the evidence showed that by the time her husband had called at the hospital it was already too late to save his life. The arsenic was already in his system in such a quantity that he would have died whatever was done. This meant that his death was not caused by the doctor's breach of duty of care and so the claim failed.

## Intervening events

In the same way as in criminal law, an intervening event can break the chain of causation. For example, you fall down a badly repaired step at college and hurt your leg, and you are taken by car to hospital. On the way, the car is involved in an accident and you suffer head injuries. It could be said that 'but for' your fall you would not have been in the car and suffered the head injury. However the real cause of the head injury is the car accident, not the step. The car accident is a *novus actus interveniens* for the leg injury. The principle to be applied is whether the injury or damage was a reasonably foreseeable consequence of the original negligent act or omission.

## 24.3.2 Remoteness of damage

Where factual causation is proved it must be shown that the damage is not too remote from the negligence of the defendant. The rule comes from an Australian case decided by the Privy Council: *Overseas Tankship (UK) v Morts Dock and Engineering Co. Ltd* (1961). This case is more commonly known as *The Wagon Mound* (1961).

### The Wagon Mound (1961)

Fuel oil had been negligently spilled from the defendant's ship on to water in Sydney harbour. It spread towards the claimant's wharf where welding repairs were being carried out to another ship. Two days later the oil caught fire because of sparks from the welding. The fire spread to the claimant's wharf and burnt it down.

It was decided that, although damage done to the wharf by oil being spilled was reasonably foreseeable, fire damage was not reasonably foreseeable. This type of damage was too remote from the original negligent act of spilling the oil.

A large tanker in dry dock port of Gdansk

The test for remoteness of damage that comes from this case is that the injury or damage must be **reasonably foreseeable**. This is the test of legal causation.

## Type of injury foreseeable

The defendant will be liable if the type of injury was foreseeable, even though the precise way in which it happened was not. This is shown by the cases of *Hughes v Lord Advocate* (1961) and *Bradford v Robinson Rentals* (1967).

### Hughes v Lord Advocate (1963)

Post Office workmen left a manhole unattended, covered only with a tent and with paraffin lamps by the hole. The claimant, an eight-year-old boy, and a friend, climbed into the hole. As they climbed out the boys knocked one of the paraffin lamps into the hole. This caused an explosion which badly burnt the claimant. The defendants denied liability claiming that the injuries were too remote, but the court decided that the boy was able to claim for his injuries as it was foreseeable that a child might explore the site, break a lamp and be burnt. The type of injury he suffered was foreseeable, even though the explosion itself was not foreseeable.

## Bradford v Robinson Rentals (1967)

The claimant was required by his employer to take an old works van from Exeter to Bedford, collect a new van, and drive it back to Exeter. He had to do this in an extremely cold winter and neither van had a heater. As the windscreens kept freezing over, he had to drive with the windows open. The claimant suffered frostbite and was unable to work. The court decided that the employers were liable for his injuries, even though the injury he suffered was very unusual. Some injury from the cold was reasonably foreseeable.

Sometimes the court will find the type of injury was not reasonably foreseeable. An example of this is the case of *Doughty v Turner Asbestos* (1964).

## Doughty v Turner Asbestos (1964)

The claimant was injured when an asbestos lid was knocked into a vat of molten metal. A short time later a chemical reaction caused an explosion of the metal which burnt the claimant. Scientific knowledge at the time could not have predicted the explosion and so the burn injuries were not reasonably foreseeable. It could be foreseen that knocking something into the molten metal might cause a splash but the claimant's injury was caused by something different.

## Take your victim as you find him

This rule means that the defendant must take his victim as he finds him. So, if the type of damage is reasonably foreseeable, but it is much more serious because the claimant had a pre-existing condition, then the defendant is liable for all the consequences. In negligence this is known as 'the eggshell skull' rule. A similar rule operates in criminal law where it is known as the 'thin skull rule'.

The operation of this rule is illustrated in the case of *Smith v Leech Brain and Co.* (1962).

## Smith v Leech Brain and Co. (1962)

Because of the defendants' negligence, a man was burnt on the lip by molten metal in a factory. The man had an existing pre-cancerous condition. The burn eventually brought about the onset of full cancer and the man died. His widow claimed against the defendants. The court decided that as a burn was reasonably foreseeable, and because of the eggshell skull rule, the defendant was liable for the man's death.

**Figure 24.4** Causation and remoteness of damage

| Principle | Case | Judgment |
|---|---|---|
| Factual causation | *Barnett v Chelsea and Kensington Hospital Management Committee* (1969) | 'But for' test – but for defendant's act or omission, the injury would not have happened |
| Remoteness of damage | *The Wagon Mound* (1961) | Injury or damage can be claimed if reasonably foreseeable |
| Foreseeability | *Hughes v Lord Advocate* (1963) | Consequence foreseeable even if exact cause of injury not foreseeable |
| | *Bradford v Robinson Rentals* (1967) | Consequence foreseeable, even if more severe |
| | *Doughty v Turner Asbestos* (1964) | Consequence not known so injury not foreseeable |
| Eggshell skull/Take your victim as you find him | *Smith v Leech Brain and Co.* (1962) | Defendant liable for all consequences of negligence |

Negligence has to be proved before the special rules of claims of psychiatric injury and negligent misstatement. These torts are covered in Book 2.

## Activity

1 Because of his fault, Tariq's van and Rhona's car were involved in an accident which resulted in Rhona suffering injuries which have affected her mobility. She is no longer able to work as a cycle courier or play sport. Consider whether Tariq is liable for all of Rhona's injuries.

2 Polish Limited had developed a new floor polish that it was testing. Jade, a secretary of the company, did not know about the test and slipped and fell on the highly polished surface of the test area and fell down the stairs breaking her leg. She was admitted to hospital where she developed a rare medical condition that was missed by Dr Hari, an inexperienced junior doctor. As a result, her leg had to be amputated. Consider whether Polish Limited would be liable for the injury caused to Jade.

3 William was sorting out some files which were on a high shelf next to the open window in his office. As he could not reach the files easily, he used a pole to push them to the end of the shelf and then tried to catch them as they fell. William failed to catch a heavy file which fell out of the window onto Robyn who was sitting outside in her car. The car's sunroof shattered and Robyn suffered a broken collarbone. Because of the injury she was unable to work as a freelance hairdresser and had to cancel a planned skiing holiday. Consider whether William would be liable for all the injuries and damage suffered by Robyn.

## 24.4 *Res ipsa loquitur*

The burden of proving the negligence is on the claimant, on the balance of probabilities. In some situations it is difficult for the claimant to know exactly what happened, even though it seems obvious that the defendant must have been negligent. An example of this is where, after an operation in hospital, a patient is found to have a swab left inside him. The patient does not know exactly how the duty of care was breached as he would have been unconscious throughout the operation. He only knows that after the operation there is a swab inside him and he suffered injury as a result.

In such a situation, the rule of *res ipsa loquitur* can be used. This means 'the thing speaks for itself'. The claimant has to show:

- the defendant was in control of the situation which caused the injury
- the accident would not have happened unless someone was negligent and
- there is no other explanation for the injury.

If the claimant can show these three points, then the burden of proof moves to the defendant who has to prove that he was not negligent.

An example of this rule is *Scott v London and St Katherine Docks* (1865).

### Scott v London and St Katherine Docks (1865)

The claimant was hit and injured by six heavy bags of sugar which had fallen from the defendant's warehouse. The claimant did not know, and could not prove, what had happened to make the bags fall. He could only show that he was injured by the falling bags.

The elements of *res ipsa loquitur* were present:

- The sacks fell from the warehouse which was under the defendant's control.
- Heavy sacks do not fall unless someone was negligent.
- There was no other explanation for the sacks to fall.

The court decided that the defendants were liable as they were unable to prove that they had not been negligent.

### Tip

You must know all three elements of negligence thoroughly, including all the precedent cases. These three parts are duty of care, breach of duty and loss or damage. Each point that you make for each element must be supported by a precedent case.

## 24.5 Defences to a negligence claim

For A-level, you need to understand two main defences which can be raised by a defendant in a negligence claim:

- an allegation that the claimant has partly caused or contributed to his injuries and/or
- an allegation that the claimant has consented or agreed to accept a risk of harm and voluntarily taken it.

A defendant can allege either or both of these defences.

### 24.5.1 Contributory negligence

The Law Reform (Contributory Negligence) Act 1945 provides that any damages awarded to the claimant can be reduced according to the extent or level to which the claimant had contributed to his own harm.

This means that both the defendant and the claimant are each partly to blame for the injury suffered by the claimant. The amount of blame will be decided by the judge. The judgement will first set the full amount of the damages as if there was no contributory negligence. The judge will then decide the percentage that the claimant is responsible and then reduce the full amount by this percentage. It has to be appreciated that this is a part defence and it will only result in a reduction of the amount of damages.

### Sayers v Harlow Urban District Council (1958)

A woman was trapped in a public toilet when the door lock became jammed. After unsuccessfully calling for help, she tried to escape the cubicle by climbing through the gap between the door and the ceiling. She stood with one foot on the toilet seat and the other on the toilet roll holder. The holder gave way and she was injured. The court decided that the local council was liable for its negligent maintenance but the damages were reduced by 25 per cent because of the way she tried to escape.

It is possible for there to be a 100 per cent reduction in damages.

### Jayes v IMI (Kynoch) Ltd (1985)

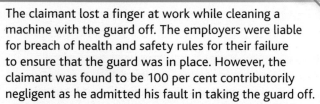

The claimant lost a finger at work while cleaning a machine with the guard off. The employers were liable for breach of health and safety rules for their failure to ensure that the guard was in place. However, the claimant was found to be 100 per cent contributorily negligent as he admitted his fault in taking the guard off.

The defence is commonly used in claims for injuries or damage suffered in road traffic accidents. Damages can be reduced where a motorcyclist fails to wear a crash helmet or a driver or passenger in a vehicle is not wearing a seat belt.

### O'Connell v Jackson (1972)

Damages were reduced by 15 per cent when the rider of a moped was injured and suffered greater injuries because he was not wearing a crash helmet.

### Froom v Butcher (1976)

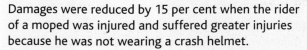

The driver of a car suffered greater injuries than would have been the case if wearing a seat belt. His damages were reduced by 20 per cent.

### Stinton v Stinton (1993)

The damages were reduced by one-third for accepting a lift from a drunk driver.

The claimant knew that the driver was over the limit. If the passenger does not know this, or it would not have been obvious to a reasonable person, the court may decide that an injured claimant was not contributorily negligent.

### Badger v Ministry of Defence (2005)

The claimant died of lung cancer aged 63. The defendant admitted a breach of statutory duty by exposing the claimant to asbestos dust, but argued that damages should be reduced because if the claimant had not smoked cigarettes he would also have been unlikely to die of lung cancer at such a young age. Because the claimant was aware of the risk from cigarettes from 1971, the court reduced damages by 20 per cent.

## 24.5.2 Consent (*volenti non fit injuria*)

Consent or *volenti* is a full defence, when the claimant accepts a voluntary assumption of the risk of harm. Simply translated, it means that no injury is done to one who consents to the risk. If it is successful, the claimant will receive no damages.

To succeed, the defendant has to show:
1  knowledge of the precise risk involved
2  exercise of free choice by the claimant
3  a voluntary acceptance of the risk.

One restriction on the use of the defence is s 149 of the Road Traffic Act 1988, which provides that the defence cannot be used for road traffic accidents. This is because of third party insurance.

The defence will not apply merely because the claimant knows of the existence of the risk; he must have a full understanding of the nature of the actual risk.

### Stermer v Lawson (1977)

Consent was argued when the claimant had borrowed the defendant's motorbike. The defence failed because the claimant had not been properly shown how to use the motorbike, and did not therefore appreciate the risks.

The defence will not succeed where the claimant has no choice but to accept the risk. An assumption of risk must be freely taken and the claimant must actually voluntarily undertake the risk of harm.

### Smith v Baker (1891)

A worker was injured when a crane moved rocks over his head and some fell on him. The defence of consent failed. The workman had already done all that he could in complaining about the risks involved in the work taking place above his head. He had no choice but to continue work and did not give his consent to the danger.

Where a person has a duty to act and is then injured because of the defendant's negligence, *volenti* will not be available as a defence. The duty means that the claimant had no choice but to act. This is particularly relevant in rescue cases.

### Haynes v Harwood (1935)

When the defendant failed to adequately tether his horse, the policeman who was injured trying to restrain the animal was not acting voluntarily. He was acting under a duty to protect the public. The defence of *volenti* could not be used against him.

### Ogwo v Taylor (1987)

The defendant had set fire to his house when attempting to burn off paint. The claimant was a fireman who attended the blaze. He and a colleague had to access the roof space to deal with the fire, but, despite wearing breathing apparatus and protective clothing, he suffered burns from the intense heat. The defendant's argument that the claimant consented to the injuries was dismissed.

In the House of Lords, Lord Bridge pointed out:

> 66 The duty of professional firemen is to use their best endeavours to extinguish fires and it is obvious that, even making full use of all their skills, training and specialist equipment, they will sometimes be exposed to unavoidable risks of injury, whether the fire is described as 'ordinary' or 'exceptional'. If they are not to be met by the doctrine of *volenti*, which would be utterly repugnant to our contemporary notions of justice, I can see no reason whatever why they should be held at a disadvantage as compared to the layman entitled to invoke the principle of the so-called 'rescue' cases. 99

The defence of *volenti* is likely to be relevant and important in medical negligence claims.

### Sidaway v Governors of the Bethlem Royal and Maudsley Hospitals (1985)

The claimant suffered pain in the neck, shoulder and arms. Her surgeon obtained her consent for an operation but failed to explain that in less than 1 per cent of these operations, paraplegia could be caused. Unfortunately she developed paraplegia as a result of the operation and she argued that she did not consent to this. The House of Lords decided that consent in medical cases does not require a detailed explanation of remote side effects. As a result, there was no liability when the doctor had warned of the likelihood of the risk but not all the possible consequences.

If the claimant acts against the employer's orders or against statutory rules and is injured, the defence of *volenti* is likely to succeed.

### ICI Ltd v Shatwell (1965)

The claimant and his brother were quarry workers. The claimant, following his brother's instructions, ignored his employer's instructions on the handling of detonators, and was injured when one exploded. He claimed in negligence and breach of statutory duty against his employer. The court decided that, by ignoring his employer's instructions and the statutory rules and by following his brother's unauthorised comments, he had assumed the risk of injury and the defence of *volenti* succeeded.

Before the defence can be applied successfully, it must be shown that the defendant did in fact commit a tort.

### Wooldridge v Sumner (1963)

The claimant attended a horse show as a professional photographer. A rider who was riding too fast lost control of the horse, which then injured the claimant. The Court of Appeal confirmed that the rider owed spectators, including the claimant, a duty of care. However, it considered the rider had been guilty of an error of judgement in his riding of the horse but had not been negligent. There was no breach of duty, so *volenti* was not an issue.

The test of *volenti* is subjective rather than objective. It will not help the defendant to argue that the claimant ought to have been aware of the risk. The defence only applies where the claimant does actually know of the risk.

### Tip

Remember that the defendant can argue both *volenti* and contributory negligence. If *volenti* fails, the defendant may still successfully claim contributory negligence and at least reduce the amount of damages that are payable.

**Figure 24.5** Defences in tort

| | | |
|---|---|---|
| Contributory negligence is a part defence | *Sayers v Harlow UDC* (1957) | Damages reduced if claimant has partly caused her own injuries |
| Amount of contributory negligence decided by the judge | *O'Connell v Jackson* (1972)<br>*Froom v Butcher* (1976)<br>*Stinton v Stinton* (1993) | No crash helmet – 15%<br>No seat belt – 20%<br>Taking a lift from drunk driver – $33\frac{1}{2}$% |
| To consent, claimant must have a full understanding of the nature of the actual risk | *Stermer v Lawson* (1977) | No consent as the claimant had not been properly shown how to use the motorbike, and did not appreciate the risks |
| To consent, claimant must have had a free choice in accepting risk of injury | *Smith v Baker* (1891) | The claimant had complained about the risks and had no choice but to continue work |
| No consent if claimant is acting under a public duty | *Haynes v Harwood* (1935)<br>*Ogwo v Taylor* (1987) | Police or fireman did not consent to injury when doing their public duty |
| Consent in medical treatment | *Sidaway v Governors of the Bethlem Royal and Maudsley Hospitals* (1985) | Not every possible risk has to be explained before valid consent can be given |
| Consent only available if following orders | *ICI Ltd v Shatwell* (1965) | A claimant ignoring his employer's instructions and not following statutory rules cannot use the defence of *volenti* |
| Consent only available if a tort has been committed | *Wooldridge v Sumner* (1963) | Although the rider owed a duty of care there was no negligence and *volenti* could not be argued |

## Activity

Suggest which defence may be argued in each of the following situations. Suggest whether or not the defence is likely to succeed.

1 Jed is sued for breaking Raj's collarbone during a kick-boxing contest.

2 Manjit accepts a lift from Steven, who already has a car full of passengers. Manjit sits in the open boot of the car, and is injured when another car hits Steven's car from behind when it fails to stop as the traffic lights change.

3 Mohammed is injured when he went for a flight in a light aeroplane with Pierre, whom he knows does not have a pilot's license.

4 Helga fell off her horse and was badly injured during a show-jumping contest when the horse pulled up at a large fence.

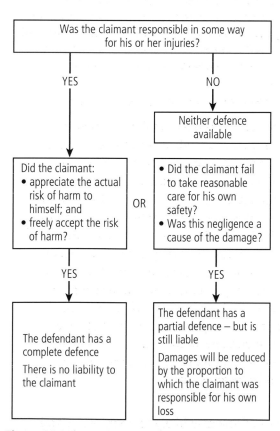

**Figure 24.6** The availability of defences of *volenti non fit injuria* and contributory negligence and their contrasting effects

## Check your understanding

**For AS and A-level:**

1 Which one statement most accurately describes the purpose of showing that a duty of care exists in negligence?

  A  To show that you care about someone

  B  It establishes a legal relationship

  C  It allows you to sue for the injuries you have suffered

  D  It gives you a bond with the person who has caused your injuries.

2 Which one of the following statements most accurately describes the meaning of breach of duty?

  A  Falling below a standard of care

  B  Breaking your promise to someone

  C  Falling over and breaking something

  D  Opening the floodgates to more personal injury claims

3 Tim is a child actor aged 7. He had an important part in a new TV drama series set in a seaside town. Eva is appointed by the TV company as Tim's nanny as she specialises in being a nanny to child actors. During a break in filming, Tim was playing close to the edge of the pier. Eva did not notice because she was checking her phone. Tim slipped and fell into the sea and was injured.

  Examine the three elements of a duty of care in negligence and discuss whether Eva owed Tim a duty of care.

**For A-level:**

1 Pat was driving her car and stopped at a set of traffic lights. Raji was driving his van behind Pat. Because he was changing tracks on his music player, Raji failed to notice that Pat had stopped and drove into the back of her car. As a result Pat's car was damaged and Sara, a passenger, was injured.

  Examine the three elements of a duty of care in negligence and discuss whether Raji owes both Pat and Sara a duty of care.

2 Amy is a waitress in a café. One morning she was showing off by carrying a large tray of hot drinks on just one hand. She was wearing high heels that day instead of her normal shoes. She fell off her high heels and the drinks spilled over a customer, Dave, who was badly burned.

  Examine the meaning of breach of duty in negligence and discuss whether Amy has broken that duty.

3 Duane asked his friend Adam to help him take his large old fridge to the local recycling centre in his van. He did not bother to secure the fridge in the back of the van as the centre was nearby. He asked Adam to travel in the back of the van and 'keep an eye' on the fridge. Unfortunately Duane went over the speed bump at the entrance to the centre too quickly. The fridge fell over, landing on Adam, breaking his leg. Adam had to have an operation on his leg but the inexperienced surgeon failed to deal with a complication and, as a result, Adam's leg had to be amputated. Adam's promising career as a footballer is now over.

  Examine the meaning of remoteness of damage and causation in negligence and discuss whether Duane caused Adam's loss and injury.

## Summary

- Negligence can be caused by an act or omission which causes loss, injury or damage to another person.
- Negligence requires proof of a duty of care owed by the defendant to the claimant, a breach of that duty and loss or damage.
- A duty of care is a legal relationship between the claimant and the defendant.
- To establish a duty of care there is a three-part test:
  - Is there proximity of a relationship?
  - Is the loss or damage reasonably foreseeable?
  - Is there a public policy reason not to owe a duty of care?
- Breach of duty means falling below the standard of the reasonable person.
- To judge whether a reasonable person would have acted in the same way as the defendant, different factors are to be considered such as the age of the defendant, and whether he is a professional or experienced.
- Risk factors may be used to judge if there has been a breach of duty, such as special characteristics of the claimant, the size or level of risk, whether any precautions have been taken, if the risk was known about at the time of the accident and any possible public benefit.
- The loss or damage must have been caused by the breach of duty.
- Causation is proved by the 'but for' test and if there has been an intervening event.
- The loss or damage must be reasonably foreseeable and not too remote. The type of injury has to be reasonably foreseeable, not the exact injury suffered. The defendant must take his victim as he finds him.
- *Res ipsa loquitur* (the thing speaks for itself) transfers the burden of proof from the claimant to the defendant. It operates when the defendant is in control of the situation, the accident would not have happened without negligence and there is no other explanation for the accident.
- The most common remedy for negligence is the payment of damages.
- Contributory negligence is a part defence where the claimant is partly responsible for causing his injuries. If successful, the judge will reduce the amount of damages by the percentage of responsibility
- Consent of the claimant is a complete defence. The consent has to be freely given and with the claimant's full knowledge of its effect.

# 25 Occupiers' liability

After reading this chapter you should be able to:
- Understand an occupier's duty towards lawful visitors as governed by the Occupiers' Liability Act 1957
- Understand an occupier's duty towards trespassers as governed by the Occupiers' Liability Act 1984

Since the 19th century the law recognised that the occupier of premises had a duty towards the safety of visitors who come onto their land. This duty developed through common law but visitors to a property were classified in different ways, and different duties were owed by the occupier. Contractors such as hotel guests were owed the highest level of duty which was a duty to ensure that the premises were fit for the purposes of the contract. Invitees, such as a customer in a shop were owed a lower duty which was to take reasonable care to prevent damage from an unusual danger. Licensees, such as a friend invited to a house would be owed a lower duty still. This was a duty to warn of any concealed danger or trap which the occupier knew about. Finally there were uninvited people such as trespassers who were owed no duty of care, except that the occupier could not deliberately or recklessly cause them harm.

Following a Law Reform Committee report the Occupiers Liability Act was passed in 1957. It provided a statutory duty on the occupier towards lawful visitors in respect of dangers due to the state of the premises or things done or omitted to be done on the premises.

Subsequently, to visitors without permission, termed trespassers, a different duty was imposed by the later Occupiers' Liability Act 1984.

## 25.1 Occupiers and premises

### 25.1.1 Occupiers

Potential defendants are the same under the Occupiers' Liability Acts 1957 and 1984 – they will be occupiers of premises who may be, but do not have to be, the owner or tenant of the premises. There is in fact no statutory definition of 'occupier'.

The test for deciding whether a person is the occupier is found in case law.

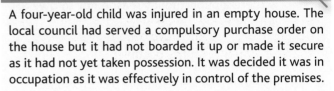

### Wheat v E Lacon & Co. Ltd (1966)

The manager of a pub was given the right to rent out rooms in his private quarters even though he had no ownership rights in the premises. A paying guest fell on an unlit staircase and died. The House of Lords decided that both the manager and his employers could be occupiers under the Act so there could be more than one occupier of the premises.

### Harris v Birkenhead Corporation (1976)

A four-year-old child was injured in an empty house. The local council had served a compulsory purchase order on the house but it had not boarded it up or made it secure as it had not yet taken possession. It was decided it was in occupation as it was effectively in control of the premises.

In practice, a decision of who is in control of premises may be influenced by whose insurance policy covers the premises and is able to meet the claim. However, sometimes, the courts will find that no one is in control of the premises, leaving the injured visitor with no claim.

### Bailey v Armes (1999)

The defendants lived in a flat above a supermarket. They allowed their son to climb out of a window to play on the roof but forbade him to take anyone else there. The supermarket knew nothing of the use of the roof. The boy took his friend on to the roof and he was injured when he fell from the roof. The Court decided that neither the supermarket nor the defendants were liable – control over the means of access (the window) was not sufficient to make the defendants liable.

### 25.1.2 Premises

There is no statutory definition of premises except in s 1(3) (a) of the 1957 Act, where there is reference to a person having occupation or control of any 'fixed or moveable structure, including any vessel, vehicle and aircraft'.

Besides the obvious such as houses, offices, buildings and land, premises have also been held to include:
- a ship in dry dock
- a vehicle
- a lift and even

- a ladder.
- The Act may not apply to every situation where the defendant is an occupier of land. For example in *Revill v Newbery 1996* the defendant, an elderly man, slept in his allotment shed as he had suffered a number of thefts. The claimant came on to the site at night intending to steal items from the shed. The defendant had an old shotgun and hearing movement poked the gun out of a small hole and fired hitting the claimant. The court, faced with a claim for compensation, decided that the fact that he was an occupier was not relevant, the claim was purely in negligence. This suggests that liability under the Act will be applied where a claimant is injured by dangerous conditions on land, or dangerous conduct that can amount to a dangerous condition if it is a continuing source of danger. It will not apply to single actions of the occupier which could have been the actions of someone other than the occupier.

## 25.2 Lawful visitors and the Occupiers' Liability Act 1957

By s 2(1) of the Act the occupier owes a lawful visitor the common duty of care. Lawful visitors can be considered separately as adults, children or workmen.

### 25.2.1 Adult visitors

Lawful adult visitors have a wide definition. They include:

- invitees – persons who have been invited to enter and who have express permission to be there
- licensees – persons who may have express or implied permission to be on the land for a particular period
- those with contractual permission – for example, a person who has bought an entry ticket for an event
- those given a statutory right of entry such as meter readers and police constables exercising a warrant.

### Key term

**Visitor** – in legal terms, lawful adult visitors are invitees, licensees, those with contractual permission and those with statutory right of entry.

### Activity

Consider which of the following potential claimants would be able to class themselves as lawful visitors for the purposes of the Occupiers' Liability Act 1957, and why.

1 Trevor is a milkman delivering milk to Archie's door.
2 Kurt is a milkman who picks flowers in Archie's garden after delivering milk.
3 Craig is making door-to-door deliveries of flyers for a pizza restaurant.
4 Iqbal has a season ticket for a Premier League team, and arrives at the ground on Sunday afternoon for a match.
5 Hannah regularly crosses farmer Giles' field, using a well-known public path.
6 Aaron, an electrician, arrives at Sana's house, as agreed, to fit some wall lights.
7 Ali is a police officer who has called at Brian's house to make routine enquiries about a recent break-in.

An adult visitor is owed the common duty of care. According to s 2(2) this means to:

> **"** take such care as in all the circumstances ... is reasonable to see that the visitor will be reasonably safe in using the premises for the purpose for which he is invited ... to be there **"**

The key point to be made is that the occupier does not have to make the premises completely safe for the visitor – only to do what is reasonable.

### *Laverton v Kiapasha Takeaway Supreme* (2002)

The defendants owned a small takeaway shop. They had fitted slip resistant tiles, and they used a mop and bucket to mop the floor if it had been raining. When the claimant went into the shop it was very busy and it had been raining. She slipped and broke her ankle. The Court of Appeal decided that the shop owners had taken reasonable care to ensure its customers were safe. They were not liable as they did not have to make the shop completely safe.

The court commented in this case that the safety of visitors to premises was not guaranteed, and that it was not feasible as the shop had taken precautions. Customers can be reasonably safe if they take reasonable care for their own safety.

### Dean and Chapter of Rochester Cathedral v Debell (2016)

The claimant was injured when he tripped and fell over a small lump of concrete protruding about two inches from the base of a traffic bollard in the precincts of Rochester Cathedral. The bollard had previously been slightly damaged by a car.

The Court of Appeal decided that:

1 Tripping, slipping and falling are everyday occurrences. No occupier of premises like the cathedral could possibly ensure that the roads or the precincts around a building were maintained in a pristine state. Even if they were, accidents would still happen. The obligation on the occupier is to make the land reasonably safe for visitors, not to guarantee their safety. In order to impose liability, there must be something over and above the risk of injury from the minor blemishes and defects which are habitually found on any road or pathway.

2 The risk is reasonably foreseeable only where there is a real source of danger which a reasonable person would recognise as obliging the occupier to take remedial action. A visitor is reasonably safe even if there may be visible minor defects on the road which carry a foreseeable risk of causing an accident and injury.

The judgements in both these cases emphasise that the common duty of care imposes a duty on the occupier to keep the visitor *reasonably safe*, not necessarily to maintain completely safe premises. The state of premises must pose a *real source of danger* before foreseeability of the risk of damage can be found.

It is possible that, if the cases had been decided in favour of the visitor, it could have opened the floodgates to a tide of claims against occupiers and created a very high level of responsibility for the safety of visitors.

A visitor may be a lawful visitor for the purposes of the 1957 Act, but if he exceeds his permission and enters an unauthorised area he may become a trespasser and lose the protection of the 1957 Act. When this happens, the rules in the 1984 Act may apply.

The duty, however, does not extend to liability for pure accidents. A duty in respect of a specific risk cannot last indefinitely where there could be other causes of the damage.

### Cole v David-Gilbert, The Royal British Legion and others (2007)

The claimant was injured when she trapped her foot in a hole in a village green where a maypole had been erected in the past. She argued that the owner of the village green had a duty to ensure that visitors were safe; that the British Legion had failed to properly fill the hole after a village fete; and that the local council had failed to adequately maintain the green. She won at first instance but failed in the Court of Appeal. The court held that since her injury took place nearly two years after the maypole had been in place, the duty on the British Legion could not last that long. Although there was no specific evidence to support this view, the hole must have been opened again by a stranger, and the incident was a pure accident.

## 25.2.2 Occupiers' liability to children

The occupier owes children coming onto the premises the common duty of care, but there is an additional special duty owed to child visitors. Under s 2(3) of the Occupiers' Liability Act 1957, the occupier 'must be prepared for children to be less careful than adults ... [and as a result] ... the premises must be reasonably safe for a child of that age'.

So, for children, the standard of care is measured subjectively, according to the age of the child. The reasoning is logical: what may not pose a threat to an adult may be very dangerous to a child. The occupier should guard against any kind of 'allurement' or attraction which places a child visitor at risk of harm.

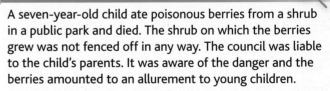

### Glasgow Corporation v Taylor (1922)

A seven-year-old child ate poisonous berries from a shrub in a public park and died. The shrub on which the berries grew was not fenced off in any way. The council was liable to the child's parents. It was aware of the danger and the berries amounted to an allurement to young children.

Where very young children are injured, the courts are reluctant to find the occupier liable as the child should be under the supervision of a parent or other adult.

### Phipps v Rochester Corporation (1955)

A five-year-old child was playing on open ground owned by the council with his seven-year-old sister. He fell down a trench and was injured. The court decided that the council was not liable as the occupier is entitled to expect that parents should not allow their young children to go to places which are potentially unsafe.

A difficulty here is that there is no age limit set as to when this rule applies.

If an allurement exists, there will be no liability on the occupier if the damage or injury suffered is not foreseeable.

### Jolley v London Borough of Sutton (2000)

The council had failed to move an abandoned boat situated on its land for two years. Children regularly played in the boat and it was clearly a potential danger. When two boys aged 14 years jacked the boat up to repair it, the boat fell on one, seriously injuring him. The claim for compensation succeeded in the High Court but failed in the Court of Appeal since it was decided that, while the boat was an obvious allurement, the course of action taken by the boys, and therefore the specific type of injury, was not foreseeable.

In an appeal to the House of Lords, this view was reversed. In their view it was foreseeable that children would play on the abandoned boat. It was not necessary for the council to foresee exactly what they would do on it. They considered that children often find ways of putting themselves in danger, which needed to be taken into account by an occupier when considering how to keep them safe.

So the standard of care owed by an occupier to child visitors is higher than that owed to adults which is probably fair, because, as the House of Lords commented in *Jolley*, children can often find ways of putting themselves in danger when on someone else's land. However, as the decision in *Phipps* shows, a parent or guardian cannot completely transfer their responsibility for the safety of very young children.

## 25.2.3 Occupiers' liability to people carrying out a trade or calling

The occupier owes a tradesman coming on to the premises the common duty of care. However, by s 2(3)(b) of the 1957 Act, an occupier can expect that a person in the exercise of his calling will 'appreciate and guard against any special risks ordinarily incident to it so far as the occupier leave him free to do so'.

The effect of this provision is that an occupier will not be liable where tradesmen fail to guard against risks which they should know about or be expected to know about.

### Roles v Nathan (1963)

Two chimney sweeps died after inhaling carbon monoxide fumes while cleaning the chimney of a coke-fired boiler. The sweeps had been warned of the danger. The occupiers were not liable as they could have expected chimney sweeps to be aware of the particular danger.

This rule, which acts as a defence to an occupier, only applies where the tradesman visitor is injured by something related to his trade or calling. If the tradesman is injured by something different, the occupier will still owe the common duty of care. This seems a fair rule as the occupier can expect a competent workman to know the possible dangers relating to his or her trade.

## 25.2.4 Occupiers' liability for the torts of independent contractors

As before, a lawful visitor is owed the common duty of care while on the occupier's land. However, if the visitor is injured by a workman's negligent work, the occupier may have a defence and be able to pass the claim to the workman. This is under s 2(4) of the 1957 Act, which provides:

> **"** Where damage is caused to a visitor by a danger due to the faulty execution of any work of construction, maintenance or repair by an independent contractor employed by the occupier, the occupier is not to be treated without more as answerable for the danger if in all the circumstances he had acted reasonably in entrusting the work to the independent contractor and had taken such steps (if any) as he reasonably ought in order to satisfy himself that the contractor was competent and that the work had been properly done. **"**

From this, three requirements will apply and all have to be satisfied:

1 It must be reasonable for the occupier to have given the work to the independent contractor. The more complicated and specialist the work, the more likely it will be for the occupier to have given the work to a specialist.

### Haseldine v Daw & Son Ltd (1941)

The claimant was killed when a lift plunged to the bottom of a shaft. The occupier was not liable for negligent repair or maintenance of the lift, as this work is a highly specialist activity and it was reasonable to give the work to a specialist firm.

2  The contractor hired must be competent to carry out the task. Presumably the occupier should take up references or recommendations or check with a trade association, if any, to satisfy this requirement. The occupier should check that the contractor is properly insured. If the contractor fails to carry appropriate insurance cover this could be a fair indication that the contractor is not competent.

### Bottomley v Todmorden Cricket Club (2003)

The cricket club hired a stunt team to carry out a 'firework display'. The team chose to use ordinary gunpowder, petrol and propane gas rather than more traditional fireworks. They also then used the claimant, who was an unpaid amateur with no experience of pyrotechnics, for the stunt. The claimant was burnt and broke an arm when the stunt went wrong. The stunt team had no insurance. The Court of Appeal decided that the club were liable as they had failed to exercise reasonable care to choose safe and competent contractors.

3  The occupier must check the work has been properly done. The more complicated and technical the work, and the less expert the occupier, the more likely that this condition will require the occupier to employ an expert such as an architect or surveyor.

### Woodward v The Mayor of Hastings (1945)

A child was injured on school steps that were left icy after snow had been cleared off them. The occupiers were liable as they had failed to take reasonable steps to check that the work had been done properly, and the danger should have been obvious to them.

If all these conditions are satisfied, the occupier will have a defence to a claim and the injured claimant will have to claim directly against the contractor. This again seems a fair rule for an occupier. It would be harsh to expect an occupier to be responsible for work carried out by competent workmen on his premises. It has to be hoped that a reputable contractor will be covered by liability insurance, and the claimant can still recover compensation.

## 25.2.5 Defences to a claim

For A-level, you will need to know the defences to an occupiers' liability claim under the 1957 Act:

- consent
- contributory negligence and
- warning notices.

### Contributory negligence

This part defence has been set out in Chapter 24. It applies to occupiers' liability in the same way as for negligence. The court will rule that the claimant is partly responsible for the injuries he has suffered. If it is successfully argued, the amount of compensation will be reduced by such amount as the court think appropriate.

See Chapter 24 at section 24.5.1.

### Consent

This complete defence has also been set out in Chapter 24. It applies to occupiers' liability in the same way as for negligence. If it is successfully argued, the defendant will not be liable to pay damages to the claimant.

See Chapter 24 at section 24.5.2.

## Warning notices

This is a complete defence to a claim of occupier's liability. The warning can be oral or written. By s 2(4) of the 1957 Act, a warning is ineffective unless 'in all the circumstances it was enough to enable the visitor to be reasonably safe'.

What amounts to a sufficient warning will be a question of fact in each case, and will be decided by the judge on the evidence. If the premises are extremely dangerous or they are unusual, the occupier may be required to erect barriers or additional warnings to keep visitors safe.

### Rae v Marrs (UK) Ltd (1990)

The premises was a deep pit inside a dark shed so a warning, by itself, was insufficient.

However if the danger is obvious and the visitor is able to appreciate it, no additional warning is necessary.

### Staples v West Dorset District Council (1995)

The danger of wet algae on a high wall should have been obvious, and no further warning was required.

## Exclusion clauses

By s 2 (1) of the 1957 Act, an occupier is able 'to restrict, modify or exclude his duty by agreement or otherwise'.

This means that the occupier will, in any warning, be able to limit or exclude completely his liability for any injury caused to the visitor. This is the case for residential occupiers, though whether an exclusion works against a child visitor may depend on the child's age and ability to understand the effect of the exclusion.

However for business occupiers this rule is subject to s 2 (1) of the Unfair Contract Terms Act 1977. This provides that:

> **❝** A person cannot by reference to … a notice given to persons generally or to a particular person restrict his liability resulting from personal injury or death caused by negligence. **❞**

In addition, s65 Consumer Rights Act 2015 provides that

> **❝** A trader cannot by … a consumer notice exclude or restrict liability for death or personal injury resulting from negligence. **❞**

These provisions mean that if there are such clauses in a warning notice, they are ineffective and cannot operate as a defence to an occupier.

### Activity

Look at the warning notices in Figure 25.1. Are either or both valid:

■ if seen on a private house?
■ if seen on a car park?

**Figure 25.1** Warning notices

## 25.2.6 Remedies

If the occupier is liable for breach of his duty, the remedy to be claimed by the visitor is damages. The court can award damages for any personal injury suffered and for any property damaged.

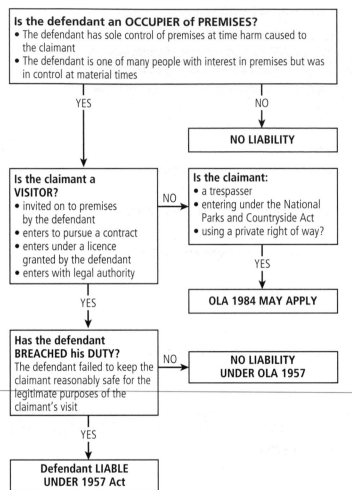

**Figure 25.2** The assessment of liability under the Occupiers' Liability Act 1957

**Figure 25.3** The assessment of liability under the Occupiers' Liability Act 1957

| Case name | Facts | Legal principle |
| --- | --- | --- |
| *Wheat v Lacon* (1966) | Visitor fell down stairs and died | Occupier is the person with control over the premises. There can be more than one occupier with control |
| *Laverton v Kiapasha Takeaway Supreme* (2002) | Customer injured in shop | The premises do not have to be completely safe. The occupier has to make the premises reasonably safe for visitors |
| *Glasgow Corporation v Taylor* (1922) | Child poisoned by berries growing on bush in park | Occupier has to protect child visitors from allurements |
| *Phipps v Rochester Corporation* (1955) | Young child injured when falling into a trench | Occupier can expect parents to supervise very young children |
| *Jolley v London Borough of Sutton* (2000) | Teenager injured when playing on boat on council's land | Occupier is liable for injuries suffered by children that are reasonably foreseeable |
| *Roles v Nathan* (1963) | Chimney sweeps killed when working in industrial chimney | Occupier can expect workmen to appreciate and guard against risks that are incidental to their work |

## Activity

1  When a visitor comes to your home, how would you explain to a member of your family what the 'common duty of care' means?

2  Discuss why children are owed a different duty of care to adult visitors. Ask a parent or another adult for his views.

3  Do you think that the defence in *Phipps v Rochester Corporation* (1955) applies today?

**Figure 25.4** Occupiers' liability to lawful visitors

| Occupiers' liability | Section/Case |
|---|---|
| Occupiers' liability is covered by two Acts: the Occupiers' Liability Act 1957 for lawful 'visitors' and the Occupiers' Liability Act 1984 for trespassers | |
| An 'occupier' is anybody in actual control of the land | *Wheat v Lacon* (1966) |
| Premises are widely defined and have included even a ladder | *Wheeler v Copas* (1981) |
| **The duty and the standard of care in the 1957 Act** | **Case** |
| A 'common duty of care' is owed to all lawful visitors | s 2(1) |
| The duty is to ensure that the visitor is safe for the purposes of the visit | s 2(2) |
| An occupier must take extra care for children, who are less careful than adults, and not put extra danger or 'allurements' in their path | s 2(3) *Glasgow Corporation v Taylor* (1922) |
| This applies to any foreseeable danger to the child regardless of what injury is actually caused | *Jolley v London Borough of Sutton* (1998) |
| Although it is assumed that parents should keep control of young children | *Phipps v Rochester Corporation* (1955) |
| A person carrying out a trade or calling on the occupier's premises must prepare for the risks associated with the trade | *Roles v Nathan* (1963) |
| The occupier will not be liable for damage which is the result of work done by independent contractors if:<br>(a) it is reasonable to entrust the work<br>(b) a reputable contractor is chosen<br>(c) the occupier is not obliged to inspect the work | *Haseldine v Daw* (1941)<br>*Woodward v Mayor of Hastings* (1945) |
| **Avoiding the duty** | **Case** |
| It is possible to avoid liability where:<br>(a) adequate warnings are given<br>(b) exclusion clauses can be relied on – subject to the Unfair Contract Terms Act 1977<br>(c) defences of consent or contributory negligence apply | *Rae v Mars* (1990) |

## 25.3 Liability for trespassers: the Occupiers' Liability Act 1984

### 25.3.1 The background of the duty

Traditionally, at common law, an occupier owed a trespasser no duty at all, other than not to deliberately or recklessly inflict injury. This rule was harshly applied, particularly to child trespassers as in *Addie v Dumbreck* (1929). A four-year-old child was killed when he fell through the unprotected cover of a wheel on colliery land. No compensation could be claimed by the parents as the child was a trespasser.

**Key term**

Trespasser – a visitor who has no permission or authority to be on the occupier's land.

The House of Lords, making use of the 1966 Practice Statement, were able to change the law and introduced a duty of 'common humanity' on to occupiers towards trespassers.

### British Rail Board v Herrington (1972)

A six-year-old boy was badly burnt when he trespassed on to an electrified railway line through vandalised fencing. BR were aware of gaps in the fencing and that children played in the area. The House of Lords established a duty of 'common humanity' which was a limited duty owed when the occupier knew of the danger, and of the likelihood of the trespass.

The Law Commission investigated this area of law in their 1975 report entitled 'Report on liability for damage or injury to trespassers and related questions of occupiers' liability'. As a result of the report, the 1984 Act was passed by Parliament and the duty of 'common humanity' was replaced by a statutory duty.

## 25.3.2 The scope of the duty

By s 1(1)(a) of the 1984 Act, a duty applies in respect of people other than lawful visitors (who are covered by the 1957 Act) for 'injury on the premises by reason of any danger due to the state of the premises or things done or omitted to be done on them'.

The 1984 Act provides compensation for personal injuries only. Damage to property is not covered, reflecting the view that trespassers are deserving of less protection than lawful visitors.

The occupier will only owe a duty under s 1(3) if:

a   he is aware of the danger or has reasonable grounds to believe it exists;

b   he knows or has reasonable grounds to believe that the other is in the vicinity of the danger concerned or that he may come into the vicinity of the danger (in either case, whether the other has lawful authority for being in the vicinity or not); and

c   the risk is one against which, in all the circumstances of the case, he may be expected to offer the other some protection.

The duty owed under s 1(4) is to 'take such care as is reasonable in the circumstances to see that he [the trespasser] is not injured by reason of the danger'.

The danger referred to in these sections is the object or part of land on which the trespasser is injured. The standard of care is an objective one. What is required of the occupier depends on the circumstances of each case. The greater the degree of risk, the more precautions the occupier will have to take. Factors

to be taken into account include the nature of the premises, the degree of danger, the practicality of taking precautions, and the age of the trespasser.

Where an occupier knows of a risk, or knows that trespassers are, or will come into the vicinity of it, there seems to be little problem in establishing liability. What often happens is interpreting what amounts to 'reasonable grounds to believe' that a danger exists and 'reasonable grounds to believe' that a trespasser is, or will come into the vicinity of the danger.

The Act appears to have given trespassers a right to claim compensation when they have been injured while trespassing. However, there have been a number of court decisions which have restricted when a duty is owed to trespassers and, if a duty is owed, whether the occupier is liable.

### Cases involving adult trespassers

When considering claims under the 1984 Act, the courts have introduced the concept of obvious dangers, especially for adult trespassers. The occupier will not be liable if the trespasser is injured by an obvious danger.

### Ratcliff v McConnell (1999)

A 19-year-old student climbed the fence of his open air college swimming pool at night and dived into the pool hitting his head on a ledge. He was seriously injured. The Court of Appeal decided that the occupier was not required to warn adult trespassers of the risk of injury against obvious dangers. In this case there was no hidden danger as it is well known that swimming pools vary in depth, and diving without checking the depth is dangerous.

The time of day and the time of year when the accident happened will be relevant in deciding whether the occupier owes a duty of care.

### Donoghue v Folkestone Properties (2003)

The claimant was injured when he was trespassing on a slipway in a harbour and dived into the sea, hitting a grid pile used for mooring boats. The grid pile would have been visible at low tide. The injury happened in the middle of winter, at around midnight. The court held that the occupier did not owe the claimant a duty of care under the 1984 Act as they would not expect that a trespasser might be present or jump into the harbour at that time of day or year.

An occupier does not have to spend lots of money in making premises safe from obvious dangers.

### Tomlinson v Congleton Borough Council (2003)

The council owned a park including a lake. Warning signs were posted prohibiting swimming and diving because the water was dangerous, but the council knew that these were generally ignored. The council decided to make the lake inaccessible to the public but delayed start on this work because of lack of funds. The claimant, aged 18, went swimming in the lake, struck his head on the sandy bottom and suffered paralysis as a result of a severe spinal injury.

In the Court of Appeal his claim under the 1984 Act succeeded. The court felt that the seriousness of the risk of injury, the frequency with which people were exposed to the risk, and the fact that the lake acted as an allurement all meant that the scheme to make the lake inaccessible should have been completed with greater urgency. The House of Lords, however, accepted the council's appeal for three reasons.

1   In order to be liable under the 1984 Act, there had to be a danger due to the state of the premises or things done or omitted to be done. In this case the danger was not due to the state of the premises but was due to the claimant diving into the water.

2   It was not the sort of risk that a defendant should have to guard against but one that the trespasser chose to run. So trespassers had to take some responsibility for their actions.

3   The council would not have breached its duty even if the claimant was a lawful visitor, as it was not reasonable for it to spend a lot of money preventing visitors being injured by an obvious danger.

The occupier will not be liable if he had no reason to suspect the presence of a trespasser.

### Higgs v Foster (2004)

A police officer investigating a crime entered the occupier's premises to carry out surveillance. He fell into an uncovered inspection pit suffering severe injuries, causing him to retire from the police force. The police officer was judged to be a trespasser on the premises. Although the occupiers knew the pit was a potential danger, they could not have anticipated his presence on the premises or in the vicinity, so they were not liable.

The occupier will not be liable if he was not aware of the danger or had no reason to suspect the danger existed.

### Rhind v Astbury Water Park (2004)

The occupier did not know of a submerged fibreglass container resting on the bottom of a lake on its premises. The claimant ignored a notice stating 'Private Property. Strictly no Swimming' and jumped into the lake and was injured by objects below the surface of the water. Section 1(3)(c) requires the occupier to owe a duty if 'the risk is one against which, in all the circumstances of the case, he may be expected to offer the other some protection'. As the occupier did not know of the dangerous objects, no duty was owed.

As can be seen the courts, in all these cases, have supported occupiers against claims by trespassers and their decisions appear to support the idea of personal responsibility, especially where the visitor has no permission to be on the occupier's land. Most of the reported cases involve the visitor suffering very serious injuries. Presumably the failure of their claims passes the future burden of caring for them on to the state.

## Cases involving child trespassers

The same statutory rules apply to child visitors as for adult visitors. The approach of judges towards claims by child trespassers is the same as for adults as can be seen by the following cases.

### Keown v Coventry Healthcare NHS Trust (2006)

An 11-year-old boy climbed a fire escape on the exterior of a hospital to show off to his friends and fell. The Court of Appeal held that, since the child appreciated the danger, it was not the state of the premises (the existence of the fire escape, which was not faulty) but what the boy was doing on it. There was no danger due to the state of the premises, and the hospital was not liable.

### Baldaccino v West Wittering (2008)

On a summer's day a 14-year-old boy climbed a navigational beacon sited off a beach as the tide was ebbing. He dived off the beacon, suffering neck injuries and tetraplegia. He was a lawful visitor to the beach but a trespasser to the beacon. It was decided that there was no duty on the part of the occupiers to warn against obvious dangers and the injuries did not result from the state of the premises. His claim failed.

Again it appears that the courts have supported the approach of personal responsibility which could be due to the ages of the children involved.

## 25.3.3 Defences

For A-level, you will need to understand defences to occupiers' liability under the 1984 Act, which are the same as for liability to lawful visitors.

### Consent

The defence of consent (also known as *volenti*) appears to be allowed by s 1(6) of the 1984 Act if the trespasser appreciates the nature and degree of the risk – more than just its existence. If successful, it acts as a complete defence.

### Contributory negligence

This defence can apply to reduce the damages payable to the claimant by such proportion as the judge thinks appropriate to reflect the claimant's responsibility for his injuries.

### Warning notice

A warning, either oral or a notice, can be an effective defence, especially to an adult visitor, if it warns of the danger in clear terms. Whether a warning will be sufficient for a child trespasser will depend on the age and understanding of the child.

#### Westwood v Post Office (1973)

The claimant, an employee of the Post Office, was injured when he entered, as a trespasser, an unlocked room which had the notice 'Only the authorised attendant is permitted to enter'. The door should have been locked. The defendants were not liable as the notice was a sufficient warning to an adult.

## 25.3.4 Remedies

If the occupier is liable for breach of his duty the remedy to be claimed by the trespasser is damages for personal injury only.

**Figure 25.5** Occupiers' liability to trespassers

| The common law | Case/Statute |
| --- | --- |
| The law was originally not to deliberately cause harm<br>Because of the harshness of this rule as it applied to children, a duty of common humanity to trespassers was introduced | *Addie v Dumbreck* (1929)<br>*BR Board v Herrington* (1972) |

| Scope of the duty under the Occupiers' Liability Act 1984 | Case/Statute |
| --- | --- |
| Duty is owed if:<br>'(a) [occupier] is aware of the danger or has reasonable grounds to believe it exists;<br>(b) he knows or has reasonable grounds to believe that the other is in the vicinity of the danger concerned or that he may come into the vicinity of the danger (in either case, whether the other has lawful authority for being in the vicinity or not);<br>(c) the risk is one against which, in all the circumstances of the case, he may be expected to offer the other some protection.'<br>The duty owed is to take such care as is reasonable in the circumstances to see that the trespasser is not injured by reason of the danger | s 1(3)<br>s 1(4) |
| Occupier does not have to warn adult trespassers of risk of injury against obvious dangers | *Ratcliff v McConnell* (1999) |
| Occupier does not have to warn adult trespasser against obvious risks if trespasser enters at unforeseeable time of day or year | *Donoghue v Folkestone Properties* (2003) |
| Occupier does not have to spend lots of money in making premises safe from obvious dangers | *Tomlinson v Congleton Borough Council* (2003) |
| Occupier will not owe a duty to trespasser he does not expect to enter premises | *Higgs v Foster* (2004) |
| Occupier does not owe a duty for danger he is unaware of | *Rhind v Astbury Water Park* (2004) |

## Activity

Discuss these points:

■ How does the duty of 'common humanity' differ from the duty imposed by the 1984 Act?

■ The approach taken by the courts towards claims by trespassers.

## Tip

You must be able to recognise whether the visitor is a lawful visitor or a trespasser, and apply the correct rules to consider a possible claim. Remember that a lawful visitor can become a trespasser if he exceeds his permission or enters a prohibited area.

## Check your understanding

1 Which one statement most accurately describes the duty owed by an occupier under the Occupier's Liability Act 1957?

   A The duty to call for help

   B The duty not to injure the visitor by reason of a danger

   C The duty not to hurt the visitor

   D The common duty of care

2 Briefly explain the conditions that have to be satisfied for an occupier to pass liability for injury to a visitor on to an independent contractor.

3 Wayne ran a cleaning business from a building on two floors. He had recently installed new flooring, himself, upstairs. Owing to his very poor work, some of the new flooring gave way and Wayne's industrial cleaner crashed through the upper floor into the room below. Yaz, a customer, was visiting Wayne's premises. The cleaner fell on her, causing her serious injuries. Advise Yaz whether Wayne has broken his duty of care to her.

4 Jimmy invited his neighbour's children to come into his garden to play with his own children in his swimming pool. Jimmy had just finished cleaning the pool surround which was still very slippery. As the children ran to jump into the pool Jimmy shouted to them to be very careful.

Unfortunately one of the neighbour's children, Leon, aged 6, slipped and suffered a broken leg. Advise Leon's parents whether Jimmy has broken his duty of care to Leon.

5 Kevin owned a gym. He had recently had new exercise machines fitted and checked by a specialist firm. Eva, a gym member, was using one of the machines when it broke, throwing her to the floor and causing her to break her leg.

Examine the duty owed by an occupier of premises, and by independent contractors, to lawful visitors and discuss whether the specialist firm, rather than Kevin, would be liable to Eva for her injuries.

6 Kevin received several complaints from members of his gym that one of the diving boards in the swimming pool was unstable and not safe. Kevin put up a large sign on the entrance door to the pool, which said, 'Danger. No entry to pool until further notice'. Matty, a gym member, ignored the notice and went into the pool area. He climbed on to a diving board, which collapsed due to a defect in the support structure. As a result, Matty fell heavily and suffered head injuries.

Examine the duty owed by an occupier to a trespasser and discuss whether Kevin will be liable to Matty for his injuries.

## Summary

- Lawful visitors are owed the common duty of care by an occupier of property.
- The common duty of care requires the occupier to keep the visitor reasonably safe.
- Greater care has to be taken by an occupier towards child visitors, especially if an allurement is present.
- Occupiers can expect very young children to be supervised by their parents.
- Occupiers are liable for injury to child visitors that is reasonably foreseeable.
- Occupiers can expect workmen visitors to be aware of risks associated with their work.
- The occupier will not be liable for the work of independent contractors if:
    - it is reasonable to give the work to another
    - a reputable contractor is used and
    - if possible the occupier checks the work has been properly done.
- Lawful visitors who are injured can claim damages for personal injury and damage to property, e.g. clothes.

- The occupier owes a duty to trespassers to ensure the trespasser is not injured by reason of the danger.
- The duty is owed when:
    - the occupier is aware of the danger or has reasonable grounds to believe it exists
    - he knows or has reasonable grounds to believe the trespasser is in the vicinity of the danger or may come into the vicinity of the danger
    - the risk is one against which he may be expected to offer the trespasser some protection.
- The occupier will not be liable if the trespasser is injured by an obvious risk or the injury occurs at an unusual time of day or year. The occupier is not required to spend considerable amounts of money in protecting the trespasser from obvious dangers.
- Trespassers who are injured can claim damages for personal injury only.

# 26 Remedy of compensatory damages

## 26.1 Compensatory damages for physical injury and damage to property

In a tort claim the court can award a successful claimant compensation for the injuries he has suffered or damage to his property. This award is known as damages.

As we saw in Chapter 23, the aim of the award of damages is to place the claimant in the same position as if the tort had not been committed as far as money can do so. This is possible where the claim is for damage to property. However, if the claimant has suffered disabling personal injury, this is not possible.

### 26.1.1 Pecuniary and non-pecuniary loss

Pecuniary loss is a loss that can be easily calculated in money terms, for example the cost of hiring a car while the claimant's own car is being repaired.

Non-pecuniary loss is loss that is not wholly money-based. This can include:

- pain and suffering as a result of the accident
- loss of amenity or a change in lifestyle, such as not being able to play a sport.

### 26.1.2 Special and general damages

#### Special damages

These are amounts which can be calculated specifically up to the date of the trial or settlement.

In other words they are the pecuniary loss. This could include the cost of repairing a vehicle and the hire costs of a replacement, or replacing damaged clothes or bags. Any loss of earnings while recovering from the accident could also be claimed.

#### General damages

These are non-pecuniary losses and are looking forwards from the trial or settlement date. They can include:

- an amount for pain and suffering
- loss of amenity
- future loss of earnings
- future medical expenses including adapting a house or car to be suitable for a severely injured person and paying for specialist care.

These amounts are, to an extent, speculative, and evidence will have to be obtained to support the claim. This will include medical evidence of the effect of the accident on the victim and how long the suffering or injuries will take to heal, if at all. For future loss of earnings and future medical expenses there will have to be an annual calculation of the loss, and this will be multiplied by the number of years of the loss. For example, five years' loss of earnings at £25,000 each year will lead to a total loss of earnings of £125,000. As explained below, the claimant will be expected to mitigate the loss, so if he can work part-time or at a lower rate, this will be deducted from the award.

### 26.1.3 Lump sums and structured settlements

When the courts make an award for pain and suffering and loss of amenity, they can only award a lump sum. This also has to be a once-only award. The claimant cannot come back to court to say that he has exhausted the damages.

This can be unfair to the claimant whose condition in the future might become worse. Also, where a large award is made for future medical expenses, there is the problem of inflation.

On the other hand an award of a lump sum might be unfair to the defendant if the claimant's condition improves considerably and there is no longer a need to pay for care.

To deal with these situations the Damages Act 1996 allows for structured settlements to be set. It allows parties who settle a claim to agree that all or part of the damages can be paid as periodical payments, that is, so much a month or a year. This is arranged by the defendant (or more likely his insurer) who will purchase an annuity through a financial company, which then pays a set amount at regular intervals to the claimant.

The Damages Act also allows parties to agree that the payments may be made for life or for a specific period (such as for ten years), and the amount can be reassessed at intervals to ensure that its value in real terms is maintained. This type of settlement protects the claimant whose condition may become worse. At the same time it can also be fairer to the defendant who will only have to pay while the claimant's condition requires it. The courts have no power to order such structured settlements.

## 26.2 Mitigation of loss

The claimant is entitled to be compensated for his loss, but he is under a duty to keep the loss to a reasonable level. This is called mitigation of loss.

For example, the claimant cannot claim for private health treatment for the injury if there is suitable treatment available under the NHS. On the other hand, if treatment is only available privately, the cost of the private treatment can be claimed.

The same principles apply to property damage. If property has been damaged beyond repair, the cost of replacing that property can be claimed. Replacing the item with a more expensive replacement would not be allowed.

## 26.3 Examples of damages awards

The three case examples below show how damages can be awarded.

### Activity

Read the three case examples carefully, then answer the following questions about each one:

1 Was this a fair award?

2 What award would you accept if this happened to a member of your family?

3 Can the principle of the award of damages in tort (to put the claimant back in the position he was in before the accident) apply to this case?

### Case study 1: Damage to hair and hair loss

The claimant was a regular client at her hair salon, attending every four weeks to have her hair bleached. Usually the salon used foils to apply bleach to her hair, but during one visit a stylist recommended that, for the health of her hair, the bleach should be applied directly on to her roots. This was agreed, and the treatment was also carried out on three subsequent visits to the salon.

After the fourth treatment, the claimant found that her hair broke and snapped when she washed it. She raised this concern with the salon on her next visit, but was reassured that this was not connected to the treatment, and her hair was bleached in the usual way. However, clumps of her hair broke off during hair washing.

This caused serious distress to the claimant as her hair was left much shorter than her preferred length. After different attempts to style her hair and cover the damage (which caused further hair loss), she left the salon and pursued a claim for the damage caused by the mistreatment. Reports from a consultant dermatologist and a clinical psychologist showed that the claimant had suffered from loss of hair over the crown and fringe, and an itchy and dry scalp with some scabbing that tended to weep when scratched. Further, the damage had caused the claimant to experience low moods, poor self-esteem, social avoidance and anxiety. The claimant received £5,750 from the salon in a full and final settlement.

Source: Adapted from www.jmw.co.uk/services-for-you/personal-injury/beauty-injuries/hair-injuries/success-stories/hairdressing-compensation/

A hairdresser applying colour in a salon

### Case study 2: Delay in treatment results in brain damage

A 36-year-old woman suffered injuries caused by a delay in emergency treatment and has been awarded compensatory damages of £5 million in the High Court. The claimant collapsed at home and her partner phoned 999. However, the ambulance would not come within 100 metres of her home without a police escort, as the address was (wrongly) described as 'high risk'.

The delay to treatment lasted 100 minutes. By the time the ambulance and paramedics arrived at her home, the claimant had suffered brain damage caused by deprivation of oxygen and a cardiac arrest.

The claimant had previously worked as a genetic scientist, but now requires constant care in a specialist medical unit as a result of her injuries. She received a £1.4 million lump sum payment and annual payments thereafter.

Source: Adapted from www.worthingtonslaw.co.uk/ articles-downloads/2014/june/5-million-damages-awarded-for-paramedic-delays

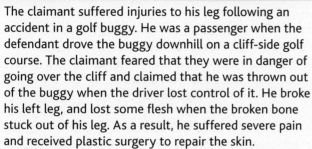

## Case study 3: Broken leg and loss of flesh in golf buggy accident

The claimant suffered injuries to his leg following an accident in a golf buggy. He was a passenger when the defendant drove the buggy downhill on a cliff-side golf course. The claimant feared that they were in danger of going over the cliff and claimed that he was thrown out of the buggy when the driver lost control of it. He broke his left leg, and lost some flesh when the broken bone stuck out of his leg. As a result, he suffered severe pain and received plastic surgery to repair the skin.

However, the defendant denied responsibility for the accident, saying that the claimant jumped from the buggy while it was travelling at no more than walking pace down the hill.

The claimant was unable to work for over a year because of his injuries. He was self-employed, and claimed for loss of earnings as well as compensation for his injuries. Eventually, a settlement was negotiated out of court between the defendant and the claimant, with full and final payment of £27,987.50 made to the claimant.

Source: Adapted from www.jmw.co.uk/services-for-you/personal-injury/success-stories/broken-leg-and-loss-of-flesh/

## 26.4 Injunctions

The A-level course covers injunctions as a remedy.

After damages, the most common remedy in tort is an injunction. This is generally an order of the court to stop doing something. If the person on whom the injunction is placed fails to follow the terms of the injunction, they will be in contempt of court and can be punished with a fine or imprisonment for a maximum of two years.

### Key term

**Contempt of court** – the failure to follow an order of the civil court. The court can order punishment if the failure is serious or continues for a period of time.

An injunction can be ordered during the case, for example to disclose documents or not to continue an action until a trial has taken place. Most commonly, an injunction can be ordered as a final order, known as a perpetual injunction. This can be ordered, for example, in a nuisance case to ensure that a person does not continue to cause a nuisance to neighbours, perhaps by banning an activity outright or within certain hours.

A less common form of injunction could be a mandatory injunction, which will order a party to carry out a certain action. This again could be used in a nuisance action, for example to install sound-proofing or an extractor to remove offending smells.

Injunctions will often be the main reason a nuisance case is brought, as the aim of taking the action is to stop the nuisance continuing.

However, following a ruling of the Supreme Court in the nuisance case of *Coventry v Lawrence* (referred to in Chapter 11 of Book 2) fewer injunctions can be expected to be granted. The court criticised the tendency to mechanically apply existing principles and award an injunction. Instead, the Supreme Court endorsed a more flexible approach when awarding a remedy. If the approach suggested by the Supreme Court is adopted in practice, it is likely that fewer injunctions will be granted and that damages will become a more common alternative remedy. This could include cases when the loss or inconvenience suffered is slight and the impact on the wrongdoer is severe.

### Case study 4: injunction granted

A final injunction has been awarded against a Birmingham council tenant (PR) who has been responsible for causing nuisance and annoyance to local residents.

PR was handed a two-year Nuisance and Annoyance Injunction which means that he cannot:

1 use or threaten to use violence, harass or intimidate any person

2 enter his road in Birmingham

3 cause nuisance or annoyance in the road, including but not limited to fighting, shouting, verbal abuse, swearing, arguing or causing criminal damage.

If any of the conditions at 1 and 2 are breached during the next two years, the terms of the injunction allow his immediate arrest and return to the court within 24 hours.

Neighbours complained of his antisocial behaviour, which included verbal abuse to residents and visitors (particularly insulting people of ethnic origin or with a disability), drinking and taking drugs outside of the property and encouraging large groups of youths to congregate there. PR also encouraged retaliation, resulting in street fights and objects being thrown through his windows.

Source: Adapted from http://birminghamnewsroom.com/full-injunction-granted-against-antisocial-neighbour/

## Check your understanding

Peter, aged 30, was involved in a serious road accident in which he suffered serious injuries.

His doctor has told him that it will be some time before he can work again, and he cannot expect to continue his job as a vet for large animals. His solicitor has told him that he is likely to receive substantial damages as the accident was the fault of the other driver.

Advise Peter on the principles a judge will use when deciding the amount of damages to be awarded to an accident victim and the damages he could claim and how he is likely to receive his compensation.

## Summary

- Damages are the usual remedy awarded in tort.
- The aim of awarding damages is to put the claimant back in the position he was in before the tort, so far as money can do so.
- The claimant is under a duty to mitigate the loss.
- Special damages can be specifically calculated and cover losses up to the date of the court hearing.
- General damages are awarded for the future and cover loss of future earnings, future medical expenses, loss of amenity and pain and suffering.
- Damages can be paid as a lump sum or by structured settlement over a period of time.
- Injunctions can be awarded in specific types of cases, e.g. nuisance.
- An injunction can be awarded ordering a person to do something, or not to do something.

# Practice questions

## English legal system questions

1. Explain what is meant by a unanimous verdict of a jury in a criminal trial and when a jury has to reach a unanimous verdict.

2. Gary, who is currently unemployed, has been arrested on suspicion of wounding.

   Explain the different forms of legal advice and representation available to him.

3. Explain the way civil cases are dealt with in court.

4. Detailed health and safety rules are needed for using a new form of technology.

   Explain why delegated legislation might be the most suitable form for the new rules.

5. Explain one reason why only a limited number of reforms proposed by the Law Commission result in legislation being passed.

6. Using an example from either civil and/or criminal law, explain how judges can avoid following a binding precedent and discuss why it may be advantageous for them to use this approach

7. Explain the role of the law making institutions of the European Union and discuss the impact of European Union law on UK law.

8. Explain the alternative methods of dispute resolution and discuss the benefits of these alternative approaches.

9. Explain the ways in which judicial independence is maintained and discuss why it is important that we have a system of judicial independence.

## Criminal law questions

1. Adam wanted to scare his friend Billy who was a keen mountain bike racer. He knew that Billy would be coming down a trail and decided to hide in the trees near the bottom of the trail to surprise him.

   As Billy came down at high speed Adam jumped out and shouted at Billy. Billy swerved and put on his brakes, but unfortunately lost control of his bike. He fell off his bike and suffered some bruising and a sprained wrist.

   Advise Adam as to his criminal liability for an offence under the Offences Against the Person Act 1861 s 47. Assuming he decides to plead not guilty, suggest whether Adam should opt for trial in the magistrates court or crown court.

2. Frank saw Geela near him on the top deck of a bus. As she passed him to get off, he started to racially abuse her and threatened to pull off her hajib. Geela was frightened by this and in her rush to get off the bus, she fell down some stairs and suffered a broken ankle.

   Advise Frank as to his liability for an offence under the Offences against the Person Act 1861 s 18. Assuming he is convicted, assess the factors the court would take into account when sentencing him.

3. Lisl was enraged by Mo and Nazir who had been convicted of grooming young girls. When she saw them near a children's playground, she ran towards them and shouted' Stay away from here!'. She then sprayed them with a pepper spray causing them to cough and their eyes to weep for a short time.

   Lisl is due to be tried in the Magistrates Court.

   Advise Lisl as to her liability for an offence under the Offences Against the Person Act 1861 s47. Assuming she is convicted, assess the likelihood that a non-custodial sentence might be imposed on her.

4. Carol believed that Dina had stolen her boyfriend. On an evening out at a nightclub she saw Dina going into the toilets and followed her in. She shouted 'Hey' and as Dina turned round, she threw some acid in her face. Dina was blinded as a result of the attack.

   Some of the acid splashed on the floor and caused slight burns to Ella who was standing nearby.

   Consider the criminal liability of Carol for the injuries to Dina and to Ella arising from the incident with acid.

5. Hari ran towards Iris shouting abuse and threatening to beat her up. This frightened Iris who roughly pushed Hari away. Hari fell over and banged his head. An hour later Hari suffered a bad headache but went home to rest.

   Two months later, Hari collapsed and was taken to hospital. Doctors found that Hari had suffered brain damage in the fall. Medical opinion was that Hari would not have suffered this brain damage if he had been treated at the time of the fall.

   Consider the criminal liability of Iris for the injuries suffered by Hari.

6. Jamal wanted to teach his neighbour's four year old son, Ken, a lesson to stop him kicking other children, including his own young son. Jamal explained to Ken that it was wrong to kick others, and said to him 'How would you feel if I kicked you?' Before Ken replied, he kicked the boy, intending to only hurt him slightly.

   Unknown to Jamal, Ken had very brittle bones and the kick shattered his leg which then required amputation.

   Consider the criminal liability of Jamal for the injuries suffered by Ken.

## Tort law questions

1. Amy is a waitress in a café. One morning she was showing off by carrying a large tray of hot drinks with just one hand to customers on the pavement outside. She lost control of the tray and the drinks spilled over a passer-by, Dave, who was badly burned.

   Suggest why Amy owed a duty of care in negligence to Dave

2. Tim is aged 7. Eva is Tim's nanny. Tim was playing in the park. Eva did not notice him go into an area of the park that was fenced off for safety reasons because she was checking her phone. Tim slipped and fell into a hole and was injured.

   Suggest why Eva breached her duty of care in negligence to Tim

3. Wayne ran a cleaning business from a building on two floors. He had recently installed new flooring, himself, upstairs. Owing to his very poor work, some of the new flooring gave way and Wayne's industrial cleaner crashed through the upper floor into the room below. Yaz, a customer, was visiting Wayne's premises. The cleaner fell on her, causing her serious injuries.

   Advise whether why Wayne has broken his duty of care in occupier's liability to Yaz and assess the sources of funding available to Yaz to bring her case against Wayne.

4. Jimmy invited his neighbour's children to come into his garden to play with his own children in his swimming pool. Jimmy had just finished cleaning the pool surround which was still very slippery. As the children ran to jump into the pool Jimmy shouted to them to be very careful.

Unfortunately one of the neighbour's children, Leon, aged 6, slipped and suffered a broken leg. Advise Jimmy as to his liability in occupier's liability to Leon and assess the different sources of advice and representation available to Leon.

5. Kevin owned a gym. He had recently had new exercise machines fitted and checked by a specialist firm. Eva, a gym member, was using one of the machines when it broke, throwing her to the floor and causing her to break her leg.

Advise Kevin as to his liability to Eva under the Occupier's Liability Act 1957 and assess the different ways this dispute could be resolved.

6. Pat was driving her car and stopped at a set of traffic lights. Raji was driving his van behind Pat. Because he was changing tracks on his music player, Raji failed to notice that Pat had stopped and drove into the back of her car. As a result Pat's car was damaged and Sara, a passenger, was injured.

Consider whether Raji would be liable in negligence to both Pat and Sara.

7. Kevin received several complaints from members of his gym that one of the diving boards in the swimming pool was unstable and not safe. Kevin put up a large sign on the entrance door to the pool, which said, 'Danger. No entry to pool until further notice'. Matty, a gym member, ignored the notice and went into the pool area. He climbed on to a diving board, which collapsed due to a defect in the support structure. As a result, Matty fell heavily and suffered head injuries.

Consider whether Kevin will be liable to Matty for his injuries.

8. Duane asked his friend Adam to help him take his large old fridge to the local recycling centre in his van. He did not bother to secure the fridge in the back of the van as the centre was nearby. He asked Adam to travel in the back of the van and 'keep an eye' on the fridge.

Unfortunately Duane went over the speed bump at the entrance to the centre too quickly. The fridge fell over, landing on Adam, breaking his leg. Adam had to have an operation on his leg but the inexperienced surgeon failed to deal with a complication and, as a result, Adam's leg had to be amputated. Adam's promising career as a footballer is now over.

Consider Duane's liability for Adam's injury and losses.

# Glossary

**Actus reus** – this is an act, an omission or a state of affairs that is the prohibited conduct in an offence.

**Advocacy** – the art of speaking in court on behalf of another; conducting a case in court as the legal representative of another person.

**Assault** – an act which causes the victim to apprehend the infliction of immediate, unlawful force with either an intention to cause another to fear immediate unlawful personal violence or recklessness as to whether such fear is caused.

**Assault occasioning actual bodily harm** – an assault which causes actual bodily harm to the victim (V) and the defendant intends or is subjectively reckless as to whether V fears unlawful force or is actually subjected to unlawful force.

**Battery** – the application of unlawful force to another person intending either to apply unlawful physical force to another or recklessness as to whether unlawful force is applied.

**Bill** – the name for a draft law going through Parliament before it passes all the parliamentary stages to become an Act of Parliament.

**Binding precedent** – a decision in an earlier case which must be followed in later cases.

**Causation** – a link between the defendant's act or omission and the injury, loss or damage caused to the claimant.

**Cause pressure group** – a pressure group that exists to promote a particular cause.

**Challenge to the array** – a challenge to the whole jury on the basis that it has been chosen in an unrepresentative way.

**Civil claims** – claims made in the civil courts when an individual or a business believes that their rights have been infringed in some way.

**Civil law** – the law concerned with the relationship between individuals.

**Claimant** – the legal term for a person or organisation who has suffered loss or damage and is bringing a civil claim for compensation to the courts.

**Codification** – bringing together all the law on one topic into one complete code of law.

**Consolidation** – combining the law from several Acts of Parliament into one Act of Parliament.

**Contempt of court** – the failure to follow an order of the civil court. The court can order punishment if the failure is serious or continues for a period of time.

**Damage** – this is a legal concept. It asks the question, has the defendant's breach of duty led to the injury or property damage suffered by the claimant?

**Damages** – the payment of money by way of compensation. The aim of damages in tort is to put the claimant back in the position he was in before the tort, so far as money can do so.

**Defendant** – the person who has caused the loss or damage.

**Delegated legislation** – law made by some person or body other than Parliament, but with the authority of Parliament.

**Denunciation** – expressing society's disapproval of an offender's behaviour.

**Deterrence** – giving a punishment aimed at putting off the defendant from re-offending because of fear of punishment or preventing other potential offenders from committing similar crimes.

**Directed acquittal** – where a judge decides there is insufficient prosecution evidence to allow the case to continue. The jury is directed to find the defendant not guilty.

**Dissenting judgment** – a judgement given by a judge who disagrees with the reasoning of the majority of judges in the case.

**Distinguishing** – a method by which a judge avoids having to follow what would otherwise be a binding precedent.

**Doctrine of precedent** – following the decisions of previous cases, especially of higher courts.

**Due diligence** – where the defendant has done all that was within his power not to commit an offence.

**EU directives** – these are issued by the EU and direct all Member States to bring in the same laws throughout all the countries.

**EU regulations** – laws issued by the EU which are binding on Member States and automatically apply in each member country.

**Golden rule** – a rule of statutory interpretation. It is a modification of the literal rule and avoids an interpretation that is absurd.

**Green Paper** – a consultative document issued by the government putting forward proposals for reform of the law.

**Horizontal direct effect** – consequential in relations between individuals. This means that an individual can invoke a European provision in relation to another individual.

**Indictable offence** – an offence that has to be tried at the Crown Court.

**Injunction** – an order of the court to stop doing something, e.g. to stop making noise after 10 p.m. Failure to follow the court order can lead to further sanctions, including possibly imprisonment. An injunction can order a positive action, e.g. to move a muck heap to avoid causing a smell nuisance.

**Intention** – a decision to bring about, in so far as it lies within the accused's power, the prohibited consequence, no matter whether the accused desired that consequence of his act or not.

**Lay magistrates** – these are unpaid, part-time judges who have no legal qualifications and hear cases in the Magistrates' Courts.

**Legal aid** – government help in funding a case.

**Liable** – the judge's decision that the case against the defendant is proved and that the defendant should pay compensation.

**Literal rule** – a rule of statutory interpretation that gives the words their plain ordinary or literal meaning.

**Mediation** – using a neutral person in a dispute to help the parties come to a compromise solution.

**Mens rea** – the mental element (guilty mind) or the fault element in an offence.

**Mischief rule** – a rule of statutory interpretation that looks back to the gap in the previous law and interprets the Act so as to cover the gap.

**Negligence** – an act or a failure to act due to the fault of the defendant which causes injury or damage to another person or his property.

**Negotiation** – the process of trying to come to an agreement.

**Neighbour principle** – the person who is owed a duty of care by the defendant. It is not the person living next door. According to Lord Atkin it is anyone you ought to have in mind who might potentially be injured by your act or omission.

**Non-pecuniary loss** – loss that is not wholly money-based. This can include pain and suffering as a result of the accident, loss of amenity or a change in lifestyle, such as not being able to play a sport.

*Novus actus interveniens* – an intervening act to break the chain of causation.

*Obiter dicta* – this means 'other things said'. So it is all the rest of the judgment apart from the *ratio decidendi*. Judges in future cases do not have to follow it.

**Original precedent** – a decision on a point of law that has never been decided before.

**Pecuniary loss** – a loss that can be easily calculated in money terms, for example the cost of hiring a car while the claimant's own car is being repaired.

**Persuasive precedent** – a decision which does not have to be followed by later cases, but which a judge may decide to follow.

**Prosecutor** – the legal term for the person or organisation bringing a criminal charge against a defendant.

**Purposive approach** – an approach to statutory interpretation in which the courts look to see what is the purpose of the law.

*Ratio decidendi* – the reason for the decision. This forms a precedent for future cases.

**Reasonably foreseeable** – a danger which a reasonable person should predict or expect from his actions.

**Reformation** – trying to reform the offender's behaviour so that he will not offend in future.

**Rehabilitate** – trying to alter the offender's behaviour so that he will conform to community norms and not offend in future.

**Remedy** – the way in which a court will enforce or satisfy a claim when injury or damage has been suffered and proved. In tort law the remedy will usually be damages or occasionally an injunction.

**Reparation** – where an offender compensates the victim or society for the offending behaviour.

**Repeal of an Act of Parliament** – the Act ceases to be law. Only Parliament can repeal an Act of Parliament.

**Retribution** – imposing a punishment because the offender deserves punishment.

**Rights of audience** – the right to present a case in court on behalf of another person.

**Sectional pressure group** – a pressure group that represents the interests of a particular group of people.

*Stare decisis* – this means 'stand by what has been decided and do not unsettle the established'. It is the foundation of judicial precedent.

**Statutory instruments** – rules and regulations made by government ministers.

**Strict liability** – a civil action where fault of the defendant does not need to be proved.

**Strict liability offences** – offences where *mens rea* is not required in respect of at least one aspect of the *actus reus*.

**Subjective recklessness** – where the defendant knows there is a risk of the consequence happening but takes that risk.

**Summary offence** – an offence that can only be tried in the Magistrates' Court.

**The reasonable person** – this used to be said to be 'the man on the Clapham omnibus'. Now it is considered to be the ordinary person in the street or doing a task.

**The three-part test** – an update of the neighbour test to show who is owed a duty of care in negligence. All three parts have to be satisfied in order that this test is satisfied.

**Tort** – this is a civil wrong, and tort law compensates a person who has been injured or whose property is damaged. The word 'tort' comes from the French word for 'wrong'.

**Trespasser** – a visitor who has no permission or authority to be on the occupier's land.

**Triable-either-way offence** – an offence that can be tried in either the Magistrates' Court or the Crown Court.

**Tribunals** – forums used instead of a court for deciding certain types of disputes. They are less formal than courts.

**Ultra vires** – it goes beyond the powers that Parliament granted in the enabling Act. Where any delegated legislation is ultra vires, then it is not valid law.

**Vertical direct effect** – an individual can claim against the Member State even when a directive has not been implemented by that state.

**Visitor** – in legal terms, lawful adult visitors are invitees, licensees, those with contractual permission and those with statutory right of entry.

**White Paper** – a document issued by the government stating its decisions as to how it is going to reform the law.

# Index